PRINCE OF WALES'S OWN, THE SCINDE HORSE.

1839-1922

PRINCE OF WALES'S OWN, THE SCINDE HORSE

COLONEL E. B. MAUNSELL

The Naval & Military Press Ltd

Reproduced by kind permission of the Central Library,
Royal Military Academy, Sandhurst

Published by
The Naval & Military Press Ltd
Unit 10, Ridgewood Industrial Park,
Uckfield, East Sussex,
TN22 5QE England
Tel: +44 (0) 1825 749494
Fax: +44 (0) 1825 765701
www.naval-military-press.com
© The Naval & Military Press Ltd 2005

In reprinting in facsimile from the original, any imperfections are inevitably reproduced and the quality may fall short of modern type and cartographic standards.

THE BATTLE HONOURS

"Meeanee"
"Hyderabad"
"Cutchee"
"Mooltan"

"Goojerat"
"Punjaub"
"Persia"
"Central India"
"Abyssinia"

"Kandahar, 1880"
"Afghanistan, 1878–80"
"Kifl"
"Iraq, 1920"

THE GREAT WAR

"Somme, 1916"
"Morval"
"Cambrai, 1917"

"France and Flanders, 1914–18"
"Megiddo"
"Sharon"
"Damascus"

"Palestine, 1918"
"N.W. Frontier, India, 1914–15, 1916"

DEDICATION

To
The Undying Memory
of
Those Beloved Members of The Brotherhood
of
The Scinde Horse
Who
Fell Asleep on The Field of Honour

"Then said he, 'I am going to my Father's. . . . My sword I give to him that shall succeed me in my Pilgrimage, and my courage and skill to him that can get it.' . . . And as he went down deeper, he said, 'Grave, where is thy Victory?' So he passed over, and all the trumpets sounded for him on the other side."

FOREWORD

COLONEL MAUNSELL has given in the following pages a clear and succinct history of the Scinde Horse. It is a fine record of an old Indian Silladar Cavalry Regiment, and one that is unsurpassed in a service which is renowned for brilliant achievements.

Tradition is an undefinable quality which is of incalculable value to the military formation which possesses it; and the tradition of the Scinde Horse is closely associated with the name of that remarkable man and soldier, John Jacob. Jacob had no direct relations with the Scinde Horse until some time after its birth, but to him is due the honour of infusing into it the spirit which, through various fortunes and occasional periods of partial extinction, has never died, and which flamed as brightly as ever when fanned by the breath of the late War.

It is a matter of good fortune that this tradition has been strengthened by the recent amalgamations brought about as the result of the reduction of the Indian Cavalry, since the 35th Scinde Horse and 36th Jacob's Horse have come together again after their separation in 1846.

The old 36th Jacob's Horse fought with distinction in France and subsequently took part in the great cavalry operations in Palestine which culminated in the total defeat of the Turkish Army in September and October 1918.

The 35th Scinde Horse, denied the opportunities of service against the Germans and Turks, played a leading rôle during the Arab Rebellion in

Mesopotamia, and added to the reputation it had gained in the old days under Jacob, especially in the combat of Kifl, 1920.

In recognition of the fine services of these two Regiments, the 14th Scinde Horse was honoured by the appointment of His Royal Highness The Prince of Wales as Colonel-in-Chief of the Regiment.

The Great War and the Arab Rebellion have shown that the same spirit exists as in the days when Sir Charles Napier wrote:

"This is a very rare and glorious instance of perfect discipline as well as courage on the part of the Scinde Horse and, in the mind of the Governor, stamps both the Scinde Horse and its Commandant as first-rate soldiers, prompt, resolute, and obedient," and we, of the Regiment, may rest assured that it will continue to maintain the same high standard as when the conqueror of Scinde penned the above words.

G. DE S. BARROW,
GENERAL.
COLONEL, PRINCE OF WALES'S OWN,
THE SCINDE HORSE.

July 1926.

PREFACE

In making up The History of The Scinde Horse, I have based the account on the following authorities:

The Period prior to The Great War—

Digest of Services, 1st Sind Horse. Digest of Services, 2nd Sind Horse. "Records of The Sind Irregular Horse." "The Conquest of Sind," by Sir William Napier. "History of The 22nd Foot." "John Jacob," by Shand. "Views and Opinions of John Jacob." "Frontier and Overseas Expeditions" (Official). "The War in The Punjab" (Official). "The Rebellion in Central India, 1857–58" (Official). "History of The Second Afghan War, 1878–80" (Official). Certain papers on the Action at Maiwand, and regarding the Bombay troops, collected by Lieut.-General Sir Robert Scallon. "History of The 3rd (Queen's Own) Bombay Light Cavalry." Personal reminiscences of various officers, including my own.

The "Records of The Sind Irregular Horse" contain, in great detail, a description of events prior to the expedition to Persia in 1857, and my account of this period is necessarily rather of the nature of a précis.

The Period of The Great War—

The greater part is from personal recollections of France and Palestine, which are backed by the War Diary of Jacob's Horse and by the War Diaries of other units and formations, kindly placed at my disposal by The Committee of Imperial Defence, in addition to a brief history of the operations written by Lieut.-Colonel (now Colonel Commandant) W. G. K. Green, who commanded the Regiment from November 1915 until September 1918. The book amplifies this last, and Colonel Green has been good enough to check it for accuracy.

For the account of the Cambrai and Épéhy operations, I am indebted to the following officers: the late Major-General A. A. Kennedy, Commanding 4th Cavalry Division; Colonel Malise Graham, 10th Hussars,

PREFACE

G.S.O.I. of the Division; Brigadier-Generals Moreton Gage and Patterson; the late Brigadier-General Neil Haig, and Colonels-Commandant Beatty and Green. I have also consulted various Divisional and Regimental Histories.

The account of the final advance in Palestine until the end of the War, has been checked by General Sir George Barrow, who was in command of the 4th Cavalry Division, and by Colonel-Commandant Green, who commanded the Regiment until the morning of 20th September, and thereafter the 10th Cavalry Brigade.

The Arab Rebellion—

For the Period in Mesopotamia, I have drawn on Sir Aylmer Haldane's "Insurrection in Mesopotamia, 1920," the Regimental War Diary, and the Histories of The Manchester Regiment, 10th Gurkhas and 45th Sikhs. Much came under my personal observation, and much is also based on accounts of varying officers who were in the country.

A proportion of the History has already appeared in a modified form in "The Cavalry Journal," and the Regiment is greatly indebted to the Editor for his courtesy in allowing a free hand in making use of some of the blocks of illustrations and maps.

The thanks of the Regiment are, furthermore, due to The Secretary, The Royal United Service Institution, London, for his courtesy in allowing the reproduction of certain pictures from that Museum, and finally to Mr. K. R. Wilson for having placed his technical knowledge at their disposal, together with his most helpful advice throughout the various stages of production and publication.

A number of the accounts of operations are rather of the nature of "tactical studies," and it is hoped that, as such, they may prove useful to future generations of Sind Horsemen.

E. B. MAUNSELL, COLONEL,
LATE COMMANDANT,
PRINCE OF WALES'S OWN,
THE SCINDE HORSE.

July 1926.

CONTENTS

THE SCINDE HORSE

CHAPTER I
1838–1880

FORMATION. AN OUTLINE OF THE SERVICES OF THE REGIMENT . . 1

CHAPTER II
27TH JULY, 1880

THE ACTION AT MAIWAND 24

CHAPTER III
1880–1914

AN OUTLINE OF THE SERVICES OF THE REGIMENT. END OF THE SECOND AFGHAN WAR. MEKRAN. SEISTAN 35

CHAPTER IV
1914

EFFICIENCY OF THE INDIAN CAVALRY AT THE OPENING OF THE GREAT WAR 42

THE 36TH JACOB'S HORSE

CHAPTER V
1914

THE 36TH JACOB'S HORSE

THE GREAT WAR
1914–1918

INDIA. ARRIVAL IN FRANCE. FRANCE AND FLANDERS. BILLETING . 48

CONTENTS

CHAPTER VI
1915
FESTUBERT. NEUVE CHAPELLE. YPRES 54

CHAPTER VII
1915–1916
AUTHUILLE. BILLETS NEAR AMIENS. ABBEVILLE. WINTER . . . 65

CHAPTER VIII
1916
TRAINING AT ST. RIQUIER. NEUVILLE ST. VAAST 71

CHAPTER IX
1916–1917
THE SOMME. BEAUMONT HAMEL. CRECY 78

CHAPTER X
1916–1917
WINTER. THE GERMAN WITHDRAWAL TO THE HINDENBURG LINE . . 86

CHAPTER XI
1917
THE GERMAN WITHDRAWAL TO THE HINDENBURG LINE. OPERATIONS NORTH OF BAPAUME IN FRONT OF CROISSILLES (17TH MARCH–26TH MARCH) 92

CHAPTER XII
1917
BULLECOURT. BILLETS NEAR DOULLENS 113

CHAPTER XIII
1917
THE DEVASTATED AREA NORTH-EAST OF ST. QUENTIN. THE LINE NEAR ÉPÉHY 118

CONTENTS

CHAPTER XIV
NOVEMBER, 1917
THE BATTLES OF CAMBRAI AND EPÉHY 134

CHAPTER XV
1917–1918
WINTER IN THE DEVASTATED AREA. DEPARTURE FROM FRANCE. THE MOVE TO EGYPT 172

CHAPTER XVI
1918
EGYPT, TEL EL KEBIR. PALESTINE, THE JORDAN 183

CHAPTER XVII
1918
THE JORDAN VALLEY. THE PHILISTEAN PLAIN 199

CHAPTER XVIII
SEPTEMBER, 1918
THE GREAT ADVANCE. THE BATTLE OF SHARON. MEGIDDO. . . . 212

CHAPTER XIX
1918
BEISAN 221

CHAPTER XX
1918
THE ACTION OF ABU NAJ 227

CHAPTER XXI
1918–1921
THE ADVANCE ON DAMASCUS. FALL OF DAMASCUS. END OF THE GREAT WAR. THE RETURN TO INDIA 231

CONTENTS

THE 35TH SCINDE HORSE

CHAPTER XXII

THE 35TH SCINDE HORSE

1914–1920

SERVICE IN INDIA DURING THE GREAT WAR. ORDERED TO MESOPOTAMIA 243

CHAPTER XXIII

1920

FROM INDIA. MESOPOTAMIA. DIWANIYAH. HINAIDI 249

CHAPTER XXIV

1920

THE 35TH SCINDE HORSE

THE ARAB REBELLION

1920–1921

THE OUTBREAK OF THE REBELLION. RUMEITHA. KIFL. THE MANCHESTER COLUMN DISASTER. OPERATIONS ROUND HILLAH . 264

CHAPTER XXV

1920

NORTH-EAST OF BAGHDAD 283

CHAPTER XXVI

1920

THE RELIEF OF KUFAH 289

CHAPTER XXVII

1920–1921

THE COLUMN TO MENDALI. MOSUL. BELED SINJAR. THE RETURN TO INDIA 296

CONTENTS

P.W.O. THE 14TH SCINDE HORSE

CHAPTER XXVIII
1921–1922

AMALGAMATION OF THE 35TH SCINDE HORSE AND THE 36TH JACOB'S HORSE. H.R.H. THE PRINCE OF WALES APPOINTED COLONEL-IN-CHIEF . . 311

APPENDICES.

		PAGE
I	BRIGADIER-GENERAL JOHN JACOB, C.B.	315
II	COMMANDANTS OF THE REGIMENT	322
III	NOMINAL ROLL OF OFFICERS	324
IV	OFFICERS—THE GREAT WAR	330
V	CASUALTIES	333
VI	HONOURS AND AWARDS	336
VII	AN HISTORICAL PRÉCIS	340
VIII	A RELIC OF SIR CHARLES NAPIER	343
IX	CORRESPONDENCE—MASNIÈRES	344
X	THE SILLADAR SYSTEM	346

INDEX 348

MAPS

	PAGE
SIND AND BELOOCHISTAN	2
HYDERABAD—CITY AND NEIGHBOURHOOD	6
MEEANEE (17TH FEBRUARY, 1843)	8
KANDAHAR AND GIRISHK	20
KHUSHK-I-NAKHUD (26TH FEBRUARY, 1879)	22
MAIWAND (27TH JULY, 1880)	28
THE WESTERN FRONT, 1914–1918	75
THE SOMME BATTLEFIELD	82
OPERATIONS BEFORE CROISSILLES AND BULLECOURT	94
AREA, CAMBRAI—ST. QUENTIN—PERONNE	122
THE BATTLE OF CAMBRAI (20TH NOVEMBER, 1917)	135
THE BATTLE OF ÉPÉHY (29TH NOVEMBER–5TH DECEMBER, 1917)	143
PALESTINE	190
THE RIVER JORDAN	195
THE BATTLES OF MEGIDDO AND SHARON	214
THE ADVANCE TO DAMASCUS (SEPTEMBER, 1918)	234
LOWER MESOPOTAMIA	250
CAMP OF THE MANCHESTER COLUMN (24TH JULY, 1920)	271
OPERATIONS ROUND HILLAH	279
THE ACTION AT KUFAH (17TH OCTOBER, 1920)	292
UPPER MESOPOTAMIA	300
THE RIVER TIGRIS, KUT—BASRA	308

PLATES

H.R.H. The Prince of Wales—Colonel-in-Chief	*Frontispiece*

	TO FACE PAGE
Brigadier-General John Jacob, C.B.	1
Baluch Chief of the Jekrani Tribe in the Bolan Pass	4
Scinde Irregular Horse (1846)	5
Officer in Fighting Order (1848)	6
The Transport of an Indian Army on the March	7
Outpost Duty on The Helmund (1879)	20
Convoy Duty, with The Bolan in Flood	21
The Charge at Khushk-i-Nakhud (1879)	22
Life at Thul Chotiali, Second Afghan War (1879–80)	23
A Trooper of The Sind Horse (1880)	34
The Sortie of Deh Khoja (1880)	35
Mametz—A Cavalry Patrol (1916)	80
Stretcher Bearers—near Ginchy (1916)	81
An Indian Cavalry Working Party (1917)	136
Masnières—Bridge Smashed by the British Tank (20th November, 1917)	137
"The Other Side of The Hill"	164
The Toll of War	165
Near Hebron	188
Enab	189
Jerusalem	192
Jericho	193
The River Jordan, Ghoraniyeh Bridgehead	200

PLATES

	TO FACE PAGE
THE MOUNT OF TEMPTATION	201
THE JORDAN VALLEY—A TYPICAL STRETCH OF COUNTRY	212
THE RIVER AUJA	213
THE BATTLE OF SHARON—THE COMMENCEMENT OF THE ADVANCE (19TH SEPTEMBER, 1918)	218
VIEW OVER MEGIDDO TO THE ESDRAELON VALLEY	219
THE RIVER JORDAN AT JISR MEJAMIE	220
THE VALLEY OF JEZREEL AND MOUNT GILBOA	221
MEJDAH—CAPTURED TURKISH CONVOY	224
TURKISH PRISONERS AT BEISAN	225
BEISAN—CAMP OF TURKISH PRISONERS	226
THE FIRST TRAIN RUN BY BRITISH TROOPS INTO BEISAN	227
DAMASCUS	236
SARACEN BRIDGE AT JISR MEJAMIE	237
THE JISR MEJAMIE–IRBID ROAD	237
ARAB LEVIES NEAR PALMYRA (1918)	237
BEIRUT—CAMP ON THE SEASHORE	240
BEIRUT—THE COAST TO THE NORTH	241
BRIDGE OVER THE DOG RIVER	242
MAJOR-GENERAL SIR G. DE S. BARROW AND STAFF (1919)	242
THE DOG RIVER	243
DIWANIYAH	288
TEL AFAR	288
NAJAF	289
HILLAH	289
FIGHTING DRESS:	
"FRANCE AND FLANDERS, 1914–1918"	310
"MESOPOTAMIA, 1920–1921"	311
A RELIC OF SIR CHARLES NAPIER (I–II)	343

THE TITLES OF THE REGIMENT.

35TH SCINDE HORSE.

1839	. .	SCINDE IRREGULAR HORSE.
		Raised at Hyderabad, by Captain W. Ward.
1846	. .	1ST REGIMENT SCINDE IRREGULAR HORSE.
1860	. .	1ST REGIMENT OF SCINDE HORSE.
1861	. .	8TH REGIMENT SCINDE SILLADAR CAVALRY.
		Reverted to previous designation.
1885	. .	5TH BOMBAY CAVALRY (JACOB-KA-RISALLAH).
1888	. .	5TH BOMBAY CAVALRY (SCINDE HORSE).
1903	. .	35TH SCINDE HORSE.

36TH JACOB'S HORSE.

1846	. .	2ND REGIMENT OF SCINDE IRREGULAR HORSE.
		Raised at Hyderabad, by Captain J. Jacob.
1860	. .	2ND REGIMENT OF SCINDE HORSE.
1861	. .	9TH REGIMENT, SCINDE SILLADAR CAVALRY.
		Reverted to previous designation.
1885	. .	6TH BOMBAY CAVALRY (JACOB-KA-RISALLAH).
1888	. .	6TH BOMBAY CAVALRY (JACOB'S HORSE).
1903	. .	36TH JACOB'S HORSE.

1921	. .	35TH SCINDE HORSE and 36TH JACOB'S HORSE amalgamated:—
		35TH–36TH Prince of Wales' Own Cavalry.
1922	. .	PRINCE OF WALES'S OWN, THE 14TH SCINDE HORSE.

BRIGADIER-GENERAL JOHN JACOB, C.B.

1812—1858.

PRINCE OF WALES'S OWN, THE SCINDE HORSE

CHAPTER I

FORMATION.
AN OUTLINE OF THE SERVICES OF THE REGIMENT.
1838-1880

IN 1838 and 1839 the communications of our army in Kandahar with India *viâ* the Bolan and Sukkur were constantly harried by Baluch marauders.

It was accordingly decided to raise a special body of horse for service on the Scinde Border. The nucleus was to be a detachment of the Poona Horse, then serving in Cutch. In August 1838 the new Regiment, to be called the Scinde Irregular Horse, was embodied at Hyderabad.

The Baluch, with whom this Regiment had to cope, are, as a race, akin to Arabs. Their manners and customs are very similar, but they are credited with a high sense of honour. The Baluch of the plains were, in the days of which we write, usually mounted on a particularly hardy breed of pony, and could cover enormous distances without water. They could, moreover, fight mounted with the sword. Their sword-play was, in addition, skilful, and John Jacob records having personally seen a case of a horse's skull cleft clean in two by a sword cut.

They were also armed with matchlocks, which outranged the Brown Bess of the period.

The Hill Baluch, the Murree, and hill Boogtis, being the clans with whom the Regiment was most concerned in its early days, were also mounted, but used their animals to transport themselves only.

All Baluch prefer to ride mares, which, they say, are hardier than stallions and have, in addition, the enormous advantage of not giving away their presence by neighing.

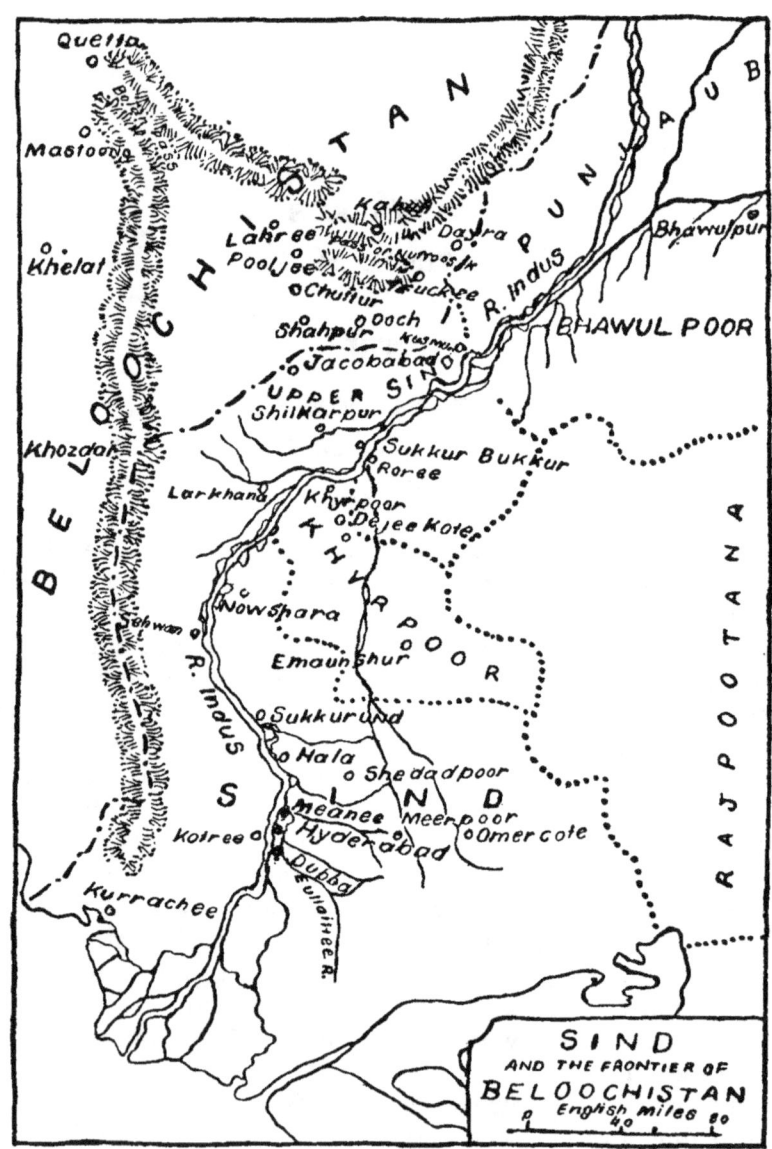

SIND AND BELOOCHISTAN.

The country they live in is a wilderness, except in a few places where there is water. The hill country is of the usual Indian Frontier type—bleak, bare and rugged, but with wider and longer valleys than is the case north of the Gomal. Cavalry can, therefore, be employed more freely than further north.

The plain country is dead flat " pat " soil, with indifferent water holes anything from fifteen to thirty miles apart, and, in appearance, might well be Mesopotamia.

The climate in the plain and lower hill area between March and the end of October is one of intense heat, ranging up to 135 degrees in the shade, and without the relief of cool nights, as is the case in Mesopotamia.

The barrenness of the country and its abominable climate made service in Scinde intensely unpopular with the Army in general. The troops were badly housed and badly looked after.

That service in the Scinde Horse was popular is attributable to the able administration of John Jacob and to the constant active service. So popular was the Corps that the price of an " assami " was frequently as high as Rs. 800. For the uninitiated it may be stated that an " assami " meant the price of the horse and a share in the baggage animal the man was bound to maintain.

In November 1838 an expedition under Major Billamore was decided on against the tribes bordering the eastern fringe of the Kutchee Plain —that is, the flat desert between the mouth of the Bolan and Shikarpore.

The mounted troops at first consisted of local levies. These proved unreliable, and a detachment of the new Regiment, under Lieutenant Clarke, was brought up.

It at once becomes apparent that the new Corps was of very different stuff and the first exploit of the Regiment occurred as follows. Clarke had just arrived in bivouac after a long march under a broiling sun, when a report was brought that a band of Baluch had left the hills on a raid. Their strength was estimated at three hundred. Fortunately, a reliable guide was found. Starting at midnight, with eighty sabres, Clarke, at daybreak, found them in a cornfield.

The Baluch had barely time to mount when they were charged and pursued for three miles up a stony river bed. Fifty raiders were cut down, the whole of the booty recovered, and several prisoners brought back.

Billamore entered the hills bordering the eastern Kutchee Plain, and penetrated as far as Deyra and Kahun.

Two very successful actions with the Boogti tribe were fought. On the second occasion the enemy were defeated with great slaughter, the victory being principally owing to the conduct of Clarke and his detachment, who highly distinguished themselves, Clarke killing four of the enemy in personal encounter, hand to hand.

The artillery, drawn by bullocks, was commanded by one Lieutenant John Jacob, an officer afterwards to be inseparably connected with the Scinde Horse. This officer made himself conspicuous by his extraordinary zeal as an explorer and by his capacity to get his guns over passes which Sir Charles Napier, in his campaign a few years later, thought practically impassable.

On Billamore's return to the plains the force was broken up, but it was shortly afterwards decided that Kahun should be reoccupied.

Accordingly, three hundred men of the 5th Bombay Infantry were installed there, fifty of the Scinde Horse under Clarke accompanying them. Clarke was ordered to return with the supply camels, together with one hundred and fifty of the infantry. Of the latter, eighty were to return to Kahun as soon as the Pass of Nuffusk was crossed. These latter were attacked by the whole Murree tribe and destroyed to a man. The Murrees, flushed with success, followed up Clarke, found him halted at the bottom of the mountain of Surtoff, and fell on him in overwhelming numbers. Clarke sternly opposed them for several hours, when his ammunition ran out. The ground was such that horsemen were useless, and the detachment was overpowered by numbers. The gallant Clarke was killed, and only few escaped to the plains.

A relief force for Kahun was sent out, commanded by Clibborn. One hundred of the Scinde Horse under Malcolm formed part of it.

It was the end of August, and the heat was terrific.

The force reached the Nuffusk Pass, where it met strong opposition from some thousands of Murrees.

The troops fought their way to the top of the pass with great difficulty and succeeded in killing over two hundred and fifty of the enemy and in repulsing their onslaught. On arrival there, however, they were too exhausted to follow up. No water could be found, and the troops became disorganized. A retirement was ordered, which was followed up by the Murrees.

Malcolm's detachment covered the move, together with some men of the Poona Horse. The force returned to the plains completely demoralized through thirst and heat, and the fact that any of the infantry got back at all is attributed to the steadiness and gallantry of the detachments of the Poona and Scinde Horse covering them.

The Regiment lost seventy men out of a hundred, and eighty-five horses, in this *débâcle*. One of the guns that was lost is now in the possession of the Regiment, having been recovered some ten years later.

BALUCH CHIEF OF THE JEKRANI TRIBE IN THE BOLAN PASS.

1838.

SCINDE IRREGULAR HORSE.

1846.

Kahun was left to its fate and capitulated shortly after. The garrison was allowed to march out with the honours of war, drums beating, colours flying, and with its only gun.

The Murree Baluch behaved both chivalrously and kindly in this affair.

The Regiment had performed such good service that its strength was raised to six hundred sabres.

In late 1841 the whole border was in a blaze, as the news of the destruction of our Army in Cabul and of our various reverses in Afghanistan was well known. John Jacob was placed in command of the Regiment, and in Political Charge of the Kutchee Frontier.

He instituted an aggressive policy of striking before the raiders could strike, and surprising them before they could surprise. The result was apparent almost at once.

Among the minor patrol episodes that occurred was that of Naik Munshi Ram, who, when he had only seven men with him, was attacked by forty raiders. He lost half his strength, but succeeded in getting his wounded and dead away. The fight put up by this small party had a great moral effect.

In October of 1842 England's Army crossed from the mouth of the Bolan. Since leaving Quetta it had been harried all down the pass. When, however, it entered the Kutchee Plain, its troubles ceased, thanks to the influence of John Jacob and his Regiment.

Orders were received that Khanghur (now Jacobabad) was to be permanently garrisoned by the Scinde Irregular Horse.

It was then a mere cluster of hovels, and now has ten thousand inhabitants.

At the end of November 1842 the Regiment was ordered to Sukkur to form part of Sir Charles Napier's Army in its conquest of Scinde. Until that date it had never been together as a unit, and the men had never been regularly drilled and trained. The Indian officers were men, however, who had learnt their earlier soldiering in the Mahratta wars and were not novices. The constant petty skirmishes and hard life led on the Kutchee Desert made the unit a tough one, as the subsequent campaign proved.

An escort of the Regiment had accompanied Sir Charles Napier previously in his interview with the Mirs of Scinde at Hyderabad. He describes the troopers as " wild, picturesque fellows, very like stage banditti." That, however, was before Jacob put them into uniform.

Napier had resolved to seize Emaun Ghur, a desert fortress some eighty miles south of Sukkur.

All that could be learnt of it at the time was that it lay six marches or so off, that water was scarce, and the country a desert. The garrison

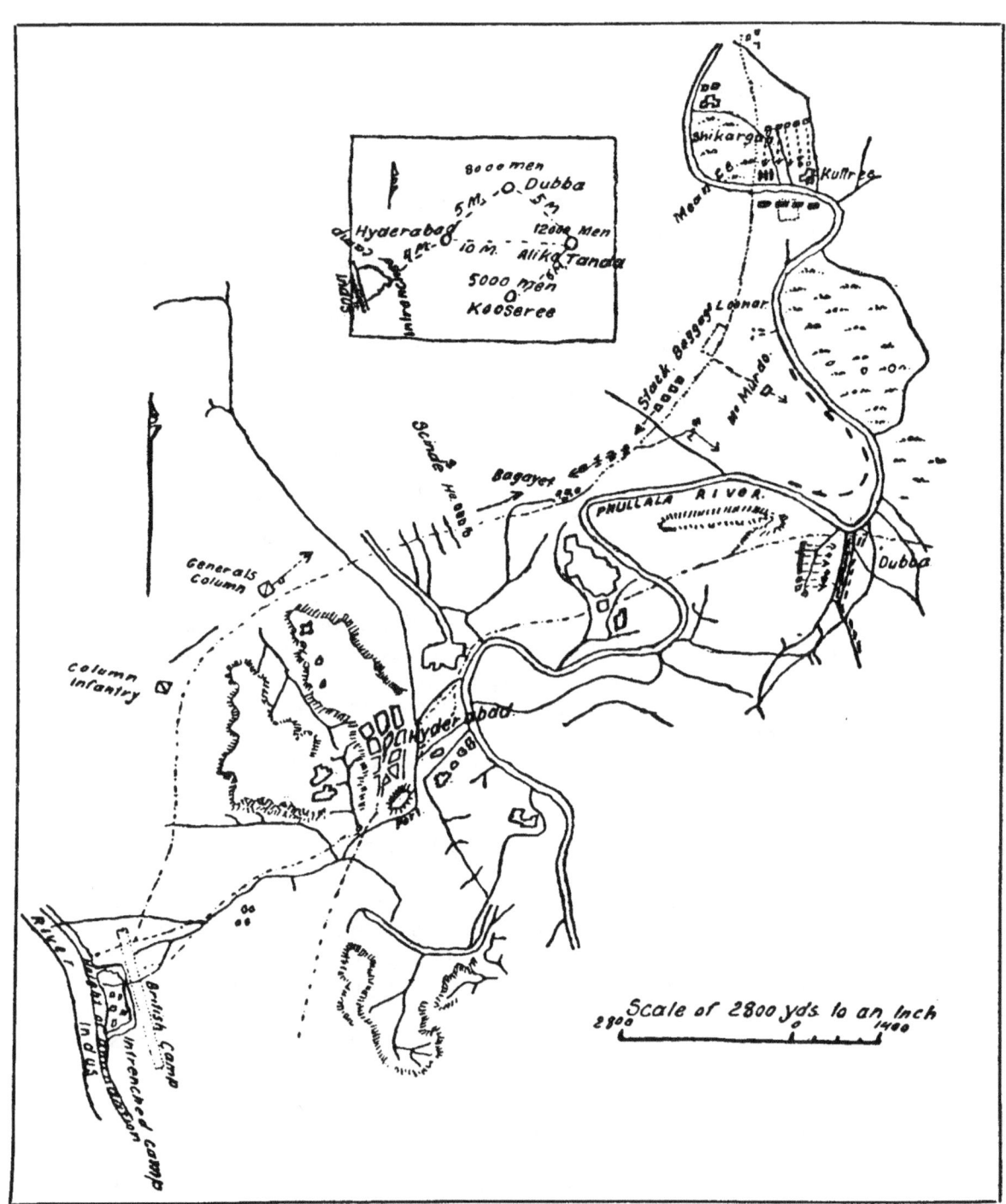

HYDERABAD—THE CITY AND NEIGHBOURHOOD.

OFFICER IN FIGHTING ORDER.
1848.

*Royal United Service Institution.
By kind permission.*

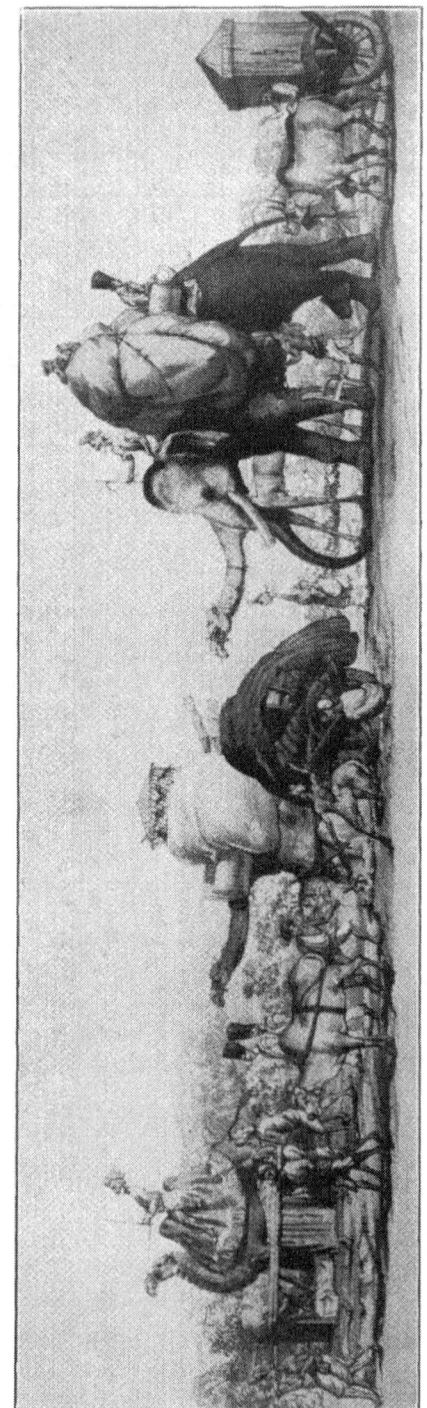

THE TRANSPORT OF AN INDIAN ARMY ON THE MARCH.

was reported as two thousand men, with numerous bodies of mounted men in the neighbourhood who might poison or destroy the wells. As it was obviously out of the question to move the whole army there, Napier arranged to take two hundred of the Scinde Horse and three hundred and fifty of the 22nd Foot. The latter were mounted on camels.

The General pushed forward, finding the water even more scarce than had been expected. In consequence, one hundred and fifty of the Horse were sent back; the remainder, under Jacob, carrying out the reconnaissance for Napier. The fortress was found abandoned and was duly destroyed.

Jacob's energy and the general enterprise shown by the men of the Scinde Horse on this expedition greatly impressed Sir Charles.

The army slowly advanced towards Hyderabad, mustering about three thousand fighting men all told, but hampered by some twenty thousand followers and an indifferent transport.

Sir Charles Napier commented bitterly on the enormous baggage train and on the herds of hangers-on that accompanied the army. This was, however, the normal feature in all wars in India from time immemorial. Sir Arthur Wellesley and, later on, Lord Roberts were the only officers who seem to have really grappled with the problem. Sir Charles himself, and John Jacob, by their personal examples set their faces against the cumbersome impedimenta that officers were in the habit of dragging about, but with scant success. It must, at the same time, be remembered that the lines of communication were not organized as they would be now, and the armies were largely "flying columns" carrying about all their requirements with them.

The desert flank was guarded by the Regiment, the right flank by the Indus.

On the 17th February the army advanced towards Meeanee. Firing was heard to the left front of the column, and Jacob was sent forward to discover and watch the enemy. Jacob soon found the Baluch Army drawn up in a strong position in the bed of the Fullaillee nullah, protected by the banks, with a dense jungle on their left and the village of Kotree on their right. The hostile artillery opened on the Regiment, which drew up in line five hundred yards in front of the position—a very trying situation, as may be imagined, for a newly-raised irregular corps. The battle began in earnest about an hour and a half later.

Napier had but two thousand men, a large camp guard having been left. The enemy was estimated at eighteen thousand.

He attacked, and a desperate battle followed.

The fight had lasted three hours, and by then Napier's reserves con-

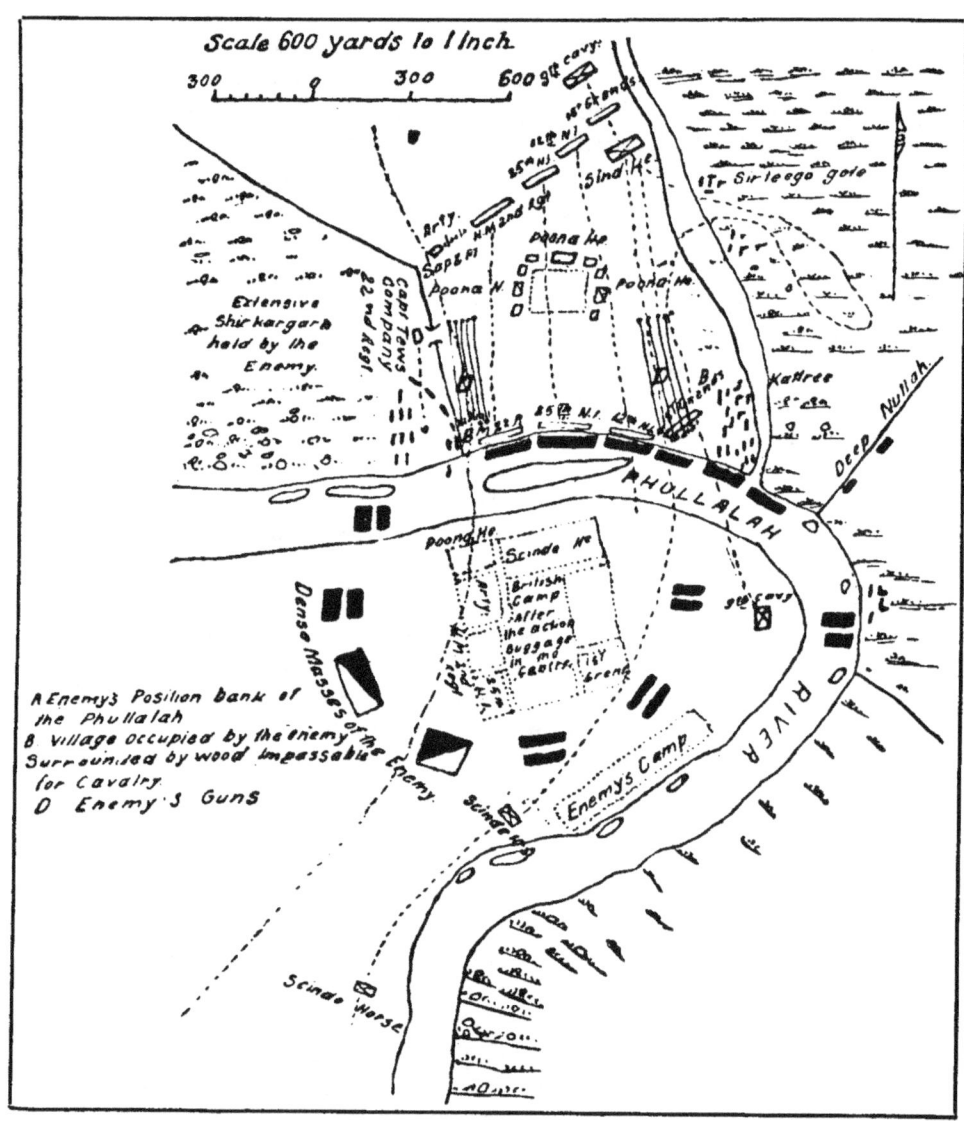

ACTION AT MEEANEE, NEAR HYDERABAD.

17TH FEBRUARY, 1843.

sisted solely of the cavalry. Napier saw his attack held up in the centre and on his right, but considered a charge on his left likely to bring about a decision.

Orders were sent to the Bengal Light Cavalry and to the Scinde Horse to charge the hostile right. The two regiments advanced with great dash over ground so broken that over fifty horses of the Scinde Horse came down. The Regiment moved on the hostile camp, which was duly captured, large numbers of Baluch being slain.

The charge decided the action, and the enemy opposing the infantry fell back. The pursuit was carried out by the Scinde Horse and Bengal Cavalry for three miles.

In this battle the Regiment captured the enemy's principal standard, which was dark green with Mir Nuseer Khan's name on it.

As a reward for its services in this action, the Governor-General ordered other standards, of the colours of the military ribbon of India, red, yellow and blue, to be prepared, with the words "HYDERABAD, 1843," inscribed thereon. When the despatches, describing Meeanee, first reached the Governor-General the battle was referred to as that of Hyderabad, but was, later on, changed to Meeanee. There were eight of these standards, one per troop. Of these, four went to the 2nd Regiment when it was formed. The four in possession of Jacob's Horse at the time of the amalgamation in 1921 are the original standards, those of the 1st Regiment having been destroyed in a fire in the Mess in the late "seventies."

The army moved on Hyderabad, halting at the Residency, four miles out.

The Mirs were panic-stricken, and hastened to make their submission.

Despite this, the country teemed with armed men, sullen and willing to fight again.

Ten thousand fresh warriors had joined since the battle, but, finding the Mirs too cowardly to move, they went off in disgust to join the forces collected under one Sher Mohamed, a few miles out.

By now the hot weather was beginning, and the army sick rate increasing by leaps and bounds.

Napier had, moreover, to find a garrison for Hyderabad Fort. He considered it advisable to await reinforcements and formed an entrenched camp, but in order to maintain the *morale* of his troops made them camp in the open beyond.

Sher Mohamed was reputed to have under him some twenty-five thousand men, within ten miles of Hyderabad.

The delay had heartened him, and the malcontents of the country thought the British had shot their bolt.

On the 24th March, however, reinforcements having arrived two days before, the army moved out, five thousand strong, the Scinde Horse in advance. The route was through very close country. The enemy was found in position at Dubba, eight miles from Hyderabad. He was strongly posted, the position having been cleverly prepared by an African ex-slave, and Jacob had great difficulty in locating the enemy.

The battle, known as the Battle of Hyderabad, began at 9 o'clock. Napier was extremely sensitive regarding his right flank, where the country was very close. He accordingly posted the Scinde Horse and the 3rd Bombay Cavalry there to protect him.

The attack began, Napier being with the 22nd Foot on the extreme left. Suddenly a horseman galloped up from the right and reported that the cavalry were charging.

Napier was at first greatly annoyed, thinking his flank was in danger, but no hostile move came from the jungle on his right. The cavalry came into view in wild career in the hostile left rear. He at once ordered the infantry to charge and, after a brisk combat, the victory was won.

What had happened was that Stack, commanding the two cavalry regiments on the right, had seen the enemy moving off to reinforce their right to meet the infantry attack. Thinking they were in retreat, he ordered the charge.

The enemy was pursued for several miles, large numbers being cut down. The Scinde Horse had nearly succeeded in capturing Sher Mohamed, that Chief's elephant being within view, when the pursuit was called off by the senior cavalry officer on the spot, presumably on the grounds that the troops were too much dispersed. This error enabled Sher Mohamed to get away and so prolonged the campaign.

Napier quickly reorganized his Army, and two days later started in pursuit, moving on Meerpore. The temperature had stood at 110 on the day of the battle, and it was daily getting hotter.

Sher Mohamed fled to his desert fortress of Omercote, whither the army could not follow him owing to water difficulties. A detachment of the Scinde Horse and 25th Bombay Infantry was, however, pushed ahead and, ten days after the battle, Omercote surrendered, the detachment having marched a hundred miles through the desert.

Sher Mohamed, nevertheless, succeeded in getting away.

To Jacob and his regiment was assigned the duty of hunting him down.

Arrangements were made for his pursuit by converging columns, but the combination broke down and Jacob was left to his own resources.

The heat by now was intense.

Sher Mohamed had made up his mind to fight, and selected Jacob's detachment as being the weakest. An encounter took place on the 14th June at the small village of Shahdadpore, but the enemy, although estimated at four thousand, had lost his nerve and, on the Scinde Horse moving out to attack him, broke and fled in every direction.

This action crowned the conquest.

It was on this day that Sir Charles Napier, pushing forward to the sound of the cannon, was struck down by the heat, and only after copious bleeding pulled round. The general attributed his recovery to the arrival of the news of victory.

In 1845 Napier decided on his campaign against the Boogties. The theatre of operations was to be the same as that of Billamore's campaign of 1839. The Regiment accordingly marched back to its old haunts about Jacobabad.

To open the campaign it was decided to make a dash for the desert village of Shahpur, where a gathering of hostile Sardars was reported. The village was forty-four miles from Jacobabad by the route taken.

Jacob, however, seized it, despite a strong resistance, after a most skilful march, a feat Napier mentioned in his dispatches.

The Scinde Horse were employed in keeping the plain area quiet and did not actually accompany Napier into the hills. There were, nevertheless, several spirited encounters with marauders, notably the action of Jemadar Gafoor Mohamed. This officer, with twenty men, was treacherously fired on by a greatly superior number of Baluch. He promptly charged, and after a stiff fight, succeeded in utterly destroying the hostile party.

The Regiment, on conclusion of the expedition, returned to Hyderabad after an absence of seven months.

It was then decided to raise a second regiment, to be also commanded by Jacob. This corps was generally known as Jacob's Horse before the amalgamation, the First Regiment being the Scinde Horse.

It was formed in 1846 by splitting the first regiment into two. At this period the composition of the corps was almost entirely of men from Hindustan, the Mussulman predominating. Jacob held strong views on the recruitment of Pathans and Baluchis. He also considered the Sikhs were inferior as soldiers to Hindustanis. It is quite probable that the best classes of these races did not care for service in Scinde and that a good class of recruit was not forthcoming.

It is of interest to note, however, that Hindustanis are once more being recruited in the regiment.

By now, Upper Scinde was in a state of chaos.

The troops stationed there were shut up in mud forts and were inactive. Raid had succeeded raid and no man's life was safe. To such a pitch had the passive conduct of the troops reached that they had to be rationed as on board ship, no supplies being procured locally, everything coming up by convoy.

A highly successful raid by no less than fifteen hundred Baluch had penetrated the British posts to within a few miles of Shikarpore and the cavalry regiment sent in pursuit had shirked engaging them.

John Jacob was then placed in charge of the frontier and the Scinde Horse marched up from Hyderabad.

A different *régime* at once became apparent. The forts were abolished and troops kept constantly on the move. A thorough intelligence system was inaugurated and a service of expert Baluch trackers and guides introduced.

In February Dafadar Rahim Bux with eighteen sowars came upon two hundred raiders late in the evening. He charged them without hesitation, dispersing them and cutting down many.

In May, at the hottest time of the year, a body of raiders was reported to have carried off some camels from a point thirty-five miles away. Jemadar Somail Khan, commanding nearest the post, started in pursuit and, after a march of seventy miles, came up with them close to the hills. The camels were recovered but the raiders managed to get away.

In September the Boogties began to give trouble and several raids took place. Lieutenant Merewether, on the 1st October, hearing that the whole tribe had entered the plains, took about one hundred and twenty sabres and came upon them to the number of some seven hundred in some broken ground, with heavy jungle a short distance to their flank. He moved between them and the jungle, when they quitted the broken ground to attack him. He charged and overthrew them with tremendous loss, pursuing them to the foothills. The destruction was so great that only one hundred and twenty Boogties are said to have escaped. The remainder of the tribe then made its complete submission.

In this action we are told that the carbine did great execution.

Jacob had by now thoroughly organized the corps. Judging from contemporary accounts, it was far better equipped than most irregular horse, and a letter from Lord Melville from the Punjab in 1853 states other regiments were beginning to copy it. Its system of transport, in particular, was excellent, each man being compelled to maintain his own, none ever being hired. It was half camel and half pony, no carts being allowed. The men, in the cold weather, were clothed in an olive-green coat reaching to the knee, with pantaloons of the same colour, and long boots of English leather. The belts and pouches were of black leather. All ranks had poshteens. The British officers wore silver helmets and do not appear to have suffered from the sun.

The uniform remained the same until after the Second Afghan War, and officers continued to wear the silver helmets as late as 1885. It was stated that they were as sunproof as the helmets normally in wear in India prior to the introduction of the " Kitchener " pattern. The plume worn in full dress was white for the First Regiment, primrose for the Second, and black for the Third.

In the native ranks the pagri was red and, as the older native officers had previously served for a long time in the Mahratta Horse, tied in Mahratta fashion.

The carbine was carried on a hook on the belt, muzzle down, with a steadying strap round the leg.

It was not until 1850, however, that Jacob introduced the double-barrelled carbine and, for officers, the double-barrelled pistol made by Messrs. Swinburne & Co., of London.

Jacob believed in the cutting sword in preference to the thrusting. He had had his arm nearly broken at Meeanee while running a Baluch through the body. As a result the men had curved tulwars, the blades being made in England. He emphasized the importance of wooden scabbards so as not to dull the edges.

The horse furniture was of native pattern, the Hussar saddle being introduced in 1871.

Every man carried a leather water-bag under his horse's belly, apparently a novelty, judging from inspection reports.

The regiments could get on the move, complete with transport, for a long campaign, in twelve hours,—a feat few, if any, irregular corps in the neighbourhood would seem to have been able to do.

This capacity was suddenly tested when the urgent demand came from Herbert Edwardes for assistance before Multan in September 1848.

At this period the organization was of strong troops, not of squadrons.

In order to furnish men it was decided to send two troops of the First Regiment and three of the Second, so as to make up a complement of five hundred sabres without disorganizing the arrangements for the protection of the frontier. They marched under Lieutenant Merewether, Jacob being required to remain as Political Officer.

Shortly after arrival at Multan a large body of the enemy was encountered outside the city and charged. Apart from this action, duties were such as might be expected from cavalry with a besieging force, being chiefly escort duty.

After the storming of the town the Scinde Horse marched with the Bombay column to join Lord Gough's Army, which it reached, after a forced march, two days before the Battle of Gujerat.

It was posted on the extreme left during the advance to that battle.

During the action the British left was threatened by a large body of Afghan Horse, estimated at four thousand, and extremely well mounted.

Sir Joseph Thackwell ordered the Regiment and a squadron of the 9th Lancers to attack them.

The charge was brilliantly executed, a great number of Afghans being slain. Two standards were captured on this occasion. This charge was greatly commented on in the House of Parliament, among others by the Duke of Wellington.

The Regiment, with the other cavalry, followed in pursuit till late at night, capturing several guns.

The day following the battle, the Scinde Horse advanced with the Bombay column, crossing the Jhelum ten days later.

It was an advanced picquet of the Corps that received the Sikh chiefs when they came in to surrender outside Rawal Pindi.

The pursuit of the Afghan element was carried on as far as the mouth of the Khyber, the Regiment accompanying the advanced cavalry.

Several skirmishes with Afridi and other raiders took place between Peshawar and the Khyber, but the raiders were in every case unsuccessful when they encountered the Scinde Horse.

From old despatches it appears that its discipline, dash and organization excited great admiration in the Punjab.

On the Scinde Border, meanwhile, the balance of the Corps was hard put to it, as the Punjab Army detachment did not rejoin for a year.

Among other extraordinary patrol exploits, however, is that of Ressaldar Fateh Maneer, who, with forty men, marched one hundred and twenty-seven miles in twenty-eight hours in pursuit of raiders, the party unfortunately losing their tracks at the end.

In April 1849 a body of Baluch, estimated at some four hundred and fifty men, marched forty miles in the night and attacked Kusmore, where there were some forty of the Scinde Horse and some Jutt encampments close by.

The enemy's information was evidently good, for they knew the geography of the camp and were, apparently, aware that a new relief had marched in late that evening and that there would be a good deal of movement of transport in consequence.

The country was very close and the enemy's approach was comparatively easy to conceal. About fifty succeeded in penetrating the post by a rush at 3 a.m., and a desperate fight was the result, the Scinde Horse losing very heavily; but the resistance was so stout that the enemy cleared out. Meanwhile the relieved forty men, under Ressaldar Karam Ali, heard the firing when about four miles off. The Ressaldar, leaving eight men with his transport, instantly turned about, and galloped back; it was getting light when he came upon about three hundred Baluch horsemen driving off at least ten hundred camels. Aided by the bad light, he instantly charged, killing many and recovering the whole of the plunder.

In September, a party chased some marauders sixty miles and caught them up in the hills. The booty was all recovered, but the robbers escaped up a mountain.

The effect of the enormous amount of hard work on the limited numbers available caused great sickness in the Corps, and, in October, Jacob had to ask for the return of the detachment then at Peshawar.

This detachment arrived in early 1850.

As an example of the high *morale* existing, the conduct of Jemadar Doorgah Singh is given.

This officer received a report that some camels had been carried off near his post. He started off with twenty men and found the tracks. Having proceeded about thirty miles at a very fast pace, seven of his horses having dropped dead from exhaustion *en route* he came upon the enemy.

The latter abandoned the camels, but continued the flight. The jemadar clung on to them till he had only two sowars and a Baluch guide left with him. Just then about fifty Baluch appeared, but the jemadar and the two sowars attacked without hesitation, but were literally cut to pieces. The Baluch guide alone escaped, severely wounded. The place of the jemadar's death is pointed out to this day with unfeigned admiration by the Baluch, and is known as Durga Kushta—no small tribute to an Indian officer of Irregular Horse.

In the meantime Ressaldar Hyder Khan, of a neighbouring post, heard that Durgah Singh had moved out. He saddled up and, moving out with due prudence, succeeded in arriving on the scene of the jemadar's death very shortly after him, recovered the wounded and booty, and returned without losing horse or man.

In April 1853 Ressaldar Shaikh Karim, at Kusmore, received information of a party of raiders.

It was two in the afternoon, and intensely hot.

He started with forty men and some Baluch Guides in pursuit. Owing to the heat several horses had to be left behind *en route*, but the ressaldar caught the raiders up by nightfall. The latter numbered some eighty men, the Scinde Horse then numbering thirty.

Nevertheless, the ressaldar ordered the charge, when the enemy turned to meet it, and a hand-to-hand combat in the dark ensued. The enemy, however, made off to hills close by, where there were several footmen.

With exhausted horses, the officer could not follow. A great many of the enemy were killed, but in the dark it was impossible to ascertain the number. The Scinde Horse lost in this affair nine killed and two wounded. The ressaldar was then thirty miles from his starting point. Nevertheless, he succeeded in bringing back the dead bodies of his comrades and some mares taken from the enemy. The stolen cattle were abandoned by the raiders during the pursuit. The detachment returned to Kusmore at three in the morning after a feat of gallantry and endurance seldom equalled or surpassed in war.

Despite Jacob's comments on the undesirability of the Baluch as soldiers, it is curious to note how bravely and well they fought when in our service as guides. In most of the patrol affairs in which the corps took part there is mention of Baluch guides being "in at the death."

The casualties in horses from heat or exhaustion appear to have often been heavy; on one occasion when Jacob had to move out with four hundred sabres to counter an expected raid, no less than one hundred and sixteen succumbed to sunstroke in forty-eight hours.

Jacob gives his opinion that on this particular day the heat was exceptional, the temperature standing at 106 in a good house. He, at the same time, states that heat alone would not suffice as an explanation, for he had on many occasions been out with parties at the hottest time of the year and nothing happened, while at other times a sudden puff of air had struck both men and horses dead even in the middle of the night.

The Baluch themselves were not immune, and many cases were reported of raiders and their horses dying.

Officers acquainted with Scinde will testify to the dread, natives have of the "Loo," or hot wind.

The Corps, like all Irregular Horse, was silladar, that is, the men provided their own horses. In the Scinde Horse the men bought the animals where they pleased, receiving, on approval by the Commandant, Rs. 100 from the Regimental Fund to assist. (See Appendix X.)

At this period the two regiments watched a frontier one hundred and eighty-five miles long, the posts being about fifteen miles apart, with average garrisons of thirty-five or forty.

There were, at most, six white officers including medical officers in the whole of the two regiments, which amounted to sixteen hundred sabres.

The responsibility thrown on the native officers was, therefore, very great.

The nearest other troops were at Shikarpore, thirty miles in rear. These were practically valueless, as they were immobile.

In 1855 the Aden Troop was formed from a nucleus supplied by both regiments.

In 1857 the aggressive conduct of Persia led to our declaring war, and an expedition under Outram was despatched. Jacob was to command the whole of the irregular horse accompanying it. The First Regiment formed part.

It landed at Bushire with one portion of the Force, and sent on a detachment up the Shat-el-Arab to Muhammera with the other. When Outram advanced against the Persians from Muhammera, the latter hastily abandoned their camp and fled.

The detachment of the Scinde Horse headed the advance in pursuit, until recalled by Outram.

Meanwhile Jacob had remained in command of the force left at Bushire.

The force was returning to India when news of the Mutiny reached

THE HONOURABLE EAST INDIA COMPANY.

Karachi. Part of the Regiment had recently landed there. Of this, two hundred sabres were sent on to Jacobabad in great haste, as the Bengal troops at Shikarpore and Sukkur were on the verge of mutiny. Merewether, commanding the Scinde Horse at Jacobabad, however, had his men well in hand, and there were no signs of trouble. It is well known that the tone of native regiments during this period was greatly dependent on the personality of the commander and the discipline prevailing. If the tone was good, native troops, even if of the same class as the mutineers, usually proved faithful to their salt. It was the same in the case of the Scinde Horse, which was, incidentally, composed almost entirely of men recruited in Hindustan, where the mutiny was at its worst. John Jacob had got into trouble four years previously through articles he had written drawing attention to the general indiscipline prevailing among the Bengal troops and prophesying a mutiny. The authorities now had to eat their words.

As the balance of the Regiment arrived it was hurried on to Bombay, whence it proceeded to Kirkee, sending a detachment down to Satara.

In November 1857 it marched from Kirkee, *via* Ahmednagar, Malligaon, Assirgarh and Mhow, reaching Neemuch on the 31st December.

While at Mhow the Regiment was present at the execution of the Maharaja of Dhar.

From Neemuch the Regiment moved on Awah, a strong fortified town not far from the present Marwar railway junction. Two other columns, from Nasirabad and Deesa respectively, were moving on the place, which was surrounded by all three columns simultaneously on the morning of the 19th January 1858.

After five days' siege operations, during which a heavy fire was maintained by both sides, a breach was reported practicable and the assault ordered for the next morning.

During the night, however, a tremendous storm raged, under cover of which the enemy escaped. The 1st Bombay Lancers and the Scinde Horse managed, nevertheless, to cut up several of the fugitives.

In February the head-quarters of the Regiment were directed to march back to Jacobabad *via* the Bikanir Desert passing Jodhpore and Jeysulmere, and striking the Indus at Rohri.

A squadron, under Major M. Green, however, remained in Rajputana. This joined the Force under Major-General Roberts and took part in the siege and capture of Kotah in March 1858. There was a large body of cavalry, a total of some fourteen hundred sabres.

On the day of the final assault, the 30th March, it had been posted to watch one exit from the town, a ford on the Chambal some seven miles distant, as it was thought the enemy was bound to be driven out that way. It so happened, however, that the enemy began to get their moveable guns out by another exit before the assault had been launched. By the time it was under way the enemy had succeeded in getting clear.

The country between the two gates was a mass of gardens and jungle, with the result that the cavalry did nothing. For some extraordinary reason the pursuit was deferred till two days later, the enemy having a start of some forty hours. As might be expected, not a mutineer was overtaken, though some guns were recovered stuck in quicksands in the Parbati River, sixty miles distant.

The mishandling of the cavalry in this affair is of interest as being an example of how not to do things. It is hard to understand why it was not divided into two bodies and brought close up to the town in the first place.

At the end of a street in Kotah was found a primitive "mitrailleuse," in the shape of forty matchlock barrels fixed in a frame and movable on a wheel.

John Jacob had been selected to command the Central India Field Force, but had not been able to get away from Bushire in time. The command, therefore, was given to Sir Hugh Rose.

The Frontier had, moreover, again begun to give trouble, and his presence was urgently required at Jacobabad. He had, therefore, to return there. In the meantime, the Second Regiment had been hard put to it with Baluch raids.

The enormous amount Jacob had to do on his return began to tell on his health. He had had no leave for years, and overwork finally killed him in 1858. He had been in Scinde almost continuously since 1839, living for the first seven years of that period in most abominable conditions of heat and discomfort. His name was held in respect, to the writer's personal knowledge, in most out-of-the-way places in Baluchistan, as late as 1900—forty-two years after his death.

In late 1857 it was decided to raise a third regiment, the nucleus being the other two.

The Frontier remained comparatively quiet till 1866, when the Murrees gave trouble. In January, a hundred sabres under Ressaldar Mir Kassum Ali encountered a large body and killed and wounded over fifty of them.

A few weeks later a party of twenty-four, under Jemadar Manover Ali, moved in pursuit of some raiders, followed up by a hundred sabres under Ressaldar Tej Singh, who caught him up just as he was preparing to engage them.

Both parties charged together, the Murrees losing fifteen killed and many wounded. The jemadar was badly wounded. Ressaldar Tej Singh, having collected the stolen cattle, once more started in pursuit, until the raiders gained the hills. He then brought his detachment back to his post, where he arrived after being fifteen hours in the saddle and covering some seventy miles.

In 1867 trouble with Abyssinia led to Lord Napier's expedition, of which the Third Regiment formed part. It was employed with the pioneer force and was thanked in despatches.

Hitherto it had not been the custom to teach irregular horse the sword exercise, but in 1870 orders were issued that it was to be taught.

In the same year further symptoms of making the service more regular were the introduction of hussar pattern saddles and evening stables. The saddles were bought in England and were of excellent quality, many being in use in the Regiment in 1900.

At the outbreak of the Afghan War in 1878 the 3rd Sind Horse formed part of General Pallisser's Cavalry Brigade in the advance from Chaman on Kandahar.

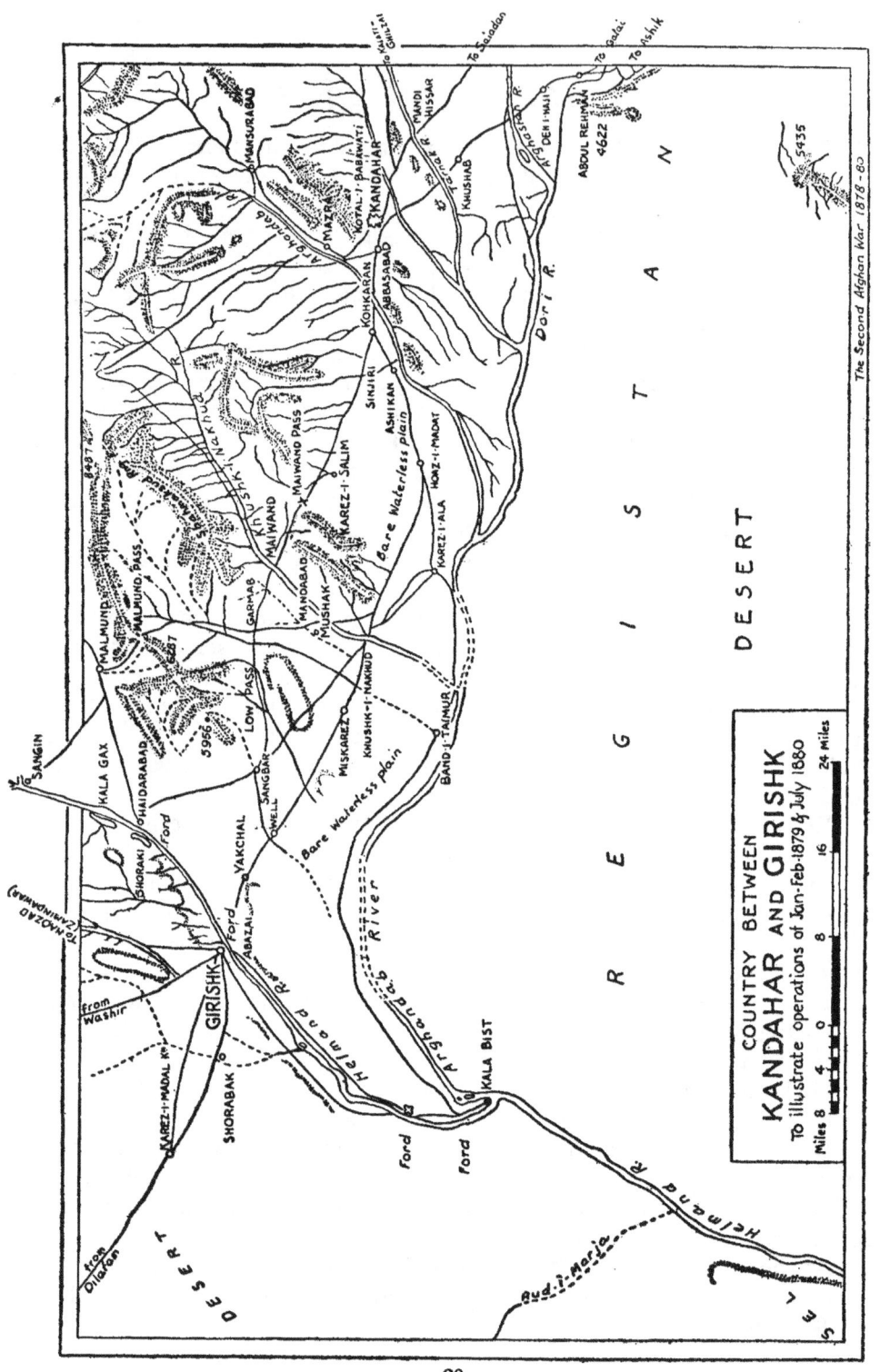

By Major G. D. Giles, Scinde Horse.

OUTPOST DUTY ON THE HELMUND.
1879.

CONVOY DUTY, WITH THE BOLAN IN FLOOD.
1879.

A skirmish took place at Takht i Pul, in which a troop took part, but otherwise Kandahar was peacefully occupied. In January 1879 a reconnaissance under Biddulph moved to Girishk on the Helmund, chiefly to tap new sources of supply. At the end of February it was decided to return to Kandahar, but meanwhile there were rumours of hostile gatherings upstream. In consequence, two squadrons of the Regiment and a hundred rifles of the 29th Bombay Infantry were detached under Colonel Malcolmson, 3rd Sind Horse, to watch the fords from Zamindawar, where the gatherings were most suspected.

This detachment then became the rearguard of Biddulph's force in the withdrawal to Kandahar, remaining one march in rear.

On the 26th February it was at Khushk i Nakhud.

As the situation seemed quiet, Colonel Malcolmson ordered a saddlery inspection in the afternoon, the saddlery being all opened out.

This inspection was in progress when the regimental grass-cutters were observed urging their camels back to camp at a gallop, while those grass-cutters who had ponies were careering in. This was followed up by a report from the escort that a large body of ghazis were approaching.

Shortly after a mass of tribesmen, with banners, was observed approaching over some high ground about a mile and a half to the north of the camp.

The infantry fell in and the saddlery inspection terminated abruptly. The hundred rifles were directed to move out and drive the enemy over the good going, away from the nullahs, which were to the north-east.

Meanwhile the cavalry got their saddlery hastily together and saddled up.

On the infantry getting the enemy under their fire, the latter edged off to their right, making apparently for the village of Sultan Ali Khan.

The Sind Horse had by now saddled up and fallen in. The two squadrons charged the hostile left centre, gallantly led by Major Reynolds.

A fierce hand-to-hand fight, lasting some ten minutes, ensued, when the enemy were forced to retreat, still disputing the ground fiercely.

Reynolds was ordered to pursue, while Colonel Malcolmson, with a portion of his men, tried to intercept a small body of the enemy who were making for Sultan Ali Khan.

Colonel Malcolmson, however, encountered a broad and deep kareze and the Afghans succeeded in reaching shelter.

Meanwhile, the rest of the cavalry and a portion of the infantry had been following up the enemy, when, as night was falling, they were called off.

The hostile strength was estimated at some fifteen hundred, of whom five hundred were ghazis and fifty horsemen.

Abu Bakka, a notorious robber chief, was reported to have been killed and some two hundred others.

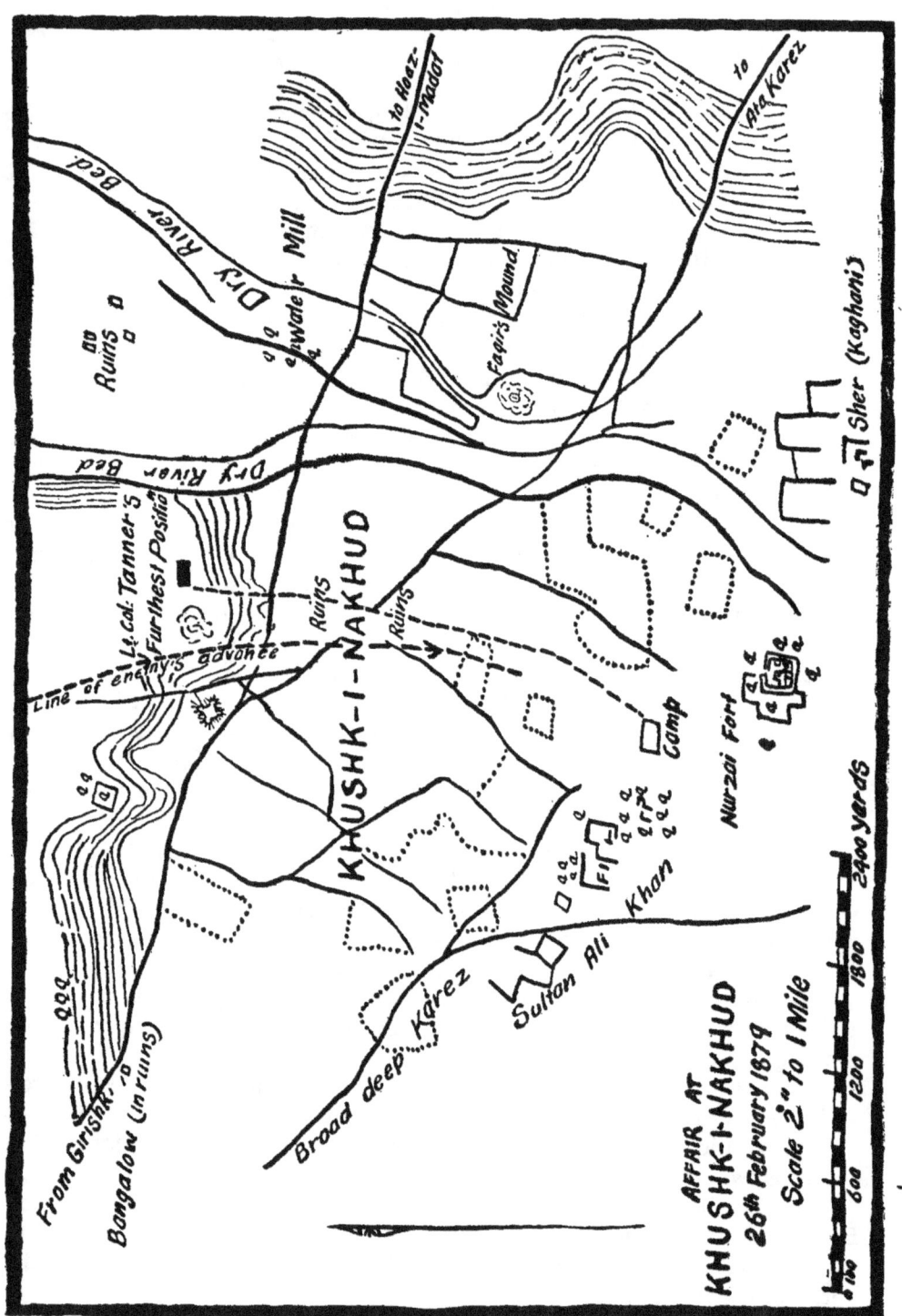

By Major G. D. Giles, *Scinde Horse*.

THE CHARGE AT KHUSHK-I-NAKHUD.

AFGHANISTAN, 1879.

By Major G. D. Giles, Scinde Horse.

LIFE AT THUL CHOTIALI, SECOND AFGHAN WAR.

1879—80.

Major Reynolds had been hit early in the affair by a bullet, but he still led his men to the attack, and so became engaged in personal encounter with the enemy, when his horse fell in a kareze, and, before he could recover himself, he was cut down and hacked to pieces.

Four of the Sind Horse were killed and twenty-three men wounded, the latter including Colonel Malcolmson. Twenty-eight horses were also lost. The casualties were thus pretty severe for a fight with Afghans.

The actual formation the charge was made in is not known, but it was, in all probability, a slap-dash affair and consisted merely in riding hard at the enemy anyhow. For this type of attack the more lines it can be made in the better, not merely for the purpose of inflicting loss, but for getting wounded men out of difficulties.

From accounts of officers who knew the 3rd Sind Horse, it was a regiment considerably above the average of native cavalry of the time and Malcolmson was one of those rare commanding officers of the period who believed in spit and polish, hence the saddlery inspection.

The employment of the infantry should be noticed.

This particular action was the most brilliant cavalry episode in the fighting in Southern Afghanistan during the whole war. Malcolmson was awarded the C.B., a great honour in those days. The charge is commemorated by a picture by Major Giles, the well-known artist, who himself served in the Sind Horse.

On the peace of Gandamak the garrison of Kandahar was greatly reduced, the troops belonging to the Force being *écheloned* as far back as Peshin, near Quetta.

When the outbreak at Kabul occurred the 3rd Sind Horse were at Khush Dil Khan, near Peshin. It had suffered much from cholera.

It returned to Kandahar in March 1880, detaching a squadron to Khelat i Ghilzai.

The squadron remained at Khelat i Ghilzai until Roberts picked up the detachment while *en route* to relieve Kandahar. It had, in the meantime, taken part in the action at Sir i Asp on the 1st July.

The Maiwand disaster took place on the 27th July 1880, and the 3rd Sind Horse had the misfortune to be involved in it. In common with other Bombay troops it was subjected to abuse and ignorant criticism.

There is no reason to suppose the Regiment had in any way fallen off since Khushk i Nakhud; a unit that has carried out a feat of arms that is the talk of the Force does not fall off, provided its officers are the same.

Maiwand and the events leading up to it are described in the following chapter.

CHAPTER II

THE ACTION AT MAIWAND.

27TH JULY, 1880

THE incidents leading up to the Maiwand disaster furnish an interesting study of the employment of cavalry attached to a small force of all arms. Future small wars in which the British Army may be called upon to take part will, in all probability, produce similar situations.

In this campaign there would have been every possibility of avoiding the disaster had the unfortunate G.O.C. made proper use of his mounted troops.

It is true that one feature, leading to the *débâcle*, was the fact that there did not exist any properly organized intelligence service under the military authorities. The whole was under the Political Officer, who acted independently of the General. To put it mildly, its nature was sketchy.

There were extraordinary divergencies, even in topographical matters, between political intelligence reports and the results of cavalry reconnaissances.

Reliable contemporary accounts, moreover, indicate that the Political Officer habitually pooh-poohed reports brought in by the cavalry.

In this connection, however, it must be borne in mind that most of these reports were brought in by officers of only some four years' service or so, while the recipients were probably well-advanced in years according to our present-day standards—for the passion the Indian authorities had for keeping men in positions for which they were too old, still existed in the early eighties. An officer of four years' service would have been, in those days, a mere child to the senior officers, and his reports might, in many cases, have been treated accordingly.

The fact remains that if the G.O.C. had only known how to employ his cavalry, he might quite possibly have averted disaster.

The events leading to the battle were, briefly, as follows:—On the 2nd July 1880 the following troops were detailed to march from Kandahar to Girishk, on the Helmund, to look out for Ayub Khan, who was advancing from Herat, and to support some Afghan levies under an official appointed by the British, termed the Wali:—

Cavalry Brigade
- 3rd Sind Horse, two hundred sabres.
- 3rd Bombay Light Cavalry, three hundred sabres.
- " E " By. R.H.A.

Infantry Brigade
- 66th Foot.
- 1st Grenadiers, Bombay Infantry.
- 30th Bombay Infantry.

On the approach of the British force, the Wali's troops mutinied and made off towards Herat.

The cavalry followed them up, but the mutineers got away, leaving their guns and camp equipment.

In view of the fact that the Helmund was very low and by now passable everywhere, and that there was a desert twenty-five miles wide in his rear, the G.O.C. fell back on the 15th July to Khushk i Nakhud, where he could block the main Kandahar route from Girishk directly, and that *via* Maiwand indirectly. The area was also a good one for supply. There were at that time no signs of any Afghan troops within thirty miles of the Helmund, but advanced bodies of Horse arrived there on the 17th.

By the 20th July the Afghan main body was along the line of that river between Haiderabad and Girishk.

The Political estimate of Ayub's strength was about fifteen hundred regular cavalry, five thousand regular infantry and thirty guns, besides tribesmen, mounted and dismounted, totalling some fifteen thousand. This estimate could only be given very roughly, owing to the fact that spies could not get through the screen of hostile tribesmen and Afghan Horse. The inhabitants, moreover, had become more and more disinclined to talk as Ayub came closer.

To enable the G.O.C. to forestall Ayub, should the latter move on Kandahar by a track other than the direct Khushk i Nakhud route, it was essential to have information of the route by which Ayub was moving at least eight hours before, so as to be able to get on the move in time.

It was not reasonable to count on this information arriving soon enough if espionage was the principal means of obtaining intelligence. Reconnaissance was the only method.

The method of despatching these reconnaissances, therefore, merits attention.

The custom was for a patrol of forty sabres to visit Sangbar, sixteen miles to the front, daily, returning at nightfall. Patrols, probably of similar strengths, visited, in like manner, Garmab and Band i Taimur, twelve miles to the north and south, respectively.

The width of front reconnoitred daily was thus twenty-five miles, with a distance of fifteen miles in the enemy's direction. To despatch patrols of such low strength such a long distance away from support was not the best way of overawing the inhabitants so as to induce them to talk. Nor was it calculated to foster that spirit of enterprise, so essential to good reconnaissance, that well-supported detachments would have had.

Furthermore, these weak parties could hardly be expected to make prisoners of the well-mounted Afghan Horse, for, under the stress of hard work in a desert country on indifferent rations and in extreme heat the horses wore out rapidly—and prisoners were badly wanted.

A particular point which required clearing up was whether the Afghan Horse, which crossed the Helmund on the 22nd July, belonged to an Afghan Sirdar called the Luinab, for this sirdar was known to be acting independently of Ayub. The best manner of doing so was to get some prisoners.

The first contact occurred on the 23rd July, about three miles from the British camp at Khushk i Nakhud, just as the Sangbar patrol under Lieutenant J. Monteith, Sind Horse—an officer subsequently well known in the Bombay Cavalry—was starting out.

About five hundred regular Afghan Horse were encountered. Some idea of the quality of these Afghan troopers may be gauged from the fact that, although the country was absolutely open and that they were well mounted, no attempt was made to rush the small party, which held its ground with carbine fire.

Two squadrons and a couple of guns, in camp, turned out to support Monteith, and the Afghans made off.

Two days later, on the 25th July, however, it is no matter of surprise to read that a portion of the Sangbar patrol, furnished by the Sind Horse, was overwhelmed by Afghans just outside that place, owing to the horses being too exhausted to enable the men to get away. A recurrence of such incidents might have gravely affected the *morale* of the cavalry—we know that similar occurrences did in the early days in Mesopotamia.

The same day a reconnaissance under Lieutenant Smith, Sind Horse, elicited the information that enemy patrols had reached Garmab, seven miles from Maiwand, and that Ayub was expected at the latter place on the 27th—a report which turned out to be correct.

Had the G.O.C. acted on this, he would have forestalled Ayub; but the attitude of the Political Officer towards all cavalry reconnaissances doubtless caused the G.O.C. to ignore it.

On the 26th July the Political Officer received reports confirming Ayub's probable move on Maiwand, but indicating that, if our troops marched on the 27th, they would forestall Ayub by at least a day.

The G.O.C. was evidently still under the impression that a large body of Afghan Horse reported at Garmab were the Luinab's men and not Ayub's—a point which might, as said before, have been cleared up by prisoners.

He accordingly marched on the 27th on Maiwand—and we know the result.

It is suggested that by pushing the cavalry brigade, plus a couple of horse guns, forward to the main junction of the Afghan line of advance at Sangbar, and letting it remain there, a suitable centre from which short-distance, but none the less quite effective, reconnaissances could be despatched would have been secured.

The strength of the detachment would have overawed the inhabitants and might have made them talk, prisoners might have been taken, and horseflesh would have been saved.

The Political Officer would, furthermore, be more reluctant to scoff at results of reconnaissances brought in by the cavalry brigadier than he was at those of young officers.

An objection may be raised that this was a dangerous detachment. Now, all reconnaissances are detachments, and to strew them over a front of twenty-five miles, as was done, is far more risky than to concentrate them on some important objective. With a weak force of cavalry it is impossible to reconnoitre in every direction simultaneously, and it is up to the commander of the force, not the cavalry commander, to make up his mind definitely in which direction he will make his main effort.

Taking into consideration the fact that two detached squadrons of the Sind Horse had engaged and routed fifteen hundred tribesmen, killing large numbers, the previous year in the same neighbourhood, and the pusillanimous conduct of the Afghan Horse when opposed to Lieutenant Monteith's forty sabres, the danger of a mobile detachment like the one suggested being overwhelmed was not great. The country on three sides of Sangbar was open for miles, and it would have been a very difficult matter for any force to approach unseen.

The line of advance *viâ* Band i Talmur was an unlikely one owing to supply, while the Mahmund Pass meant a long *détour*, news of which, if attempted, might be given away by the inhabitants.

The Sangbar route would, moreover, be watched at night. The dominating factor was, however, that reports from Sangbar would arrive in ample time to enable the British to get on the move and forestall Ayub at Maiwand, if necessary.

It is a natural consequence of a disaster that some scapegoat or scapegoats be found, and among them were the cavalry, who were blamed for not furnishing information.

It is a fact well known to officers who care to study war that indifferent

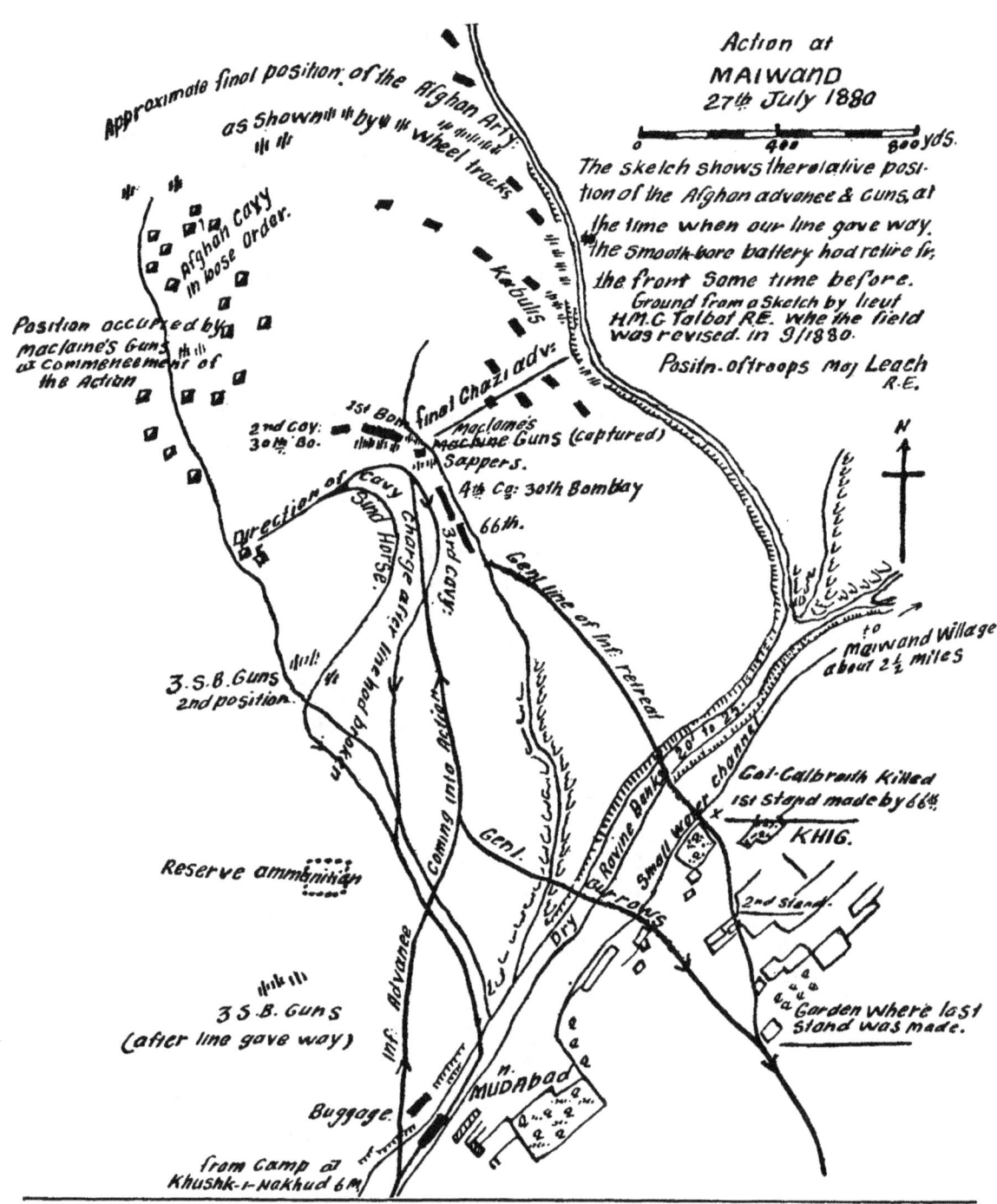

MAIWAND—Sketch by Lieut. H. M. G. Talbot, R.E.

cavalry, given some definite task to do, will produce better results than first class *personnel* given but a vague mission.

The blame in this case rests on the Force Commander primarily and secondly on the cavalry brigadier. To blame the unfortunate troops, as was done, was absurd. "A commander despatching a reconnaissance will obtain the information he deserves."

Under present day conditions the G.O.C. would in all probability have the assistance of some aeroplanes and probably some armoured cars.

The country is well suited to air reconnaissance, as there are but few trees and landing grounds are everywhere.

Ayub would have had considerable difficulty in concealing his indifferently disciplined troops, and an advance by day would be in full view. His only chance would be a night advance.

If the country is anything like the normal Baluchistan country, as it is supposed to be, armoured cars would be of considerable value over the routes some three or four miles from the foothills, viz., the Band i Taimur route, the Khushk i Nakhud—Yakchal route and the Khushk i Nakhud—Sangbar route.

The Maiwand—Garmab—Sangbar route would, in all probability, be broken up with water cuts and, close to villages, with flooded fields. Considerable saving in horseflesh would result and the cavalry could be reserved to support the cars and for those reconnaissances where identifications and prisoners were wanted. It is probable, however, that aeroplanes and armoured cars would not have much moral effect unless in very large numbers indeed. Armoured cars, moreover, as judged from Mesopotamian experience, have a habit of getting into trouble, and to expect them to supplant cavalry even in a very open country like this is ridiculous. In the intensely hot weather, again, their crews would find life almost unbearable.

The suggestion that the cavalry brigade be pushed forward to Sangbar would apply with equal force to the present day. With the great fire-power possessed nowadays there would be even less likelihood of the detachment being overwhelmed.

Improved means of signalling would, in addition, be available if trouble occurred.

The Force was to move at 04.30, but did not get clear of the ground till nearly 07.30, encumbered by a very unwieldy baggage.

The leading cavalry, the 3rd Bombay Cavalry, were not much more than half a mile ahead. The Sind Horse furnished the flank and rear guards, all not more than half a mile out. The country was very open, and there would have been but little risk in pushing the cavalry three or four miles to the front and flanks. In view of the fact that the object was to forestall Ayub at Maiwand or strike him *en route* there, the proper use would appear to be to have pushed all the cavalry not immediately required for local patrolling—say the whole brigade, less one squadron, plus a couple of horse guns—ahead to secure the place.

About two hundred or three hundred ghazis were reported to be there. Afghan Horse, in strength, were also reported to be at Garmab, but our cavalry should have found but little difficulty in coping with them.

It was intensely hot, and the unfortunate infantry marched in a most fatiguing formation.

There were constant halts to get the transport together. About three hours after the start—that is, about 10.00—a spy brought in information that Ayub's troops were in Maiwand in force.

The G.O.C. decided "it was too late to go back and that the advance must continue." What he proposed to do if he went back is not known.

Meanwhile the young British officer with the vanguard reported he could see large bodies of troops moving across his front towards Maiwand. This was confirmed by the flank guard of the Sind Horse.

It is somewhat significant of the attitude towards young officers' reports that the vanguard commander was told first of all that he was creating false alarms, and it was only after the cavalry-brigadier had himself looked through his glasses that this report was accepted.

This would be about 10.30.

The guns and cavalry were pushed forward and engaged hostile cavalry about a mile north of Mundabad.

The infantry meanwhile were suffering greatly from heat and thirst. They were, moreover, not a little fatigued owing to the unsuitable formation in which they had marched. Nevertheless they were hustled along after the cavalry without being given a chance of getting a drink at a stream which was crossed. This had a serious effect later. For some reason the infantry were halted in rear of the guns and lay down.

In the meantime, Ayub, emboldened by our delay to advance, brought up his artillery.

About noon the G.O.C. ordered the infantry to advance, which they did with the utmost steadiness.

As the fire grew hotter they were ordered to lie down, practically in a line with the horse battery.

This was the only effort at an advance.

In the meantime the cavalry, who had gone forward as escort to the guns, had remained close to them.

They were mixed up in a most extraordinary manner, three troops of the 3rd Bombay Cavalry and two troops of the 3rd Sind Horse being sandwiched in between each other and the guns, quite irrespective of regiments.

It is said that it was impossible to withdraw them as the Afghan Horse threatened to rush the guns.

This would be conceivable before the infantry came up, but not so afterwards.

The 30th Bombay Infantry were full of young recruits, and it has been stated in some quarters that a withdrawal of the cavalry from close to them might have upset them. The remainder of the cavalry were some three or four hundred yards to the left rear of the line.

The infantry lying down had a certain amount of cover, but the batteries and the cavalry were absolutely exposed.

Meanwhile the Afghans began to encircle the force, and attack the baggage, which was left close to Mundabad.

An examination of the ground some months after the battle showed that the position taken up, in absolutely open ground, had a nullah affording excellent cover—and one by which the Afghans brought up their artillery—running within six hundred yards of the front.

A smaller nullah ran about the same distance round the left flank and rear.

The position was altogether as bad a one as could be imagined. A glance at the map will suffice.

Battery after battery of Ayub's guns came into action, and their fire was very accurate. Our artillery was unable to cope with it and the force found itself a focus of fire from almost a semicircle of guns firing at ranges not exceeding eight hundred yards—the present equivalent of, say, three thousand yards.

Afghan Horse swarmed round our left flank and harassed the baggage. As they were well mounted they could evade our troopers on their tired horses.

For the first two hours of the action at all events—say till 13.00—there is no reason to suppose that our infantry would have failed to respond to an order to advance, for until then their losses had been slight, the gunners and cavalry suffering most. Horses were coming down in every direction under the shelling, and it was computed that the 3rd Sind Horse must have lost some eighty horses out of two hundred odd when the line went.

As the gun-fire began to tell, however, the morale of the unfortunate infantry, lying under a roasting sun and suffering severely from thirst and fatigue, must have begun to be affected.

As regards the cavalry, the cavalry brigadier had directed a conglomeration of men of the 3rd Sind Horse and 3rd Bombay Cavalry, who had been posted towards the right flank, to charge a body of ghazis moving round that way.

The men had moved off to charge, a fact which in itself indicates that their *morale* was not yet affected, when he counter-ordered it. The men fell back to a position in rear of the centre of the infantry.

The brigadier evidently made no attempt, even then, to sort out the troops of the two regiments and get them under their own officers in some order. The men still remained distributed by troops mixed up.

From a study of the operations, the cavalry brigadier would appear to have been absolutely devoid of initiative, though a brave man.

At somewhere about 15.00—that is, some four hours after the action began—a ghazi rush broke the left of the infantry and a panic spread along the line, the 66th alone remaining firm.

The general confusion of the battle makes things hard to follow, but this would seemingly have been the moment for the cavalry brigadier to act on his own, if ever. A counter-charge delivered at this moment might have saved things, provided it was delivered before the demoralized infantry had reached the cavalry.

As it was, the brigadier waited until the G.O.C. came up to him and asked him to charge. By then the confusion was such that orders could not be heard. Ghazis and sepoys had become mixed up with the cavalry, who were in small parties. The numbers with the brigadier did not exceed some hundred and thirty all told, consisting both of men of the 3rd Bombay Cavalry and 3rd Sind Horse. The rest of the cavalry was inextricably mixed up with the infantry and guns.

The men were, moreover, shaken by their four hours' passive exposure to artillery and musketry fire. To pretend that good European troops would not have been affected under similar circumstances would be absurd. It says much for them that they did charge, though not in the direction wanted. By this, the 1st Bombay Grenadiers were saved from utter destruction.

It might be imagined that it would have been a hopeless procedure to rally after a charge like this. Nevertheless the brigadier did collect the men again. This fact should be noticed; for, with the stream of fugitives (including British troops) and the general demoralization that existed, it would have been an easy thing to clear off with the rest.

The cavalry retired, moreover, at a walk.

As may be expected, it was the 66th Foot who held staunch and eventually saved things, in a measure, by their stand at Khig.

Nevertheless, the affair developed into a rout, though the cavalry retained their formation.

It had generally been believed that the G.O.C. had been killed, but it was not until the retreat had proceeded about two miles that he suddenly came up from the rear, riding behind the Woordie Major of the Sind Horse (both being on the same horse). About the same time three other British officers were brought in, in the same way, by men of the Sind Horse.

The Afghan pursuit petered out very soon, as the tribesmen were busy looting.

The demoralization of the infantry was such that they would not even wait by some water, as they thought the Afghans too close.

On reaching the Khushk i Nakhud River, a troop of the Sind Horse held the left bank and covered the retirement until carriage had been found for most of the wounded.

During the retreat the rear of the guns was the last point protected, and the cavalry has been criticized for not remaining further to the rear, by which means many stragglers and wounded might have been saved.

Granting that it might have been difficult to induce the cavalry as a whole to charge again, there is much evidence to show that had any attempt been made to keep it further in rear it could have been done. From accounts of officers who were present it would seem that the unfortunate Force Commander had now lost his head and received no backing from the cavalry brigadier.

An opportunity to water the cavalry at Khushk i Nakhud was let slip.

Had this been taken, the rear of the infantry would have been protected. The shakiness, which was accentuated by thirst, heat and fatigue, would have quite possibly calmed down, and many men might have been saved.

In particular, it would appear that no attempt was made to keep the cavalry behind at Hauz i Hadat, where the exhausted stragglers were watering. The excuse tendered was that the G.O.C. was afraid there might be a panic, as Afghan artillery were reported approaching. The fact that a troop of the 3rd Bombay Cavalry did actually remain on there till the stragglers were clear indicates that the G.O.C. exaggerated the state of demoralization.

This troop reached the neighbourhood of Kandahar at 14.00 next day, some six hours after the G.O.C. arrived there, which is of itself a sufficient indication of the spirit of the men.

On this disastrous day no less than nine Indian ranks were awarded the Order of Merit in the 3rd Sind Horse alone—a very high proportion considering only some two hundred and twenty sabres were engaged.

The more one reads of the miserable affair, the more painful becomes our display of leadership, and, until Kitchener reformed the Army in India some twenty-five years after Maiwand, the Bombay troops were subjected to abuse and ignorant criticism as being inferior fighting material.

It must be remembered, however, that, until then, inter-Presidential feeling ran high. A peculiar brand of *esprit de corps* of gloating over mishaps to other units was, furthermore, very prevalent right up to the beginning of the Great War.

Again, Hensman, a writer who accompanied the Punjab part of the Army, seems to have written largely with the idea of boosting the portion he was with, while not taking into sufficient account the incompetent leadership of the Bombay troops.

Had the Bombay troops had a man like Roberts in command, the tale would have been very different.

A peculiar feature with regard to the criticism was that the composition of the units at Maiwand included really comparatively few Bombay-enlisted men, and of these there were hardly any Mahrattas and no Rajputana Rajputs. One infantry battalion was recruited entirely from the Punjab, while the two cavalry regiments were chiefly from the Rohtak and Delhi districts—districts which have been proved in the Great War to furnish some of the very best horse soldiers in India.

" In war it is the man, and not the men," and the man was absent.

THE BATTLE HONOURS

"MEEANEE"	"PUNJAUB"
"HYDERABAD"	"PERSIA"
"CUTCHEE"	"CENTRAL INDIA"
"MOOLTAN"	"ABYSSINIA"
"GOOJERAT"	"KANDAHAR"

"AFGHANISTAN, 1878–80"

A TROOPER OF THE SIND HORSE.
1880.

By Major G. D. Giles, Scinde Horse.

THE SORTIE OF DEH KHOJA.

KANDAHAR, 1880.

CHAPTER III

AN OUTLINE OF THE SERVICES OF THE REGIMENT. END OF THE SECOND AFGHAN WAR. MEKRAN. SEISTAN.

1880–1914

ALMOST immediately after Roberts had relieved Kandahar he fought the battle which routed Ayub.

In this action the Bombay troops watched the Baba Wali Kotal on the right.

When the Afghan army broke the Bombay Cavalry Brigade, consisting of the 3rd Bombay Cavalry and 3rd Sind Horse, was directed to push through the Kotal in pursuit.

Several parties of the enemy were engaged and some hundred Afghans were killed. Most of Ayub's army had, however, dispersed. This latter feature is always one to reckon with in small wars, and for this reason cavalry must be far quicker jumping off than is necessary in the case of war with regular troops.

The Bengal Cavalry Brigade on the extreme left found itself hung up by bad ground and also failed to come up with any formed bodies.

The Regiment pursued as far as Mansurabad, some fifteen miles, returning long after dark to bivouac. Maiwand was thus to some extent avenged.

In 1882 certain reductions were made in both the Bengal and Bombay Armies, many regiments being disbanded.

The 3rd Sind Horse, being the junior Regiment in the Bombay Cavalry, was broken up, large numbers of its officers and men being absorbed in the two older regiments.

From accounts of officers who knew the Regiment, it was reckoned as being one of the best units in the Bombay Cavalry, both in war and sport.

A very long and deadly period of peace followed, but the regiments were constantly furnishing escorts to Sir Robert Sandeman and other Political Officers in all parts of Baluchistan and in parts of Persia.

There were many alarms of forays and sundry minor skirmishes, but little more.

Life in this detestable country included all the disadvantages of active service with none of its excitements. Sir Robert Sandeman had, by his able administration, deprived us of the latter.

In 1887 General Luck, a well-known cavalry officer of the time, held a camp of exercise of the Sind Cavalry Brigade at Sibi, one of the first of its kind.

This camp of exercise was much talked of and did an enormity of good. At its conclusion, as a test of endurance, he ordered the First Regiment, now the 5th Bombay Cavalry, and the 7th Bombay Lancers, a newly raised unit, to march across the desert between Sibi and Jacobabad, the principal scene of the exploits of the Sind Horse in its early days.

The Sind Horse completed the distance, one hundred and eighteen miles, in forty hours, marching *viâ* the foothills.

The 7th Bombay Lancers marched a slightly shorter distance, alongside the present railway line, in thirty-six hours.

It is believed that the length of this march is nearly a record. The Sind Horse lost no horses as a result of it, extraordinary to relate.

In 1893 the class composition of the Regiment was modified, the enlistment of Sikhs and Pathans commencing.

The composition at this period became one squadron Sikhs, one Pathan, one Hindustani Mussulman, one of Rajputs and Mussulmans of Rajputana.

The recruitment of Derajat Mussulmans, in lieu of the Hindustanis and Rajputs, commenced a few years later and continued until the end of the Great War, when the recruitment of Mussulman Rajputs again commenced.

In 1899 trouble suddenly broke out in Mekran. A small force was hastily despatched by sea from Karachi. Fifty sabres of the Second Regiment, then the 6th Bombay Cavalry, under Lieutenant Naylor, formed part but arrived after the rest had disembarked at Pasni.

Mekran differs from the rest of Baluchistan in that in the few districts where there is much water the chief product is dates. In other respects it has all the same objectionable characteristics with a few of its own thrown in.

The Mekrani is a mixture of Baluch, Arab and negro, the last admixture being due to slaves. He cannot be said to be a formidable fighting man, with the exception of certain of the maliks who are really brave men.

The normal form of "war" consists in raiding, followed up by a pursuit at very safe range, for it is not the etiquette to suffer casualties. On this occasion, however, the Mekranis, who had not previously felt the power of the British raj, opposed the advance at the southern entrance of the pass leading to Turbat from Pasni, at a point called Gokh Prusht. Their number was estimated at fifteen hundred, armed in the main with matchlocks, but with a few Martinis and Sniders. (At this period Indian troops had only Martinis.)

The cavalry had not arrived when the action opened, having only reached camp, after a series of double marches, that morning. On hearing the gunfire, it saddled up at once and arrived in time to take a prominent part in the attack, being detached to act dismounted from some high ground on the enemy's right. The Mekranis were routed, leaving some two hundred dead on the ground. No pursuit was possible owing to the mountains. Subsequently many forts were destroyed, and there was the usual hard marching in this particularly noisome country.

Things quietened down slightly, but trouble recommenced soon after the troops had returned to India.

Mekran is some five hundred miles away from the British garrison at Quetta and is a difficult country to get at even from the coast, owing to the intervening mountains.

The only so-called forces in favour of law and order were some Baluch levies, under the local governor, termed the Nazim. With these, the dominant motto in war was "safety first." No action must be fought at a closer range than twelve hundred yards, for men had been occasionally hit at that distance.

The country being suitable and times dull, certain of the more enterprising maliks had carried out some highly successful raids, and, on their conclusion, had promptly retired, usually to Persian Mekran, where they could not be pursued. The "grand coup" had been a raid into British territory which bagged some ten thousand head of cattle, sheep, goats and camels, and these from places as much as one hundred miles inside our frontier. The bitter pill of this affair had been that the Nazim had been led some eighty miles off in the wrong direction by a skilfully engineered feint.

All Mekran, Persian and British, was laughing in its sleeve at this official. Arrangements were accordingly made with the Persian Government for a small force of British troops, under Major Tighe (the late Sir Michael Tighe), to co-operate with a Persian force and restore some degree of order. As it would, in all probability, be a difficult matter to capture the chief offenders, their baronial castles were to be destroyed.

These castles are built more on the lines of Europe than of the North-West Frontier and are extremely strong. With resolute garrisons they would be most formidable even against field howitzers. All are in the midst of date palm groves.

Major Tighe's force was composed of fifty sabres of the First Regiment, then the 5th Bombay Cavalry, under Lieutenant Maunsell, a section of a mountain battery, a section of Sappers and Miners and four companies of the 27th Baluchis. The last two units went by sea to Gwadur.

The cavalry and guns marched from near Jacobabad, moving via the Mulla Pass, in which there was constant trouble owing to horses dropping shoes in the stony river-bed, and in which the river would sometimes be forded some fifteen times a march, Khozdar, and Nal to the Kej Valley in Mekran. The distance was six hundred miles, covered in six weeks, through a country which was, in its last half, a desert, with little and bad water and nearly always difficulty in fodder supply. The final march was sixty miles in thirty hours for the purpose of joining the 27th Baluchis in the attack on Nodiz. This was a fort in which a band of outlaws had been invested by the Nazim's levies for the last month. The investment had been in accordance with the traditions of this gallant body of men. Only one casualty had occurred, and that on account of a gross breach of etiquette on the part of the besieged, who had taken an unfair advantage of a period not normally devoted to "war." The fort was well rationed up, both for men and animals, and we found many maunds of dates in it. There were cows, goats, donkeys and even a camel or two as well, all in good condition. A kareze ran under the walls and there was plenty of good water. The besieged, indeed, were perfectly happy in the confidence, based on all previous experiences of Mekrani "war," that the besiegers would soon tire of the investment and go away. The Nazim's presence was rather annoying, but that was all, for it was seemingly quite possible to go out at night. There was but little doubt that this appreciation of the situation would have proved correct had the Nazim not learnt of the approach of Tighe's force. Furthermore, this official had a grievance against the outlaw chief on personal grounds, for it was this man who had engineered the coup which brought ridicule on the Khan of Khelat's officer.

The besieged had heard of British troops coming in the course of their daily chat with the levies, but seemingly disbelieved the yarn or thought themselves strong enough to cope with them.

Otherwise it is hard to account for their hanging on until the 27th Baluchis actually arrived on the scene, for the leaders were undoubtedly brave resolute men, and men, moreover, who had shown themselves endowed with no little skill and dash. There would not have been the least difficulty in breaking away in the night, and but little in doing so by day. As things turned out, they played into our hands and enabled us to make a bag which would have been next to impossible had they taken to the hills, for the people were all in league with them. The 27th Baluchis assaulted the fort after a short but inadequate bombardment by the two mountain guns. They were met in the small breach effected by a charge of swordsmen and had to wait for a further bombardment. Two British officers and about twenty-five men were killed and wounded in this effort.

The back of the resistance was, however, broken by the two leaders of the outlaws being killed. A prolonged steady shelling by the two mountain guns, which were brought up to one hundred yards range, caused the garrison to surrender as a second assault was starting. The guns had fired some hundred and fifty rounds, but had only made a breach four feet wide in a mud wall three feet thick. The shells had set fire to the roof of the "keep," and this was the final cause of the surrender. There is but little doubt that if it had not been for the artillery we might have lost very heavily indeed, and might even have failed altogether.

All Mekran was sitting on the fence and things might have been highly unpleasant. As would be expected, the cavalry merely played the part of spectators in the affair.

The next phase was to join up with the Persians. The force was now to be a flying column carrying three months' rations. No fewer than four thousand camels were required for the odd nine hundred rifles and two hundred horses and mules composing it.

The march was through the normal desolate Baluchistan scenery and the camels, all miserable brutes, died continually. The country was quite quiet, which was just as well, for the column strung out to some ten or eleven miles.

The Sind Horse detachment went on ahead with the Political Agent to join up with the Persians who were near the outlaw fort of Magas, while the 27th Baluchis destroyed another fort called Irafshan.

Magas was a most formidable-looking place, still in outlaw occupation. There was a truce on, as the Persians were negotiating with the garrison over a surrender. Our allies' "troops" were a truly wonderful army, and their morning "parades" afforded the greatest interest, not to say amusement. Very wisely perhaps they had not ventured within a mile of the fort.

Its garrison, however, had heard the news of Nodiz, with numerous and startling embellishments. It is believed that Nodiz was the first fort that was ever taken in Mekran otherwise than by treachery, bluff or starvation. They evacuated the place before the infantry came up. On going over it, it is not too much to say that all of us felt the greatest relief at their having done so. It was enormously strong. The walls were some fifty feet high and far too thick for mountain guns to have the least effect. With a garrison to put up a show like Nodiz it is more than doubtful if we could have tackled it with the means at our disposal. The only hope would have been howitzers. One must, in dealing with Orientals, at the same time, remember that, as a rule, the stronger the defensive works the less formidable are the people, and, in the days of Lake and Wellesley, British troops did not hesitate to attack places like Aligarh, Ahmednagar and Gawilgarh, which were held by brave men. Had Magas put up a resistance we might have been in a very nasty position indeed, for the sea was two hundred miles off and no help by land could be expected from nearer than Quetta, which was six hundred miles away. Furthermore, in those days the only form of communication was by tribal messengers.

Great difficulty was experienced in blowing up the fort, and the question of the supply of gun-cotton became acute as there were more to be destroyed. The Persians, fortunately, had a lot of gunpowder.

The force then moved on and destroyed sundry other places. The inhabitants had cleared absolutely away into the mountains and the villages were quite empty.

There had been, all along, difficulty in feeding the odd two hundred horses and mules of the cavalry and guns, and, as the serious work had now been finished, it was decided to send them back to Quetta. Before they went, the cavalry were sent off on a kind of " de Wet " hunt after an outlaw named Mahomed Umar. As the whole country was friendly with this gentleman, the effort was farcical. One marched for " miles and blinkin' miles " for days on end, on wild-goose chases. The government had only put five hundred rupees on the man's head and would pay nothing for intelligence. So far from doing any good, this effort might well have lowered the prestige of the Sirkar. The game of " ragging the troops " by furnishing bogus information which forms such a favourite pastime at Peshawar, Dera Ismail Khan and other places where raids occur, might well have occurred here, but with more serious consequences, for we were living on prestige to a great extent, and if this had gone we might have had to fight our way out of the country. After a certain number of futile and hard marches we adopted the plan of compelling the informer to accompany the troops, or if this was thought inadvisable, the intelligence or political official who advised the trek. This proved most efficacious, and the writer recalls Colonel Barrow (now Lieut.-General Sir George Barrow) advocating the same process as a protection from unnecessary turn outs at Tank in 1911.

It is believed that the Sind Horse were the only troops who had ever been seen in these out-of-the-way parts of the earth, and, extraordinary as it may appear, the name of John Jacob was known to many, although he had died over forty years before.

If the march down to Mekran had been hard, the return was worse, for the country was all desert as far as Khelat. The water varied from the crystal clear stream impregnated with salts, to the two-hundred-feet-deep well, with no means of lifting the water beyond our picketing ropes, and the water all sulphuretted hydrogen. The men and syces would continually have to go out after a long and tiring march and scrape together stuff called grass. It was, moreover, getting hot. The horses' shoes were worn down to thin plates and were always coming off. A search would then have to be made for the fallen shoe so as to have it made up again into tips. By the time one reached Quetta nearly all the horses were shod with tips, remade by the farrier, who, for a wonder, could make shoes. The men's boots were worn out and the gunners made up grass shoes.

The officers'-mess stores had run down to one tin of porridge and one of sardines per week, with no liquor at all beyond tea. One lived on tough chicken, goat, rice, onions and chupattis for more than a month.

By the time the detachment reached Quetta, the cavalry had marched eighteen hundred miles in six months and had not lost a horse or mule.

In 1904 the Seistan Boundary Commission, under Sir Henry MacMahon, left Quetta. Fifty sabres of the First Regiment, under Lieutenant Landon, formed part of the escort. The climatic conditions were worse than those of the Mekran parties, for the Seistan Desert is one of the coldest and the hottest parts of the earth. The conditions of hard marching and general discomfort were identical. This detachment was away, without relief or leave, for no less than two and a half years.

The men of the Sind Horse greatly distinguished themselves by their cheery behaviour through this trying time. Certain other troops mutinied at the conditions.

A large amount of space has been devoted to the description of the very minor affairs of Mekran and Seistan, but it is thought that some personal account of the type of work our regiments had been carrying out for years on the Baluchistan Border will be in place in the Regiment's history.

The detachments in these cases had been commanded by young British officers, but most were of weaker strength and under native officers. In only very rare instances was there any fighting. It was the same old tale of continuous hard marching, bad food, bad water and violent contrasts of heat and cold. The last is very trying, for the temperature always drops enormously as soon as the sun goes down. This type of service is far more irksome to troops than the normal brand of fighting Indian soldiers meet with, and has no glory attached.

In 1905 Lord Kitchener reorganized the whole army in India. To the immense joy of all ranks we ceased to be local regiments.

There is not the slightest doubt that localization is extremely bad for troops, particularly if there is no fighting. Officers fight shy of units stationed in a dull hard country, which is, in addition, expensive to live in, and everything trends to a narrow outlook.

We know that certain prominent civil officials were opposed to de-localization on the grounds that our men knew the country. It takes but little time to learn this, and it does troops who have lived in comfortable cantonments an enormity of good to go out to a rough country and be knocked about a bit.

CHAPTER IV

THE EFFICIENCY OF THE INDIAN CAVALRY AT THE OPENING OF THE GREAT WAR.

1914

AT the outbreak of the Great War soldiering in India was considerably behind that at Home, and the Indian Cavalry lagged far behind the British in general efficiency.

The difference had been greatly accentuated in the years following the South African War.

With this behind and the German menace ahead, the Home authorities had set their house in order, with the result that the original British Expeditionary Force was the finest body of troops the world had ever seen.

This had been largely due to the extreme care displayed in the selection of commanders and staffs, and there is reason to suppose that the best British Service officers either avoided going to India or were retained at Home prior to the outbreak of the War.

In India things were very different. Owing to the absence of a sufficiently ruthless system of elimination of the unfit there were many men in high places not up to their work. The passion of the Simla hierarchy for the retention of men past their day, which had proved so ruinous in the Sikh Wars and in the Mutiny, still held good, though not, of course, to the same extent. The authorities appeared oblivious, in some particularly blatant cases, to the fact that because a man had once been a good soldier, fit both physically and mentally, he might not still be so when he received a new appointment. The effect of prolonged residence in a bad climate and under conditions which tend to deteriorate the normal man was ignored.

The happiness and lives of men, but above all the honour of a regiment, seemed, not infrequently, to be secondary to the unpleasantness that might be caused by passing over some individual who could but prove to be a bad, weak, or enfeebled commanding officer.

Many instances can be quoted of regiments, once famous, having their fair name besmirched owing to such appointments.

If there was a large proportion of commanding officers who were too old, the brigadiers were even worse. The changes that occurred in the command of Indian formations in the first eighteen months of the War speak for themselves.

As a consequence of this most pernicious system India can be safely said to have been ten years behind the times, as judged by British Expeditionary Force standards.

The country was dominated by the "small war" fetish, and but few Indian Army officers ever dreamt that they would find themselves fighting in Europe, or against any enemy that fought on European lines for that matter.

The principle that "if you can kill the cat you can kill the kitten" was not appreciated.

The contrast between Home methods and those existing in pre-War India was painfully evident when officers attended staff rides and manœuvres in England.

The higher training in India was markedly behindhand. It is not a difficult thing to recall some extraordinary performances on manœuvres, particularly when some commander who had spent his life on an office stool got going.

It was not altogether to be wondered at, therefore, that one occasionally heard the caustic query as to whether it was the function of the general to train the troops, or the troops to train the general.

Despite the absence of much inducement to fit themselves to meet a European enemy, the great majority of Indian Army officers were keen enough on their job and only required to be put on the right lines and be shown, by some competent senior officer in whom they had confidence, the standard to be worked up to.

There were, however, far too many seniors who were only second class—and their subordinates knew it. It will, therefore, be understood that although in most cases the troops worked hard enough, the work was frequently misdirected through lack of capable supervision.

This was more marked in the cavalry than in the infantry, owing to the general ignorance of the arm on the part of so many of the generals. In a number of Indian cavalry regiments the work done was not merely inadequate, but was superficial and lacked thoroughness, and the generals had to leave second-class commanding officers to their own devices as they did not possess the necessary knowledge to put them on the right lines.

Much of the work did not amount to more than an hour's squadron drill in the day, if that. It was common to find units that could drill fairly well, but which were extraordinarily bad at field work. Poor field work was, indeed, the rule and not the exception, even in good regiments.

Regiments appeared to be judged more by the sporting character of their officers than by the latter's professional capacity. It is, indeed, hardly an exaggeration to say that a regiment with a good polo team might almost be said to have been able to snap its fingers at inspecting officers. There is, certainly, something to be said for the method, for most good soldiers are good sportsmen. It was, however, greatly overdone and the correct balance was not maintained. It by no means signifies that because a few British officers are good polo players or shikaris that the Indian ranks are either disciplined, trained, or in hard condition.

It is, indeed, curious to note how extraordinarily sticky certain units, whose officers were, in time of peace, great thrusters, proved to be.

A notion existed that the Indian cavalry soldier could not be worked up to British standards, despite the example of the native mountain batteries, which were simply excellent. The War, however, showed that, given time and live men as commanders, he could be made to run the British regular trooper very close indeed. The regiments from France had nothing whatever to learn from the mounted troops they came alongside in Palestine, and could show the way to most.

In every respect, except horsemastership and horsemanship, the Indian cavalry were far behind the British regular and—and this is the point—to a quite unnecessary degree.

General Barrow, Colonel of the Regiment, together with many other Indian cavalry officers who served with British cavalry in the early days of the War, is emphatic that the Indian cavalry could never have done what the British did from the Battle of Mons until the end of the First Battle of Ypres.

They probably could have, had they been trained to the standard attained by the regiments in France by the end of 1916.

At the same time, it is only fair to state that General Barrow is of opinion that the Indian cavalry were, even in 1914, ahead of the French, and he saw much of the latter. The French cavalry were trained for shock, pure and simple, and looked down on any dismounted work as *infra dig*.—the job of mere " pousse caillous." They would not even demean themselves by digging trenches at the First Battle of Ypres. They were, moreover, extremely bad horsemasters and had a very low standard of musketry.

Not merely was the higher training of officers in India behindhand, but the individual training of the men also. Recruit instruction was not by any means remarkable for either its thoroughness or adequacy in scope. Instructors, hard enough to get even now, were few and far between, and usually indifferent. The result was that men were passed into the ranks long before they were fit for it, as judged by British cavalry standards.

When once a man joined the ranks his individual training might almost be said to have ended, for, owing to the colossal amount of leave allowed, the time of the men during the hot weather and rains was almost entirely taken up in exercising horses. The amount of leave granted was, in the writer's opinion, simply ridiculous. A man got away for seven months every three years in addition to two months every year. On return to the unit he had usually forgotten much of what he had ever been taught.

In the winter months work was confined to troop, squadron, regimental and brigade training.

As the time was always broken into by Christmas holidays, "weeks," visits by big functionaries and sundry festivities, a great deal of the work was rushed through in a superficial manner, and much time was lost in endeavouring to make good defects in individual training.

Foot work, the basis of all training, was extraordinarily bad. There was, and still is, a prejudice against it.

As a natural consequence, the ground work in essential matters like musketry was flimsy. Fire control and fire direction may almost be said to have been a sealed book. It may be argued that musketry returns were not too bad. The answer is that, on the word of an Inspector of Musketry with whom the writer discussed the matter, but little reliance could be placed on them.

The sowar on his feet was a ridiculous object. His arms drill was slovenly to a degree.

Slipshod sentries, slack guards, and the appearance of five men walking four different steps, as was the rule and not the exception, had a great deal to do with the attitude of British troops in 1914 and 1915—that of a scarcely veiled contempt.

The babel of noise that accompanied work at ration dumps, embussing or debussing, loading up carts or similar jobs, did not help matters.

It behoves Indian cavalry officers, jealous of the good name of their service, to see that this state of things does not recur.

As a result of the inadequate individual training nearly the whole of the N.C.O.'s were quite incapable of imparting instruction, and a number of Indian officers as well.

The proportion of either who could read a map was very small.

There were numbers of Indian ranks who were too soft and too old to stand the strain of active service, and who, moreover, did not want to go when the chance came.

It was a matter of the greatest difficulty to get rid of incapable Indian officers owing to lack of support from the higher authorities. It was almost equally difficult to weed out bad N.C.O.'s unless one lay for them in a manner that was hardly consonant with one's position. Brigadiers in most cases appeared to walk in terror of using that most effective weapon for assisting commanding officers to pull regiments together, the power of summary dismissal or reduction. The consequence was a commanding officer in a bad regiment might find himself saddled with Indian officers and N.C.O.'s who were working harm, but against whom it was a matter of great difficulty to get tangible evidence for trial.

The " bhai bandi " that is the curse of any body of troops, British included, who are recruited within very narrow territorial limits, often makes the obtaining of evidence very hard.

In Indian units, moreover, a trial by court martial, even if resulting in conviction, may sometimes do more harm than good.

With the rage for economy then prevailing it might have been obvious that the Government was paying men not worth their keep.

It will, therefore, be appreciated that, with the Indian officers only partially trained, and, what is worse, brought up under the slipshod traditions of the " Irregular Horse," discipline was by no means of the precise and strict nature a great war demands. Jacob's Horse was, in this respect, far above the average, and necessarily so, for had it not been the case it would have been a general nuisance, composed as it was of the most turbulent races in India.

Under these conditions is it to be wondered at that, in the early days of the War, the Indian cavalry, on fronts other than France and Palestine, did not in all cases exactly cover themselves with glory?

Numerous instances of stickiness, lack of dash, and even misconduct, occurred throughout the War. Much was evidently due to faulty handling on the part of British officers, and this, as may be expected, reacted on the rank and file.

More, however, was undoubtedly due to insufficient training and discipline. The gallantry of their British officers in no way made up for these deficiencies, as the poor fellows found to their cost.

Now, it is a curious thing, but misconduct was almost unheard of in the regiments trained in France. The dash of the men was universally commented on.

It is submitted that this was due to three things, leading, discipline and training, and these were, in the main, brought about in France and not in India.

It must, however, be remembered, that the regiments in France were, with the exception of a couple who were engaged at Festubert, Christmas 1914, and one at High Wood in 1916, not seriously engaged until 1917. They had, therefore, over two years to pull together, much of the time under young and excellent generals.

Herein lies the solution, for the class of Indian recruited in the cavalry included none of the useless creatures with which some of the unfortunate infantry were cursed. The men were the pick of the fighting stock of India.

It may be urged that the Indian cavalry had always done well in previous wars. It must, however, be remembered that these affairs hardly ever threw much strain on the troops, and did not, as a rule, demand a very high standard of efficiency. The regiments that had shone in them had, moreover, been fortunate in having really good men in command, or were units with a very great tradition behind them which enabled them to stand much hard work and strain.

A great war or prolonged service in a hard country and bad climate would cause weaknesses to appear very quickly. An indifferently disciplined unit, and one, above all, which had " lived soft " in comfortable cantonments, would soon crack and break—and we know this happened. With the above defects at the outbreak of the War it is easy to account for the strong antipathy that existed at General Head-Quarters and in many high places in France against India and anything that emanated therefrom, for certain very senior officers had seen with their own eyes the state of affairs and the difficulty in getting a move on.

As regards the attitude of British regular troops towards Indians, much was due to ignorance, and this was not confined to those who had never been in India. Little or no effort had been made to make them learn something about the sepoy, with the result that nearly the whole of British rank and file, together with a large proportion of the officers, were prone to categorize the lot as the same as their syces and line boys. They were almost incapable of distinguishing between the useless creatures who were to be found in some of the infantry units now disbanded, and good Indian troops. Furthermore, the Indian Corps had not received altogether fair treatment—the state of affairs can be seen in Sir James Wilcocks' book—and had been placed in a series of impossible situations.

Certain Indian troops, who had lost most of their British officers, had failed. The additional strain had fallen on the British troops, and the tales of failure did not lose in the telling. We know that white troops frequently failed under similar circumstances later in the War.

All this had to be lived down by the Indian cavalry, and it was to the credit of the service that the regiments finally left France with a very good name indeed.

CHAPTER V

THE 36TH JACOB'S HORSE.
THE GREAT WAR.
1914–1918
FRANCE AND FLANDERS.
INDIA. ARRIVAL IN FRANCE. BILLETING.

1914

AT the outbreak of the Great War the 35th Scinde Horse (formerly 1st Sind Horse) were at Dera Ismail Khan, and the 36th Jacob's Horse (formerly 2nd Sind Horse) were at Cawnpore.

The composition of both Regiments at the time was, on paper, the same, viz. one squadron Pathans, one Sikhs and two of Mussulmans of the Derajat.

In practice, however, there was a considerable difference, owing to the two units recruiting different sub-clans of the above classes.

The 35th remained in India during the whole War, combining the jobs of furnishing drafts for France and Internal Security.

There were present with the 36th Jacob's Horse at one period, no less than two hundred men of the 35th, including some of the finest Indian Officers in the Regiment.

Owing to the fact that, at the opening of the War, Regimental Depots could only furnish young recruits for drafts, units that did not proceed on service were directed to supply reinforcements. This system lasted until about mid 1916, when the Depots began to send men. As the casualties were very low in the Indian cavalry, the problem was not a very serious one.

Jacob's Horse received drafts from the 16th, 21st, 23rd, 35th and 37th. The number supplied by the 35th exceeded the total of the rest put together.

These reinforcements were chiefly Pathans and Sikhs, and it was not until Jacob's Horse Depot began to send them that the Tiwana and Derajat squadrons received men in any number. Both of these squadrons had a number of Pathans in them in consequence.

The lack of definite link units in cavalry, resulted in the " three regiment group " system now existing.

The 36th proceeded to France in October 1914, forming part of the Lucknow Cavalry Brigade, 1st Indian Cavalry Division.

The Brigade consisted of the King's Dragoon Guards, the 36th Jacob's Horse and the 29th Lancers, together with " U " Battery R.H.A.

Lieut.-Colonel R. E. Roome commanded the Regiment.

4TH CAVALRY DIVISION, FRANCE

(On arrival, known as 1st Indian Cavalry Division).

Royal Horse Artillery.

" A.", " Q.", ' U." Batteries.

LUCKNOW CAVALRY BRIGADE.

King's Dragoon Guards.
29th Lancers.
36th Jacob's Horse.
Jodhpore Lancers (after April 1917).

MHOW CAVALRY BRIGADE.

Inniskilling Dragoons.
2nd Lancers.
38th Central India Horse.

SIALKOT CAVALRY BRIGADE.

17th Lancers.
6th Cavalry.
19th Lancers.

After a most uncomfortable period at Orleans, the Brigade moved up to Lillers, where it was billeted for a few days, when it moved off to the Prevefin area, where it remained till March.

The men were well received by the French. In only very rare instances did one come across objectionable inhabitants, and the first case occurred at Lillers. Here a genteel individual announced he would not have any officers or anyone else billeted on him. He moreover threatened to stab the French interpreter. When he found some thirty jawans with dirty boots clumping upstairs to his attics, which had been told off to them as billets, he showed signs of collapse, and had to be supported away.

One occasionally ran across good ladies who would threaten the billeting parties, waving their arms and screaming "Jamais de troupes chez moi, jamais de troupes," or "Pas de chevaux, pas de chevaux," but the sowar, with that remarkable capacity possessed by most Indians of pretending not to understand the inconvenient, would proceed to put his horses under cover regardless, the lady subsiding into helplessness.

The Mussulman soldiery were at first inconvenienced by the pigs, and the more devout individuals would not even utter that terrible word "soor," but alluded to them as "janwars."

The French Algerian troops, on the other hand, were extraordinarily slack in their religious observances. They drew the line, however, at actually eating pork. French officers said, humorously, that although they never drank alcohol, they none the less occasionally got drunk.

Their dealings with these troops generally seemed much on the same lines as ours, though they had a big proportion of French N.C.O.'s with them.

The French peasantry preferred Indian troops to any other, and occasions arose when they wrote in and asked to have them, as their behaviour was so good. The men were more docile than the British, and they gave infinitely less trouble than French.

It seemed that the peasantry greatly preferred either Indian or British troops to their own. The discipline of the last named in billets appeared, according to the inhabitants, to leave much to be desired, and one heard complaints of the mysterious disappearance of chickens and eggs, while the cow's milk supply seemed to diminish to a remarkable degree. The British, on the other hand, had plenty of money to throw about and a considerable surplus of rations.

The general form of French village life followed very much the same lines as that of the home-life of the Indian soldier.

There was the community of interest of both being entirely farmers, and conversations ran on farming, price of dairy supplies, cattle, and similar topics.

A number of the men learnt French and spoke it extraordinarily well. It was not, indeed, an unheard, of thing for Indians to explain themselves to British officers, who could not speak Hindustani, in French.

Among other attainments was the acquisition of equine French. This was rendered necessary owing to the farm horses disdaining to understand words like "hath," "uth," or "chal." "Gee up" and "whoa" were equally valueless. As the Gallic horse had a penchant for stealing English corn it became also necessary to learn French terms of abuse. Once these were acquired the animal became quite affable and reasonable.

Doubtless it was merely putting into practice the custom of his masters in " taking it out of the foreigner."

After being in the same billets for some time the French peasants seem to have gained a very genuine liking for them. Sowars frequently rode over to visit old friends if they happened to be in the neighbourhood subsequently. A number of men would willingly have remained on in France, particularly Pathans, and would have settled down to the French country life extremely well.

Billeting cavalry in winter was not an easy feat. There were few villages capable of holding more than one squadron, if the horses were to be stabled under cover. The consequence was that a regiment be strewn over a large area with villages sometimes two miles apart. Squadron officers' messes, therefore, became the rule and remained so till we arrived in Palestine in 1918.

Even when in the devastated area the difficulty in accommodating more than five or six officers at table under cover, made a continuation of the system imperative.

The adjutant also had a good deal more complicated staff-work to do when getting the regiment on the move than when it was all in one place.

The jawans were allowed to go in to both Abbeville and Amiens when we were in their neighbourhood in 1916 on the distinct understanding that they did not wander about with their pugaris on the backs of their heads and chew food all over the place.

At first they showed a disposition to converse at the tops of their voices with each other on either side of the street and walk about hand-in-hand like a lot of children.

They got out of this and by the end of the year did nothing which could possibly move the most pluperfect sergeant-major in the world to wrath. Their chief hobby seemed to be to hang about cheap jewellers' shops and buy watches. British officers going on leave would be handed about a dozen gaudy-looking timepieces in a state of hopeless disrepair, which the men fondly imagined would return as good as new. Old Braun, our very popular interpreter, was also a victim in this respect.

A further passion indulged in was the purchase of nickel-plated spurs, and what was worse, in some cases, nickel-plated bits. The spurs were the bane of one's existence whenever one wanted orderlies, etc., to turn out extra smart, for until 1921 they always appeared, if they could possibly do so—on the plea that the ration ones had been lost.

The contrast between the sowars from France and the sepoys from India was most noticeable in Cairo and Jerusalem, the former strong, well-set-up men, smartly turned out, and the others slopping about all over the place.

The sowar, by the time he left France, had dropped many of his finnicky Indian notions as regards food. While Hindus and Mussulmans drew the line at beef or pork respectively, they undoubtedly ate a great deal of normal French food—English rations did not suit.

They became very Europeanized in many respects, getting their hair cut at French barbers' shops, using scent and safety razors and even reading French newspapers.

The Woordi Major, when once questioned as to a certain Indian officer, stated, " Wuh bilkul gentleman ho gya "—" He's quite the little gentleman."

The Indian officers had proper billets for themselves after British officers had been accommodated, and, not infrequently, would follow a British officer as a room became vacant.

At first there was certain trouble owing to their penchant for holding durbars in their rooms with one or two hangers-on massaging their ankles and others squatting by, after the old Silladar fashion. This was put a stop to and, by the end of the War, they held aloof from the men like British sergeants, to the great improvement of discipline and self-respect.

In the summer months it became customary for men and horses to be entirely in the open and not in barns, unless it rained heavily, when the men would go inside. In the winter this was obviously impossible.

In 1917 Indian officers were allowed to go on leave to Paris, where their conduct was always admirable. A Parsee in business there was very good to them.

In billets a feature much appreciated by the men was the abundant supply of milk obtainable. The Sikhs, in particular, would be seen soon after arrival going round with their canvas horse buckets bargaining with the various " muddums " for it. These buckets, incidentally, had probably been just used for watering horses at some filthy horsepond. The Mussulman troops were, surprising to state, far more tricky as regards their eating in France than were Sikhs or Hindus. The pig question was at the bottom of it.

The excellent feeding, good climate and hard work the men had to do, made them physically some of the finest Indian troops ever known.

Constant trench digging, wiring and road making made the sowar an all-round handy man, welcomed by every sapper officer in the country. Finally, and above all, the removal of the far too numerous products of long service in India, British and Indian, enabled the Indian soldier to progress in a manner which was little short of amazing, with the result that he eventually left France with a great name—and a name well deserved.

As the pack-mule transport of Indian cavalry, with its attendant horde of undisciplined scallywags in the shape of syces, obviously did not suit Continental conditions, we had wheeled transport organized as under :—

"A" Echelon. A.T. mule carts with Indian drabis. The disadvantage of this was its inability to move out of a walk.

"B" Echelon. G.S. horsed wagons with British drivers.

These last had been hurriedly enlisted, put into khaki and called soldiers.

If one was to judge from their conduct in the five months they were with us, they must have been the very sweepings of the slums.

In British units there is machinery for dealing with men of this type, but in Indian units there is none.

As a consequence they did not go far from rivalling the unenviable tradition of the "Wagon Train" of the Army of Flanders of 1794, who rejoiced in the soubriquet of "The Newgate Blues."

They gave so much trouble that, to our relief, native drivers from the R.H.A. Ammunition Columns were substituted.

These proved simply excellent, hard working, good drivers and as brave as lions.

The A.T. carts were replaced by limber wagons and we put our own men on to drive them. There was a certain amount of opposition to this, based on the extraordinary notion that the sowar had his "izzat" lowered by acting as transport driver.

The pre-war sowar was, in many instances, a pampered individual as regards the duties he could be called upon to perform, and the idea that a good soldier should turn his hand to anything did not exist.

Work with the transport was unpopular, not on account of loss of prestige, but because the man had two animals and a cart to look after instead of one horse. It meant, furthermore, a good deal more irregular hours and much exposure to bad weather.

The men, however, got off guards and much nasty work.

In France it was by no means a safe job, as the roads were constantly and regularly shelled.

CHAPTER VI

FESTUBERT. NEUVE CHAPELLE. YPRES.
1915

THE Regiment was first in action in the trenches at Festubert, in January 1915, losing heavily getting into them, as it had to pass in front of some blazing haystacks which lighted up the whole country. The trenches were full of water, in some places almost waist deep, and the communication trenches could not be used at all.

At that period, however, certain generals held the idea that it was wrong to evacuate them for this reason, quite regardless of the fact that the Germans themselves would not want them, unless they were of vital tactical importance to either side, which they were not.

The consequence was casualties from trench feet were very heavy indeed, both in the King's Dragoon Guards and in the Indian units. The total casualties from enemy fire and trench-feet combined were heavier than any suffered at any one action for the rest of the War. The K.D.Gs. had no fewer than eighty men evacuated on account of trench-feet, and Jacob's Horse some ninety, quite apart from those men laid up for three of four days. Some of the men evacuated did not return for four or five months, some not at all.

It is true that a very large proportion of the casualties might have been avoided by knowing better how to deal with the cases. At that time, however, the necessary measures were not generally so well known as they were later. It is, however, practically certain that the casualties would have been lighter had the Germans occupied the trenches and had we attempted to retake them.

As regards evacuation of wounded, Lieutenant Owen Jones was hit in the arm in the morning and was in hospital in London that night, which is "some work." Regiments went into the line stronger on this occasion than they did later on, their strengths averaging about three hundred as against two hundred and seventy afterwards. Much of this was due to the anxiety of individuals to go into action at this period. This particular itch, however, died down pretty soon.

In 1914 the French would say, " Les officiers anglais vont à la guerre comme au sport, et se laissent être tué." There was much truth in this.

The French motto "Voir sans être vu, tuer sans être tué" was certainly not acted up to by many in those days, with the result that valuable lives were lost. This was the result of the "small wars" in which officers had taken part—comparative safe shows in which the hostile fire was a mere flea-bite.

For Neuve Chapelle the Division moved up to the Bois des Dames. There was some notion prevalent that a "break through" was possible, but it seems difficult to imagine how cavalry could have acted with all the dykes and wire about. This was the first great bombardment the Regiment, or any Indian cavalry regiment, for the matter of that, had ever heard. There were many moves up in after times for the great "G" in Gap that never occurred until Cambrai, when, owing to faulty arrangements of people higher up, the cavalry were too late.

On the 22nd of April the Regiment was at Liettres, close to Aire. We heard a most unpleasant rumour that, although we had taken Hill 60, the Boche had attacked with some poison gas north of Ypres and that the line had gone. There was a bit of "the French have let us down" in the tale, but the "Old Army" was rather fond of saying this, and we did not pay much attention to it. We began to learn later on, however, that whenever we heard bad news it was more likely to be true than not.

It struck us that the "Iron ration," as we called the Indian Cavalry Corps among ourselves, owing to its never having been employed, might get rather more fighting than it wanted very shortly, and being put on half-an-hour's notice to move, added to the impression.

Not until the evening of the 24th, however, did we move—and we carried out a march that officers who took part in it will never forget. It seemed that the whole corps was on one narrow cross-country road, with almost innumerable branches, cross roads and level crossings.

It became very dark and began to rain. Trains seemed to be at every single level crossing we came to, rushing troops up to the battle. The gates would shut almost without warning, and one felt lucky if one did not get shut in on the line with some snorting engine within a yard. As the head had kept moving, those cut off by the gates would be left some distance behind—sometimes quite half a mile. No men had been dropped at these places, with the result that one had only the gregarious sense of one's horse to let one know which way to go. One would proceed to career wildly, often along greasy cobblestones, to catch up—horses coming down at intervals. If the road was straight one could see the sparks thrown up by the horses' shoes some way ahead. This effort would be followed by a sudden halt as one hit the croup of the animal in front.

At one point, the "A" echelon baggage of the Jodhpore Lancers was met with carts upset in every direction and positive mountains of blankets and kit all across the road. The Jo Hukums, as they were called, were a very scallywag crowd in those days—very different from what they were a year later.

The whole of the "A" echelon baggage in the Indian Cavalry Corps at that time was A.T. mule carts, limber wagons not having been issued. It is not known whether march orders forbade the sandwiching in of transport which could only move at a walk, or not. It is probable, however, that the old Jo Hukums were then above such details—after all even the best staff cannot deal with super men.

The climax was reached when we noticed officers flashing electric torches outside the doors of some cottages we were passing. They were billeting parties. They gaily informed us that their brigade had overshot the mark and was now retracing its steps towards us. Having proceeded about a quarter of a mile further on we met this army—retracing their steps as expected—the passing point being a very narrow lane with deep ditches on either side and pitch dark. The confusion may be better imagined than described. Horses and men were pushed into the muddy, filthy dykes, and our unfortunate brigadier only just escaped drowning.

None of us had the foggiest idea of where we were bound for, and one brigade, commanded by one who is now a very distinguished officer, described a complete circle, eventually hitting its own tail.

By daybreak, however, we succeeded in reaching billets, extremely relieved that we were not immediately required.

The detail of orders is not known to the writer, but it is suggested that officers should have been told where they were going to at all events and a much stronger route picqueting party detailed, particular attention being paid to the level crossings.

To be perfectly frank, the march left a rather unsettling impression of the capacity of the staff.

The Regiment found itself at Oxelaire, a small village under Cassel, and we fully expected to be rushed closer up to the line. Nothing happened for the next couple of days however.

A railway line ran close to us and a simply astounding number of trains carrying French troops up to the battle passed by. The French were now beginning to turn all their troops out in the *bleu horizon*, which was to become famous. Their equipment, from being the very second class stuff it was at the beginning of the War, was also improving enormously.

On the 28th the Division moved close up behind the battle to about St. Jan der Biezen, across the Belgian Frontier. While passing through Steenvoorde, quite a distance behind the line, the roar of the bombardment was tremendous—we did not hear the like till Cambrai and Sharon.

Moving over the cobble-stones of these French and Belgian towns was most nerve-racking and horses were always slithering about, sometimes coming down. In this connection, the first casualty the writer recollects in the War was at Rouen about the 14th August 1914, when a man of the Carabiniers had his ankle broken by his horse falling a couple of hundred yards from the ship from which the squadron had disembarked.

En route to St. Jan der Biezen we passed over the high ground at Cassel and saw a sight, the like of which we had never seen, and never saw again—a seemingly endless column of lance points and horsemen stretching both in the Ypres direction and away from it.

In Steenvoorde we met Colonel Cartwright, the former commandant of Jacob's Horse, at that time A.A. and Q.M.G. of the Northumberland Territorial Division. He told us that the Division had already lost over four thousand men and had only been in France ten days.

We met numbers of refugees from Ypres, Vlamertinghe and Poperinghe, extraordinarily English in appearance—and singularly objectionable.

The "brave Belge" of these parts was, to our mind, a disgusting creature, totally devoid of any sense of patriotism. Large numbers of perfectly able-bodied men were knocking about who should have been soldiers, and we knew the number of Belgian spies was enormous.

In point of fact the French in the early days of 1870 were not much better and only became patriotic as a whole through conscription and propaganda.

While we were at St. Jan der Biezen the French counter-attacked and retook Steenstrate. Their guns were quite close to us. The whole of the first night we were there the "75's" were at it, the system of fire from the sound appearing to be rather that of the parade *feu de joie*—a rolling fire from a very long line of guns, firing in succession from one end or the other.

We rode out to have a look at Poperinghe, which had had some 17-inch shells dropped into it. This was the first time we had ever seen the effect of a really big shell bursting on a house, and we were rather disappointed.

The crisis of the battle passed and we were not employed. We returned, accordingly, to our area south of Aire, not altogether sorry to get out of Belgium.

During May there were several sudden moves up towards the line south of Bethune as a result of the Festubert battle.

The staff work was now better and hitches but seldom occurred. The reports we received about this battle were not exactly encouraging, and we were obviously losing heavily with nothing to show for it.

We did not know at the time that we were involved rather more deeply than was wished in order to help the French out of their difficulties in their Vimy Ridge offensive rather to the south.

Most unsettling reports began to filter back as regards shell shortage, and we heard of many cases where our unfortunate infantry were simply mown down by machine guns within thirty yards of their own wire.

We began at this period to be a bit sceptical about our formerly much-talked-of rides in pursuit of the beaten Hun, and began to see that so far from our moving up to go through the *G* in Gap we were more likely to be employed in stopping one in our own line.

Life behind the Line certainly had its monotony and boredom relieved by these turns out.

It is, at the same time, difficult to speak temperately of the absence of any effort, in most Indian cavalry brigades, to get officers more abreast of the times.

No less an authority than Lieut.-General Barrow has stated that the whole of the cavalry from India, including the British cavalry, was behind that trained at home in this respect.

In a very large number of units little more than horse exercise was done. In most, there was a want of a common doctrine to work on as there was no one senior enough to direct it.

In the Indian units especially, there was an enormous leeway to make up, particularly with regard to stimulating the intelligence of the Indian ranks in field work, at which most were decidedly weak.

The consequences of this loafing showed themselves to the full when the two Indian Cavalry Divisions were put through a very detailed inspection in the spring of 1916 at St. Riquier. This inspection resulted in many changes in command and, incidentally, in giving for a time the unfortunate Indian Cavalry a very bad name.

One has heard it said by many that it was just as well that it was not seriously employed as cavalry in 1915—for in their heart of hearts many officers had considerable doubts as to its being equal to a severe or prolonged trial.

It is to be clearly understood that the Indian Regiments in France were no whit worse than those in India. It was the Indian system which was so far behind the British that unfortunate units suffered, and suffered in many cases, through no fault of their own.

By the end of May 1915 the whole of our infantry were badly in need of a rest, and it was resolved to relieve them, in part, by cavalry in the Salient.

The 1st Indian Cavalry Division was moved north, its horses being left in the area west of Cassel.

The country was extraordinarily pretty, not at all unlike England. There were, moreover, numerous detached farms, a feature which is uncommon further south. The inhabitants were very pleasant, speaking a Flemish dialect which is very similar to English.

The Regiment went to Erkelsbrugge-Bollezele, very comfortable billets. From here a trench party embussed for Vlamertinghe.

For officers who had not been in the line hitherto the gradual deterioration of the countryside as one got closer up was most noticeable. From Poperinghe onwards the country was most dreary, though Ypres was fair to gaze on from a distance.

At Vlamertinghe some of our cavalry were met coming out of the line and waiting to embuss on our 'buses.

They had had a bad time and some regiments had lost very heavily. They made no bones about their relief at getting out of it and told us we would probably get it in the neck as well, which was not encouraging. In particular they had commented on the gas.

At that period we had merely pads soaked in chemical we were to wrap round our nostrils and mouths. The prospect of being gassed was not alluring in consequence.

Accommodation was found for us in some remarkably verminous huts at Brandhoek, close to Vlamertinghe.

Our rest that night was not of the quietest on account of the shelling in the neighbourhood. The high explosive "Crumps," crumping even half a mile away, shook the ground.

The matutinal speech of a deeply affected private of the Dragoon Guards in the hut next to us, to the effect that he had been unable to obtain adequate repose owing to the dreadful explosions of the big bombshells in close proximity to his devoted head, at intervals of every ten precise seconds the whole night without intermission, was, in a measure, correct.

The above are not the exact words used, but give some idea of the situation.

Our own guns were perforce silent. They were limited to three rounds a day—for every round had to be husbanded to meet emergencies.

Terrific excitement was caused one evening by the announcement that a 9·2 Howitzer close to us was about to fire her weekly ration of two shells that night.

The Indian troops were kept in reserve for a few days, prior to going up into the line in support.

The term "reserve" in France indicated, under most circumstances, an enormous amount of digging, wiring and carrying, often under most nerve-racking and dangerous conditions. Not infrequently one lost more men on this type of work than if one were right up in the front.

On the night of the 1st–2nd June Jacob's Horse had to send up a big carrying party to Hooge Chateau. The King's Dragoon Guards held the place the following day, with the utmost gallantry, under a bombardment which had opened at 05·00 hours and continued till 17·00. The Germans had then attacked, but had been driven out again. The K.D.G. casualties amounted to no less than seven officers and seventy-nine other ranks killed and wounded out of about two hundred.

Considering the fact that the Germans had put over some seven thousand shells on an area not two hundred yards square, the wonder was that there were not more. In point of fact most of the casualties were caused by machine-gun fire when counter-attacking some Germans who had entered the Chateau. The number of men dazed and partially stunned by this bombardment, though not actually wounded, was very great.

On the 31st May some officers of Jacob's Horse had been detailed to go up to the trenches just south of the Chateau, then held by the 3rd Dragoon Guards and Leicestershire Yeomanry, while others went to the trenches about Zouave Wood. The ostensible object was to learn the trench routine of that part of the line.

So far as the officers with the 3rd Dragoon Guards were concerned, their experiences were confined to helping dig out men buried by trenches blown in, dodging shells and dressing wounded men. Shelling, steady and extremely accurate, had lasted some seven hours that day, shells falling at the rate of about one in fifteen seconds on the very restricted area held. It was mostly 4·2, with some 5·9 thrown in. Trenches were blown in repeatedly, sometimes burying men. One had to set to to dig the man out at once or he would get suffocated. This was, of itself, a dangerous job, for Boche snipers abounded in the trees ahead.

The place was, furthermore, occasionally swept with shrapnel, which fortunately did but little damage.

Our own guns hardly fired ten rounds that day, so short was the ammunition supply.

The coolness and aplomb of the long service regular soldier under this strain was extraordinary.

Externally, at all events, the men showed but little sign of it, though this had been their third consecutive day in this health resort.

The non-regular troops were visibly more affected.

The 31st May and the 2nd June 1915 were rightly described in the *Daily Mail* as "The Days of the Dragoon Guards."

At this lapse of time there may be, in some quarters, a tendency to forget what the "Old Army" had to go through in those days of early 1915, when K.I. was coming into being and when the British working man persistently went on strike for more pay.

To sit for days, and, in some cases for weeks, in trenches overlooked by the Hun, and be shelled, without being able to reply, sometimes for hours together, was a strain which could, in all probability, have been endured by British regular or good Prussian troops only.

It is doubtful whether the troops of any other nation had this extraordinary capacity for passively standing punishment.

The very first French official communique of the whole war, reporting the Battle of Mons, hit the nail on the head with prophetic accuracy as regards the British soldier: "Les troupes anglaises ont donné. Ils ont déployé toute la solidité et l'impassabilité de leur race."

Naturally all moves up to Hooge and Zouave Wood had to be made at night—a most eerie and extraordinary experience to those who had never been in the Salient before. One seemed to be surrounded by the Boche, whose flares went up continually on either side. The place was lighted up quite brightly one second and dark the next, while dropping bullets came from every conceivable direction. There was steady shelling of roads nearly the whole night, and certain particularly hot spots would be passed as quickly as possible.

The dead-white appearance of the transport drivers, crouching low over their horses' necks as they neared points which machine guns or snipers were known to favour and the general uncanny appearance of everything caused by the flares, made a picture one had never seen before and, certainly, so far as other parts of the lines we were in subsequently were concerned, were never to see again.

At this period we noticed that troops in the line abused, quite unjustly as it happened, our gunners for not replying to the shelling.

They praised in eloquent terms the French artillery, forgetting that the latter had usually lots of ammunition, while we had only enough to meet grave emergencies.

Ypres was a ghastly spot.

The sickly stench of partially buried horses killed shortly before, filled the whole atmosphere.

On the 3rd June Jacob's Horse went into the support line at Yeoman's Post, about twelve hundred yards S.W. of Hooge, remaining there for the next three days. There was the usual dropping rifle fire from three sides all the time and some light shelling. Casualties were, however, light.

Lice in this delectable neighbourhood were everywhere.

What this place would have been like had it rained is impossible to imagine. Fortunately the weather was glorious.

We noticed, at this time, that the continual preaching of the offensive spirit to unfortunate troops in the line, by big people who lived well behind, was greatly resented, and to our way of thinking quite naturally so. It was rather hard to understand the reasoning which demanded that men supplied with five rifle grenades, and bad ones at that, should make themselves aggressive towards an enemy far better posted and equally skilled, who had a hundred.

After its tour in the Salient, the Regiment returned to its verminous city of palaces near Vlamertinghe.

The Boche had a most objectionable habit of shelling this sanctuary, and on three occasions the place had to be hastily evacuated. Once the sole inhabitant left was one Shakur—a gentleman more generally known later on as " Shakoo "—a mess cook.

This individual was brewing tea when the shelling began, and while it was in progress, was seen to go into the mess kitchen, produce cups and a teapot and then go out to try and serve tea to the officers who were, together with all the rest of the troops, lying down under cover outside the camp area. There were the corpses of men of the 8th Hussars who had just been killed within fifty yards of him.

Shakur was a remarkable character whose normally objectionable habits continually got him into trouble. He and a Madrassi cook were aspirants for the Regimental football team, which consisted of the Colonel, two other British officers, two British batmen, and some jawans. This team nearly won the Divisional Cup early in 1916.

A very considerable number of the other domestics, however, started on a non-stop race for Calais. One of them was brought up, still going strong, the far side of St. Omer.

Vlamertinghe Church was burnt down finally when the Regiment was there.

It was at Vlamertinghe that one first heard the great war jibe of the old soldier to the newly arrived units : " Are we down-'earted ? " " Naow." " Well, yer blanked soon will be."

It was at Vlamertinghe also that the first indication that Mr. Atkins' notion on causing his light to shine before women (the aim and object of all soldiers since the dawn of history), differed from that of the " Indous," as the French called the jawans. With great vulgarity he followed up parties of our men parading in " shirt-sleeves " with shouts of " 'Ullo, Johnny, yer shirt's 'angin' out."

This led to the first of those drastic reforms which were shortly to shake the Indian Cavalry to its foundations, for it resulted in no less a measure than compelling the men to tuck their shirt-tails inside their breeches.

In connection with raiment, it was later in the War when the Naga Labour Corps landed at Marseilles. The men had all been issued with clothes on the ship. It was a warm day when they left the docks to march to the camp, some seven miles. The Naga left fully dressed, but feeling the heat, proceeded to gradually strip off his garments. By the time he passed the top of the Cannebiere he had divested himself of his coat, shirt and vest, which he put on his head. When he reached La Valentine his nether garments had also been removed, to the immense joy of the whole neighbourhood, who followed these famous gentry in crowds.

Among other points brought out by this time was the impossibility of the British officers of Indian units counting on Indian servants in time of danger. They might find themselves absolutely stranded in the messing line with no one to cut up meat or cook. The result was batmen were sanctioned from the British Cavalry. Many of these men stayed on till the end of the war with their Indian units and took the greatest pride in their achievements. There was a good deal of weeding out to be done, however, and several very bad bargains were struck. One good result arose, nevertheless, from these bad bargains, and that was that officers' orderlies began to learn the very simple jobs required of a batman. From 1915 onwards, very few officers had British soldiers as personal servants. They were, however, almost indispensable in officers' messes, for it was not reasonable to employ the Mussulman soldier in cooking pork for instance, or the Sikh or Hindu in cutting up beef.

The idea that the Indian soldier has his " izzat " lowered by acting as a servant on service or manœuvres is a relic of antiquity.

It was about the time of the Second Battle of Ypres that a number of Yeomanry officers were attached to Indian Cavalry units in France. The idea was that they should form an additional reserve of officers and should receive some training as well. Their value as a reserve of officers was largely discounted by their ignorance of the language and of Indian habits and customs. At the same time, we found that the jawans got on with them extremely well and would have followed them anywhere in battle—for these Yeomanry officers were drawn from a good type of British gentry.

They were, unfortunately, very ignorant of soldiering. We found it a little disconcerting to find a Yeomanry major knowing considerably less than a regular subaltern of four years service.

The manner in which the average Indian cavalry unit loafed in billets through early 1915 seriously handicapped these officers learning anything.

Had they joined us in 1916, things would have been very different. Most had, however, left us by the end of 1915, being recalled to accompany their regiments to the Dardanelles or to Egypt.

Of the three officers with Jacob's Horse, one, Lord Kesteven, was killed by a shell fired by a submarine at the transport carrying his regiment to Alexandria. The other two, Robinson and Robertson, came through the War safely.

A number of Yeomanry officers who had been all through the Beersheba–Jerusalem operations subsequently went to the Indian Cavalry, taking permanent commissions. They were of excellent material but astonishingly ignorant, considering the amount of service they had seen.

It was about the middle of 1915 also, that we began to receive the earlier batches of officers of the Indian Army Reserve—a body who exercised a profound influence on the service as the War went on.

Drawn from every type of " sahib " in India, and from every conceivable profession and Government Service, the Indian Cavalry has a deep debt of gratitude towards these officers.

There were, naturally, some very famous characters, varying from one known as " Popoff," who fought the War, splendidly attired, at one of the bases, to " Tin Eye " Gordon, an old friend from Sind, whose hitherto unpublished work, entitled *From Subaltern to Field Officer—and Back Again—In Six Weeks : The Story of a Soldier's Life* earned him eternal glory, being a true and accurate account of this great man's career.

Neither of these were with Jacob's Horse.

A particular feature of these officers, with very rare exceptions, was their extraordinary sense of discipline. In civil life most had occupied positions of considerable importance, with numbers of men working under them, either as managers of tea gardens—for the planters joined up in force—or as civil engineers running big works, or as members of big manufacturing firms. Furthermore, they were, in almost every case, men of the world who had knocked about a bit, but who found themselves serving, sometimes in the same squadron, under officers who were very much their juniors in age. It was the public school training that did it.

The Lucknow Brigade was particularly fortunate as regards them, as the number of decorations received will show. Speaking from memory, the 29th Lancers alone received two D.S.O.'s—a great honour for subalterns—and three M.C.'s for some dozen I.A.R. officers with them.

In certain cases, regiments, and good ones at that, received the I.A.R. somewhat coldly, professional prejudice and snobbery—the latter a rather common weakness in the pre-war Army—being at the bottom of it. This fact sufficed to show that the regiments had not been properly blooded.

CHAPTER VII

AUTHUILLE. BILLETS NEAR AMIENS. ABBEVILLE. WINTER 1915-16.

1915

IN August 1915, the Division moved south into the area north-east of Amiens, which our newly formed Third Army was just taking over from the French.

The march led through beautiful country and was carried out in glorious weather.

The country was far more interesting than Flanders, and much more suited to cavalry work.

The " I " Branch of the Army hoped that it would be possible to run a telephone line *via* the bed of the Somme through the German lines. We had had telephonic communication with Lille for some time and it was thought possible that it might also be worked in the Third Army opposite which the Boche was supposed to be very slack.

A party of Afridis and Bangash from the regiment under Captain Gavin Jones was accordingly placed at the disposal of " I " Branch.

It was to work in the Somme Valley about Vaux.

The task, however, was an impossible one. The Boche was fully on his guard and nothing could be effected. One or two minor patrol actions took place in which the men showed up extremely well.

In connection with stalking and patrolling a curious idea was found prevalent among many officers of British units who ought to have known better, namely that all Indians are super-men in these respects.

There was a tendency, therefore, to sometimes give them tasks which might baffle a Red Indian of fiction.

In the cavalry there are very few Indians who are anything much out of the way in their capacity to move noiselessly, as was discovered at the Schools for Sniping that were started in 1916. They are usually better than Europeans, but that is all. It is possible that Gurkhas and Trans-Border Pathans may greatly excel, but the only Trans-Border Pathans enlisted in the cavalry were Adam Khel Afridis, who live in a country surrounded by British Territory and extremely peaceful, so far as Frontier matters go.

The Division took over a portion of the line about Authuille, facing the afterwards historic Chateau of Thiepval.

A feature that struck us about here was how comfortable the French had made themselves. Hurdlework booths and shanties had been erected at all sorts of places, usually where some particularly fine view was obtainable. This was particularly noticeable about Vaux on the Somme. Here they must have been in full view of the Germans. We learnt that hardly a shot had been fired on this sector by either side since the Battle of the Marne, nearly a year before. There had been a temporary lapse when the French attacked Hebuterne and Thiepval in the spring, being successful at the former place but failing at the latter.

A curious feature was the first indication the Germans had that we had taken over from the French was by picking up a Lee-Enfield bullet. The British had been in the line three or four days before this occurred.

It is not generally realized that on the greater part of the French front things were usually extraordinarily quiet. They had a definite fighting zone and a definite quiet zone, and there seemed to be a mutual agreement on the subject with the enemy.

On the greater part of the British front things were comparatively warm. In certain respects this may have been due to enormous advantages of ground possessed by the Germans, but there was an uneasy impression abroad that a certain amount was due to the attitude of some British commanders, who, seemingly, always wanted to be thought aggressive, quite regardless as to whether it really paid or not. After all, the idea that "moral" benefits by troops being ordered to infuriate an enemy vastly stronger than themselves does seem rather a ridiculous one, though it undoubtedly existed in some quarters.

It obviously paid the enemy to be aggressive.

On our taking over the sector we did wake things up slightly, but for what reason it is rather difficult to follow, as our guns were still limited to three rounds a day.

To pretend, however, that the line was at all a hot spot would be too ridiculous for words.

It is understood that the original intention was that the Indian troops were to be put into the sector about Vaux, but the French, who were to the south of the Somme, objected to having native troops next to them—a retaliation to protests of ours against Algerian troops being on our left when the first gas attack at Ypres occurred.

Thiepval Chateau still had its walls standing and the beautiful fir woods were almost intact.

The view was magnificent right up the valley of the Ancre towards

Pys and Irles. A greater contrast than the horrible brown wilderness it was after the Somme could never be imagined.

Air reports of the period continually drew attention to train-loads and barge-loads of timber being brought up. It was generally thought that these were for winter hutting. That the timber was meant for roofing dug-outs was not thought of.

One particular disadvantage of taking over from the French was that they never seemed to do any work on rear lines of defence worth speaking of. Although they had been in this portion of the line since the Marne there was little or nothing behind the front line.

The same thing occurred south of the Omignon in 1917, with the result that we were badly let down by them when the great German offensive of March 1918 took place.

As usual, when the cavalry were not in the line, it had to furnish big working parties. These were by no means unpopular, for we were getting bored with loafing about behind the line and we felt we were doing something at all events, towards helping things on.

In September the whole Corps "stood to" for the Loos Battle. As we were on half an hour's notice for something like forty-eight hours on end we were a little anxious. Some optimists thought a *G* in Gap was certain, but most thought this was more likely in our own line. We did not know till a long time after, of the abominable manner in which the battle had been fought, more particularly the way the reserves had been mishandled. We heard that some of the New Army Divisions had behaved brilliantly, while others had failed terribly.

As Sir Archibald Montgomery told us, it had been a case of either half-baked troops caught on the crest of the wave doing brilliantly, or others, equally good in reality, but caught in the trough, doing badly.

These New Army Divisions had now been training for about a year, and were the very pick of Britian in so far as material was concerned.

As a result of the battle, many New Army Divisions had regular brigades and battalions brought into them as stiffeners.

We learnt, shortly after, that the cavalry was to be drawn on for commanding officers and seconds-in-command of battalions.

In November, accordingly, a number of officers went off. Majors Fagan and Davidson, and Captains Gavin Jones and Allardice left us. Captain Allardice was killed on the fateful 1st July 1916, the first day of the Somme.

It was in the summer of 1915 the machine gunners of units were grouped into Brigade machine-gun squadrons.

For the winter of 1915–16 the Indian Cavalry Corps was moved right back to the area between Abbeville and Eu.

Here, at long last, some effort was made to start systematic training for trench warfare. There was much to learn, chiefly as regards modifications in the pre-war systems of trench construction, which had not contemplated the employment of heavy artillery or bombing. The enormous wiring had not, moreover, been foreseen.

Nevertheless, the old manuals were sound enough as a foundation if the average officer had really known them thoroughly and not depended so much on sapper assistance.

Bombing also was taken up seriously. Our own Division was comparatively lucky as regards accidents, but Captain Owen Jones of the Regiment was blown to pieces while taking a class.

There were all sorts and conditions of bombs, and to this day it seems amazing that more of the men were not killed.

As there was a considerable shortage of dummies to practise throwing with, a squadron commander, afflicted with a brain wave, conceived the idea of big round pebbles from the sea shore. A dafadar with a pack mule was accordingly despatched to a place on the coast called Ault, about six miles from Franlieu, where the Regiment was billeted. The place is remarkable for a very high tide.

The report of the dafadar on his pilgrimage was somewhat ridiculous. He was an extremely bovine Sikh and took the matter most seriously and as with a grievance. His complaint was, that he had found some ideal pebbles by the water's edge but the water, for some unexplained reason, kept rising and drove him back. He had found one or two other suitable places where there was a large supply of stones, but on each occasion he had had to quit for the same reason. Finally a " Franci chokra " had begun to poke fun at him and tell him he would be drowned if he stayed where he was any longer. It was both mysterious and aggravating.

The same day the colonel and adjutant with their orderlies visited St. Valery, at the mouth of the Somme. A most extraordinary phenomenon occurred here. The whole of the water ran out of the river, and ships that were floating when the orderlies arrived were on the mud when they left. There was much discussion on these events in the Regiment.

It should be noted that the pebble experiment was a huge success, and the men's capacity to throw bombs was enormously increased thereby.

Franlieu had been in occupation of the Germans in 1871, and the owner of the local chateau had some tobacco which he said had been left by a German officer who had been billeted there. This was produced with due ceremony and smoked.

It was noticeable that in hardly a single instance was there definite evidence of German troops in occupation in France in 1871, being anything other than well behaved. One grew, moreover, very sceptical of the many yarns of German atrocities in the Great War. One had only to visit Amiens and the villages about after the Germans fell back after the Marne to see that most of the stories were mere propaganda. That certain instances did occur is undoubted, but that they were magnified a hundredfold is equally so.

This winter, also, despite violent opposition to a hitherto almost unheard of violation of Indian Cavalry traditions, we got down to making the men march in step.

Some officers had been inspired to this effort in 1915, their spirit of emulation having been aroused by the spectacle of a martial formation, jocularly known as the "Aerated Bread Company," but officially entitled the Army Bearer Corps, moving through our village *au pas cadencé*, headed by a very military gentleman in the shape of a Bengali doctor.

Their appearance was most imposing, and the thunder of their hobnail boots could be heard for miles, so much so that jealous individuals said that the employment of steam rollers on the roads was unnecessary.

1916

In March 1916, the Division shifted to the valley of the Authie, about eighteen miles north of Abbeville. The Regiment moved into a filthy village called Boufflers, which had been previously occupied by French artillery.

It was to the château of Breuil, two miles from Boufflers, that the King of France, with only four companions, rode after the Battle of Crecy. In answer to the challenge at the gate, he said: "Open, it is the fortune of France." Here he had a meal and then departed (Froissart).

Crecy was quite close.

The French never cleared away the dung from their horse-standings seemingly, for there was a layer some nine inches deep of it in the barns. The stench clearing it out was appalling, and the veterinary officers were, not unjustifiably, anxious about an epidemic of mange.

The peasants had been properly "disciplined," and hardly dared to make a complaint at first. The attitude of the normal French officer to the peasantry seemed to be "Think yourselves jolly lucky we are not Prussians."

The simple villagers soon recovered their nerve, however, and their capacity for putting in claims for *dégâts* was fully up to the best traditions of the Picardy peasant.

It should be noted that in those days Indian regiments had no sweeper personnel, all the work, including filling in latrines, being done by the men themselves. In connection with French horsemastership, it was astonishing how bad it was in the first two years of the War. One hardly ever saw a decently turned out horse. Mange, sorebacks and galls were common. It was a known fact that Sordet's Cavalry Corps, after the Mons retreat, had sorebacks innumerable. Their cavalry would sit on their horses' backs for hours on end and never dream of dismounting.

As regards sanitation, we only followed up one French unit—a cuirassier regiment of repute—which had really cleaned up its billets and filled in its latrines. The passage of French troops was almost always signalized by dirty, foul ground.

While at Boufflers we went to a lecture at the Third Army School at Auxi le Chateau on bayonet fighting. The subject was bloodcurdling to a degree. An officer in Scotch costume dilated on how to kill Boches, accompanied by a dreadful man in a tin hat who seemed to follow up every remark of the Scotch officer by most horrible growls, grinding of teeth and pointing a rifle with a fixed bayonet at us.

The final dénouement was a furious wrestling match between the two, when the Scotch officer suddenly drew a table fork hidden in his adversary's puttie and held it to his throat. The gentleman with the tin hat then threw up his hands. It was a great relief to see the officer win, for in the minds of some of us the man with the tin hat was behaving in a most improper manner towards his superior officer.

Speaking seriously, however, Major Campbell, the officer in question, did an enormity of good with regard to training in the *arme blanche* in general. It became a live thing and not the old deadly drill.

At the same time it is worth considering whether much of the time devoted to it would not have been better spent in teaching the men how to shoot. We know that the Army went " bomb mad " after Loos, and that it was no unusual thing for the British soldier to attempt to hold up a hostile attack by throwing bombs when the enemy was more than seventy yards off. Our casualties, indeed, from our own bombs were often serious.

The Lewis-gun and Hotchkiss rifle were employed on numberless occasions when the rifle would have been more suitable.

The normal infantry soldier after 1915, had no idea of shooting, and his idea of attacking seemed to be to walk straight forward to the objective.

When there was no barrage, or when the barrage was not a very strong one, the casualties became simply enormous owing to the inability of the troops to use their own fire power.

CHAPTER VIII

TRAINING AT ST. RIQUIER. NEUVILLE ST. VAAST
1916

IN the spring of 1916 the Indian Cavalry formations were sent in succession to a training area near St. Riquier, about seven miles north of Abbeville. Here many divisions, French and British, had been fattened for the slaughter. In it, the French, in particular, had rehearsed their 1915 offensives on Laurette and on the Vimy Ridge. One spot was pointed out as having represented Ablain St. Nazaire, where there had been most bitter fighting in the real battle. The area had a few shallow trenches. These were not obstacles to horses, but our entrenching mules gave a good bit of trouble. We had pack horses issued in consequence.

Taken on the whole it was as ideal a spot as could be imagined for any kind of training. It even went so far as to have a hill with three trees from which big generals could watch proceedings. Two of the trees were withered. It is said that they had wilted when they heard the dreadful words used by some of the generals when things went wrong.

There was a great contrast between the work done when we went into this area the first time and when we visited it just before the great September attack on the Somme.

As stated previously, the higher training of all officers in the two Indian Cavalry Divisions was far behind that of those trained at home, but, except in one or two brigades, nothing had been done to improve it in 1915.

Attention had certainly been paid to making the sowar more handy on his feet and in improving the *laissez-aller* discipline prevailing in the majority of Indian regiments. March discipline had attained a very high standard. A large number, moreover, of the products of long service in India, British and Indian, had been weeded out.

These factors, combined with the issue of very many remounts to replace the useless animals which swarmed in the Silladar cavalry, had rendered the Indian troops of infinitely more value than they had been on landing in October 1914.

What was now required was field work, and lots of it, for the Indian is extremely hard to train in this respect.

Unfortunately, the majority of our brigadiers seemed unable to rise beyond the close order work we had done before the War.

Much most valuable time had been wasted in brigade drill on the sands at Cayeux in the winter. A relieving feature of these parades had been the immersion of certain unfortunates in quicksands.

The effects of training on these lines showed themselves at St. Riquier.

Suitable formations for artillery fire were unknown, and no doctrine existed as regards coping with the machine gun. The proper working in of fire with movement, was a sealed book, and the very word liaison was unknown.

Furthermore, the pernicious doctrine of long foot advances as contrasted with the rapid mounted advance in loose formation had crept in.

It was disconcerting to find oneself standing in mass on an exposed hilltop in full view of ground supposed to be in enemy occupation and within three thousand yards of a powerful artillery.

That murmurings arose was inevitable, and in May we learnt, with relief, that many changes were to be made in commands.

That these changes were necessary was undeniable, and an enormous improvement soon became noticeable throughout the two Divisions.

At the same time the method of effecting the removal of the senior officers responsible was objectionable in the extreme. To insult, as was done, men who had served the State loyally and well for some thirty years and who, owing to India being some ten years behind the times, found themselves in positions they were not quite up to, is a matter that cannot be discussed temperately.

It was generally known, moreover, that some of these officers had already realized their limitations and had applied to be relieved, but without success.

Furthermore, some quite good men went with the rest. It seemed more by good fortune than by anything else that some of these had a second chance on another front, where they did well.

At the same time, there is but little doubt that April 1916 was a most important period in the advance of the Indian Cavalry to efficiency.

It was said, with a good substratum of truth, that it was trained in France and made its name in Palestine.

The Brigade went to the St. Riquier area three times in 1916 and the Regiment was fortunate enough to be billeted in Gapennes on all three occasions.

The *maire* of this village was a remarkable character, and one of the most jovial and pleasant Frenchmen we came across during the whole War. He was a great wag and, like many of his countrymen, had an idea of humour far in advance of the corresponding class of Britisher. We found, incidentally, that very large numbers of bourgeois and working-class French were extremely witty people. Their wit, moreover, was by no means necessarily of a prurient nature.

On visiting Gapennes the third time, just before the September attacks on the Somme, we inquired of this gentleman what kind of troops he had had billeted on him.

He replied that he had had good troops and he had had bad troops, both English and French, but that no troops were so *mechant* as that distinguished and excellent regiment, the Inniskilling Dragoons, whose name we saw chalked up on a wall close at hand. He said he had especially kept the chalk marks to remember it by.

Scenting a yarn, we listened further. It transpired that the *jeunes officiers* had a gramophone which opened at réveillé and never ceased till long past midnight. Requests for a cessation of fire had merely resulted in invitations to the *maire* and his comfortable spouse and daughter to join in a dance they were wont to indulge in. Furthermore, they had acted a play in which the most prominent character had been a burlesque of the *maire* himself, garbed, however, in the fireman's helmet and carrying the village crier's drum.

Finally, they had made attempts to carry off both the *maire's* lady and daughter in the brigade car which was going into Abbeville.

Never were there such gay dogs as "les sixième dragons d'Inniskilling."

It was at Gapennes that Shakur, the mess cook, had a difference of opinion with one of the British batmen at the ration stand, and a still greater difference with his squadron commander because he returned therefrom with his nose wrapped up in the *Daily Mail* and minus the rations.

The Paris edition of the *Daily Mail* was always eagerly sought for and provided much up-to-date information.

Altogether, we look back to our days in the St. Riquier area as some of the best we spent in the whole War.

It was on return from St. Riquier in May that Bt. Lieut.-Colonel Moreton Gage, D.S.O., 5th Dragoon Guards, was sent to command the Lucknow Cavalry Brigade. Under this officer vast strides were made towards efficiency, and the present standard of war fitness of the Scinde Horse is very largely due to his sound and admirable system of training.

A school of sniping was started shortly after, under an officer of the King's Dragoon Guards, who ran a similar school later on at El Arish in Palestine. It was a curious thing what very bad shots most Indians proved to be. The British were far better. It is true that the telescopic sights puzzled them, but, even after discarding them, the picked Britisher was the better man. Indians were rather better at crawling and hiding, but not markedly so.

This particular school was of extremely good value and it is a pity it has dropped out since the war ended. Most valuable lessons in camouflage were gained at it.

In June 1916 dismounted trench parties of the Lucknow Brigade went into the line opposite the Vimy Ridge. Jacob's Horse took over Neuville St. Vaast, in support. On this particular sector mine warfare was in vogue. Owing to the careless mining methods of the French, the Germans had gained a great lead and the British had serious difficulty in making up lost ground. Mines and camouflets were continually going up.

The Indian Cavalry were employed on mining fatigues, being scattered about in parties of fifteen men or so all along the front. The work was trying, and by no means too safe, owing to accumulations of carbonic gas.

Nevertheless, a special report was sent in on the staunchness of a party of the Regiment on the occasion of a German mine going up unexpectedly, despite the fact that they had no officers with them and that no one in the neighbourhood knew any Hindustani. On another occasion Ressaldar Mmd Nur and seven men of " D " Squadron rescued some miners who had been overcome with carbonic gas—a very dangerous service for which this Ressaldar was deservedly rewarded.

Neuville St. Vaast was a charnel house and the trenches filthy to a degree—quite unnecessarily so. The men did an enormous amount of work in cleaning them up and making them both more secure and more habitable.

Partially buried French and German dead were everywhere, and the place swarmed with enormous rats.

The communication trenches were constantly blown in and were regularly machine-gunned at night when reliefs came up.

The Boche had perfect observation and could see any daylight movement along them. For mining, a large amount of timber baulks had to be carried up, and these drew fire as soon as they showed above the parapet. In the more advanced trenches they were visible at night even, as the enemy flares lighted the ground up.

The Germans were then preparing to meet the Somme offensive. The result was the Vimy sector was quieter than it might have been.

The men were on excellent terms with the Lancashire miners they worked with.

It was here that the men first had steel helmets issued. The prestige of these was enormously enhanced by some machine-gun bullets glancing

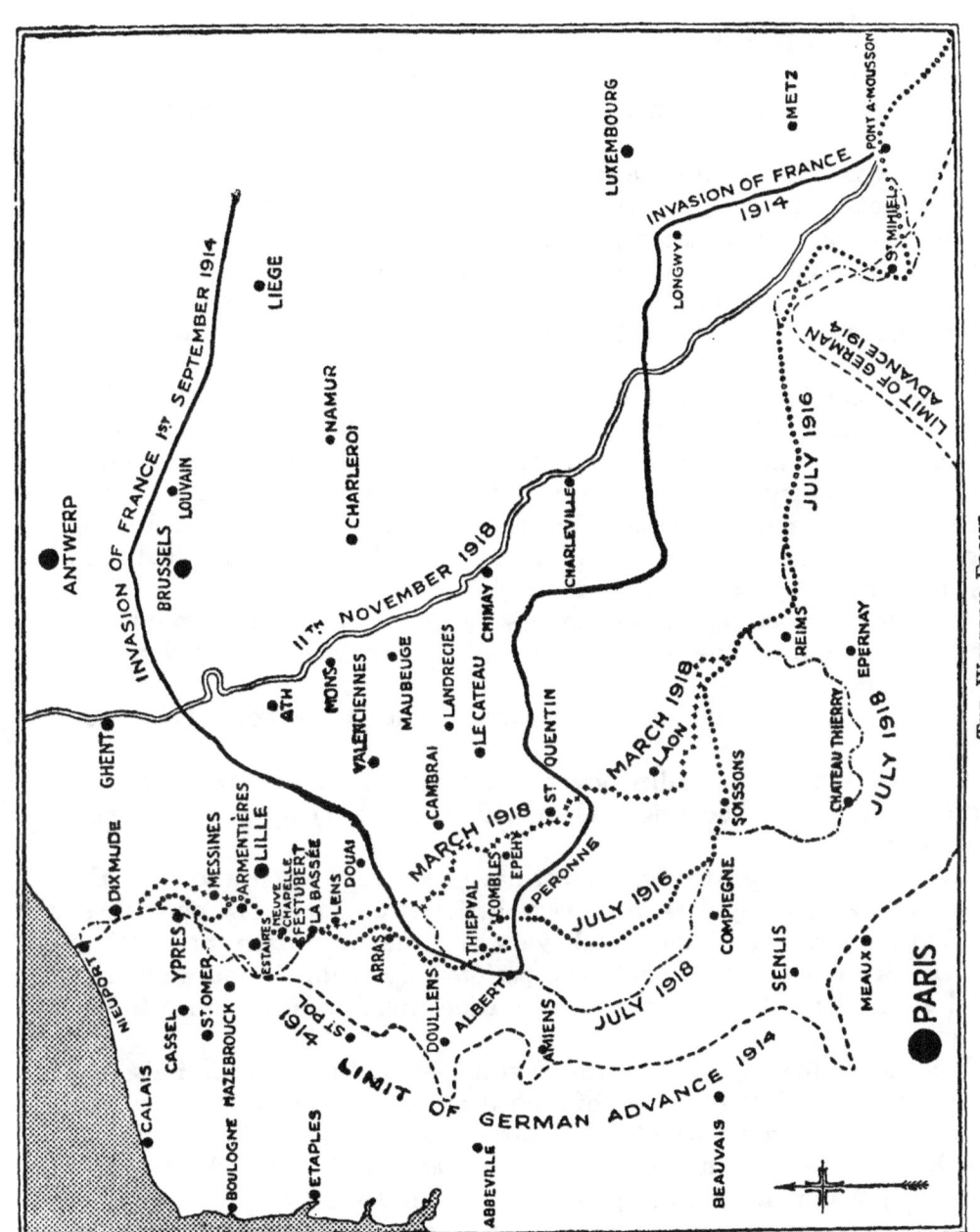

The Western Front.
1914–1918.

off when the men were moving up. Odd helmets found lying about were eagerly pounced upon. The Sikhs did not wear them.

So far as we British officers were concerned we were delighted at the men doing so. We were made far less conspicuous thereby. In the early days we wore loongis and a more abominable head-dress could never be devised. They were no head-gear for a white man.

Hotchkiss rifles had just been issued to the Indian Cavalry, but it was as well that at that time they were not required for serious use, as a very exaggerated value was placed on their efficiency and the teams were only partially trained. There was a fair amount of shelling going on, but the Boche seemed to use only light stuff, except for strafing our batteries.

It seemed as though he had shifted his guns south to meet our concentration for the Somme.

What Neuville St. Vaast would have been like under heavy shelling is hard to imagine, for most of our dug-outs and cellars were very sketchy, though strong enough for 4.2's. We came to the conclusion we would rather be in open country than run the risk of being buried alive. There were some big caves under the village, but these had only one or two exits and might prove death-traps in case of an assault. We heard this had been the case in the big battle of April 1915.

The Boche observing officers were very quick to spot parties offering good targets, and on one occasion some of the Regiment had a very unpleasant time.

Fortunately only field-gun fire was used, or casualties would have been very heavy.

One could quite well realize how trying it must have been to live in this portion of the line for a considerable period, with the enemy watching every movement.

In winter or rainy weather it must have been very much worse, for the trenches became quagmires after very little rain. Lines of approach to the Vimy Ridge were under full view all the way from St. Eloi to Neuville St. Vaast. Movement was, perforce, by night, if one wanted to avoid going along the muddy communication trench which seemed to run for miles.

We were relieved by the 60th Division—brand-new Territorials just landed, very raw, but keen and of a good class. Several of the men who relieved us were employees of John Barkers and Harrods. We next met this Division again in the Jordan in 1918, very much changed, and commanded by Major-General Sir John Shea, Scinde Horse.

To listen to our Sikh gas expert dilate on the Vermoral Sprayer to the relieving cockney, who may have been, for all we knew, a chemist by profession, was most illuminating. The explanation was delivered in mixed Punjabi and French, and was accompanied by gestures in demonstration. Its clarity was assisted by the fact that the demonstrator had lost two front teeth. We came to the conclusion that the Londoners could not fail to be greatly impressed with the vast scientific knowledge possessed by the Indian.

We left Neuville before we expected to, and were rather excited thereby, for we knew the Somme offensive was to begin at any moment. The flashes in the sky to the south by night showed there was a bombardment raging, the like of which no man had seen, though we heard nothing. We were confident there was to be *G* in *Gap* all right, a thing we hoped for and yet dreaded—for no sane man likes battle.

On return from Neuville St. Vaast the Regiment was inspected by Sir Douglas Haig. He expressed great satisfaction at the appearance of men and horses. At the same time he observed that the value of Indian units would be enormously increased if only they had a proportion of British N.C.O.'s who could take the place of officers knocked out. Any Indian Army officer with experience of prolonged heavy fighting will endorse the soundness of this remark. The only proviso is, the British N.C.O.'s must be very carefully selected, otherwise they would become the bane of one's existence like our old friends the transport drivers.

CHAPTER IX

THE SOMME. BEAUMONT HAMEL. CRECY.

1916-17

1916

ON the 1st July 1916, the historic opening of the Somme battle, the Division moved up in reserve behind Gommecourt.

This portion of the attack was, however, a failure, the 56th Division, close behind whom we were, losing some five thousand men. It is understood that the failure was due to lack of training of the troops and to the Germans being more ready for the attack in this quarter than he was further south.

It was rather a shock for us to hear, in confidence, that, despite the reiterated statements in public that the British soldier of the New Armies was better than the Boche at " close in " fighting, the Boche was the better man in reality. It was a matter, at bottom, of the professional versus the amateur, and no amount of individual courage could make up for the difference.

The 4th Cavalry Division, the new name of the Division, was then distributed behind the sector north of the Somme battle by brigades.

A mining fatigue party again went up to the line, this time near Roclincourt, but did not have such an exciting time as that which went to Neuville St. Vaast.

In August the Brigade shifted to close behind the northern end of the Somme battle front of the 1st July, and resided in a particularly smelly village named Gaudiempre.

It sent up a party to put in gas at Fonquevillers—a nerve-racking and highly unpleasant task.

The prospect of one of the gas cylinders being hit and bursting was a far from attractive one.

While about here certain officers seized the opportunity of visiting the Notre Dame De Laurette spur—a trip well worth taking. The view was magnificent and it was quite understandable why the French attached such importance to it in the April 1915 battle.

The view towards Lens and that towards Arras was an absolute contrast, the former being all factories and collieries, while the latter was entirely country.

We went to hear the 56th Divisional Concert Party, "Bow Bells," with its great prima donnas Glycerine, Margarine and Gelatine.

These three "ladies" were of surpassing beauty and of impeccable virtue. The performance was an excellent one, as might be expected from London Territorials.

Our Division had only regular troops and the musical talent was decidedly mediocre. One noticed that the "New Army" and Territorials had a far higher standard in this respect.

It is doubtful whether the good old songs about mother-in-law, kippers, drink and bad smells would have gone down with them. It is certain that the sentimental ballad like "Only a burd in a gaolden kyge" and lasting to twenty verses would have been a complete frost. "Sic transit gloria mundi."

We were put on to a fascine and hurdle-making job in some woods a few miles behind the line. We were, in very truth, "Les domestiques de l'Armée," as an aggrieved French cavalry officer told the writer. The French cavalry were doing the same, and, as they thought no "small beer" of themselves and were generally reputed to have made themselves objectionable to their own infantry before the War by their airs and graces, they felt their "fall" greatly. We did not regard it as a fall, and were only too delighted to do something other than loaf.

Long columns of very fine-looking infantry passed south continually, on their way to the Somme. One could not help feeling sorry for them, for we all knew what lay ahead. They were the first batches of Territorials and the men of K.I.—the best blood of the Empire.

They were usually singing—the battle song of the Somme—"The only Girl in the World." To this day there is always something rather horrible in hearing it.

Together with the chaff and banter usual when bodies of troops meet, there was something we heard for the first time—directed against the British cavalry of course, for the jawan did not indulge in badinage with British troops. It was destined later on to become singularly offensive, particularly as the quality of our infantry deteriorated. It was "Never bin over the top, 'ave yer."

This jeering at the cavalry ceased entirely after the debacle in March 1918, and the feeling went the other way. It had become apparent that the British trooper was the first fighting man in Europe, and to him, in no small measure, was due the salvation of the Third and Fifth Armies, amid scenes of demoralization that baffle description.

At the same time, it was quite easy to understand that infantry soldiers, back from the boredom, monotony and, usually, the danger of the line, should feel resentment at seeing troops who had been out of it for long periods together, living in comfortable billets and beautiful country. The normal man in the ranks would not, in all probability, know that the cavalry had had a great hand in saving the situation at the First and Second Battles of Ypres.

One more mining party went up to the line, and at the end of August the Division moved right back to the training area of St. Riquier, following just on the heels of our old friends the 56th Division, who marched out in pouring rain singing, as Atkins does whenever the weather is bad, at the tops of their voices.

Here, once more, the regiment went to Gapennes and learnt from *Monsieur le Maire* all about " le plus méchant regiment " and the fireman's helmet.

This particular training was of exceptionally good value, and General Allenby came down and gave his views.

It is probable that the Indian Cavalry was about at its best at this period, for, in 1917, it was in the line continually, and many of the trained squadron commanders had gone off on various jobs, being replaced by comparatively untrained I.A.R. or War Babies. Here we saw the Tanks practising preparatory to their appearance in the great battle. On the hard chalky soil their performances seemed almost uncanny, especially when they walked through a copse with comparatively thick trees.

The enthusiasm of the crews was also most heartening. Our disappointment was great when we saw them a couple of weeks later stuck in the greasy craters of the Somme battlefield.

After a most interesting and instructive week in the training area the Division moved up to the Somme battle via the valley of the Authie and thence to Querrieu.

It had been in April 1914 that Major Maunsell, in common with other Staff College officers, had done a scheme for the defence of Querrieu Chateau —rather a strange coincidence.

The whole of the 4th Cavalry Division was bivouacked about Querrieu for the 14th September. It was a most unpleasant, raw day.

The next day it went into close bivouac three miles S.S.W. of Albert, close to Dernacourt.

The whole of the British Cavalry in France—five Divisions—were up for the battle.

The Regiment was fortunate enough to be in a field with stooks of corn. These proved a Godsend when it began to rain.

FRANCE AND FLANDERS.

*The Imperial War Museum.
By kind permission.*

MAMETZ—A CAVALRY PATROL.
July, 1916.

*The Imperial War Museum.
By kind permission.*

STRETCHER-BEARERS—NEAR GINCHY.

12th September, 1916.

The bivouac was most congested, three brigades of cavalry being packed in between a railway embankment and a road. Traffic along the road equalled that of The Strand at the busiest time of the day.

We were lucky in not being shelled, for the bivouac would have been a positive shambles. The German gunners apparently had their hands full.

We were fortunate enough, also, to have great air superiority, for no hostile planes appeared by day.

A plane came over one night and dropped half a dozen bombs close to us. One burst in a troop of the 3rd Hussars and killed ten horses and a couple of men, besides wounding a number of others. The other bombs did no damage, fortunately. They were not, it is understood, of the 106 fuse type that burst horizontally and which did such damage later on.

The first step to be taken was for officers to get to learn the lie of the land, and numerous reconnaissances went up to the line. It was no easy matter to find the way, as all landmarks has been obliterated. Certain villages such as Guillemont, where the bombardment had been colossal, had practically disappeared, slight mounds and tree-stumps alone marking the sites.

On the evening of the 17th September it began to rain, and the whole country became the most appalling quagmire imaginable. The unmetalled tracks, churned up by the passage of horses and vehicles, became practically impassable, and our reconnaissances had the greatest difficulty in moving at all.

The bivouac became a sea of mud, and the disgusting smell of mud and horse-dung mixed pervaded the atmosphere.

Operations were, for the time, held up. It would have been a most difficult matter to bring cavalry through the maze of trenches by the cavalry tracks.

H.R.H. the Prince of Wales, our future Colonel-in-Chief, was seen here bicycling along a filthy muddy road and hanging on to the tail of a lorry for a tow. He was then a platoon commander in the Grenadier Guards, and had it not been for the number of decorations he wore there was nothing to distinguish him from any other young officer.

The dismounted reinforcements of the 4th and 5th Cavalry Divisions were employed on the track leading in the direction of Flers and Leuze Wood. This was no pleasant task, for the Boche persistently shelled the route, and parties that came under observation were always in for a warm time. A number of casualties occurred in consequence. In fact, on one occasion we had to reinforce the reinforcements. The staunchness of the men under shell-fire was, however, remarkable, and belied the nonsense occasionally heard about good Indian troops not being able to stand shelling.

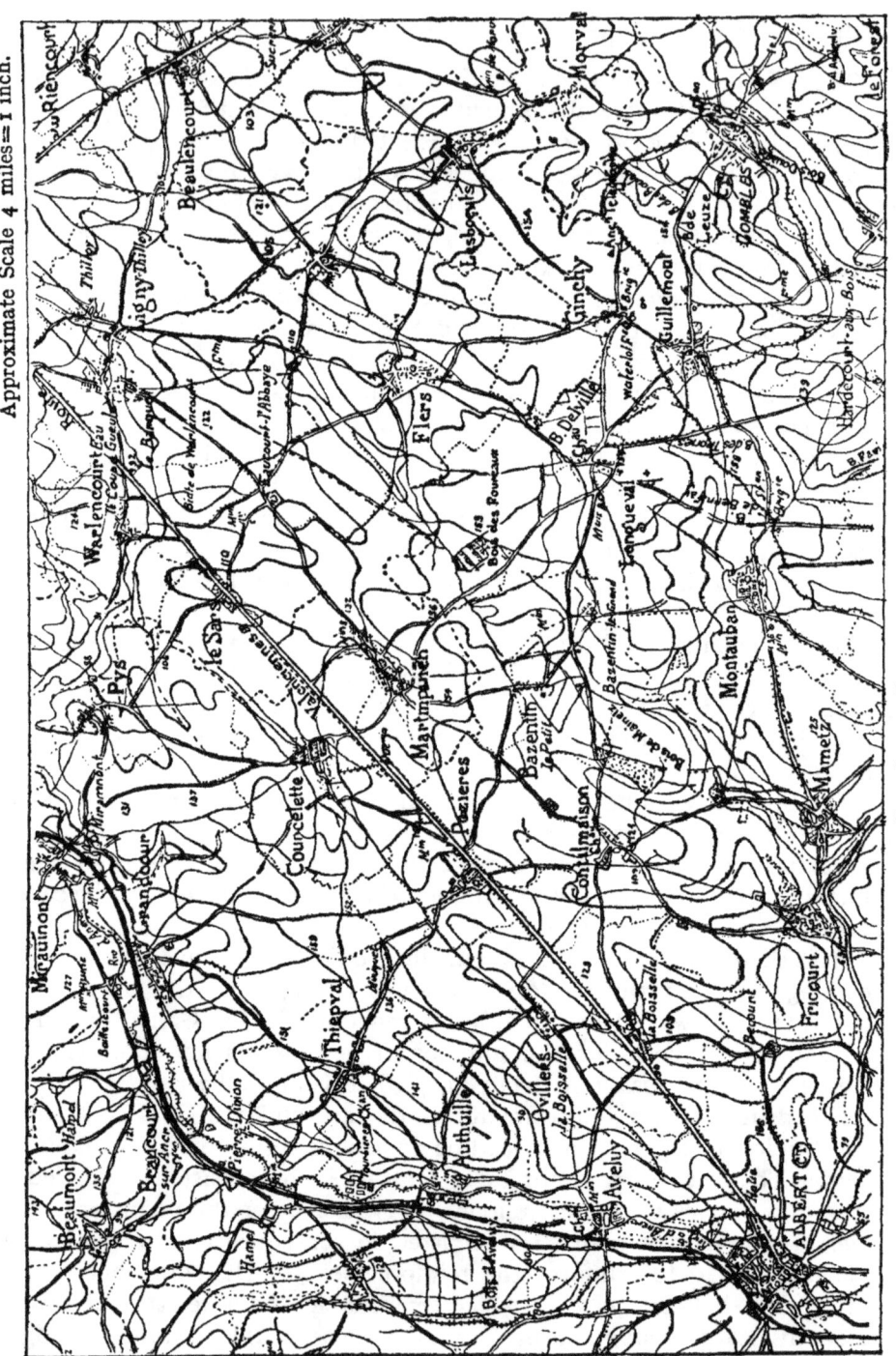

THE SOMME BATTLEFIELD.

The dismounted men of the Regiment saw a good deal of the Guards. The astonishing manner in which these famous troops kept up their traditions for smartness under the most adverse conditions greatly impressed them. A story was current that these worshippers of "The Great God, Discipline," had advanced at Loos with the platoon-sergeants calling the step.

On the morning of the 21st September, however, the weather cleared and preparations were made for a great attack, to take place on the 25th.

The operation envisaged the capture, *inter alia*, of Guedicourt, Les Bœufs and Morval. In the event of success the 4th Cavalry Division was to move forward, through Guedicourt, to seize Ligny-Tilloy, with a view to attacking the enemy in rear towards the west and also to intercept his reinforcements from the north and east.

The Mhow and Sialkot Brigades were moved up in the early morning to Bois De Bernafay and Mametz respectively, the Lucknow Brigade remaining in reserve, at one hour's notice, at Dernacourt.

The operation was not completely successful, and the opportunity for cavalry action was again lacking. The two advanced brigades returned to Dernacourt in the evening.

On the 26th September the Division began to move back out of the battle area. Only the Lucknow Brigade remained. At midday, sudden orders were received for the Brigade to move forward. The King's Dragoon Guards moved to Trônes Wood, the remainder of the Brigade to Mametz.

As Guedicourt had now been taken, it was thought that an opening for cavalry might offer. The XV. Corps' duty squadron (19th Lancers) had been despatched to Guedicourt on a reconnaissance to find out what was going on in the neighbourhood, as the infantry and flying corps reports had been so varying.

The squadron commander, Captain Fitzgerald, told us that evening that he galloped over most poisonous ground, full of shell craters, to get there, as he thought he would get shelled to nothing if he went along the track. What amazed him was that no horses came down.

The squadron had a brush with some Germans outside the village, which he said he found unoccupied by either our own people or by Germans.

He had lost a few men, but his led horses had been caught by 5·9's in a hollow road marked on the map, and had had thirty-two killed and sixteen wounded. He thought he would have been wiser to have left the animals in the open, well opened out, and subsequent experience showed this to be the best course in circumstances where the place of concealment is obvious to the enemy.

As the enemy was definitely ascertained to be massing not far from Guedicourt, the 19th Lancers squadron was recalled.

There being now no opportunity for cavalry, the Lucknow Brigade was directed to follow the rest of the Division out of the line.

The Division was withdrawn right back to the area about Crecy, north of Abbeville.

A curious feature about our stay at Dernacourt had been the comparative silence.

At Neuve Chapelle and Second Ypres the roar and thunder of the guns had been tremendous, though we were farther away from them than we had been at the Somme.

At Dernacourt, within three miles of the greatest bombardments of history, almost the only thing that we heard was a French 15-inch gun on a railway truck about half a mile away.

The country round Abbeville is of considerable historic interest with regard to previous wars in which the English were engaged, particularly with relation to the campaigns of Crecy and Agincourt.

Crecy was only some fifteen miles from Abbeville, and Hesdin, close to Agincourt, some twenty-five.

According to available records the country round Crecy is much the same now as it was then, except that the forest of Crecy extended closer to the village.

It added much to the interest of life to study the history of Abbeville.

The name Lagache—that of the prisoner of war who showed Edward III the ford of Blanche Tache over the Somme—is still common in these parts.

We were twice billeted within a couple of miles of the ford—now a ford no longer, as the Somme has been canalized.

A fact not noted in English histories was that Edward took a very bad knock trying to force the passages at Abbeville, apparently just about where the Rouen road leaves the town. The English were fairly up a tree when the ford was given away.

It is remarkable also that, in these chronicles, no mention is made of Amiens—nasty inhospitable people those Amienois of those times!!

We had Cromwellian regiments billeted in Abbeville in the winter of 1658–59. They formed part of the force " Old Noll," sent over to fight beside Louis XIV against the Spaniards. These troops were, for a time, under the orders of the Marquis de Castelnau, the ancestor of the French general. According to the Abbeville writers they made themselves highly unpopular by their behaviour in the church of St. Vulfram, for it is recorded that they not merely lighted their pipes at the altar candles but even danced during the services—Puritanism with a vengeance. These were the Regiments who fought the battle of the Dunes and who stormed Ypres—feats of arms which astonished Europe. It was they who were first dressed in red—the "redcoats" of the Model Army.

One small village, Airaines, near which we were billeted, was, according to Edward III's mess bill, the place where his cook purchased a chicken and a bottle of wine.

While in the Crecy area a boar-hunt was arranged, after a good bit of formality had been gone through with the Prefect, for all hunting was forbidden.

A rich owner of beet factories had a pack of hounds which used to hunt the forest in time of peace.

The whole Division turned out and we had a very pleasant morning. It was the same as any other woodland hunting. The hounds, however, were not fit and were done up after a comparatively short gallop.

While in this area also much very high-class training was put in.

In October, our doctor, Captain Munro, I.M.S., was recalled to India. He had been with us since the outbreak of the War, and we felt his departure a great deal.

At the end of October the machine gunners of the Division went up to the line opposite Serre and Beaumont Hamel. They were twenty-seven days in the line without relief and took a very important part in the Beaumont Hamel battle of the 11th November. The Lucknow Brigade machine gun squadron greatly distinguished itself on this occasion, the gunners of the 29th Lancers and Jacob's Horse smashing a German counter-attack delivered under a very heavy bombardment.

Lieutenant Howell, Jacob's Horse, was gassed, and Lieutenant Falconer, 29th Lancers, wounded, while Jemadar Ghulam Khwaja, Jacob's Horse, was killed.

The Lucknow Brigade squadron on this occasion collected no less than two M.C.'s, one D.C.M., five M.M.'s and two I.O.M.'s, which was pretty good for about seventy men in the line. These " mixed " machine-gun squadrons were broken up in the winter of 1916–7, " all British " personnel being substituted.

For the first four months of 1917, which included the operations before Croissilles and the Battle of Bullecourt, the squadrons were, in all probability, of less value than the " mixed " ones, as the men were only moderately disciplined and knew nothing about horses. A " mixed " organization was, however, in many ways unsatisfactory.

The Beaumont Hamel battle had demonstrated the staunchness and skill of Indian machine gunners to the full.

Prior to the battle a ridiculous incident occurred at the pow-wow of unit representatives. The code word of one formation was " blinker." Its representative, rather a famous character, forgot it, and announced himself as " stinker," to the huge glee of the assembled company.

CHAPTER X

WINTER 1916–17.

THE GERMAN WITHDRAWAL TO THE HINDENBURG LINE.

1916

IN the winter of 1916–17 big working parties were sent up to about Longueval and Delville Wood.

They were employed in laying light railways and preparing roads for the offensive it was hoped would come off in the spring.

As is well known, the preparations all came to naught owing to the Germans evading battle on this part of the line by falling back out of the Somme salient to the Hindenburg Line.

The work was gruesome in the extreme, as corpses lay in every direction about a foot below the surface, the stench in many cases being appalling.

There was a certain amount of long range shelling, but the casualties were light.

The Regiment shared dug-outs with the New Zealanders. At first we were a little afraid the men might be maltreated, but we were very soon shown to be wrong, for a kinder or nicer lot of men than these magnificent Colonials could not be found on earth. We had to stop the men sponging on them, or they would have got all their tea, sugar and cigarettes.

Incidentally, the only people prone to be unfair to Indian troops were British regulars, with the exception of gunners, who had always come in close contact with Indians.

In 1914 and 1915 there was usually an uneasy suspicion that the men might get more than their fair share of dirty work if no British officer of their own was present. There was a particular type of British service officer, fortunately rare, who adopted the " damned nigger " attitude. In no small number of instances this was due to ignorance, and this ignorance was not confined to officers who had never been in India, for some who had were just as objectionable.

It must be remembered that there were very highly placed officers indeed who, in those years, made but little effort to conceal their attitude towards Indian troops.

This died down in mid 1917, and by the end of the year had completely ceased. Épéhy had shown them what Indian troops could do if only they were given a fair chance.

In the back areas, when working parties were up in the line, the men with the horses had a very hard time, particularly when the animals were scattered about in twos and threes in villages.

Training was impossible, except for officers' tactical rides.

Among the men, and usually among the officers, it was far more popular to be up in the line or on working parties than going through the drudgery of watering, feeding, grooming and exercising a number of horses day after day.

1917

In January 1917 it became intensely cold, and we had one of the hardest winters known in Europe for years.

The Indian troops, properly clothed and well fed, were perfectly fit. The experiences of the War, indeed, showed that the idea of their not being able to stand cold was nonsense, provided they had enough clothes. The pre-War scale, being run in the huckstering spirit of John Company, was skimpy and quite inadequate.

We amused ourselves sliding on various ponds, and the spectacles near Abbeville, where the whole population turned out, were most entertaining.

It was at this time that an officer rejoined from sick leave in England. A devoted aunt had presented him with a bottle of sloe gin, very rare and precious. He had also brought a bottle of Mars Oil for his boots.

His horror and surprise may be imagined when he discovered that his Indian batman had anointed several pairs of his boots with the sloe gin. History does not relate whether either the batman or the officer drank the Mars Oil as a consolation.

In view of the prospective renewal of the Somme offensive, combined with another from the Arras direction, an elaborate sand table of the Mory Ridge and country to the north of Bapaume had been prepared in billets, and several most instructive exercises took place on it.

It was of great interest to compare it with the actual ground when we went forward in March, and it proved of great value, even to the Indian officers.

The Boche, however, with that lack of consideration for others which had made him so universally unpopular, had destroyed several of the landmarks and features which had endeared the sand table to every one. He had actually shown the want of taste to go so far as to remove a whole copse which had figured very largely in our indoor exercises.

Furthermore, there was reason to suppose that he had even altered the shape of the Mory Ridge itself in order to thwart us, for the sand table showed the eastern slope to be steep, whereas we found it a very gentle one.

Certain insinuations that the sand table was inaccurate were quite uncalled for.

Seriously speaking, however, the inaccuracy in detail of contouring in the French published maps was extraordinary. Those made up by our own Intelligence were far superior.

A definite system of training reinforcements at the Bases was, by now, well in progress. At Rouen a very excellent " bull ring," as the troops called it, had started, from which the Indian Cavalry profited greatly. They had the great good fortune to have some sergeants of the Guards to put ginger into them in their footwork, which sorely needed it, for the normal sowar, on his feet, was a ridiculous object.

The young officers just arrived from Quetta and Wellington Cadet Colleges, had a very sound grounding in trench work at Rouen, which proved a Godsend when they went up to the line. Unfortunately there was not enough time to train them in cavalry work. This latter had to be picked up when they joined their units, and even then could not be done very thoroughly. The majority of these officers, though of first-class material, who had seen great operations of war, were, by the Armistice, still insufficiently ground in their jobs as horse soldiers.

The Divisional and Corps schools, which were being established about this time, did a great deal of good, certainly, but time was not available to produce the finished article.

So far as our village was concerned, we were rather alarmed at the arrival of some French troops who were to be put on to widening the railway. Previous experience of " poilus " of this type showed they were not very pleasant neighbours owing to their peculiar notions on sanitation.

While beside the railway one day we noticed a train, with what seemed to be Oriental troops in a kind of French uniform, who interested our men greatly. They were the Portuguese, who were just arriving. They were not impressive.

The strain of war was, by now, becoming noticeable as far back as Abbeville. Prices had gone up greatly and coal was very short. The French were largely dependent on English coal. It was quite pitiable to see long queues of wretched Frenchwomen waiting, in the bitter cold, outside the coal merchant's stores in Abbeville. It was at this juncture that the high-souled patriot, the Welsh miner, elected to go on strike.

In early February 1917 we heard rumours that the Boche was falling back on our Somme front, though for what reason we could not imagine.

We certainly suspected that we had a big offensive in preparation, owing to the railways and odd work we had been put on to about there.

In view of the bitter weather, however, we did not expect to have to do anything for a month at least, and carried on the normal routine of training in billets.

The Brigade was then billeted in the area we were in the previous winter, about six miles south-west of Abbeville, the Regiment being at Quesnoy le Montant.

On the evening of the 25th orders were received for a march next morning. A pretty general impression existed that this was the normal practice march which would be over by lunch-time, and some of us only packed up portions of our kit, and marched without having had breakfast.

To our disgust, however, we found ourselves moving right out of the Divisional area, never to return.

We marched some forty miles that day—with light hearts but aching stomachs—to a village named Naours.

The hard frosts and subsequent thaws had so affected the roads that our " B " echelon baggage could not get along with our blankets. The result was that a night of most bitter cold followed.

We were in considerable alarm for the next night, should the march be continued, for we were now only some ten miles in a direct line behind the battle front, and the roads were even worse.

Fortunately the Army did not require us to move for the next two days, and our kits fetched up.

At Naours there was a big underground village, the main street of which must have been about a quarter of a mile long. It had been a historic place of refuge in the old days, especially when the Spaniards were in the Low Countries and constantly fighting the French.

In this part of France, it will be remembered, there were many villages with huge subterranean galleries.

At Arras and Neuville St. Vaast, for instance, there were enormous caves, capable of accommodating several hundreds of men each.

The reason for the sudden move up, was that there were definite signs of a German withdrawal on the Somme front, and the Fifth Army wanted a cavalry brigade handy to push forward the moment it occurred.

The Brigade then moved to some huts near Becourt, passing through Albert en route. The roads were in a very bad state.

The cold at night was intense, despite many layers of blankets.

The next two days were spent in reconnaissances for possible lines of advance through the crater area. Those who have not actually seen what this was like in mid-winter, can have no conception of what it meant.

The shell holes touched, and the country was almost impossible to move over on foot in parts, much less ride. There was every chance of being swallowed up by the mud and slush if one left a recognized track, and the shell craters were so deep that a horse might get drowned if it fell in.

A battery the Australians had got into position by the Butte de Warlincourt, had been manhandled off a light railway, together with its ammunition, as horses could not even move singly.

The general outcome of these reconnaissances was that it would pay best to move up the Ancre Valley, by the main Miraumont Road, which was, for some extraordinary reason, comparatively little damaged.

The Boche had withdrawn all his field guns and most of his 5·9's. His shelling was nearly all by 8-inch from very long range. These shells could be heard coming for what seemed ages before they arrived, and to be anywhere near their business end was a most alarming experience. They were, indeed, far more alarming than damaging. The ground was so soft that it rather smothered them. An enormous fountain of mud and stones was raised by each burst.

The Hun, however, still hung on to his line, protected by masses of wire, and infantry reconnaissances could make no progress.

The enormous strength of his line enabled him to hold very long stretches with a ridiculously small number of men.

For some reason we heard only vague rumours of the far-famed Hindenburg Line, and, in so far as the Fifth Army was concerned, there seemed to be an apparent ignorance of where the German withdrawal was going to stop.

The actual troops in the line were very far from holding any illusions as to the German being a beaten man, and it was generally heard that he was falling back *pour mieux sauter* rather than from hard necessity.

As an immediate advance seemed improbable, the Brigade was withdrawn some fifteen miles to billets. It fortunately managed to get its horses under cover before a violent snowstorm began.

The 29th Lancers, in the meantime, were detailed to leave a big road-making party at Bazentin. This party was moving along the road near Pozières one morning when an 8-inch shell burst at the head of the column, blowing to atoms a British officer, two Indian officers and fifteen men. The remainder carried on to their work.

This party was relieved on the 14th March by one from the 36th under Major Maunsell.

The main Albert-Bapaume Road, on which we were working, had been shelled persistently since the opening of the Somme battle, seven and a half months before, and was now in such a state that it could hardly be described as a road. The enormous craters on either side of it, all full of water, had absolutely rotted away all the foundations and necessitated an enormous amount of work.

The portion we were working on, moreover, was in full view of the Hun lines about Bapaume, and any big gathering of men was certain to be treated to shelling.

Although 8-inch Howitzers are not great at rapid fire, and would hardly deign to worry about parties of five or six, we were careful to see that we did not offend them.

Quite close to the huts we were in at Bazentin was a Russian gun the Huns had evidently brought over from the Eastern Front and abandoned.

CHAPTER XI

THE GERMAN WITHDRAWAL TO THE HINDENBURG LINE. OPERATIONS NORTH OF BAPAUME IN FRONT OF CROISSILLES MARCH 17th TO MARCH 26th, 1917.

March 17th

ON the 17th March the working party had got back to Bazentin, tired after a hard day's work, and had just turned in to sleep when an urgent order was received to join the Regiment which had moved up with the horses to Albert. Great difficulty was experienced in getting transport, but eventually an Australian sergeant lent a G.S. wagon, which helped greatly.

The men marched at midnight, very heavily laden up with winter clothing it was too risky to leave dumped, and reached Albert just as dawn was breaking. The march was enlivened by a highly technical discussion—discussed at the pitch of the jawans' voices—on the rival merits of killing a Boche by " cut one " or by " cut two." No decision was come to on this very vital point.

The Regiment was found to be under orders to move at once, and no time was available for a rest, or even a meal.

The Brigade was to push through in pursuit of the Germans, who had fallen back at last.

Fortunately a few ration biscuits were found—the hopes of luscious frizzling bacon had hitherto buoyed up the hearts of the officers of the working party, and they were a poor substitute.

While on the move, the experiences of the party with the horses were also learnt. Orders had been suddenly received the previous day, while the horses were at exercise, to move up to Albert, a distance of some twenty-two miles. This entailed an enormous amount of work, dumping kits and getting animals saddled up in marching order with only one man to four horses. The King's Dragoon Guards lent a squadron to help in leading the animals. Albert was not reached till long after dark and the lines were not down till midnight. In addition, rations for three days had to be distributed and put on each saddle. As can be imagined, there was little rest for anyone that night. Nevertheless, the cheeriness of the men was extraordinary, and spoke wonders for their physical fitness.

March 18th

The brigade moved along the Ancre Valley, past Miraumont, through the German front line, to Logeast Wood.

The Boche had made an inundation close to Achiet le Petit, which compelled the R.H.A. battery to go all the way round by Irles. This was "A" Battery, the "Chestnut Troop."

At Achiet le Petit we entered former German territory.

Some delay occurred at Logeast Wood, and the brigade did not move forward till 16·00.

In the meantime it was of interest to see the German lines. There was much that gave one furiously to think.

The better read and more travelled British regular officer knew, in his heart of hearts, that it was not reasonable to suppose that the magnificent material of the New Armies could, with the limited period they had had for training, have officers of the same quality as the Germans. Certain stories told in confidence by staff officers who really knew what they were talking about regarding the Somme Battle showed that it was largely the case of the professional versus the amateur.

There was, moreover, much scepticism about the published statements that the German had lost more heavily than we had. We knew that the enemy moral at the end of 1916 was not what it had been, but that was all.

Here, behind the old German line, the evidence before us of his skill and thoroughness in entrenching and wiring, and, above all, of his amazing salvage system, was overwhelming.

We had the gravest doubts whether the British soldier could have been induced to put in so much work, and were quite certain that what he might have put in would not have been of nearly such high quality, taken on the average whole. It is understood that prisoners-of-war helped materially, but a great deal was done by German troops.

The manner in which the actual withdrawal was conducted gave ample proof that the enemy was by no means a beaten man.

No officer of the brigade imagined for one instant that the Boche would not fight on the Hindenburg Line—that mysterious line of which there was so much talk.

It was with no little astonishment that one heard that a certain high personage held the view that he might fall back beyond it. That there was something in this rumour was confirmed by orders that were received a day or two later.

THE OPERATIONS BEFORE CROISSILLES AND BULLECOURT.

The country round the Bois de Logeast was quite clean and devoid of shells craters, but the villages were all more or less derelict, and it was found that nearly all the intact houses had delay action mines in them.

That the Boche was not altogether devoid of humour, was shown by the fact that, during the withdrawal, a German Town-Major who had been inundated with complaints from luxury-loving individuals regarding his billets, had left the complete file of correspondence on the table of his late residence addressed to the relieving British Town-Major with the words " For necessary action " written thereon.

In the villages there were stick grenades lying about in every direction, all detonated, and several accidents occurred—none, fortunately, to the men of the Regiment.

A particular feature was the care which the German had bestowed on the graveyards, regardless of whether the grave was German or British. The talk of " Corpse factories " had always been regarded as mere propaganda by more knowledgeable officers. In all probability, it really alluded to the German method of disposal of horses' carcasses, which, like many other things, we afterwards copied.

While waiting at the Bois de Logeast the King's Dragoon Guards brought in the tallest and lankiest Boche one had ever set eyes on.

The boy must have been 6 feet 6 inches high and about 33 inches round the chest.

The Brigade advanced at 16·00 from Logeast Wood on Ervillers.

The Regiment furnished the advanced guard.

" B " Squadron (Captain Carpendale) and a section of M.G.s was despatched independently on a reconnaissance *via* the Mory Ridge to see St. Leger, Ecoust and Croissilles. This squadron put in some extraordinarily fine work in the evening and during the night.

The enemy had evidently been slightly hustled in his withdrawal, for these villages were not as much destroyed as they might have been, and a number of explosions occurred.

One feature that struck one particularly was the amazing capacity of the men to find their way about in absolutely strange country at night over quite long distances.

Advanced patrols of the vanguard came into contact with the enemy at dusk, two coming under machine-gun fire at about one hundred and fifty or two hundred yards range. Their losses in each case amounted to two men and one horse.

This was the first indication we had that the machine-gun is by no means as formidable to cavalry as was supposed, provided the patrols kept moving.

In both cases the patrols had not been well handled, the scouts being too close in and the body of the patrols bunched.

Further experience in the following days showed that casualties were almost negligible, provided the men moved fast and well opened out. Our experiences with Turks down in the Jordan later on were the same, but in the present instance we were up against first-class German troops, every bit as good as good British. The German rear detachments consisted of both mounted and dismounted parties. The mounted men belonged, so far as we could ascertain from marks on saddlery of a horse we caught, to the 14th Uhlans.

Darkness having come down, we halted with posts in close contact with the enemy about a mile south-west of the line Ecoust-St. Leger-Boyelles.

Jemadar Alam Sher, " C " Squadron, did some excellent work while fronting a Uhlan picquet of superior strength. We bivouacked in the open. It fortunately did not rain, but was pretty cold.

March 19th

At 06.30 the advance was resumed.

The King's Dragoon Guards were directed on the Mory Ridge, our " B " Squadron coming under their orders.

" C " Squadron, Jacob's Horse (Captain Farquhar) advanced on St. Leger and Croissilles, and " A " Squadron (Captain Blacker) moved on Boyelles.

The brigade covered, therefore, a front of some six miles, the 29th Lancers being in reserve.

For the case of a reconnaissance which might demand " tearing aside the veil " or for a break through in pursuit of a beaten enemy, this extension would obviously be too great. In this case, however, we were not following up a beaten enemy—he was anything but beaten. There was little object in trying to rush him seriously, for such action would lead to heavy loss with no compensating advantage.

All that was really wanted was to see where he meant to come to a standstill. If we could cut off small parties or succeed in hustling him with small loss to ourselves, so much the better, but the time for incurring heavy loss to attain great ends was not yet.

Further to the south, in the Fourth Army area, where the 5th Cavalry Division was operating, opportunities were greater, for there were far fewer lines of defence, and odd trenches with wire, than there were with us. We came upon strongly wired lines every couple of miles or so, and all the villages were wired.

Nevertheless, in the Fourth Army area, the higher command fully realized the nature of the German withdrawal, and kept a tight hold on the cavalry.

"A" Squadron bumped the enemy in Boyelles very soon, but in too great strength to do anything. A troop that managed to get into the village was driven out almost at once.

"C" Squadron became engaged with Uhlans and Jägers within ten minutes of the start. These gradually fell back through St. Leger on Croissilles, after putting up a fire fight at about one hundred yards range just S.W. of the former village. The shooting on neither side was brilliant, for a colossal expenditure of ammunition resulted in two German casualties only, while Jacob's Horse lost no one. The coal-scuttle helmet of one of these Boche is now in the Mess—first blood in open war. The keenness of the jawans was wonderful.

Some cyclists and a troop of Yorkshire Dragoons came up about now. They were the vanguard to the 18th Division from the Miraumont direction. They were followed up by infantry.

"C" Squadron attempted to push on to Croissilles, moving by the northern slopes of the Sensee Valley in which both St. Leger and Croissilles lie.

The advanced troop was heavily fired on.

A dismounted advance was attempted, but was frustrated, largely by the sweep of machine guns posted about the southern corner of the village on the other side of the valley.

Farquhar, Dallas and Jemadar Abdul Samad were all hit, together with a number of men.

It was obvious that the place was too much to take on with cavalry alone.

Risaldar Sadiq Mohamed extricated the squadron, displaying the greatest coolness in doing so. He and Jemadar Alam Sher furthermore got all the wounded away under a very heavy fire, assisted by some of the men.

Major Maunsell was sent to take over. He at once liaised with the infantry and ascertained that they were not pushing any further ahead of St. Leger that day.

He dispatched patrols to find a way round Croissilles on its northern side. These all reported they could make no progress.

It was of interest to watch the skill with which one of these patrols worked, galloping widely extended against the flanks of a suspicious point and drawing fire. The commander was Dafadar Ahmed Khan, subsequently Woordi Major of the 35th. He put in some excellent patrolling that night as well.

To the south of Croissilles, "B" Squadron and the King's Dragoon

Guards had a series of minor affairs, but also found no further advance possible. Ecoust blocked the way. Here the Uhlans made one or two slight attempts to catch our patrols and scouts, but nothing more. It would have profited them but little if they had, for we were better mounted.

A German horse we captured showed signs of having had very little corn. Its saddlery, though quite serviceable, was not nearly of the same quality as ours.

It was remarkable how quick the German was in stripping dead horses. If he could not strip them in time, he took the feed bags at all events.

All this pointed to a very fine discipline, and we speculated whether the British soldier would be as good. Certainly a very large number of our troops would not be.

The enemy withdrawal had been conducted with most admirable skill. The support lines were always occupied prior to the rear lines moving back, and all moves were covered by the fire of bodies down in position. The varying isolated lines of trenches, all wired, and the villages and copses, gave a series of *point d'appuis* to fall back on.

There was hardly space enough to give more than a couple of troops much space for extended manœuvre, and, as the Uhlans stuck very closely to their infantry and machine-gun support, it would have been extremely difficult to cut off any parties.

The most favourable opportunity would have been between Logeast Wood and Ervillers, where there was a space of about three miles clear of wire. The German had, however, this area behind him when we caught him up, or the chance would, most certainly, have been taken. By 14·00 the infantry advanced guards were up and all further attempts to advance for the day ceased. It was obvious that the enemy did not intend to fall back any further unless he was driven back.

The infantry were loud in their praises of the keenness of the Indian cavalry soldier. They had watched " C " Squadron trying to take Croissilles from a distance, but were too far off to help.

A particular feature to which attention should be directed is that Regimental and Brigade Head-quarters must keep units in the front line posted with events on either flank which might affect them. For instance, a report was sent in by " B " Squadron, to the south of Croissilles that five hundred infantry were seen just on the southern edge of the village about noon, somewhere about the time " C " Squadron tried to enter the place—exact times are hard to trace. The infantry in St. Leger knew nothing of this, nor did " C " Squadron. In fact, the matter was quite unknown to anyone who might have been affected, till after the operation.

At the same time, the fact must be remembered that the whole time of

Officers with Brigade Head-quarters seemed taken up with writing innumerable situation reports which were demanded by the Fifth Army, the Vth Corps, and even by the 4th Cavalry Division, who had now reached Miraumont.

The last named were hardly concerned with events at all. It is hard to imagine the object in calling continually for reports regarding petty fighting such as we were indulging in.

All these higher formations wanted to know was where the enemy intended to stop.

Quite possibly the Brigade reports were unnecessarily voluminous and took too much time writing.

Evening, March 19th

The situation in front of Croissilles was roughly as follows:

The enemy, holding the line Ecoust-Croissilles, about eight hundred yards in front of our posts.

King's Dragoon Guards on Mory Ridge.

"C" Squadron 36th and one troop "D" in St. Leger.

Balance 36th, immediately N.E. of Ervillers, 29th Lancers, one squadron north of St. Leger, balance near the 36th.

Vanguard 18th Division, St. Leger.

Leading Brigade 18th Division, Ervillers.

Lucknow Cavalry Brigade Head-quarters and Head-quarters leading Brigade 18th Division in close proximity by Ervillers. Neither knew of the other's existence—a very grave error.

At the special request of the vanguard commander, Major Maunsell remained with him as liaison.

The first step to be taken was to arrange for patrolling for the night.

Owing to absence of proper liaison in the day, there had been great duplication and waste of power.

It may sound extraordinary, but the vanguard commander said he had no intention of sending out any patrols despite the fact that the enemy might slip off.

The cavalry accordingly took over the job, and kept in close touch with the enemy till just before the attack next morning. A curious feature, considering the tactical situation, was that no senior officer of the 18th Division seems to have visited the vanguard from the time it halted till midday next day. At any rate cavalry officers who were actually with the vanguard commander during this period never saw or heard of one. A young brigade-major came up in the afternoon and Major Maunsell asked him to get into direct touch with Lucknow Brigade Head-quarters, which were somewhere near Ervillers. This was not done.

A senior officer visiting the vanguard could have learnt at first hand the nature of opposition, and might have done something to bring up more guns, or have helped in other ways. In view of the fact that there was not a single regular officer with the vanguard and that the whole of the officers comprised in it knew little or nothing of open war, this precaution would appear to have been doubly necessary.

The habits of trench warfare had, at this time, become so firmly fixed in the minds of even regular soldiers, that this omission seems understandable.

On the other hand, the Fifth Army Commander was up, as well as the 7th Divisional Commander, whose Division was only just beginning to debouch from the Puisieux direction.

Night, March 19th–20th

As it began to rain and sleet it was decided to put " C " Squadron and a troop of " D " under cover on the outskirts of St. Leger.

This was a rather risky move, both on account of shelling and booby traps. The former was a certainty, the latter a possibility.

There might, in addition, be difficulty in getting the men to turn out quickly.

There was, on the other hand, a whole battalion in front and a counter-attack under the strategic conditions, seemed unlikely.

The abominable weather decided it, and the risk was worth it, for the men secured a full night's rest after no sleep to speak of for two nights.

The rest of the Regiment, indeed the whole Brigade, spent a most uncomfortable and miserable night in wind, rain, sleet and mud.

St. Leger must have been a very pretty village in the dip between two hills. It had several intact houses. Whether they had delay action mines in them is not known, but certainly none went up that night, and the cottages Battalion Head-quarters were in had their cellars all clear. It rather seemed as though the Boche had evacuated the place sooner than he really intended.

A particular feature that struck one first of all was the extraordinarily good messing arrangements in the infantry, and the regular routine for meals. They fed far better than we did.

A second thing was, what a fine bag the Boche would have got with one, for him, lucky shell, on the battalion mess where there must have been at least some twenty-five officers collected together.

A further feature was the absence of any German 5·9 shelling, although we were nearing the Hindenburg Line, Croissilles being merely an advanced work of it. We had been able to see in the afternoon the great masses of brown wire on the heights somewhere south of Fontaine, which proclaimed it.

The shelling was confined to light field howitzers, firing both common shell and H.E.

The Ervillers Road was shelled intermittently, no damage being done.

The regimental bivouac had the misfortune to receive a couple, resulting in the colonel's orderly being wounded and a couple of horses being killed and one wounded. St. Leger was shelled almost continuously from the moment we entered it on the 19th March till the brigade went back to billets, but with light stuff only. It would be of interest to know how many shells it received. During the first twenty-four hours there must have been the best part of some three thousand, and the damage done was almost nil. Not a single horse and only one man was hit on the night of 19–20th, although a whole battalion and squadron were in the village.

It is true the shells were not heavier than 4·2's, but one would have thought some casualty would have occurred. In so far as "C" Squadron was concerned, particular care was taken to see that not more than four horses were put into any one building and that they were kept absolutely on the fringes of the village. The wisdom of this was shown by the fact that the Yeomanry put a squadron into big buildings towards the centre of the village a couple of days later and lost some forty horses, either through shell fire or delay action mines.

The extraordinary regularity and method of the shelling got rather on the nerves.

Having reached one corner of the village, it would reopen at the diametrically opposite corner and work steadily up and down, covering thereby, the whole village. At a certain stage one would know that the next group of four shells would drop near—this was the trying stage. When this had passed one was immune for the next twenty minutes. The nonchalance of the infantry officers, to whom this was a mere bagatelle after Miraumont, which had been persistently crumped by big stuff, was extraordinary. The only precaution taken was to play bridge close up to the wall windows were on, so as to avoid the chance of a splinter.

Mr. Atkins, needless to say, was quite unaffected. One has often felt disposed to smile, when doing schemes in later days, at the ridiculous claims put forward by some officers as to rendering villages untenable because they happened to have a couple of Howitzer batteries on their side.

During the night patrols from both the 36th and 29th brought in regular reports showing that the enemy was still hanging on.

The cool precise manner in which these reports were brought in and delivered by the N.C.O.'s commanding, greatly impressed the infantry.

The writer can recall the appearance of the keen, dark faces, under their steel helmets, and the waterproof capes streaming with rain and covered with mud.

Odd reports from both patrols and people dropping in during the night seemed to indicate our troops in rear were all converging on the same village. Australian, 18th Division and 7th Division indentifications were located within a couple of miles of St. Leger.

The vanguard commander intended to advance at 07·00 on the morning of the 20th.

A written message to this effect, was sent off at 23.30 by Major Maunsell to Cavalry Brigade Head-quarters. This was followed up by a verbal one by Captain Mercer, 29th Lancers, at about 00·30 hours, 20th instant.

The first message only reached Cavalry Brigade Head-quarters at 05·30, the orderly having wandered about all night looking for the report centre and eventually going to his own regiment, who managed to forward it. A similar fate betook that carried by Captain Mercer. Acknowledgment of both messages had not been pressed for, unfortunately, as it was considered certain that they had arrived.

Brigade Head-quarters were last known to be in an easily found spot.

The signal officer had, however, omitted to mark the position of the brigade report centre, either by lamp or sentry, and the staff had gone off into a dug-out not far from the road to escape the abominable weather.

This error was a serious one, but one which will constantly occur in war if the organization of a head-quarters is not carefully run in respect to catching orderlies and messengers. Over-worked staff-officers cannot do everything. The human machine cannot work without a rest for a long time together without something cracking.

The Brigade was strung over a front of seven miles at 05·30 and a co-ordinated effort to help the infantry was a matter of great difficulty.

The message having been received at 05·30, the time necessary for the Brigade to swallow it, get orders out to units, and for units to get on the move when the infantry were some way off, did not allow much margin in hand, if the latter were to attack at 07·00. Nevertheless, all that was possible was done and an officer was promptly sent off to St. Leger to tell Major Maunsell the brigade could not be up to help by that hour.

The Horse Battery and such machine gunners as were not with units got under weigh. The former went into action in time, but the latter arrived very late.

Meanwhile, on receipt of information, at about 06·30, that the cavalry brigade could not be ready to help by 07·00, Major Maunsell made every effort to induce the vanguard commander to wait for half an hour or so.

The company commanders were all present and evidently expected postponement.

The latter officer, however, after some hesitation, announced his intention of carrying on.

The only thing to be done was for Major Maunsell to get into touch with the 29th, the nearest cavalry, ask them to co-operate, and send " C " Squadron, 36th, along with them.

Major Meynell, the officer commanding the 29th squadron on outpost, at once agreed in so far as his squadron was concerned, and the remainder of the Regiment followed him up as soon as his action was known.

A message was also sent off asking the Horse Battery and M.G. squadron to come up.

The orders to the infantry had amounted to little else than to walk straight forward in the normal trench to trench attack formation of that period in France. This meant a succession of lines at about four paces extension and seventy yards distance. This might have been suitable to advances of say two hundred yards behind a strong barrage, but was quite out of place in an attack over some eight hundred yards of open, with no covering fire at all to speak of.

The front of attack was, altogether, about half a mile, the companies attacking roughly along the slopes on either side of the Sensee, which were swept by oblique machine-gun fire.

The fire of the vanguard Field Battery had been arranged in a haphazard manner, with no thought-out plan for concentration on certain points for certain times as would be done now. The Horse Battery commander did not have time to liaise with the vanguard commander and had to join in as best he could.

Both the vanguard battery and the Horse Battery were not too flush with ammunition, and the battery commanders were, seemingly, apprehensive of getting up more. It seemed they were unnecessarily so, for the Horse Battery certainly indulged in odd straffes some time after the affair was over.

It must, however, be remembered that gunners in France at this period had been accustomed to having some three hundred rounds a gun ready to hand to play with, and doubtless felt a bit at sea when it came down to about seventy. The four machine guns with the vanguard were in a position on the Ervillers side of St. Leger and could only fire at some sixteen hundred yards range. Their firing, under these conditions, could only amount to vague plastering of Croissilles and would have been about as effective as blowing peas. There could be no concentration on likely points for machine guns, as was the dominating consideration. There had been discussion on the position for machine guns the evening before, and Captain Mercer, 29th Lancers, a M.G. expert, had actually pointed out some good forward positions to the youth in command. There had been a slight protest from the vanguard commander at the long range, but nothing was done to insist on more forward action.

The greatest error of all was to take on frontally a very strong position. An attempt to pinch the enemy out by the high ground and not by the slopes on either side of the Sensee would, it is submitted, have been better.

Although the vanguard had been in position since 13·00 the previous afternoon, there had been, to the positive knowledge of cavalry officers present, no attempt on the part of the vanguard commander to reconnoitre the ground.

It was obvious to any officer with the slightest degree of training in open war—that the attack, as conceived, must fail.

Furthermore, the excellent quality of the officers and men made it certain that there would be no half measures and that losses would be correspondingly heavy.

The whole conduct of this miserable affair was a model of how not to do things.

It was an admirable illustration of the impossibility of untrained officers, however brave, taking on open war under European conditions, without heavy casualties which could be obviated with a certain degree of skill.

At 07·00, accordingly, the attack started.

The aplomb of the infantry was a thing to witness and make one feel proud of being of the same race. The enemy was evidently expecting them, for, as soon as the leading line topped the crest on the northern slopes of the Sensee a heavy machine gun fire opened from the opposite side of the valley at a range which was probably some eleven hundred yards. There cannot have been much less than eight or ten guns, firing from both sides of the valley.

A couple of batteries of Field Howitzers also opened. One shell killed an officer and six or seven men of the infantry. Otherwise the losses from artillery fire were almost negligible.

About six hundred yards from Croissilles, the casualties began, and one could see the men drop as the machine guns caught them.

There seemed no attempt to advance by parties making small rushes, as we had been taught before the war, and as we do now. It was a steady advance without firing, many of the men having their rifles slung in the traditional trench war fashion.

The infantry advance had started before the 29th and "C" Squadron 36th had had time to get into action. Both the latter now attacked along the high ground to the north of St. Leger, starting from about the ruined mill, close to which place the led horses were left.

The arrangements for these were not particularly good and the writer remembers finding those of "C" Squadron, 36th Horse on the point of stampeding owing to their having been brought too far forward into full view of the enemy. Proper handling of led horses is a point to which far greater attention should have been paid in training.

The cavalry attack was by alternate rushes covered by their own fire.

It soon became obvious, however, that the opposition was far too formidable to offer any hope of success, and the advance was brought up about in line with the infantry. Attempts to "turn" Croissilles from the north by a long detour proved abortive. Throughout the attack the covering fire by guns and machine guns showed itself quite inadequate. The gunfire, in particular, was attenuated to a degree. The fear of running short of ammunition seemed to obsess the battery commanders, though it is hard to see how it would affect things if they did, for there was ample strength to cope with a counter attack.

As regards the machine guns, the squadron commander (Major Simonds, Scinde Horse) had taken the precaution of reconnoitring for positions the previous evening, and this stood him in good stead when he received sudden orders to come into action.

As any young subaltern who had passed his promotion examination could have foretold, the whole attack collapsed within ten minutes of the start.

A number of the unfortunate infantry were pinned down all day by the fire and only made their way back after dark. The admirable bearing of the men on getting back to St. Leger was a thing to witness.

This particular battalion—7th or 8th Northamptonshire—was an excellent one of the K1 type. All that was wanted to make them first class was knowledge, and there had been no time to obtain it.

The vanguard commander himself was a man with every attribute a good soldier requires except that. One could not help feeling immense admiration for these men, coupled with a feeling, almost of stupefaction, at their appalling ignorance of open war.

The casualties in this affair amounted to some one hundred and thirty men of the Northamptonshire Regiment, ten or fifteen of the 29th and two of the 36th. It is doubtful if the enemy lost five men.

On the whole, it was just as well that the cavalry were late, and could not take a more prominent part in proceedings. The whole 7th Division attacked later on, and failed. What was wanted was lots of artillery, and it was useless to attack without it.

At the same time, a properly conducted attack would have resulted in far lower casualties and would have guaranteed the possession of good jumping-off places for the final thrust when more guns came up. Quite possibly some lodgement might have been effected in the enemy's line which might have loosed his hold.

For officers who had been well trained in open war, as all the regular cavalry officers were, nothing could be more trying than to witness mismanaged affairs, like that described, without being able to do more than advise. In view of the fact that most of the senior New Army officers in the infantry at this period were men who had seen very heavy fighting—far more than we of the Indian Cavalry—though of a purely trench war type, it was rather hard to get them to understand that open war, without a tremendous artillery to help one, was a very different thing to that to which they had been accustomed. In trench fighting the degree of skill in handling a battalion was hardly the equivalent of that required for handling a company in open war.

It is as well that this should not be forgotten.

We learnt subsequently, that many petty failures, leading in some cases to relatively heavy losses, had occurred on the front of our advance. We heard of one before Le Verguier in particular.

The advance in this portion of our front had now become stabilized, the German having no intention of going back any further until he was driven back.

In so far as the brigade was concerned, not much more was done than tap up and down the lines and establish the fact that the enemy was still in position.

It seemed to us that we were doing quite an unnecessary amount of this sort of thing, and losing good men and horses without adequate return.

The cavalry brigadier was continually getting orders to despatch patrols to confirm reports sent in by the brigade about an hour previously.

Fifth Army Head-quarters seemed obsessed with the idea that the enemy was about to fall back behind the Hindenburg Line.

A very fine piece of patrolling was done by Lieutenant Johnson, Jacob's Horse, in the Henin direction, north of Croissilles. He combined skill and dash in such a way as to enable him to secure a host of useful information, as well as avoid any casualties.

It became necessary to recall the patrol after dark, a matter of some difficulty, as may be imagined, in a strange country. Nevertheless one Sowar, Taj Mohamed, succeeded in doing so. This man was a ginger-headed Pathan, well known in the brigade. He later on distinguished himself in Mesopotamia, in particular at the Kifl debacle, where he was seen rallying fugitives at a culvert by the process of kicking them and threatening them with the bayonet if they moved back.

In obtaining information on this type of operation the limitations of air reconnaissance were most marked. Most of the aeroplane reports were of no value whatever. In particular, it was dangerous to rely on a report that such and such a place was not held. We had much confirming experience of this in 1920, in the Arab Rebellion. Where large masses of troops are in question, things may be, and probably are, different, though many cavalry officers, now in very high positions, had reason to mistrust the Air Force after Palestine experiences. The German had, just then, better planes than we had. We saw two of ours shot down in quick succession, and very horrible sights they were too. We consoled ourselves, however, with the thought that the flying men, in both cases, died quickly, and there was no lingering death.

One of our planes, however, did extremely good service to a "D" Squadron dismounted patrol, which was getting into difficulties with some Germans. It swooped down on the latter, machine-gunning them, and enabled our men to get away.

Throughout the whole of our stay in the neighbourhood of Ervillers, there was great difficulty in getting up rations owing to the state of the roads. The first issue we had was on the 21st March—we had gone over on the 18th. Horses and men had none at all left when they arrived. The men had lived on biscuits mainly, with condensed milk or jam in a limited quantity in addition. They had none of their normal Indian food. The Mussulman troops said they could carry on if they got a big cigarette ration. Sikhs would have eaten cheese, but the Mussulmans would not touch it, as they suspected pig fat.

On our return to billets a committee sat with a view to fixing up a tinned mutton ration. The Indian officers agreed to this, but when it came to the point, ratted, religious prejudices being too strong in some quarters. The horses had merely their saddle blankets, but having been in first-class condition when they started, were able to carry on without hurt, for the weather could not possibly have been worse, what with rain, sleet and hard frosts at night. Had they been in the same condition when they started on the break through in Palestine in September 1918, it is quite probable no casualties would have occurred from exhaustion at all, and even then they were very low.

It may be as well to state that all horses had been clipped.

Despite the rain, we had difficulty in getting drinking water. The Boche had destroyed all the wells or had filled them with filth. All the horse-ponds had been poisoned, and one could smell the chloride of lime, or whatever it was, in every village. We got drinking water by draining wheel ruts, but the horses had to wait till a well was opened up.

The following tactical points cropped up and should be appreciated by all officers:

(1) The importance of liaising with neighbouring units. This was a comparatively new feature in our training, and but little attention seems to have been paid to it in England before the War, and absolutely none whatever in India.

Our own Brigade Head-quarters offended in this matter, for it was within half a mile of the Infantry Brigade Head-quarters in Ervillers without being any the wiser.

The evil consequence of lack of co-operation between units has been shown in the Croisilles affair.

Unless this point is continually drummed in in peace training, there seems a very good chance of it being again overlooked in war.

Cavalry officers should find but little difficulty in liaising with infantry, and should understand that it is up to them rather than the footslogger to do so.

(2) The value of high training in the rank and file, in gaining information and in saving casualties.

There was a marked contrast between the results obtained by the regular troops and the Corps Cavalry (Yeomanry) for instance.

It was quite easy to spot the trained articles from the untrained from a distance. The manner in which the latter stood about inviting shellfire, and the inexpert manner in which they approached tricky places was marked.

The King's Dragoon Guards, in the whole period they were out, only lost three or four men, and sent back excellent reports. The Yeoboys doing precisely the same work, had far heavier casualties than our units.

Two of the Yeomanry squadron commanders had been attached to us for a month in the winter. They were perfectly frank in regard to their lack of knowledge, and bewailed the fact.

They were in no way to blame, for they had no one to train them in their own unit and could not possibly expect to pick up enough in a month's attachment, when our men were all up in the line. The blame rests on the higher authorities, for there were ample cavalry officers kicking their heels between battles to have trained them. The material to work on at that period was simply first class.

These yeomanry, to the best of the writer's recollection, had not even wire-cutters. Our own were bad enough and soon got out of order cutting the very thick German wire.

In point of fact, Corps Cavalry require a really higher standard of training than brigaded cavalry, for their job means far more patrolling and far less fighting. The reverse was actually the case, for the yeomanry brigaded with regular regiments in France were extraordinarily good.

(3) The value of proper use of field-glasses, used in conjunction with some ruse to get the enemy to show himself.

(4) The value of covering fire, or fire down ready to open, both to give reconnaissance confidence and to distract attention.

(5) There was a tendency, due to inadequate co-operation in training, to leave machine guns attached to a unit in the lurch, forgetting all about them when the operation was over. From reading accounts of subsequent actions in 1918 even this was by no means uncommon. This is far less likely to happen when units have their own guns than when guns are attached from a machine-gun squadron.

(6) Neglect to cut wire or prepare routes in the neighbourhood of where one was halted, so as to get away quickly should a burst of shelling occur or should one be suddenly called upon to move in any given direction.

(7) The importance of having some capable and responsible individual with the led horses. The enemy almost invariably started shelling the neighbourhood where they had seen a big group of horses.

A big combined operation for the attack on Ecoust and Croissilles was to take place on the 26th March.

As a result of our various reconnaissances it was obvious that this was not to be taken on light-heartedly. The 7th Division was to do the job. It is understood that its artillery was not all up and that the divisional commander, who had reconnoitred the whole front most carefully in person, was opposed to attacking until it had arrived.

We were to co-operate in the attack, follow through, and then reconnoitre and seize the Hindenburg Line if the latter was not strongly held.

It would be of interest to know the real grounds for supposition that the enemy would not hold the latter.

We know, as a fact, that the Fourth Army down south held no such illusions, and it has been a matter of speculation to this day as to how they ever existed in the Fifth Army. To our great relief, however, the attack was postponed and the brigade ordered to return to billets.

The 7th Division, on receipt of peremptory orders from the Army to attack, did so a few days after we left, and was bloodily repulsed.

In the week we had been operating we had been able to test the training we had received in the past year, and results were highly satisfactory.

A particularly gratifying feature had been the way it had permeated the Indian ranks, and the very high standard of efficiency they had reached.

The keenness and dash of the men had excited comment among all the British troops. We picked up a great deal more useful knowledge than we did, on the whole, in operations in Palestine. With the Turk, one could usually afford to take liberties—but never with the German.

Here there was a bigger mixture of all arms present and far more artillery.

Unfortunately, owing to the various points d'appuis being wired, opportunities for mounted action were absent.

In the 5th Cavalry Division operations further south, the 8th Hussars and the Canadian Cavalry Brigade had minor affairs.

The Regiment lost two British officers wounded, one Indian officer killed, and twenty-seven I.O.R.'s—killed, wounded and missing. Three of the missing rejoined after the Armistice. They had been well treated as prisoners. Seventeen horses were killed and eleven wounded.

It should be noted that the proportion of British Officer casualties to those of Indian ranks proved high throughout the War, averaging one British Officer to fifteen I.O.R.'s. The proportion of Indian Officers was even higher, working out to one in eleven.

A curious feature with regard to casualties when mounted patrols were used was that men's casualties and horse casualties, taking a number of patrols together, worked out at about equal. This proved to be the same in the Jordan in 1918 where the casualties of seven patrols in June and August worked out to a total of fourteen I.O.R.'s and twelve horses.

From the very nature of operations in France men's casualties exceeded those of horses by a very great proportion.

In the final advance in Palestine the 10th Cavalry Brigade had ninety-one battle casualties in horses and seventy-seven in men, not a very great difference. From the writer's recollection of exercises at the Staff College before the War, battle casualties of men and horses in cavalry engaged in purely mounted work, worked out about equal as a rule.

It is estimated that our total casualties on the 19th, 20th and 21st March amounted to about sixty from the Lucknow Cavalry Brigade, seventy from the Corps Cavalry (Yeomanry) and one hundred and thirty from the Infantry battalion, a total of some two hundred and sixty.

The only known Boche casualties were one killed, one wounded and two prisoners. Judging from the great weakness of our fire and the amount of cover available, it seems probable that the enemy did not lose more than a dozen men all told.

During these operations two incidents occurred, which to our minds anyhow, seemed humorous. We did not imagine they would appear so to the victims.

It is to be borne in mind that in war, some idea of the comical, even if accompanied by tragedy, is a gift not to be despised.

The first was the terrible result of ambition.

Durbara Singh, a portly Sikh, of benevolent appearance and fatherly demeanour, used to drive the regimental drag in the days of peace at Cawnpore.

When war came, he was given the job of driving the mess-cart, which he did with great success.

Inspired, possibly, by some ill-timed reference to the career of Sir William Robertson, he desired to return to the ranks, hoping therein to establish a bubble reputation at the cannon's mouth.

With the mischance that occasionally checks the career of one who might otherwise become great, however, he found himself the leading scout of a patrol detailed to search a copse. On rounding the corner his bridle was seized by a Hun and he was led away captive. He, and all other Indian prisoners apparently, went to a camp near Berlin. They were well treated, and he subsequently wrote to the colonel, giving his best salaams to the sahibs and his pals, concluding with the words " Takra ho jao, ham jitenge " (Keep up your spirits, we'll win yet). He also asked for a special brand of chilli which he said he did not get in his rations. He, in common with other Indian prisoners, afterwards passed down to Roumania, where he worked in the fields. When the Bulgar collapsed he rejoined the British *via* the Black Sea.

The German officer in charge of the prisoners had been for many years in Cawnpore, his wife being very good to them and continually saying how she wished she was back in India.

Durbara Singh returned to his duties as brake orderly on rejoining after the Armistice, his fatal attack of ambition having been cured.

The second instance was a capture, under similar circumstances, of a " C " Squadron jawan, who had, after enormous difficulty and heavy bribes, been persuaded to cook for the sahibs. The manner in which his squadron commander had been in the habit of describing succulent dishes cooked by this treasure had made the more credulous officers mouths water, while the more cynical had nearly created breaches of the peace by their observations.

The fact remained, however, that the man was the squadron pride. News of his capture was not received with the gravity it should have been, and there is reason to suppose that one of the junior " C " Squadron officers had, in an unguarded moment, expressed his relief at the man's departure from the culinary department. He is even supposed to have thanked the troop commander for having placed the man in such an advanced post of honour as leading scout—a modern version of the tale of Uriah the Hittite.

Nevertheless, some officers live in hope of finding him running a restaurant rivalling Henri's or the Carlton in his native town of Dera Ismail Khan.

The Brigade, less the King's Dragoon Guards, who remained out between Ervillers and Mory till relieved by the 17th Lancers a few days later, moved back to Aveluy, to a filthy camp of huts in which good and valuable material was lying about in every stage of neglect.

The Regiment put in an enormous amount of work in cleaning up and in salvage.

Whatever the papers said, the waste that went on in France was little short of a scandal. Salvage of every description could be picked up all over the place where troops of mediocre discipline had been hutted. From one's recollections of early 1915, it must be confessed that the Regular had not set too good an example in this respect.

From here officers went round to see the famous German point d'appuis of the Somme Battle—Thiepval, the Zollern and Stuff redoubts, as well as the gruesome craters of La Boisselle, into which the dead had been thrown and where the rain had washed all the earth off. It was a mournful wilderness of horrible desolation. Enormous rats still swarmed in the dug-outs about Thiepval and the Zollern, and it was not by any means too safe to enter them.

A most unfortunate accident occurred to a troop of " A " Squadron while exercising. A horse trod on a buried rifle grenade, with the result that three horses were killed and two men wounded.

Two of our nights were enlivened by Hun planes laying eggs on the Fifth Army Head-quarters at Albert. The thundering detonations of the bursting bombs made one say mentally, " Thank the Lord they are not near us." No damage was done.

The air was often very foul, and, what was worse, there were said to be danger of deserters in hiding, British, Australian, French and even German, men not above committing murder if they thought to profit. None of us saw any, but it was a known fact that a gang of these desperadoes had taken up quarters not far from Albert at one time.

We know from Sir Nevill Macready's memoirs that, owing to the absence of the death penalty in certain Overseas forces, there was no check on a certain type of ruffian who could only be brought to reason for fear of it.

CHAPTER XII

BULLECOURT, BILLETS NEAR DOULLENS.

ON the 8th April, the Brigade, following up the rest of the 4th Cavalry Division, moved up to Irles for the first battle of Bullecourt.

The great Arras-Vimy offensive was to begin next day, and the Fifth Army was attacking in conjunction in a north-easterly direction on Bullecourt.

The weather was appalling, rain, sleet and most bitter cold, with a biting wind.

The bivouac at Irles was in a dreadful state, with enormous shell-holes full of water all over it.

One crater close to the officers' mess tent was twenty-two feet in diameter and must have been fifteen feet deep.

There were only fifteen tents for the whole Regiment. The men, by this time, were, however, very handy at running up shelters with waterproof sheets, and made themselves comparatively comfortable. At 02·30 on the 10th April the Division moved forward to positions of readiness, echeloned from about Mory back to Sapignies, the Lucknow Brigade being at the last-named place in reserve.

The attack did not come off and we moved back in a blinding snowstorm to Irles. Three officers and the Trumpet-Major, who were riding at the head of the Regiment, were slightly frostbitten in the face. The beauty of the Trumpet-Major's nose—always of a bibulous appearance—was slightly impaired by the catastrophe.

At 03·45 next morning we again moved forward to the same positions.

This day the Australians attacked with Tanks, without a preliminary bombardment.

All went well at the very start, but there was no weight in the attack. There were not, apparently, sufficient men detailed to "mop up."

The enemy, who had retired underground when the tanks passed over them, came out again and cut off the Australians who had penetrated the line.

It is understood that some three thousand casualties, all real good Anzacs, were incurred.

As the attack progressed the 17th Lancers, Sialkot Brigade, followed it up along a valley running towards Bullecourt from the Mory Ridge.

They came under a very heavy shell fire, not shrapnel fortunately, but trotted through it with the steadiness worthy of this famous Regiment.

They lost astonishingly few horses and only two or three men. Experience showed that, provided there were no obstacles to impede movement, an artillery barrage seldom inflicted much damage on moving cavalry.

Almost simultaneously the 17th learnt that the enemy was still in Bullecourt, and the advance was ordered to halt, very providentially as it turned out.

The whole effort on the part of the Fifth Army was a costly failure, and we heard rather bitter comment on the attempt ever having been made with so weak a strength available. This was not the first time we had heard murmurings against the Fifth Army and some of its offensives.

It was this affair that caused the Australian distrust of Tanks that was not overcome until the success at Hamel in April 1918.

The dismounted cavalry reinforcements had the job given them of preparing a route through the trenches and wire.

In so far as our own line was concerned there was little or no work to be done, as there was hardly any wire and no trenches to speak of.

In front, however, lay the Hindenburg Line. Some serious hitch had occurred in the issue of wire-cutters, for Major Whitby, 19th Lancers, on taking over command of the party just as the attack was commencing, found there were none. The Indian officers, with a touch of unconscious humour, gravely consoled him with the fact that no one would get into trouble as they had been duly indented for.

He arranged to borrow some from the 17th Lancers who were close by.

The party then advanced across No Man's Land, towards a couple of Tanks, which were thought to have been ditched.

There had been a good deal of machine gun and artillery fire all the time, but now it increased out of all proportion, and it became evident that it came from the Tanks. Signals to cease firing had no effect. Nevertheless, the leading portion consisting of men from Jacob's Horse and the Jodhpore Lancers, still pressed forward. Captain Graves, Jacob's Horse, had been hit in the stomach early in the advance, but carried on most gallantly. It then became obvious that the Germans were using the Tanks as strong points, and it became a matter of extricating the party which was, by now, within fifty yards of the German wire.

By the mercy of providence a heavy snowstorm came down. Under its cover, Jemadar Wazir Singh, Jacob's Horse, and Jemadar Sheo Nath, Jodhpore Lancers, together with a few jawans, succeeded in carrying off the wounded, including Captain Graves. The action of these men was gallant in the extreme, and would, doubtless, in any war other than the Great War, have gained some of them the Victoria Cross. In France, however, it was not the policy to give this decoration for saving wounded men, and quite rightly so, for many a good man has been killed trying to rescue another who might be better left where he was.

Lieutenant Ogley, Jacob's Horse, was awarded the Military Cross for gallantry on this occasion.

The Regiment lost nearly 30 per cent. of its reinforcements in this unfortunate affair, and Captain Graves died two days later.

The night following the battle was a dreadful one. It began to snow and sleet. The men had rigged up shelters in some trenches, and as darkness came on it was impossible to see what was shelter and what was ground.

Some most ridiculous things happened, owing to people walking on top and falling through on to the men underneath. The Regiment had been put into an old line of trenches where the 13th Australian Battalion normally rested. These latter had gone up to the battle, but in the night the remnants began to trickle back. In some cases the men had had to walk eight miles through the snow.

The battalion had gone over the top with five hundred men—good Anzacs of Gallipoli—and by the time we left, over twenty-four hours after the battle had finished, not more than fifty came in.

It is impossible to speak too highly of these men. They were physically the finest troops we had ever seen, well above Guards standard, and most were of extremely good class, though serving as sergeants and privates. It struck one what a waste of officer material there was among them.

They were astoundingly cheery, though some could hardly move from exhaustion.

There were none of the Sydney larrikin type with this lot, though we gathered that these were exceptionally good.

They were unanimous in their distrust of Tanks.

The lurid flow of language of some of the Aussies in conversing with our British batmen, when they thought they were out of our hearing, was striking. To the horror of a stout officer in the Regiment (who had been brought up in a country parsonage) his own squadron representative chimed in with certain expressions, which, had they been used by his maiden aunt's parrot, would have inevitably resulted in the bird having its neck wrung. To hear a deceased comrade alluded to in certain terms was novel to say the least.

This particular man we all thought a very genteel individual—until that moment.

There was a possibility of our having to line the Mory Ridge to check a big counter-attack that was expected in some quarters. This very fortunately did not materialize as the Hun had his hands full opposite the Vimy Ridge and about Arras.

As we were not moving fast we were able to bring up horse rugs round the animal's necks. This precaution saved enormous casualties in horses from exposure. It is understood that further north numbers of poor beasts dropped dead in the bitter weather.

Many casualties undoubtedly occurred owing to bad horsemastership, and those of the machine gunners, very raw, and only partially disciplined, were serious. Particular difficulty was experienced with their transport. Captain Channer, Jacob's Horse, was in charge of the Brigade " A " echelon wagons. He had the greatest difficulty with the machine gunner drivers.

They had little idea of driving, and none whatever of looking after horses. Their regular nucleus of late King's Dragoon Guards gunners did all that men could do to get a move on with them.

It must be remembered, however, that the nights were pitch dark and driving was very tricky and difficult, particularly at points where the Germans had blown craters in the roads. Carrying on with half-disciplined men, was no easy feat. Sir Douglas Haig very truly observed that improvising mounted troops from classes not accustomed to horses was a matter of the greatest difficulty.

These men, however, began to improve enormously as time went on.

They did excellent work in the great battle of March 1918.

At the start off they seemed to be machine gunners first and cavalry soldiers second, whereas the reverse should be the case.

While at Sapignies the concussion of the great bombardments some twelve miles to the north was such that bits of mud fell in from the sides of the trenches and roofs of dugouts.

A few days later, while in billets some eighteen miles back, it was even worse—window-panes and glasses rattling everywhere.

The actual noise was not so great as it was at Ypres or Neuve Chapelle.

In August 1917 the concussion from Passchendaele was noticeable even as far as Lewes in Sussex, though no actual sound could be heard.

For the six weeks following the German withdrawal to the Hindenburg Line, delay action mines were continually going up. One cross-road we had passed over several times was lifted about an hour after we had gone over it.

We learnt that the house in Gommiecourt in which Lucknow Brigade Headquarters had confidingly spent the night of March 19th had disappeared two days later, burying a number of unfortunates. The Town Hall of Bapaume also followed its example.

In this case the Town-Major and his staff, as well as a number of members of the French Chamber of Deputies, were killed. French officers had but little sympathy for these latter, and expressed a wish that the whole chamber might " sauter " as well. The normal French officer had even less use for his politicians than we had.

With regard to labelling dug-outs as " Dangerous, not to be entered," certain astute officers made use of the device to protect private dumps in areas they had evacuated. The ruse was highly successful.

On our return from the battle, the first halt was in the huts at Aveluy, which we had cleaned up after so much trouble. They had been unoccupied since we left. Nevertheless, on our departure next morning, the gentleman described as the Town-Major reported them as having been left dirty—presumably in revenge for our having salved some £2,000 worth of stuff on our previous visit. Some extraordinary creatures were met among these Town-Majors, of every possible category and age.

One or two were bad cases of shell-shock, or rather nervous break-down. In particular an unfortunate boy whose battalion had been destroyed at the assault on Thiepval on the 1st July 1916 was much to be pitied, although his inefficiency was most aggravating.

Later on in the year a remarkable character in one Colonel Reid, aged 70, who formerly commanded the Highland Light Infantry, was Town-Major of Athies, in the devastated area. He, despite his years, was a Town-Major of the very best type.

The Division returned to billets in the area south-east of Doullens, where the time was spent in getting the horses back into condition.

The regiment went to Vauchelles. The dreadful weather and no cover had told a good bit on the weedier animals.

The billets at Vauchelles were the last to be occupied by Jacob's Horse until just before the Indian cavalry left France. A Divisional School was here, that of a very fine Yorkshire Territorial Division.

The Officer Commanding complained that the saddest part of running a school was that such an enormous number of the best students became casualties so soon. Just then his Division had had bad luck in the Arras battle, which was at its height. The barrage fired against a strong east wind made so much dust on the dry ground that blew back in the men's faces, that they had been partially blinded and missed several machine guns. These latter punished them badly from behind when they had passed. This was the Division's first great attack. In this area the concussion of the bombardments about Arras was felt in an extraordinary manner.

It probably passed down the valley of the Authie.

CHAPTER XIII

THE DEVASTATED AREA NORTH-EAST OF ST. QUENTIN.

THE LINE NEAR ÉPÉHY.

IN mid-May, the Cavalry Corps moved into the devastated area between the Omignon and Épéhy.

It was to take over portions of the line from the infantry.

The area was a remarkable example of thoroughness in laying waste a country in such a manner as to make it serve a military purpose and hamper industry when peace came. The articles in the papers giving vent to their horror of Hun depravity may have been good propaganda. From the point of view of " la grande guerre," in which the aim was to knock out another nation completely, and not merely gain certain terms, it was hardly a recognition of common sense.

From the Somme about Peronne to the German outposts of the Hindenburg Line, a distance of some seven miles, there was hardly an intact house. This is also applicable to both Peronne and Athies which were small county towns. As one neared the line some of the villages had not a wall left more than four feet high and all the cellars which might be used as splinter proofs had been knocked in. Whole woods, notably Grand Priel Wood and those about Jeancourt, had been felled and the trees entangled in such a manner as to render it a matter of great difficulty to find cover from the air for batteries.

Trees had been felled for long distances across roads which gave covered lines of advance and had been left standing at points like cross-roads so as to give good ranging marks.

The only thing we scored in was that, by the destruction of villages, we had a good bit of material for repairing roads—always a difficulty in the chalky downland country we were working in.

We were seriously hampered in the winter of 1917–18 as regards accommodation for troops.

The area had, however, the immense advantage of our being able to work across country without continual straffes over damage to crops. One could ride for miles without finding any obstacle other than an escarpment or sunken road. As a cavalry country it was excellent, and we made full use of it when out of the line.

There is but little doubt that had the two Indian Cavalry Divisions been retained in France instead of being sent off to Palestine a fortnight before the German attack on the 21st March 1918 they could have done most excellent work in this area—for the worst part of the " break through " occurred south of Épéhy and south of the Omignon.

It is quite within the realms of possibility that the enemy might never have crossed the Somme.

The 4th Cavalry Division usually occupied the area Devise–St. Christ–Le Mesnil, about three or four miles south-east of Peronne.

There was a village in it called Mons en Chaussée which the French cavalry, covered by a bombardment of two batteries of 75's, had " galloped " in August 1914. Lieutenant-Colonel Shea, Scinde Horse (now Lieut.-General Sir John Shea), who was then a G.H.Q. staff officer, was an eye-witness of this very dashing feat of arms.

It is curious, but none the less true, that none of us knew anything about this affair.

Near Vadencourt there was a small cemetery containing the grave of a French soldier of 1870, and another of a British soldier dated August 1914, the last named evidently a straggler who had lost his way, for the British Army had retreated by a line further to the south.

As the villages were all smashed up—not by bombardment but by demolition—we had to run up shelters from the debris. There was certainly a good bit of this, but the difficulty was to find stuff that was not more or less broken or riddled with holes.

There were, close to St. Christ, a number of dug-outs, enormously deep and extraordinarily well constructed. These were the extreme rear elements of the German Somme defences. They were, however, not healthy to live in and we did not use them. Only very few tents were available. In an ordinary summer the absence of good cover might not have mattered, but that of 1917 was a wet one, as we were to learn to our cost at the dreadful Passchendaele battle, the most horrible of the whole War. The number of poor wretched men who, though only slightly wounded, perished through being smothered in the mud or drowned in shell craters was enormous.

A good many senior officers began to suffer from rheumatism and lumbago.

The troops in this portion of our front were mostly " B " class Divisions, or what seemed to us to be " B " class, for they were not nearly of the same quality as those we had been with before.

Incidentally, in our service, the distinction between "A" class, or "troupes d'assaut" Divisions in contradistinction to "B" class, whose job was merely to occupy the line, was not, in theory, admitted. In practice, however, it was.

There was not much difficulty in distinguishing between the two categories when one took over or handed over trenches. The precision and care of one lot compared very favourably with the others.

In France there was a great "esprit de division" and "esprit de peloton" as differing from the "esprit de bataillon" which was the rule in the "Old Army." It permeated in a most extraordinary degree right down to the men.

The line down here differed from the normal trenches we had been accustomed to. It consisted merely in the posts where the picquets had dug themselves in when our advance was brought up against the outworks of the Hindenburg Line at the end of March.

Their siting and construction were ample indications of unskilled and not too well disciplined troops.

To watch the working parties of these latter mooching and slopping about, and rivalling the British workman in his best efforts at "ca' canny" was something that made one think. Above all, the inertia and lack of authority of most of their officers was the disquieting symptom.

We were now beginning to reap the fruits of the delay in introducing conscription, whereby men are allotted the jobs to which they are best suited when their nation goes to war.

Owing to its non-introduction we had lost numbers and numbers of men as privates who would now have been first-class officers or N.C.O.'s had they only been more widely distributed.

A visit to a German Prisoners' camp to look at the depraved and degraded Hun, as the newspapers called him, was far from reassuring. They were, frankly, bigger, stronger and better disciplined than the men we were now getting into the Army.

The method we were adopting for strengthening the line was a copy of the German system we found at Passchendaele. That is to say it was a number of small posts arranged chequerwise in considerable depth as differing from lines of trenches. The Germans had found that lines of trenches were easier for the hostile artillery to range on than these posts.

The main line of defence was about a mile back from the front line but was only marked out when we took over. We worked steadily on this for the rest of the year.

An objection to the posts was that it was so difficult to move about when there was any shelling in the neighbourhood. On one occasion the writer recalls a battery being crumped with 8-inch quite three-quarters of a mile off and the splinters flying all over the place. Two men were hit moving over the open, just outside where we were.

A further objection was that the enemy might cut the wire between posts if it was dark or foggy, and then attack them from the rear—as he did on the 21st March.

Posts, again, might get smothered individually and the garrisons destroyed owing to their not being able to get clear by some connecting trench. One could not help feeling that the forward garrisons would be properly in the soup in the event of a big offensive and would only get away under very favourable circumstances.

Between Pontru and Hargicourt, which was the portion we held, "No man's land" averaged from four hundred to six hundred yards wide. The Regiment was usually just to the north of Pontru.

The whole area was clean and devoid of battle debris. Above all, there were no trench rats—the most loathsome of loathsome animals.

There were a good many wild duck in the Omignon and fellows could occasionally get one or two.

We used to go into the line as a heterogeneous formation described as the Lucknow Battalion, Mhow Battalion or Sialkot Battalion, according to our brigades.

One of the regimental C.O.'s commanded this outfit and a squadron commander his own particular regiment. A brigadier commanded the two battalions in the line. The average strength per regiment was about two hundred and seventy, or, roughly, a little more than half the unit's strength.

The system was not particularly satisfactory, but it is doubtful if any other method could have been devised.

The average tours in the line were ten days in front, ten in support, and ten back with the horses.

A feature in our system of occupying the line and in construction of works was the disadvantage of too frequent turnover of brigadiers.

The writer can recall one particular bit of trench being dug out and afterwards filled in with wire on no less than two occasions in three weeks owing to relieving brigadiers not being in agreement. One brigadier would advocate the construction of a large number of small posts, with the idea of inducing the enemy to distribute his fire, while another only wanted a few. Furthermore, regiments would occupy one portion of the line for ten days and, after a rest, would go into another, returning later on to find work on which much labour and thought had been expended absolutely changed.

In view of the fact that it was of paramount importance to get the line

Approximate Scale 4 Miles = 1 Inch.

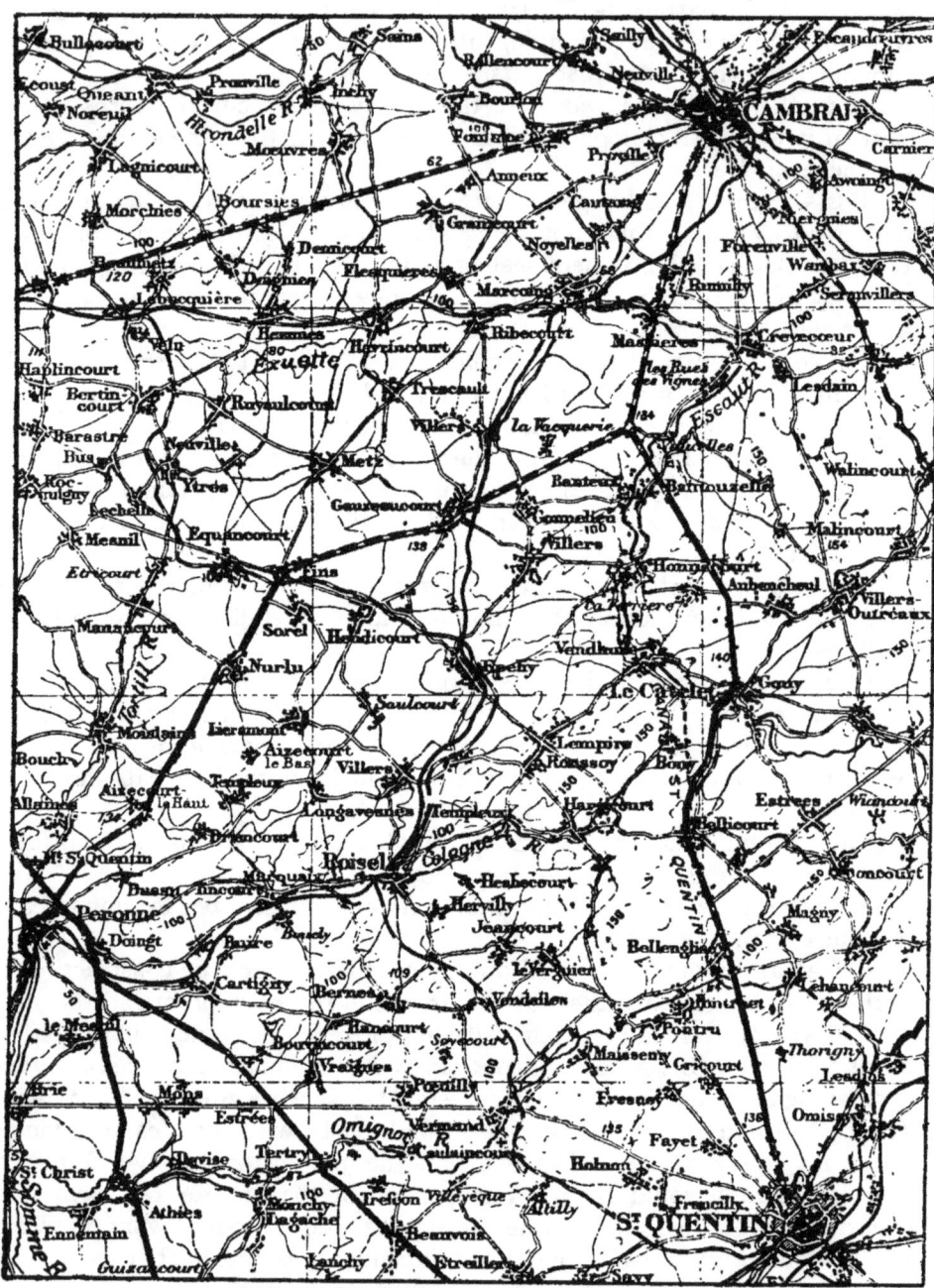

THE AREA CAMBRAI—ST. QUENTIN—PERONNE.

strengthened quickly so as to ease tired and indifferently trained infantry who were expected in, it is submitted that it would have been better to have adopted the German principle of keeping the same troops in the same sectors as long as possible. It is not as though we were in a hot bit of the line where troops required to be shifted to quiet sectors at intervals.

The line was quiet and the German did little to make himself unpleasant.

He used to register his guns to get the error of the day on the tumulus, north of Pontru, and anyone desirous of obtaining a rise in his profession could do so between the hours of 06.30 and 08.00 by standing on top of it.

The Boche artillery officer who hit did not cause any resentment whatever. It was the gentleman who missed who made himself unpopular. Most amazing feats of agility on the part of grave and dignified officers took place sometimes, when some wretched young observing officer made a miss.

The French were to the south of the Omignon. The entente between the jawan and the poilu was in a measure inconvenient, for the French apparently regarded chupattis, ghee, and other Oriental delicacies in the light of the very best dainties and would flock to a "langar" just on the boundary between the zones.

Here a sort of young volcano would arise owing to their zeal to assist the cooks, which the Boche might, or might not start shelling.

For a large part of the time Mangin's Division—a reserve division, but one, none the less decorated with the Croix de Guerre—was there. Very fine well-set-up men they were too. The French officers were rather amusing in connection with the divisional commander. While behind the line they said the men used to throw a chest and say, "Nous sommes de la division Mangin," while up in it they used to curse him as an inconsiderate thruster.

The German did not worry the front-line posts with artillery, except in Hargicourt, which was an unpleasant spot. He used, on the other hand, to do a good bit of shelling of the main line, particularly north of Le Verguier. But little damage was done, however. He also used to make himself objectionable by shelling the support posts about three hundred yards back from the front line—probably because they were head-quarters.

The stuff was usually 4·2 howitzer with occasional 5·9 and, though frightening, did not actually do much damage. These support posts were out of sight and the shelling was entirely by aeroplane photos.

The Boche, with his normal nastiness, was inconsiderate as to time, for one was usually trying to get a sleep in when he began, and on occasions the batman bringing breakfast had to move with such speed that one's meal was distributed on the ground.

He did not really become angry till towards the end of September when, by a series of pin-pricks in the shape of raids, the Canadian Cavalry Brigade, more familiarly known as Canucks, had annoyed him.

Battalion and company head-quarters then became quite uncomfortable.

There was a certain amount of machine-gunning of the front line at night, when working parties were out wiring and digging. We were unnecessarily slow in retaliating by shelling the emplacements. Later on we did so with great success. The enemy would then counter-straffe—usually the next day —with artillery, on head-quarters.

A certain number of patrol affairs took place in the very wide " No man's land," where we had the advantage.

The Indian trooper was, by then, every bit as good a man as the Boche; it is idle to pretend this was the case in 1914–1915. When we first went into the line one or two cases occurred of our own patrols fighting each other, the liaison between the despatching units being faulty. A glorious battle took place on one occasion between two British cavalry patrols, fortunately without casualties. Mutual identification was brought about, however, by a very Scotch gentleman on one side inviting a member of the opponents to " Come over heere, ye square-headed Blinkey."

Young officers used to like going on patrol, though one does not pretend they liked the fighting part of it.

In this connection it should be remarked that the German patrols were almost always commanded by Feldwebel, in other words, sergeant-majors. In both the French and German services far more use was made of N.C.O.'s to perform certain duties than was the case with us.

We continually employed officers in jobs which a properly trained N.C.O. should be able to do with ease.

It must be remembered that the " Old Army " never before had any difficulty in replacing officers from what is generally known as the " gentry " as it was so small. Furthermore, the N.C.O.'s of the Regular Army were almost invariably pretty much of the working class. The lower middle class of the nation had nothing to do with the Army, though it went into the Navy, usually in specialist ratings.

The consequence was that the regular N.C.O. might not be able to get the same amount of work out of the man as a man of rather superior social standing, properly trained, might. This resulted in our employing officers. When the New Armies were raised the tradition stuck, and officers continued to do jobs N.C.O.'s should have been able to do.

In the New Armies this should, it would seem, have been unnecessary, for there was ample material of the very best kind to select from.

In the Great War, the officer class ran dry and the disaster to the Fifth

Army, in the opinion of many who kept their eyes open, was in part due to the terrible falling off in the class of officer.

By the above it is by no means intended to imply that officers should always hang about the rear and never show themselves. There are, however, numberless jobs an N.C.O. can supervise just as well provided he gets it on the neck if they are done badly and if he is really backed up by the men being jumped on if they don't play up to him.

There were certain instances of patrols being sent out commanded by very young British officers, who were quite untrained. Indian officers would have done just as well in their very limited scope. One or two poor boys, who would have been worth their weight in gold with a little longer experience, became casualties under what the writer thought at the time, and still thinks, were conditions under which they should not have been detailed.

The Cavalry Corps carried out several raids on a largish scale. On any other front than France these raids would be considered more in the light of battles than raids, such was the concentration of gun and machine-gun fire.

The Canadian Cavalry Brigade, 5th Cavalry Division, was probably the most conspicuous in this brand of enterprise and was uniformly successful. This particular brigade had first-rate material.

The Royal Canadian Dragoons was a regular regiment with a number of ex-British troopers in the ranks. The Canucks were disciplined far above the average run of Colonial units and were on excellent terms with the Indian troops. They alluded to the jawans as "Wogs." This was, in those days, a term of endearment, rather on the lines of the expression used by sailors in Johnson's Dictionary. Now, as we all know, it is one of opprobrium.

The biggest raid carried out in the 4th Cavalry Division was by the Inniskillings on Cologne Farm—a place to become famous in the great attack on the Hindenburg Line in 1918.

To give some idea of its extent with regard to weight of artillery and machine-gun support, it had seventy-two guns and forty machine guns on a front of about three hundred yards only.

The pulverizing bombardment and its suddenness quite upset the Boche and no retaliation at all took place till next day, and even then he only became nasty in the evening.

Like all properly run raids it had been rehearsed time and again behind the line and nothing was left to chance.

The enemy casualties were probably heavy, for a number of dug-out entrances were blown in on the occupants, who, if they were not actually buried alive, must have had a terrible time getting out after it was over— if they ever did. Men who have gone through an experience like that are seldom of much good for fighting for months after. A curious feature was that the enemy thought we had permanently occupied the Farm. It was extraordinary to watch enormous fountains of earth spouting up from it the whole of the following afternoon.

In the evening the Hun retaliation began and a big working party of Jacob's Horse came in for some very heavy 5·9 shelling. The writer was present, and did not like the experience at all. By one of those extraordinary strokes of luck that occur in war no casualties resulted.

The majority of the raids carried out by the 4th and 5th Cavalry Divisions were successful and the moral effect was good. One found certain cases where there was a tendency to doubt whether the casualties were really worth it. After all, on this particular sector, it was not a case of the Germans being very likely to attack and it is doubtful if the information given by the prisoners can have been of much real value.

Though in our particular case the moral effect was, in general, good, it was by no means always the case in France, even if a success was achieved.

There was a certain type of commander—not confined to the British—who thought he must do something to justify his existence. When a raid was ordered by men of this kind there was frequently an uneasy feeling that troops were being sacrificed to gain a bit of credit for the commander.

In late 1914 and in 1915 there were a number of affairs, badly thought out and not properly rehearsed, which resulted in serious loss and no adequate gains. The moral effect was far from beneficial.

In fighting a military people like Germans one could take no chances and an officer who might be brilliant against irregulars might become a positive danger in France.

A school of thought existed that " going over the top " did men good. It undoubtedly did so, provided the troops were not badly hammered in the process. Unfortunately, in very many cases, even after most elaborate preparations, Fortune did not smile, and very serious loss was sustained. It has often been a moot point whether troops fight better after having been shot over, or whether they do best fresh to battle. There are limits either way it would seem.

With Indian troops, there is but little doubt that they would be distinctly the worse for having been severely punished. On the other hand, even in really good Indian regiments there are, not infrequently, men who believe in the Bengali motto " Sir, in peace the military is a very honourable profession, but in war it is too dangerous to be adhered to." By troops being shot over this category of gentleman becomes eliminated.

The Hun hardly ever raided us. He wanted to be left alone in this sector.

He knew, moreover, that he had cavalry up against him—" long service regular troops of high moral and discipline, well skilled in patrolling," as one of his captured communiqués put it.

It would, therefore, be obvious that no offensive on our part was contemplated about here.

Raiding an Indian unit would be hardly worth the bother as the prisoners would know absolutely nothing. Nevertheless, attempts were made to raid the 29th Lancers at the beginning of June on two successive nights, the first attempt being accompanied by a very heavy minnie bombardment. Both were met by well-delivered bayonet charges in which the jawans showed wonderful dash. In repulsing one, a British batman who was cooking dinner at the time, joined in—whether he sloshed the Hun with his saucepan after the manner of an Irish cook is not recorded. Possibly he frightened them off with the threat of compelling them to try his culinary effort.

There was a horrible fascination in watching a raid accompanied by a big bombardment. In this sector the nights were nearly always pretty quiet—a machine gun stuttering here and there only was the rule, together with a little shelling from time to time.

There would be nothing whatever to indicate anything unusual, when, with a simultaneous crash from hidden batteries within two or even three miles' radius of the point to be raided an appalling burst of fire would open. The whole sky would blaze with gun flashes and the objective would be smothered in the flame of the bursts. To some, this first burst of fire would be terrifying for the moment—one can quite well imagine what it must have been for the raided. When once this was got over there was an extraordinary sense of exhilaration—indeed, as an exceedingly polite, but at the same time very jovial, corporal of the Inniskillings explained, " Faith, sorr, 'tis the barrage that lifts ye forward, sorr ; ye can't help it."

An incident combining humour and pathos occurred about this time owing to one of the men receiving reports from the Punjab that his spouse was not following the example of Penelope when Ulysses was on his wanderings.

The damsel had no fewer than four lovers. Furthermore, she was dispensing the proceeds of five milch buffaloes in riotous living and wanton entertainment of these gentry.

The dafadar, with considerable emphasis, described her to his squadron commander in terms which, in homely Anglo-Saxon, would be the equivalent of something canine and feminine. He furthermore requested him to write to the Deputy Commissioner with the view to the administration of a dozen strokes of the rattan—to be applied weekly—(it was not clear as to whether the D.C. himself was to be the executioner—possibly this addition to the duties of the I.C.S. was one of the causes in the falling off of recruitment to that great service.) To be perfectly frank the lady seemed to fully deserve it.

The problem was a difficult one for us to settle, for one could not send the man off on a week's leave as might have been done with British troops. Furthermore, to act on these lines might result in a whole crop of faithless wives. The only thing to do was to communicate with the Deputy Commissioner, who, we learnt later, was overwhelmed with similar tales from men overseas.

The ressaldar, in connection with this affair, made a somewhat ingenuous remark. " You know, sahib, this affair of —— is very troublesome. He takes it greatly to heart. Supposing some man (evidently just as one gentleman might say to another) says ' Ha, ha, your wife has four lovers ' —— might get very angry and even hit him. Then there would be a fight and things would become very unpleasant."

We learnt that the affair settled itself quite amicably on the man's return to India.

Life in the devastated area, whether up in the line or back with the horses, was, obviously, not so comfortable as in billets. The shacks we ran up about Le Mesnil, where the horses were, were not properly rainproof and the wind fairly whistled through the chinks.

Our feeding, moreover, became gradually worse and worse as 1917 went on and as food supplies got shorter. The excellent fresh eggs, butter and milk we had in abundance in billets were now no more. We had to rely on the Canteen at Peronne, three miles away, for more interesting diet than rations.

These last were as good as anyone could possibly expect, but had fallen off in quality since 1916. In order to get a real good " blow out " one had to get a joy ride in to Amiens in the Brigade car or take a very slow train from Villers Carbonnel—the latter a real Sabbath-day's journey.

There were some excellent restaurants in Amiens—Armeens the jawans called it. At one, the Cathédrale, was the renowned Marguerite, a waitress of extreme discretion, known to the whole British Army. The presence of this charmer must have gained a fortune for the old crocodile who ran the place.

A *déjeuner* with a bottle of wine—all very good it must be admitted —might run to fifty francs, which was far higher than Paris.

Amiens had been, since 1915, a sort of Metropolis for the Army, and the shopkeepers must have coined money.

There was always a feeling of lurking satisfaction that the German shelling in April of 1918, must have caused many of the creatures who battened on the Army pretty serious financial loss.

As regards food in general, one could always get better food in France than in England after the middle of 1917, when the submarine torpedoing became really serious. The French, as a people, are nothing like so well disciplined as the British and it seems doubtful if it would have ever been possible to enforce the same restrictions as we had at home. At Marseilles there was no attempt, beyond some very mild bread rationing, at enforcing anything.

With regard to the men's feedings, an experiment was made in giving them a bread ration. Their complaint was, however, that in an hour or so its effect had entirely passed away unless they were given about four loaves apiece a day. The chupattis stuck inside them better (as any British officer who has had the misfortune to have to live on them for any length of time can vouch, they certainly stick all right). In the trenches the men took over from British troops all the thermos food carriers, and other trench stores in connection with feeding, quite regardless of any caste notions and made full use of them.

They dug and filled in latrines—often including those of troops they had relieved—all themselves.

They had thrown over completely the idiotic notions possessed as to these things before the War and realized that it was a point of honour for good soldiers to do any mortal job called for.

In mid-1917 a remarkable document appeared in France with the object of attracting officers to the Indian Army. Many comments on this wonderful effusion appeared in *Truth*, it will be remembered. It descanted on the joys of life in the East, of what a healthy country it was and how rich one could grow out there. It was possible to keep a long string of racehorses and polo ponies for a few rupees a month and one could shoot tigers, lions and elephants off one's back veranda. As for snipe, it was the rule to bring back several hundred couple every morning for breakfast.

We were greatly edified with its appearance, for it made life for Indian Army officers in France so much easier to have this document thrust before one as a monument of up-to-date Indian official effusions.

The author of this masterpiece is a hero as yet unknown. He nevertheless deserves a place on the pinnacle of fame already occupied by those brilliant raconteurs, Louis de Rougemont, Baron Munchausen and Doctor Cook.

There is a yarn to the effect that he was a War Office wag, having a dig at Simla—a visit to the War Office at this period amply revealed the good will existing between it and the Simla hierarchy.

The Line near Épéhy

In August the Division took over, for about a fortnight, the portion of the line east of Épéhy.

The chief interest in this was that the German break through after Bourlon Wood took place here.

The defence of the front line was complicated by the fact that it coincided with the ends of spurs dropping, steeply in some cases, into the St. Quentin Canal.

The width of the valleys and also that of the spurs made cross-fire of machine guns a difficult matter. Furthermore, this would involve putting a larger number of machine guns forward than might be advisable.

Such fire, moreover, demanded a high standard of efficiency in the gunners themselves—and it is doubtful if they possessed it. The machine gunners in our service were not, at that time, a " corps d'élite " as we now recognize them. It is a definite fact that the infantry machine gunners we found in this sector, actually had their guns laid on our own lines when the writer and the machine-gun squadron commander visited their posts. They were blissfully ignorant of the fact.

As for artillery, the flat trajectory of guns impaired their usefulness in ability to shell these ends. The only remedy was a very large proportion of howitzers.

It will be seen, therefore, that it was a comparatively easy matter for the enemy to assemble close up to our line and rush the picquets. With raw troops this might lead to a panic—and we know it did.

The battalion we took over from—a cavalry brigade in the line was about the equivalent of a strong battalion—had just been raided.

It had the " wind up " properly, and it was almost pathetic to see the company that had " copped it " scuttling out on relief. The company commander said there was every prospect of another raid, though for what precise reason it was rather hard to discover, except for the fact that the prisoners taken may have blown the gaff regarding a contemplated offensive some two or three miles to the south and the Boche may have wanted confirmation.

On going into the portion of the line raided we were not surprised to see why the Germans had met with such success. The trench was some ten feet deep—an enormous depth—and fire-steps were only few and far between. On getting on to the latter it was hard to see more than five yards. The wire was all knocked about owing to minnie shelling. There was a solitary deep dug-out, clearly marked on aeroplane photographs, close to the point of the spur attacked. The Boche had shown considerable skill. He had put a concentration of about half a dozen heavy minnies on to the point, together with some light ones. The British had done the worst possible thing under the circumstances, viz., retired to the dug-out without leaving any proper sentries.

The enemy, who had nothing whatever to stop him, merely walked to the mouth and invited its contents to come out, with the alternative of a bomb. The whole thing was over in under five minutes and the Boche had made a bag of thirty prisoners.

Good troops would have easily repulsed him.

The patrolling in " No man's land " had evidently been of a remarkable character, for none of the information handed over was correct. It seemed highly probable that it had not amounted to much more than the patrol lying up in a shell hole a few yards in front of our own wire, quite a common occurrence with the bad officers we were getting in the infantry. Good patrolling would have effectually prevented a raid.

Our patrols encountered no enemy in this sector, though they were out every night and all night. On one occasion a patrol of the 29th Lancers, commanded by a well-known character in the brigade, one Falconer, a I.A.R. officer, attained the dignity of being praised in Hindustani from the German trenches. The praise was, however, accompanied by a couple of rifle grenades, which Falconer reported as having rather cramped his style. The recipient of the report happened to be a rather serious-minded officer and Falconer was told off for not being sufficiently official.

The " minnies " were a nuisance, and the big fellows were distinctly alarming, though if one really analysed their effect it was chiefly frightening.

A man of the 17th Lancers was being removed to the rear suffering from " shell shock " owing to a succession of them bursting close by. While on the way back he was wounded by a splinter. The effect was extraordinary, for the man broke loose from his comrades and dashed back to the front-line trench to " do in the blinkin blinker wot fired that blinkin minnie."

An exceedingly good bit of work was done in broad daylight by Ressaldar Abu Khan, Jacob's Horse, an Afridi. This officer volunteered to crawl out into " No man's land " by day to spot a " minnie " emplacement. He did so, and, furthermore, spotted a lot of Germans on the St. Quentin Canal bank, enabling the gunners to shell both the minnie and the Germans.

The extraordinarily acute vision of the Afridi and Bangash element was very evident on this occasion, for the men could spot the projectiles leaving the ground.

Apart from this " minnie " shelling, the sector was even quieter than our normal one by Pontru.

While we were in it, two points, to become famous in the final great advance by the Fourth Army, namely the Knoll and Guillemont Farm, were attacked by our infantry. We could see the battle about two miles to the south, or rather we could see the glare and shell bursts over the intervening ridge. The initial attack was a success and a most remarkable communiqué appeared in *Comic Cuts* anent it. The communiqué omitted to remark that the Germans had counter-attacked and had not merely retaken these points but some of our original front line as well. Deluded simpletons regarded this as a breach of faith on the part of " I " Branch. More sophisticated individuals, however, took care to read the German communiqués as well as our own. In order to get at the real truth one had to halve the total of both, for we were just as good liars as the enemy—and some of our politicians could knock spots off any German in this line.

It is as well that officers should realize that communiqués are primarily intended for the public in general, troops in general coming second and those troops actually involved last.

Our stay in this sector threw a good bit of light on the astonishing success of the German counter-attack on the 30th November, for, if the unfortunate division that took over only a short time before the attack was disposed in anything like the manner the troops we took over from, anything might have happened if the patrolling was bad. We know that patrolling generally was not a strong point of the troops in France at that time.

Having seen the front line we could easily understand how tired troops, just after a bad doing about Bourlon Wood and Passchendaele, and fresh to the sector, might break if the front line was suddenly rushed as it was.

We know, in point of fact, that the actual German assault took place after daybreak and patrols could not be in " No man's land " then.

At the end of August we returned to our old area about Le Mesnil.

In early September troops who had been in the Passchendaele battle began to arrive in our area. They had been badly knocked about but still retained a good tone.

It was most refreshing to hand over trenches to smart alert officers and N.C.O.'s as contrasted with many we had been with lately.

At the same time it would be idle to say that they were highly trained troops, even in points of trench construction.

We were greatly annoyed at finding trenches we had laboured hard over impaired by elementary misdemeanours like undercutting parapets for shelters, for with any shelling this invariably meant trenches crumbling in.

At this period the battalion commanders were, in the main, non-regular officers and had but little experience of anything but very static war. The average degree of military knowledge was distinctly mediocre in anything that involved skill of manœuvre.

Senior regular officers told us how difficult it was to get anything done with the half-baked battalion commanders and not even half-baked platoon leaders. Everything had to be on the cut-and-dried lines and nothing could be left to the man on the spot as it had been found, time and again, that he did not possess the necessary knowledge to meet with a situation not absolutely catered for.

In the case of the artillery, the senior officer had attained a degree of skill equalled on no other front, though the battery commanders knew but little beyond the mechanical work of fighting a battery, These latter would have been very slow in a moving war.

The tremendous casualties in officers of the infantry had resulted in a falling off in quality which began to affect discipline. The chief wonder was that it did not fall off more.

We were, by the autumn of 1917, getting pretty well down to bed-rock in the man-power line.

Von Hindenburg, in his book, says the War was fought, in its later stages, by brave militia. This statement hits the nail on the head. As may be well imagined, the braver they were the heavier their casualties.

Many operations, where even moderate skill would have resulted in comparatively small losses, proved enormously expensive.

In very truth we realized the meaning of Rudyard Kipling's lines :—

> "And what did ye think they should complish?
> Warfare learnt at a breath?
> Knowledge unto occasion at the first far view of death?"

At the end of September Lieutenant Braithwaite was wounded on a patrol action and Major Maunsell was gassed.

In October 1917 the King's Dragoon Guards were recalled to India. We were sorry to lose them from the Brigade, for they had been with us since the beginning of the War.

A farewell dinner was given at the Restaurant Godebert at Amiens.

It is understood that their principal job was to act as a training depot for the new cavalry being raised out there.

CHAPTER XIV

THE BATTLE OF CAMBRAI.
THE BATTLE OF ÊPÊHY.
November, 1917

THE BATTLE OF CAMBRAI

FOR the Cambrai Battle, the Lucknow Brigade was detached from the 4th Cavalry Division and attached to the III Corps.

Its task was to have been to cross the Canal d'Escaut at Masnières or east of it, behind the 2nd Cavalry Division, and make good the high ground north of Esnes, three miles east of Crèvecœur.

From here raiding parties were to be sent south and south-east, the Jodhpore Lancers being detailed to raid a divisional head-quarters at Ligny, six miles east of Crèvecœur. From about Esnes the Brigade would be in a position to protect the right flank of the 2nd Cavalry Division, whose job it was to isolate Cambrai from the east and south-east while the 5th and 1st Cavalry Divisions did the same from the east, north-east, and north.

As is well known, the cavalry operations missed fire, greatly to the disgust of all cavalry soldiers.

The Brigade moved, after dark, on the 19th November, to Longavesnes, two miles west of Villers Faucon, where it bivouacked. The next morning it moved up to Heudicourt.

At 13.15 it followed the 2nd Cavalry Division through the Hindenburg Line and, as it got dark, bivouacked about La Vacquerie, close to the cavalry track. It had rained hard the whole day. It was hoped that an opportunity to advance would occur on the 21st, but it did not, and the Brigade returned to the 4th Cavalry Division at Fins in the evening, reaching bivouac, after much wandering about, at 22.00. The Division had come up from the Devise area that morning.

Jacob's Horse had on 20th inst., despatched two patrols under Lieutenants Stroud and Blakeney, to liaise with the infantry and reconnoitre the crossings over the Canal d'Escaut about Crèvecœur and Masnières. These patrols did most excellent work, keeping close behind the leading infantry. They found the crossings held.

A report from one, received at Lucknow Brigade Head-quarters at 12.40, stated that the cavalry track was through to a point three thousand yards

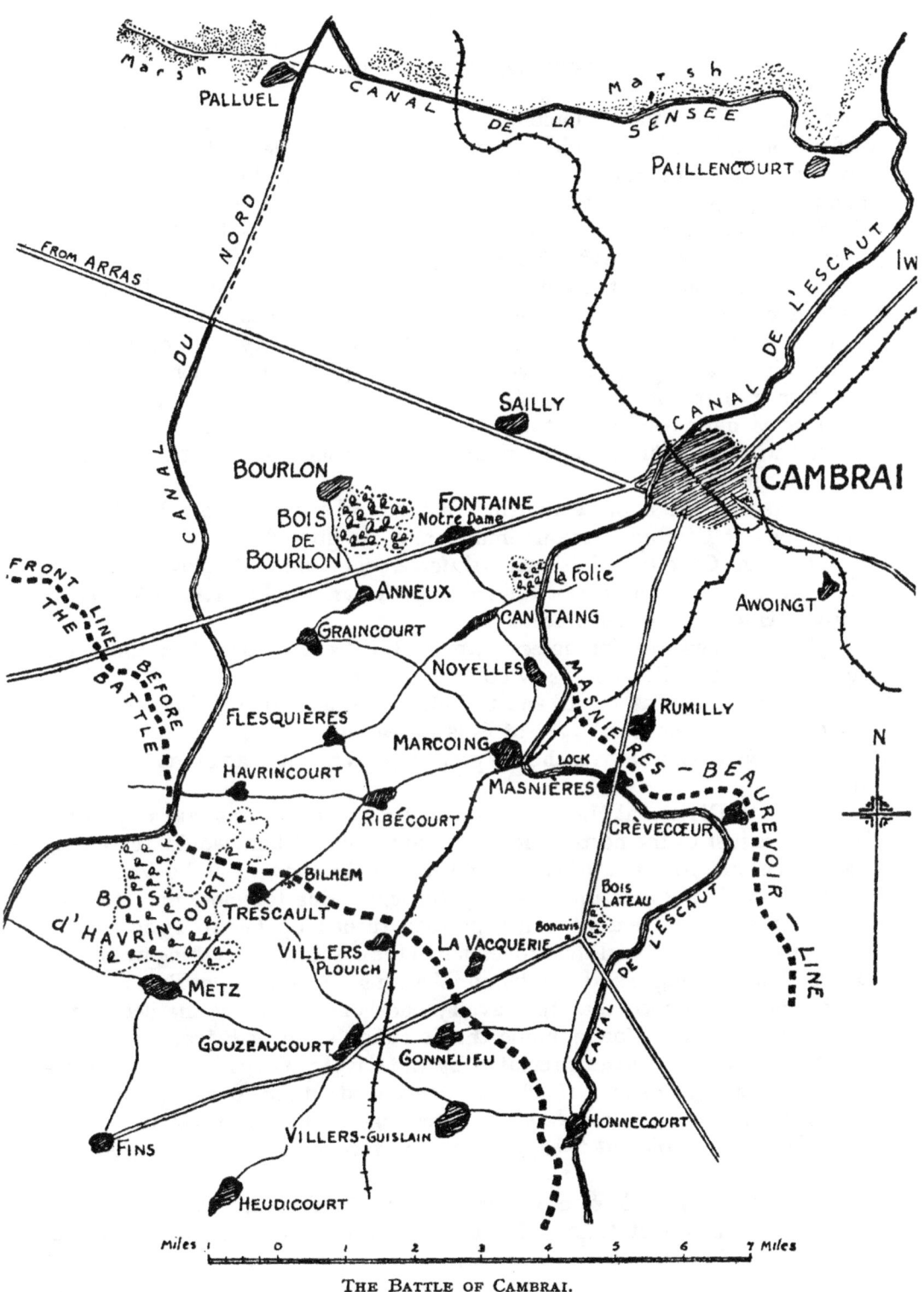

The Battle of Cambrai.
20th November, 1917.

east by north of Villers Plouich and that the attack was going well. The orderly bringing this report had ridden at least five miles and could not have left much less than an hour before, which would make the hour of dispatch about 11.50 (the original message is not with the Brigade War Diary). This confirms Captain Watkins' statement (referred to later) about the Cavalry track being ready before 11.30.

In connection with these patrols, experience at the Somme and at Arras had already shown the enormous value of cavalry liaison patrols to keep commanders informed of the progress of the fight. They were of infinitely more value than reports from even infantry brigade commanders dependent on their own infantry.

This is more or less natural, for the infantry outlook is necessarily limited when they are engaged in fighting and their mobility not one-sixth that of the cavalry.

In view of the many comments that have been made on the Cavalry operations at Cambrai certain timings may be quoted.

The 4th Cavalry Divisional reinforcements were employed on the Kavanagh track, under Major Reynolds, 37th Lancers, Lieutenant Watkins, Jacob's Horse and other officers.

The track was fit for horses through the German first line about an hour and a half after zero—say 08.00.

It was through as far as and including the last line of trenches of the Hindenburg system north-east of Bois Lateau at 11.00.

There were no other trenches to prepare gaps through as far as the Canal d'Escaut.

The 12th Divisional History shows that Bois Lateau was taken by 11.00 and points just to the north of it before that hour. There would, therefore, have been but little risk of cavalry pushed as far forward as La Vacquerie at that time losing men unnecessarily through being too close up. Nevertheless, not a man, except a few patrols, turned up before 13.00.

At that hour the battle had rolled far to the east and everything was quiet where Major Reynolds and Lieutenant Watkins were—north of Bois Lateau. Both officers imagined that the cavalry had gone round by another route, when General Seely, Commanding the Canadian Cavalry Brigade, rode up.

In the Diary of events circulated by the Cavalry Corps it is stated that the 5th Cavalry Division arrived in its concentration area over an hour late, having been held up *en route* by level crossings. That is to say, instead of arriving at " zero plus $2\frac{1}{2}$ " e.g., 09.00 as it was supposed to, it arrived at 10.00.

No mention is made of any level crossings in the 5th Cavalry Division War Diary or in any of its Brigade Diaries. Furthermore, the whole of these

*The Imperial War Museum.
By kind permission.*

A INDIAN CAVALRY WORKING PARTY.
July, 1917.

German Official Photograph. *The Imperial War Museum. By kind permission.*

MASNIÈRES—BRIDGE SMASHED BY THE BRITISH TANK.

20th November, 1917.

diaries make it clear that the Division was saddled up and ready to move at 08.50, ten minutes before the hour appointed.

The Canadian War Diary goes so far as to state that the Brigade " bivouacked for the night of the 20th south of Dessart Wood, N.E. of Fins," that is to say in its allotted concentration area, having marched from Boully west of Tincourt at 12.50.

The Amballa Brigade arrived " at daybreak "—the 18th Lancers of this Brigade at 06.24 and the Secunderabad Brigade at 05.00.

The order from the Cavalry Corps to move forward, issued at 11.40, was received by the 5th Cavalry Division at 11.50. The Division moved at 12.05, the Canadian Cavalry Brigade leading.

This brigade reached Masnières at 13.39—ten miles in an hour and a half, which is, in itself, some tribute to the manner in which the Kavanagh track was prepared.

The situation in Masnières at this hour was that the 88th Infantry Brigade and one tank had succeeded in gaining a footing in the village under a certain amount of hostile artillery and machine-gun fire.

The tank attempted to cross the canal, but the bridge gave way and the tank fell in—very gradually it is stated. One of the crew lost a wig of which he was inordinately proud and a considerable amount of correspondence appears to have taken place with a view to his receiving compensation for the same. A bridge a little further to the east was found half demolished and was made fit for cavalry by 15.30—all under rifle and machine-gun fire —and a squadron of the Fort Garry Horse crossed.

Colonel Patterson, then commanding the Regiment, states it only took five minutes to get over and has given his opinion that if it had been vigorously supported the whole operation would have worked out as planned.

He furthermore states that he personally galloped over, on receiving the order to recall it, and penetrated more than a kilometre inside the Beurevoir-Masnières line.

This line was wired, but was only dug out in parts. It was not then held at all and such enemy as was encountered by the squadron was extremely shaken.

The enemy had not at that hour brought up any fresh troops.

A study of the Canadian Cavalry Brigade War Diary leaves one with the conviction that Colonel Patterson has a great deal of reason on his side.

The squadron spent the night inside the Masnières-Beurevoir line, in a chalk pit. The only Germans encountered in the neighbourhood were working parties and no difficulty was met in dispersing them.

All night long German lorries could be heard arriving in Rumilly and it must have been galling to a degree to the officers to feel that they were not being supported and that such an opportunity was being let slip.

There is every ground for supposing that these lorries were bringing up reinforcements, for an attack made by the 29th Division at 11.00 next morning was met by a strong counter-attack and but little progress was made.

There is considerable uncertainty as to who actually gave the order to hold up the advance. In an article in *The Cavalry Journal*, by General Pitman, it was reported to be General Greenly, commanding 2nd Cavalry Division, who had arrived at Masnières. General Greenly, however, denies it. (See Appendix IX)

It is extremely easy to be wise after the event, but it is at the same time submitted that but little harm could have ensued had we established a strong bridgehead with the Canadian Brigade. The main point to which attention is drawn, however, was the fatal loss of two hours in ordering the cavalry up.

Supposing the Canadian Cavalry Brigade had been at hand when Bois Lateau fell it is quite within the realms of possibility that the canal crossings might have been rushed and the bridges saved, when everything would have turned out as planned.

A point to which attention might, however, be directed, is the limitation of advance for tanks when it becomes a matter of crossing bridges. In this particular case the gallant thruster did more harm than any good he could have done had he got over.

It has been reliably stated that Cambrai was the Tanks' last chance. Had they proved a failure that day the Corps was to be abolished. Taken as a whole, however, it must be admitted that they had not had much of a chance before as they had usually to operate over greasy muddy ground.

At Cambrai, they were to take the place of a preliminary bombardment, the guns opening an intense fire at zero. This latter was most dramatic, for until zero—06.20—there was none of the heavy shelling that usually preluded attacks apart from the barrage. Then some ten hundred guns opened simultaneously along the whole front and the tanks went forward, each pair preceded by an officer to show them the way—for the blindness of tanks is extraordinary.

Certain tanks were detailed to assist our working parties clear the wire.

The passages made by them did not enable the horses to get through.

They were provided with grapnels and were of great value, especially if the wire had been cut before. Even after they had cleared a space, however, the denseness of the grass tangled up with odd bits of wire, iron stakes, etc., required a lot of clearing.

It was most unpleasant working in their neighbourhood until the infantry had advanced some way, as they drew fire of every description, with the result that on one occasion work had to be stopped for some twenty minutes. A certain number of casualties occurred.

The trenches of the Hindenburg Line were some fifteen feet wide at the top and some nine feet deep. They therefore took some ramping and bridging.

Incidentally it had only been ascertained shortly before the battle that they were of this width and our tanks could only negotiate some seven feet. The tanks therefore carried big fascines which they dropped in. Despite this, a number got ditched, chiefly where they went over "dug-out" entrances.

The 4th Cavalry Divisional Pioneer Battalion, as the dismounted reinforcements were called, put in most excellent work, following the leading infantry and tanks as close as possible, and getting the wire cleared and trenches bridged or ramped in record time. The jawans were splendid.

Lieutenant Watkins, Jacob's Horse, was specially mentioned in Divisional Orders.

The failure at Cambrai bore good fruit, however, at the Battle of Amiens on 8th August 1918. On this occasion special care was taken for the impulse for the forward move to come from the leading brigadier, with the result that a great success was achieved.

As a contrast, had the orders laid down for the Sharon Battle of 19th September 1918 been adhered to, the Turks would, in all probability, have had time to man the Musmus Pass in the Mount Carmel Range. As it was we only won the race by an hour.

The Battle of Épéhy

The 4th Cavalry Division returned to the area by the Omignon on 23rd November.

In the early dawn of the 25th it moved north to Villers Faucon, standing by for a continuation of the Cambrai Battle, but moved back the same afternoon.

Things quietened down and preparations were made for taking over the normal trench sectors, the Lucknow Brigade being in reserve about Devise.

All this time there had been the rumblings of battle to the north, and it was known that there was dirty work going on about Bourlon Wood.

On the morning of 30th November, however, a heavy drum fire was heard. In France no one as a rule paid much attention to this, and it was thought to be merely a straffe rather out of the normal. Certain brigades were exercising horses. The 7th Dragoon Guards (5th Cavalry Division) were at the divisional baths, and the Mhow Brigade were actually riding up to take over the trench sector south of Hargicourt.

Suddenly the word came that there had been a very heavy attack on the VII Corps front about Honnecourt and to the north of it and that the line had gone. Incidentally this information did not get down to regiments, though from the urgency of the subsequent moves and the general confusion it was pretty certain that the Hun had given us something rather unexpected.

The Cavalry Corps Commander telephoned to the Third Army, pointing out that the best use for the cavalry was a counter-attack from about Ronssoy-Épéhy on Villers Guislain, and the Third Army issued orders accordingly.

He and the 4th and 5th Cavalry Divisional Commanders motored on ahead to 55th Divisional Head-quarters at Villers Faucon.

The 5th Cavalry Division moved off at 11.30 from Estrées en Chaussée, the Amballa Brigade leading.

This Brigade trotted without a check for eleven miles, through Roisel and on to Villers Faucon.

Here a short halt was made, and a very welcome one, for, owing to the speed of the movement, officers had only rather hazy ideas of where they were.

Everywhere was the utmost confusion. The fog of war dominated everything. Demoralized and panic-infected men were in all directions. Never had the Indian sowar seen British soldiers in such a state.

Troops of high moral and discipline alone could have remained unaffected.

At 13.30 the Amballa Brigade received orders to act as advance-guard to the Division, which was to move, via the west of Épéhy, with a view to attacking the enemy and closing the gap between Épéhy and the Guards, who were known to be moving down on Gouzeaucourt from the north-west.

The Guards, incidentally, had taken Gouzeaucourt at this hour, though this was not known at Villers Faucon.

The brigadier decided to move on Gauche Wood at once and discover what was between Gouzeaucourt and Villers Guislain.

The 8th Hussars were detailed as vanguard, the 9th Hodson's Horse, Machine Gun Squadron and 18th Lancers following in above order.

The 8th Hussars, soon after passing Peizière, found themselves tied up in the wire of the rear defences of our line and, shortly after, bumped the enemy about Chapel Crossing and Gauche Wood. Our own infantry were found about Vaucellette Farm.

Progress was impossible, the enemy being in great strength.

One squadron, however, succeeded in gaining a hollow road about three or four hundred yards west of Gauche Wood, where it became engaged in a fire fight with the enemy, losing Major Ryder, the squadron commander, and some fifteen men. It was shortly afterwards reinforced by 9th Hodson's Horse, who arrived just about as an attack was debouching from Gauche Wood. This attack was held up on the line of the railway.

The remainder of the 8th Hussars, after making vain efforts to advance about Chapel Crossing, joined the squadron about 16.00. The horses had been left some way to the rear.

The Regiment had received orders to take Gauche Wood. Reconnaissances, however, showed that this would be madness in view of the great strength in which the place was held.

It remained, in consequence, in occupation of the road until relieved by the 18th Lancers about 21.00.

The casualties had amounted to about forty, together with seventy-five horses and mules.

The brigadier, on seeing the 8th Hussars held up soon after passing Peizière, gave orders to the 9th Hodson's Horse to support them, working round their outer flank so as to get into touch with the Guards about Gouzeaucourt.

There was a long line of wire running approximately from the north-east end of Peizière past Revelon and thence north. Hodson's Horse had great difficulty in finding a passage. Eventually a small opening was found to the north of Revelon. Major Fraser, commanding the leading squadron, pushed through this and led direct on Gauche Wood. This wood is on the far side of a ridge from Revelon, and such had been the rapidity of the advance that the officers were still in great doubts as to their location.

There had, in addition, been the usual kind of urgings to "shove on," "what the blazes are you waiting for?" that so often accompany rapid moves of cavalry, which did not tend to help things.

There is absolutely open ground for nearly two thousand yards between Revelon and Gauche Wood. Fraser crossed this without fire being opened until he approached the wood, when he saw Germans advancing from it. He then found the sunken road in which the 8th Hussars squadron was and joined in the fire fight, compelling the enemy to halt about the line of the railway.

The remainder of Hodson's Horse found things very different, for no sooner had the second squadron cleared the wire, than a regular inferno of shelling, 5·9 and every other kind of shell, burst upon them. Diamond formation, with troops about forty yards apart, was taken up, and the Regiment moved, without a waver, across the valley.

The advance excited great admiration among onlookers.

An extraordinary feature noticed was the number of shells that burst in between the troops as distinct from those that hit. Where one hit, four or five men and horses would be knocked out.

The Regiment reached a fold in the ground short of the hollow road where there was a certain amount of cover and the men dismounted.

They then moved forward to the road and engaged the enemy.

As it was now clear that there was no hope of any further advance, the led horses were all sent back some three miles, well out of the way.

The mistake of Monchy le Preux, where seven hundred horses had been shelled to death in the streets of the village owing to no orders having been received to send them away, was not to be repeated.

The casualties of Hodson's Horse had hitherto amounted to some fifty, men and seventy horses. They included, unfortunately, both Majors Fraser and Atkinson, who had just been recalled from the command of infantry battalions, and were officers above the average.

Colonel Beatty, then commanding Hodson's Horse, is of opinion that the casualties in men would have been nearer one hundred and fifty than fifty, had this advance been attempted on foot.

Furthermore, thanks to the rapid advance, we secured the strong line of the hollow road, which had an important influence on the next day's attack.

This road had been the head-quarters of a Field Company, and ample evidence of the morning's panic was available in the shape of blankets, clothing, rations, and other debris. Thanks to these it was possible to make oneself very comfortable in the bitter night that followed.

The horses were brought away just in time, for heavy shelling began on the place they had just quitted.

This was followed by intensive shelling on the road, in addition to spasmodic rifle and machine-gun fire. The cover was fortunately very strong, and casualties were negligible.

During the operations described above, the 18th Lancers were in reserve to the north-east of Heudicourt.

At 17.00 the Regiment received orders to relieve the 8th Hussars in the sunken road. It was, in addition, to (1) reconnoitre Gauche Wood, (2) occupy it if possible, (3) if the wood was held to make preparations to attack it next morning.

The relief was duly carried out about 21.00, and the situation of the Amballa Brigade was then:—

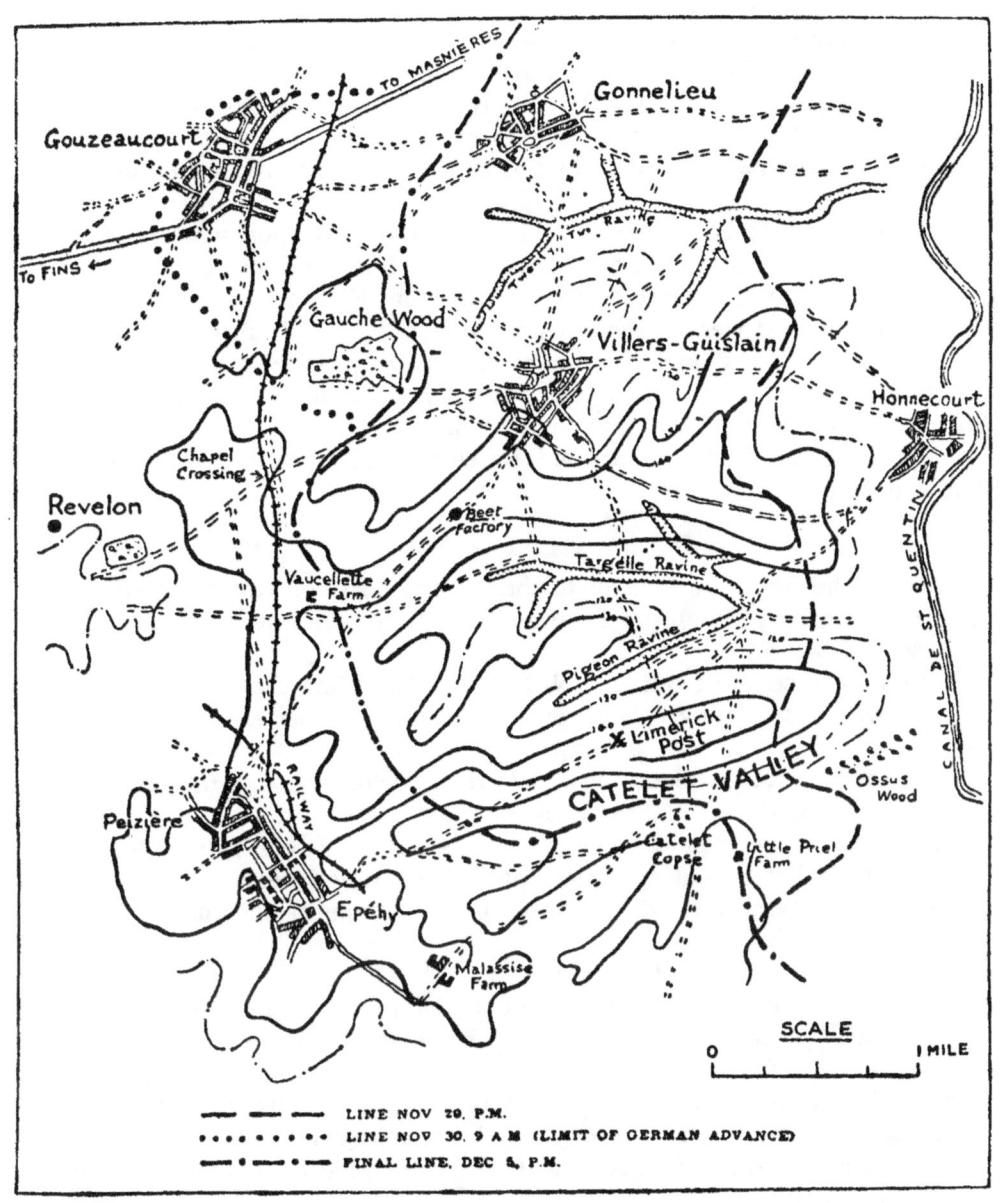

The Battle of Epéhy.
(Showing the lines on 29th November–5th December, 1917.)

In hollow road, from right to left, 18th Lancers, 9th Hodson's Horse. In reserve 8th Hussars.

A Battalion of the "Queen's" was in touch with the 18th.

The Canadian Horse Artillery Battery covered the front.

The night passed fairly quietly, but the enemy lining the railway were very much on the alert, opening bursts of fire from time to time. Their Véry lights sometimes fell right into the portion of the road occupied by the 18th.

The Secunderabad Brigade followed Amballa. It then worked round its outer flank and moved on to Gouzeaucourt, halting about a mile south-west of the place as it was found that the Guards had taken it.

Reconnaissances were made with a view to a possible mounted attack on Gonnelieu. This village was, however, heavily wired.

While waiting south-west of Gouzeaucourt it came under very heavy shell fire, which caused but few casualties.

After dark the Brigade returned to Divisional Reserve south-east of Heudicourt.

Canadian Cavalry Brigade

At 15.30 the Brigade advanced to the railway north of Vaucellette Farm, where it bumped the enemy. Progress was impossible, owing to growing darkness and wire.

Reconnaissances sent out established the fact that the Raperie (Beet Factory) was very strongly held with machine guns, as also was Chapel Crossing.

A German prisoner taken showed that he belonged to a division just brought up from the St. Mihiel sector.

Had attention been paid to the reports sent in by this brigade a good deal of futile effort would doubtless have been saved next day.

The Brigade remained in this position the whole of the night.

4th Cavalry Division

The Lucknow Brigade, at the head of the Division, reached St. Emilie at 17.00, and was placed under the order of the 5th Cavalry Division.

It was now dark.

The 29th Lancers were pushed ahead as a support to the infantry south of Vaucellette Farm, the remaining unit bivouacking north of St. Emilie.

The Sialkot and Mhow Brigades, as they came up, also halted and bivouacked in this neighbourhood.

The night passed quietly.

The general situation on the night of the 30th November–1st December was vague, to put things mildly. Units knew nothing—but thought a great deal. One thing was certain, and that was that our infantry were very shaken, in no condition to attack, and not altogether to be relied on if the enemy advanced.

We had lost the whole of our guns about Villers Guislain, Gonnelieu, and Gauche Wood, and had very few left in the neighbourhood beyond the VII Corps Heavy Artillery and the two Horse Artillery Brigades of the 4th and 5th Cavalry Division. (The Guards, in their attacks on the 30th November and the 1st December, recovered nearly a hundred guns parked by the Germans for removal near Gouzeaucourt.) Furthermore, the enemy had advanced in thousands and had suffered quite unappreciable loss. They were, moreover, ensconced in the wired-in elements of our front line, and in strong positions.

It is significant that neither the Cavalry Corps nor the 5th Cavalry Division operation orders gave the enemy's supposed position.

The general situation of our own troops was roughly as follows:—

55th Division Infantry, roughly from about Little Priel Farm to close in front of Épéhy and thence to Vaucellette Farm, positions very vaguely known.

4th Cavalry Division, near St. Emilie.

Canadian Cavalry Brigade, 5th Cavalry Division, Vaucellette Farm to the hollow road where the 18th Lancers were.

On the left of the 18th, 9th Hodson's Horse.

Secunderabad Brigade, a thousand yards south-east of Heudicourt.

2nd Cavalry Division on left rear of Amballa Brigade.

Guards Division, Gouzeaucourt.

There were odds and ends of infantry of the 55th and 12th Divisions scattered about here and there, but, as said before, they were not in a condition to attack. Their orders were to take advantage of any cavalry success.

The shortage of artillery was the most unfavourable feature as regards our counter-attacking. There were, however, a good number of tanks still available, and it was resolved to profit from this.

The tanks, however, had been very heavily engaged for some days previously. There was the inevitable confusion resultant from heavy fighting and the crews were exhausted. Very many of the machines had been badly knocked about and were in urgent need of overhaul. At the time the German counter-blow fell a number were in a dismantled state and had to be hastily reassembled by tired men.

After superhuman exertions this had been effected, and some even took part in an attack on Gouzeaucourt in the forenoon of the 30th. Most of these were knocked out and were seen to be blazing furiously when Hodson's Horse crossed to the hollow road.

The conditions for tank co-operation by the morning of December 1st were extremely unfavourable.

The machines were a long way from the point of assembly, the night was dark, time had not been available to reconnoitre the routes, and the terrain was quite unknown. The natural blindness of tanks did not make things easier.

The general confusion as to position of our own troops was such that even cavalry and infantry did not know where all the posts were.

Furthermore, a number of tanks had been strained and began to develop mechanical defects when moved.

It will, therefore, be understood that it was only natural that hitches occurred, despite the untiring exertions of their personnel.

These facts must be borne in mind, for there was a tendency to lay blame on the Tank Corps without having considered the difficulties with which it had to contend.

The Cavalry Corps was to attack the line Villers Guislain–Gauche Wood with tanks on the morning of 1st December in conjunction with the Guards Division, who were to attack the line Gauche Wood–Gonnelieu at the same time from about Gouzeaucourt.

The 1st Guards Brigade, with the 2nd Bn. Grenadier Guards on the right, was given Gauche Wood as its objective, and was allotted twenty tanks. Only two Field Artillery Brigades could be scraped together to support the whole Guards Division.

The Amballa Brigade, with six tanks, was to attack Gauche Wood from the west, supported by the Canadian Royal Horse Artillery Battery.

The Wood was thus to be assaulted from the north and west.

The Lucknow Brigade, still attached to the 5th Cavalry Division, was to attack Villers Guislain from a point about six hundred yards south of Vaucellette Farm. Nine tanks were allotted to it.

The artillery support ordered is not traceable. We know, however, that it was valueless, whatever it was.

All attacks were to be at 06.20, the cavalry being dismounted.

The Secunderabad and Canadian Cavalry Brigades were to be in mounted reserve to the 5th Cavalry Division.

On the extreme right, the 4th Cavalry Division was "to take advantage of the advance of the Tanks and seize the Villers Ridge and a line running south from a point about a thousand yards to the south-east of Villers Guislain."

The 2nd Cavalry Division was to assemble west of Gouzeaucourt by 07.00 in readiness.

Amballa Brigade

The 18th Lancers were detailed for the attack. This Regiment's war diary shows that this was actually ordered for 06.45, e.g. twenty-five minutes after the Guards on its left.

The operations are best taken in conjunction with those of the 1st Guards Brigade, and, more particularly, with those of the 2nd Grenadier Guards, who were on its right.

The Tanks detailed for this Brigade were late, those on the right not turning up until Gauche Wood had actually been entered. On the left of the brigade, however, they arrived just in time and proved of great value.

The 2nd Grenadiers waited ten minutes and then advanced without them.

There was the best part of a thousand yards of open to cross with no cover at all.

We are told that the covering artillery bombardment was "very attenuated," but that the Brigade Machine Gun support was invaluable. The 2nd Grenadiers simply made for the Wood as fast as the men's legs would carry them, no alternate rushes were made. But few troops in France at this period other than Guards would have attempted such a thing.

The enemy began to throw up his hands as soon as the battalion came near, and the Grenadiers entered the Wood, where scattered fighting took place.

Shortly after entering, a counter-attack took place on the battalion right, which was repulsed. Greatly, however, to the surprise of the Grenadiers some 7th Dragoon Guards, loaned to the Amballa Brigade from the Secunderabad Brigade, appeared from the same direction as that from which the counter-attack had come, followed by the 18th Lancers.

The battalion had by now lost all its officers but two, and a great number of men—the casualties amounted to some one hundred and fifty in the day.

As a consequence the 18th Lancer officers were asked to take over command of portions of the Grenadiers, who were scattered about in various parts of the Wood.

The advent of the 7th Dragoon Guards and the 18th proved a Godsend in the consolidation and mopping up that followed.

All these units were pretty well mixed up all over the place, but worked in with the greatest cordiality.

Tanks then began to arrive. Though their crews helped with the consolidation the actual presence of the Tanks was more a danger than an asset, for they attracted fire of every description and many casualties occurred to men standing in their neighbourhood. In consequence, they were, at 08.40, requested to withdraw. By this time, however, most seem to have been knocked out. Three were reported to have gone on to Villers Guislain, but had to return. These must have done so from near Gauche Wood, as none were anywhere near the Lucknow Brigade.

To turn to the 18th Lancers.

The Regiment was ready to advance from the hollow road at 06.40. There were no signs of the Tanks. Meanwhile a heavy enfilade fire had opened from about Chapel Crossing, which inflicted numerous casualties in the right squadron.

Some Hotchkiss rifles were brought to bear and had the effect of weakening the fire. It was then decided to advance from the left squadron, which was more sheltered by the ground than the right.

Thanks to these measures the advance, when it did begin, was carried out very cheaply.

It was not until 07.15 that the leading tanks arrived, " but seemed uncertain of their direction," for they moved north after crossing the railway, thus skirting the wood and leaving it on their right hand. Such as entered the wood did so from the north.

It is very hard to make out where the Tanks, if any, detailed for the Lucknow Brigade went. All that is certain is that the whole lot seemed very fogged as to their position, some—those actually detailed for the 18th Lancers according to the statements of officers of the 9th Hodson's Horse —running on top of the latter Regiment and killing a number of men, thinking they were in the German lines. It must be remembered that this was after dawn, and it was quite light.

It seems most probable that if any tanks were detailed for the Lucknow Brigade, they were the ones who passed through the 18th, for, as said before, the 9th were on the left of the 18th. The Tanks having passed through, the 18th Lancers went forward. This was between 07.15 and 07.30. It was carried out by alternate rushes.

A number of Germans were taken prisoners *en route*. These were being passed back through Hodson's Horse when the Tanks referred to above ran on to this regiment.

The Wood was reached with extraordinarily little loss, the enemy being absorbed with the Guards. The place was fully in our hands by 09.30, a number of prisoners being taken and very heavy casualties inflicted on the enemy.

In the history of the Grenadier Guards we read of " their great appreciation of the fighting spirit and dash of the 18th Lancers "—some chit ! for His Majesty's Guards do not say this for nothing. There are particularly warm eulogies of Colonel Corbyn commanding the 18th, who was, unfortunately, killed by a shell about midday.

A particular feature, commented upon as regards the occupation of the Wood, was that no artillery F.O.O. was up. As a result many good targets were let slip.

Furthermore, at about 14.30, our own guns began to shell what was presumably intended for "Twenty Two Ravine," but which was really the fringe of Gauche Wood itself. Later on, when the range was lengthened, the shells were still falling very short.

Very heavy 5·9 shelling began between 15.45 and 16.45—quite possibly as the Germans thought a big attack, in conjunction with one then being made by the Canadians, was in preparation.

The casualties of the 18th amounted to four British officers and thirty-seven Indian ranks killed and wounded—astonishingly light, all things considered.

Neither the 8th Hussars nor 9th Hodson's Horse were required to take part in the fighting, though the 9th had to send up a number of men to act as stretcher-bearers.

Lucknow Brigade

At 03.30 the Lucknow Brigade moved to just north of Peizière, where the horses were sent back. Here flares and other stores for trench attacks were drawn.

The Brigade then moved forward to the rendezvous ordered for the Tanks, six hundred yards south of Vaucellette Farm, which it reached at about 05.30. All this was done in the dark, and it seems a matter of questionable wisdom to have detailed a brigade consisting entirely of Indian troops, of which neither the brigadier nor any of the officers had had a chance of looking at the ground, for an attack, particularly on such novel lines as one with Tanks. The Canadian Brigade of the 5th Cavalry Division had been on the ground since the afternoon of the day previous and had not been heavily engaged. It would seemingly have been better suited to the job.

At 05.45 the brigadier (Brig.-General Gage) received a most disconcerting message from the adjutant of the Tanks stating that they could not turn up at the appointed rendezvous, but were starting at Genin Well Copse, half a mile east of Revelon, and distant over a mile from the Brigade. With this starting-point and Villers Guislain as objective they would pass about twelve hundred yards to the north of it and, what was worse, on the other side of the Villers Ridge.

General Gage, at the time of receiving the message, was liaising with Brigadier-General Seely, commanding the Canadian Cavalry Brigade, and was about half a mile from where the Lucknow Brigade was assembled.

He at once sent off orders to shift ground to the north-west, with a view to catching the Tanks in their advance.

A good deal of difficulty was experienced in finding C.O.'s in the darkness, and it was not until about five minutes before zero hour that Jacob's Horse received the order. It was a great piece of luck for the Regiment that it did, for it was about to advance regardless of the non-arrival of the Tanks.

Shifting troops in semi-darkness to a flank when close to the enemy is difficult enough when they know the ground.

It becomes doubly so when neither officers nor men have even seen it by day, and it says something for the discipline and leading in the Brigade that it succeeded in assembling some seven hundred yards to the south-west of Vaucellette Farm by 06.50 without the enemy being any the wiser.

Had the Tanks gone even moderately direct for Villers Guislain they would have been spotted from this position, for dawn was now breaking.

There was, however, no sign of them, and the tank liaison officer could not be found.

The officer commanding the section detailed originally for the attack afterwards stated that his major had changed the orders and put the whole on to Gauche Wood.

Some tanks did get near Villers Guislain, but as to whether they were from this section or not we do not know. One thing is certain, and that is they did not go direct from Genin Well Copse towards that village.

Assuming, however, that they went from the Copse towards Gauche Wood, they would have been screened from the Lucknow Brigade by an intervening spur, which would have also drowned the noise of their engines.

Incidentally it would be of interest to know what the brigadier would have been expected to do had he known the Tanks might attack Villers Guislain from near Gauche Wood.

To diverge as far north as Chapel Crossing would appear a very questionable move. He was pretty certain to get mixed up in the fighting about Gauche Wood.

Now two particular points had been stressed by the Tank liaison officer: first, that the Tanks should, if possible, cross our front line as soon as it was light, but not after; second, that the troops should follow them at not more than one hundred and fifty yards.

The natural conclusion come to by the brigadier was that the Tanks had already started so as to fulfil the first requirement, and that they had been missed while he was shifting the Brigade over.

It was obviously impossible to fulfil the second, but something might be done by shoving ahead at once.

He accordingly issued orders for Jacob's Horse to move on Vaucellette Farm and thence try and work forwards to Villers Guislain, the 29th and Jodhpore Lancers remaining behind for the time being.

A point to which attention should be drawn is that the 5th Cavalry Division had taken no steps to assist the brigadier, either by the issue of fresh orders to meet the changed situation or by sending up a staff-officer.

In view of the importance of the attack on Villers Guislain and its effect on the proposed operations of the 4th Cavalry Division to the south, it is submitted that this was throwing an unfair burden on a subordinate commander and an error in staff work.

No staff-officer from this Division visited the Brigade the whole day.

The failure of an attack on Villers Guislain by the Lucknow Brigade or its non-materialization would inevitably result—and did result—in the failure of any attempt of the 4th Cavalry Division on the Villers Ridge.

The situation confronting the brigadier was an extremely difficult one.

The dismounted strength of his Brigade amounted to about seven hundred and fifty all told, regiments averaging two hundred and thirty, and the Machine Gun Squadron about seventy.

That is to say the total strength was about the equivalent of one strong battalion.

He had learnt from the Canadian Brigade that the enemy was in great strength in front of him, that the Raperie (Beet Factory) was very strongly held with machine guns and that Chapel Crossing was also.

The Germans were, moreover, fresh troops just up from St. Mihiel.

The only British troops now between him and the enemy were some extremely shaky infantry about Vaucellette Farm. These could not be counted on to stand if the enemy advanced, and their orders were not to attack themselves, but to merely profit from the advance of the cavalry. There was the prospect of their streaming back through his own Brigade, who, with the exception of the Machine Gun Squadron, were all Indian troops, though good ones. The conduct of even the best Indian troops is always an uncertain factor when British troops break.

His left was absolutely exposed, for the Canadians had been withdrawn into mounted reserve near Genin Well Copse.

As soon as he passed Vaucellette Farm his right would also be in the air, for the attack of the 4th Cavalry Division was to be dependent upon his success.

The Tanks, if they had gone on, must be at such a distance off that they might have been knocked out before he could profit from them. Leaving, however, the Tanks out of the picture, he had no artillery under his orders.

The 5th Divisional R.H.A. had been "divisionalized" and were chiefly absorbed in the Gauche Wood attack.

The three batteries moreover had over two thousand yards of front to watch, and anyone with the slightest experience of France would know that this was a mere flea-bite.

To attempt a serious attack with neither tanks nor artillery was merely to repeat the experience of the Aubers Ridge and the Second Battle of Ypres, where the men were mown down in hundreds and could do nothing.

The main point, however, was that by not attempting to attack he might be letting down the Amballa Brigade attack on Gauche Wood.

The advance began, as stated before, at 06.45. The enemy was evidently expecting it, for no sooner had Jacob's Horse begun to show themselves than the enemy guns opened.

The Regiment was then in artillery formation well opened out. The sky was absolutely black with the smoke of bursting shells. Very fortunately they burst too high, with the result that hardly any casualties occurred.

Possibly the enemy was using guns captured from the 12th Division the day before—there had been two batteries in Villers Guislain—and did not quite get the hang of the fusing.

On nearing Vaucellette Farm the enemy machine guns opened and the casualties began.

Here were found some of our infantry, looking through periscopes, in narrow, hastily scooped-out trenches. They were a heterogeneous collection of cooks, batmen and odds and ends who had been scraped together and dignified by the name of a "composite battalion," and to them every honour is due for having stood when their comrades had bolted. Their relief at the arrival of Jacob's Horse was immense.

The Regiment then attempted to push ahead of them, but after going a hundred yards or so the hostile fire was such that further advance would have meant annihilation.

According to officers of Jacob's Horse we had no artillery support at all at this period. At about 09.00 an attempt was made to work round via the Chapel Crossing flank, under cover of the crest line, but nothing came of it.

The difficulty we were up against was to get machine guns or Hotchkiss rifles up into positions from which they could do something to answer the fire. Such, however, was the hostile superiority in this respect that as soon as a man showed himself a concentration was brought to bear that at once killed or wounded him.

A succession of efforts merely resulted in casualties.

The enemy was located in a line of trench running from about Chape Crossing to about three hundred yards north-east of Vaucellette Farm, with odd parties in shell-holes and shallow bits of cover in front, all very hard to spot.

Four machine guns were definitely located, but these were mere drops in the ocean, for the front was stiff with them.

The only thing to do was to hang on under a very heavy artillery and machine-gun fire.

It was about this stage that one of our aeroplanes evidently thought the troops in the Farm were German. It swooped down three times machine-gunning it. The last time it killed Captain Parnell, the popular and excellent Adjutant of the Regiment.

The 18th Lancers also had a very narrow escape this way, but the ground cloth was got out in time, when the plane went off.

In the far distance, somewhere between Gonnelieu and Villers Guislain apparently, it was, with considerable risk of being shot, possible to see some tanks blazing furiously. These were the only ones seen the whole day. Nothing was seen of some which were said by the 5th Cavalry Division to be approaching Villers Guislain at 08.35.

Even if they had been seen the Brigade could have done nothing more than it did.

Only a commander totally ignorant of the conditions prevailing would have ever expected it to have attempted a further advance without artillery.

4TH CAVALRY DIVISION

While the above operations had been carried out by Amballa and Lucknow Brigades the 4th Cavalry Division had been heavily engaged to the south.

The Division, less the Lucknow Brigade, had assembled north and west of Peizière by 06.00. While waiting, the Mhow Brigade came in for some shelling. A good many men and horses were hit, but it did not shift ground —there may have been no cover to shift to, for the Brigade was in mass, and this formation is only suitable when little or no cover is available except in one place.

The task of the Division was " to take advantage of the advance of the Tanks and seize the Villers Ridge and a line running south from a point about a thousand yards south-east of the Villers Guislain."

The Mhow Brigade, supported by the R.H.A. Brigade, was detailed for the attack. It was to advance " as soon as a suitable opportunity presents itself," the Sialkot Brigade closing up in support.

Under orders from the Corps Commander the attack was to be mounted.

The 4th Cavalry Division Operation Orders issued at 02.00 made out the enemy line to run not far from the west end of Ossus Wood, thence to about Vaucellette Farm.

This may quite well have been the line at the hour, though the confusion of battle makes even this uncertain.

The information was doubtless obtained from the 55th Division, who were in the sector. We know, however, that a certain post, known as Limerick Post, on the ridge to the north of the Catelet Valley about fifteen hundred yards north-west of Little Priel Farm, was evacuated at 05.00 in the morning and that the Germans at once occupied it. As to whether this was known by the 2nd Lancers (Mhow Brigade) when their attack started is more than doubtful, for Colonel Turner intended to wheel north at a point about where this post was.

The German line at the time the Mhow Brigade attacked, would appear to have been more as follows :—

Ossus Wood, thence due west on both sides of the Catelet Valley to about a thousand yards from Épéhy, where it turned north to Vaucellette Farm.

The enemy was thus in possession of the whole of the wired-in supporting posts of our original line. A line drawn roughly south-east from the Beet Factory will represent their locality. To the east of this line would be our former front-line trenches with their maze of communication trenches.

The ground for about fifteen hundred yards to the east of the railway is pretty clear of obstacles and is good open going for cavalry.

From Peizière to the Beet Factory some three thousand yards the ground is absolutely devoid of cover and every movement can be seen from the latter place, which was known to be strongly held with machine guns.

Our own infantry were in occupation of the slopes near Little Priel Farm, and their line ran thence west to roughly about two hundred yards or so parallel to the railway and to the east of it. They were all very shaky.

Brigadier-General Niel Haig fully appreciated the impossible job he had been given, as shown in the following letter :—

Copy of letter from Brig.-General Neil Haig,
Commanding Mhow Cavalry Brigade.

30.6.25.

The attack on the Villers Guislain ridge was by direct order of the Corps Commander.

I had previously received from Alfred Kennedy (Commdg. 4th Cavalry Division) an outline of what would be required of the Mhow Brigade and had carefully reconnoitred the position personally.

I came to the conclusion that any attack on this position (except by a large force of infantry prepared by a strong artillery barrage) could not succeed.

I went up to Alfred Kennedy's Head-quarters, explained the enemy's situation to him, and asked him to come down to my H.Q. himself.

Kennedy came down at once and accompanied me to the point whence I had seen the enemy's position. He had to crawl on his belly a good way, but I was able to show him the Beet Factory (i.e., the Raperie) walls and what I took to be the wire in front of the enemy's machine guns.

Kennedy quite agreed with me that an attack on this position was impracticable, and said he would go and talk to the Corps Commander on the telephone at once and explain the situation. Kennedy returned to me later and informed me that he had explained the situation carefully, that the Corps Commander was very annoyed at the delay and ordered the attack to take place at once.

I allowed the 2nd Lancers a quarter of an hour to arm themselves with their lances, which, in the hurry of moving off, had to be brought up by cart. While I was issuing my orders to the C.O.'s and squadron commanders one of the Corps Staff rode up, and when I had finished, said to me, " Then I can inform the Corps Commander that you have great hopes of success."

I took him to one side so that no one could hear, and I told him he could go back and tell the Corps Commander that I didn't think we had " a dog's earthly."

He returned and told the Corps Commander that I was not optimistic —his name was Heidemann, of The Bays, and I think he was G.S.O. 2 or 3.

I had 933 casualties among my horses.
   386 were killed,
   547 wounded (446 remained with Bde.
     101 were evacuated).

I have just looked the numbers up in my old pocket-book.

I think I have some old maps, etc., and some one visited the battlefields afterwards and told me I was quite right about the positions of the wire and enemy machine guns.

(Sd.) NEIL HAIG.

Copy of a letter from Major-General A. A. Kennedy,
Commanding 4th Cavalry Division.

Neil Haig is perfectly correct. It is not likely you would find any trace of the episode in the Corps Diary. I wanted an inquiry held, but the Corps Commander, I imagine, never sent on the letter I wrote.

On the day in question the original orders required the 4th Cavalry Division to be in a position just west of Épéhy ready to take advantage of any success gained in the dismounted cavalry and tank attack with a view to advancing and occupying the high ground east (?) of Villers Guislain.

You may recollect that the tanks failed to turn up at the hour given for the dismounted attack by 5th Cavalry Division with Gage's Brigade attached and that consequently this attack did not make much progress.

The fact was known to me when I was told that the Corps Commander wished to speak to me on the telephone.

I walked across to where were my Divisional Head-quarters and the following conversation took place between me and the Corps Commander :—

General Kavanagh. How is your attack getting on ?

Self. My attack ! Why, it has not started, as the dismounted attack has not made any progress. The tanks failed to turn up and there is nothing doing.

General Kavanagh. Rot ! You have to carry out your attack as ordered.

Self. But my orders were to take advantage of any success gained in the dismounted attack, and, as I say, there has not been any success.

Kavanagh. You have to carry out your attack at once.

Self. If you order me to do so I will try it.

I may say the Corps Commander was evidently very annoyed and, from the first, spoke very rudely. I put down the 'phone and went across to Haig. He told me what his plan was, and I said that we had to put it into execution forthwith.

The order was then given by him to his Brigade, with the result you know.

Subsequently, when we were asked for lessons learnt this day, I wrote that the chief lesson was the old one of leaving it to the man on the spot to decide the time of delivering his attack, and that it was a mistake to try and do this by telephone when some miles distant and ignorant of the tactical situation.

I do not know what the records contain, but the true story is as I say, and I more than once discussed the matter with Kavanagh afterwards. Neil Haig and Malise Graham, now commanding the 10th Hussars at Aldershot, saw all the correspondence. I may say I have always regretted that I did not, there and then, refuse to carry out Kavanagh's orders.

I thought at the time that there might be a *very* slight chance of the mounted attack gaining a little ground, and that, if it did, it would certainly help the dismounted attack to get forward, so I did not refuse.

Haig's plan struck me as sound, and I told him to carry on.

Kavanagh told me afterwards that his complaint against me was that I merely ordered the attack and did not care a damn how it was done ! This was some months later when I was acting as his B.G., G.S. during Home's absence on sick-leave.

I stood with Haig near the railway bridge at Épéhy and watched the Inniskillings advance across the bridge, then deploy and gallop towards the trenches, also their return.

I then went back to the 'phone and told Kavanagh what had happened. He said it was a gallant effort. Was it an operation of war?

Yours sincerely,
A. A. KENNEDY.

The Brigade Orders were :—

1. The 2nd Lancers were to seize Targette, Quail and Pigeon Ravines, objectives some three thousand yards east of the northern exit of Peiziére, and establish a defensive flank.

One squadron of the Inniskillings was to support them.

2. The Inniskillings and four machine guns were to follow as soon as the 2nd were seen approaching their objective and endeavour to seize and hold the Villers Guislain Ridge about a thousand yards east of Villers Guislain.

The detail of artillery targets is not known, but was probably the Villers Ridge.

At 09.35, the 2nd Lancers, followed by " C " Squadron the Inniskillings, left Épéhy by the southern exit leading over the level crossing. It was the commanding officer's intention to move down the Catelet Valley and then wheel north to the objectives. This line of advance was selected as being the most covered.

Thanks to this, the Regiment avoided the fate of the Inniskillings, who had bare open ground to pass over.

After a brilliant advance under very heavy fire from both sides of the valley it succeeded in reaching a hollow road, known as Kildare Lane, running from Little Priel Farm towards Villers Guislain, whence it was unable to move the whole day. This point was nearly a mile inside the German lines.

It was more by good luck than anything else that the Regiment was not exterminated on some wire it ran on to in the first place, and subsequently by shelling.

The dominating feature of its success in getting so far was surprise and not finding wire—for we were fighting only some three thousand yards behind our former " No Man's Land."

Attempts made to move north into Pigeon and Quail Ravines were frustrated by the deadly machine-gun fire that came from all four sides. The Regiment in consequence did not reach its objective.

For two hours it was thought to have been swallowed up by the enemy.

"C" Squadron of the Inniskillings also became tied up with the 2nd. It eventually protected their left in the hollow road. Thanks to its bombers it succeeded in repulsing a German bombing attack—German bombs being used. Had the enemy succeeded in this, they would have been in a position to work machine guns up, so as to enfilade the road, which was a mass of men and horses. We are told that one German was blown clean out of the road by a bomb thrown at him.

The full details of the operations of the 2nd Lancers is attached.

Almost simultaneously with the 2nd Lancers, the Inniskillings (less "C" Squadron with the 2nd Lancers) moved down the Peizière–Villers Guislain Road.

The leading squadron, accompanied by a section of machine guns, moved at a gallop. The remainder of the Regiment followed in a column of squadrons in line of troop columns, widely extended at a distance of about six hundred yards.

A heavy machine-gun fire from both flanks opened from the very moment the Regiment crossed the railway, and the fire grew hotter and hotter as the advance continued.

Nevertheless the squadron pushed on with extraordinary gallantry, and a few even reached the Beet Factory. Here the Germans ran out and surrounded them.

Not a man either of the squadron or the machine gunners returned.

The remainder of the Regiment pushed on to within about a thousand yards of the Villers Ridge, when the Commanding Officer (now Brigadier-General Patterson, D.S.O.), rightly realizing that no officer or man would be left alive if the advance continued, gave the order to withdraw, which the Regiment did with great steadiness.

The Regiment lost during the day six officers, one hundred and eight other ranks, and one hundred and eighty-seven horses, while the unfortunate machine gunners lost two officers, fifty-three other ranks, and eighty-four horses.

Nearly the whole of these casualties occurred in the few minutes this mad enterprise lasted.

The situation of the Mhow Brigade, within ten minutes of its attack being launched, was that one and a half of its three Regiments were out of the picture. They had nothing to show for the sacrifice in any conceivable way whatever—unless a brilliant display of gallantry be considered a sufficient result.

It is extremely difficult to imagine why the attack was ever ordered.

It may have been thought that the Tanks were approaching Villers Guislain—some did at 08.35 apparently. It must, or should have, been known, however, that they were unsupported, as the Lucknow Brigade had reached no further than Vaucellette Farm—and unsupported Tanks are useless.

A successful entry of Gauche Wood could have no influence on the enemy nearly two miles to the south.

The point of attempting a mounted attack under the circumstances seems incomprehensible.

In the case of the Inniskillings, not one single element that has conduced to success in mounted attacks, since and including the days of Napoleon, was present.

Surprise was absent, the enemy was absolutely unshaken, our fire support was totally inadequate, and even if the enemy had been reached, what could have been done to him behind wire and in trenches?

A whole cavalry division could have done nothing under these circumstances.

It may be urged that the attack was launched with a view to helping the Lucknow Brigade. This Brigade was, however, nearly a mile off, and did not even know that an attack had taken place till much later in the day. Its value in this respect may thus be appreciated.

The value of a holding attack depends largely on the length of time the pressure lasts. It is of interest to note that the Mhow attacks started at 09.35 and by 09.45 all was over—ten minutes.

There is one point, however, to which attention must be drawn, and that is that the 2nd Lancers penetrated a mile into the German line under very heavy fire from both sides of the valley they passed down.

The Inniskillings, despite the open ground they were working in, managed to get, according to Colonel Patterson's own description, to within a thousand yards of the Beet Factory and then returned.

They were thus under an intense machine-gun and rifle fire for some two thousand yards altogether in absolutely open ground.

The enemy artillery did not get going until the Regiment had recrossed the railway.

The Inniskillings certainly lost more than 33 per cent. of their strength in doing so, but the 2nd Lancers hardly lost anyone until they came on wire.

Now, in these attacks we were up against good German machine-gunners, though the actual infantry do not appear to have been anything very wonderful. The 2nd Lancers could see them bolting in all directions as they advanced. Furthermore, these gunners were organized in great depth, and were in many cases well wired in.

Is it not reasonable to suppose, therefore, that an attack by, say, two brigades might have succeeded had there been no wire, and had the enemy been so located as to be able to be got at?

At Al Mughar we were up against Turks, not certainly organized in very great depth. Here the attack started some three thousand yards from the enemy over bare ground that would hardly hide a rabbit, and the supporting fire merely amounted to one battery and a machine-gun squadron.

The Turks were in no way shaken and had been a long time in their position. The Turk individually is a better man than most Germans, though the machine-gunners may not be their equals.

This attack was a brilliant success, mainly, it is submitted, because the enemy could actually be got at.

The very loose formation in which infantry must now fight tends to make them very susceptible to a mounted charge, provided it is delivered in depth and there are no obstacles.

It is submitted that failures in mounted attacks in France can, in most instances, if not all, be traced to (*a*) obstacles, (*b*) insufficient numbers, and as a result of (*c*) insufficient depth.

In the meantime the whereabouts of the 2nd Lancers was unknown, but eventually some horses were spotted near what was thought to be Pigeon Ravine. They were about twelve hundred yards to the south of it in point of fact. It was not until 10.50—two hours after the attack—that a message, carried by a very gallant sowar, one Govind Singh, a Rajput, was received by the Brigade giving their true position.

Before this was received two squadrons of the Central India Horse were pushed down the ridge to the north of Catelet Valley, dismounted with the object of extricating them. It was not possible, however, to advance further than a point about two thousand yards east of Épéhy owing to the Germans being in occupation of Limerick Post, referred to before.

A third squadron of the Central India Horse tried to reach the 2nd Lancers by a more southerly route later in the day, but also failed.

At 13.00 the two squadrons of the Central India Horse, in conjunction with the 166th Infantry Brigade, again attempted an advance, but it failed heavily.

The Central India Horse lost five British Officers and fifty-two Indian Ranks in these efforts.

In so far as the Mhow Brigade was concerned, the 2nd Lancers were now out of the picture and were thought to have been irretrievably lost in the German lines.

The Commander of the 4th Cavalry Division (Major-General Kennedy) had been watching operations from a ruined windmill to the north of Peizière when, about midday, he was sent for by the Cavalry Corps Commander to a point to the west of that village, where the 4th and 5th Cavalry Divisional Head-quarters were.

He was then ordered to arrange a renewed attack by Mhow from the south, and by Lucknow from about Vaucellette Farm, on the Villers Ridge. Lucknow was brought back under his command.

A glance at the map will show that these two attacks, each of about the strength of a battalion at the outside, would be separated by the best part of a mile.

He anticipated bringing off this attack at about 14.00, but while the orders were being made out learnt that the 5th Cavalry Division had arranged to attack at 15.00, but in what manner he did not know. He accordingly arranged to postpone his attack so as to co-operate with the 5th Cavalry Division, adding a paragraph to his own Operation Order, " The 5th Cav. Divn. is co-operating."

This order, timed 12.40, was received by Lucknow at 13.20 and by Mhow at 14.15. The delay in getting through to Mhow is accounted for by the very heavy fire and barrage down to the east of Peizière the whole day.

In so far as Mhow was concerned a reply was sent in fifteen minutes later to the effect that the only troops that could be put in were a couple of weak squadrons of the Inniskillings and one of the Central India Horse, the rest of the Brigade being tied up and unable to move, and that an attack with so weak a strength would produce no effect. This message only reached the Division after Lucknow had commenced its advance. The result was that the latter had its right in the air.

The 4th Cavalry Divisional Order for the 15.00 attack arranged for the VII. Corps Heavy Artillery to bombard the Beet Factory.

The three R.H.A. Batteries were to engage machine-gun emplacements on the Villers Ridge.

Seemingly, this was the whole of the artillery support available for the whole day, for the 55th Division had only two artillery brigades at the opening of the Battle on the 30th November and many guns had been lost.

Whatever artillery there was, officers both of the Mhow and Lucknow Brigades are unanimous that it was too weak to produce the least impression.

There seems a degree of doubt as to whether the 5th Cavalry Division knew that Lucknow had returned to the orders of the 4th or not, for in its operation orders it inserts a boundary line between the Canadian Brigade and the Lucknow Brigade, which was now to be put in dismounted on Lucknow's left, though the latter knew nothing of it until its own attack had actually begun. The consequence was Lucknow advanced on the southern slopes of the Villers Ridge and not along the crest as it would have had it known.

LUCKNOW BRIGADE

In so far as Lucknow was concerned, the prospects of any success, in view of the morning's failure, did not seem particularly bright, mainly owing to the inability of the R.H.A. to effect anything on the enemy machine guns.

The covering fire of the M.G. Squadron, with the enemy very close, not clearly located, and in such a position that we could not get guns into position for direct fire, had amounted to plastering the area some distance in rear of whence the enemy fire came.

For the purpose of downing it therefore it was of little value. The right flank was absolutely in the air, and as at the time the attack started nothing was known about the Canadians going in on the Brigade's left, it was thought the left would be also.

The total front the Brigade could attack on, if one Regiment was to be in reserve, could not exceed some six hundred yards—we know that the Guards' frontage only had five hundred yards to a battalion. The whole strength of the dismounted brigade did not much exceed a battalion.

Jacob's Horse was to move on the Beet Factory direct up the Beet Factory–Peizière Road and thus on the south-east side of the Villers Ridge. The Jodhpore Lancers were to be in support and the 29th in reserve.

When the advance began the German fire redoubled. At least eight machine guns, in addition to those already spotted, were located. Movement along the crest was to invite certain death, and many casualties occurred in attempting it. The right of Jacob's Horse succeeded, in spite of heavy loss, in working its way about eight hundred yards east of Vaucellette Farm, every rush drawing tremendous fire.

The dash and staunchness of the men was beyond all praise, for there was very little cover. Only troops of very high quality would have gone forward in the circumstances. Above all, when once settled into cover, few would have left it to advance.

The attack was well under way, when a liaison officer from the Canadian Brigade reported to Brigadier-General Gage that his Brigade was held up on the line Vaucellette Farm–Chapel Crossing. This was the first intimation the Brigadier received that the Canadians were attacking at all. As it was there was a gap between the two brigades. He at once ordered the Jodhpore Lancers to fill it and move in a north-easterly direction.

Officers in Jacob's Horse could see the men of the Jodhpores dropping as the machine guns caught them.

This effort considerably eased the situation on the Canadian right, and they began to work forward shortly after.

So far as Jacob's Horse was concerned, it soon became obvious that a further advance meant destruction.

The fire, so far from diminishing, increased.

The Regiment was in a salient, with its right flank being caught in enfilade and the left considerably ahead of the Jodhpore Lancers.

The fire of our Horse Artillery Brigade, though directed on the machine guns to the south of the Villers Ridge, had but little effect on the entrenced emplacements, and could not be brought to bear on the machine guns which enfiladed the right.

The fire from the Beet Factory had only slightly diminished as the result of the bombardment of the heavy artillery.

All that could be done was to hang on and pray for darkness.

When this arrived, the Brigade began to dig in. The attack was watched throughout by the 4th Cavalry Divisional Commander, who was well satisfied that the troops had done all men could do.

Jacob's Horse lost one British officer, Captain Parnell, three Indian officers and ten men killed, and one British officer, Captain Farquhar, one Indian officer and twenty-three men wounded. Captain Farquhar had a most extraordinary wound, a machine-gun bullet entering between eye and nose and coming out at the back of his head. Two years after there was hardly a mark and his sight was quite unaffected.

The casualties were not heavy, thanks to the Brigadier being a man of character, who refused to push an attack which a mere schoolboy could have seen to be hopeless. From a study of various operations in the Great War there is but little doubt that if more commanders had acted in this manner many perfectly useless casualties would have been avoided. Numerous instances can be quoted of commanders, not acquainted with the local situation, issuing peremptory orders to attack, under circumstances which could lead to nothing but heavy loss to no purpose.

On occasions, it may be essential to sacrifice one body of troops in order to enable another to succeed. In the case of the Lucknow Brigade, however, it is impossible to see what good can have come out of further efforts to get forward. The only result would have been a line of corpses some hundred yards or so ahead of where the troops were held up. Furthermore, with the Brigade knocked out, there would have been but few other troops to take their place. It was not as though we had large reserves available.

5TH CAVALRY DIVISION

The attack of the 5th Cavalry Division, timed for 15.00, was confined to the Canadian Cavalry Brigade.

It was directed to advance on Villers Guislain between Vaucellette Farm and Gauche Wood.

The Brigade had the advantage of both flanks being secure and of the whole of its Divisional Artillery being available to help it, although this only amounted to three Horse Batteries.

The main factor, however, was that Gauche Wood, which had been taken by 9.30 that morning, menaced the German right rear about Chapel Crossing.

The artillery that had supported the Guards' attack on the Wood in the morning also did a good deal to assist matters.

Furthermore, the pressure of the Jodhpore Lancers on the Germans to the north of Vaucellette Farm began to tell, and by 16.50, despite an enemy counter-attack which was repulsed with heavy loss, Chapel Crossing and some prisoners, with a machine gun, fell into the Canadians' hands.

This success was followed up, and by dark the Brigade had succeeded in working well forward to a line running roughly from the south-east corner of Bois Gauche to five hundred yards north-east of Vaucellette Farm.

The prisoners taken belonged to troops brought up from St. Mihiel two days before.

The Brigade lost four officers and seventy men, mostly Fort Garry Horse.

It is difficult to imagine what was to be expected from the 15.00 attack ordered for the 4th Cavalry Division.

The morning attacks had given some indication of the hostile strength. The addition of the VII. Corps Heavy Artillery was not likely to affect things much. What was wanted was a big field-gun barrage, and without it every attempt to get forward must have been hopeless. It is to be noted that this attack was ordered by the Corps Commander in person, who had come up to comparatively close behind the battle front and who must have been fully acquainted with the situation, as he could, with no great trouble, have seen the ground through his own eyes. It was not the case of telephonic orders issued when he was a long way back as had been the case of the morning's attack.

It may be urged that the Canadian Brigade succeeded in advancing. The question is, however, what good did this do? Were the Canadians any better off than before? Was the gain of ground worth the casualties?

A particular feature of the 30th November to the 1st December, had been the splendid conduct of the Indian Cavalry, without exception, in this the greatest action in which they had ever taken part.

German Official Photograph.] *The Imperial War Museum. By kind permission.*

"THE OTHER SIDE OF THE HILL."
(German soldier at an advanced post, at Honnecourt.)

August, 1917.

German Official Photograph.]
Taken four months after the Battle of Épéhy.]
The Imperial War Museum.
By kind permission.

THE TOLL OF WAR.
Fallen Indian Cavalryman.
Villers Guislain.

March, 1918.

Their behaviour was subsequently commented on in the House of Commons.

As regards Jacob's Horse, two individuals have been specially spoken of, one was Colonel Green and the other was our popular French interpreter, " Bruno " Braun, a member of the Alexandria Bourse. " Bruno " constituted himself into an unofficial stretcher-bearer and displayed the utmost gallantry. His name was sent in for the " Croix de Guerre." The French authorities, however, were almost rude on the subject and seemed to hint that " if ever the old devil sticks his nose into a battle again and gets killed we shall visit dire punishment on him. His job is to argue with fat madames as regards billets and go in and buy groceries from French shopkeepers, not to go prancing about in the battle line."

About midnight the Mhow and Lucknow Brigades were relieved by the 21st Division and the Sialkot Brigade and bivouacked near Épéhy.

The Secunderabad Brigade relieved Amballa in Gauche Wood.

The 2nd Lancers succeeded in extricating themselves in the dark via the Lempire Road.

The night was bitterly cold. Many officers who were present say it was one of the worst they had ever experienced.

The total casualties in the 4th Cavalry Division amounted to about four hundred and fifty men and a thousand horses.

Of these the Mhow Brigade lost some three hundred and forty men and nine hundred and thirty-three horses and had nothing whatever to show for it. Furthermore, it is a known fact that among the senior officers of the Division there was a feeling that the casualties were brought about through mismanagement in high places. The actual number of men lost was not so much the point, for the percentage was not high as compared with those in the infantry. The futility of the Mhow Brigade attack and the 15.00 attack of the Lucknow Brigade were the objections mainly stressed.

Under the circumstances, is it to be wondered that a tale flew round that the attacks had been ordered so that the impression might be given that the Cavalry Corps was doing something to justify its existence, having failed to do so on the 20th November? The writer has heard this from the lips of no fewer than four brigadiers who were present in the battle.

It may be of interest to know that our dead lay out in what was evidently the " No Man's Land " after the battle, until the great German offensive of the 21st March 1918. They were then especially commented on in the History of a German Regiment which took part in it. A photograph of a dead Sikh with his horse was taken, which is now to be seen in The Imperial War Museum, and is here reproduced.

2ND LANCERS AT ÉPÉHY

By Captain Whitworth, 2nd Lancers

Dealing first with Colonel Maunsell's questions:—

(1) *What was directed on the charge?*

The charge took place down a shallow valley. At no point was the sky-line to the Regiment's right or left more than seven hundred yards distant.

The German fire was almost entirely from machine guns. There was probably a little rifle fire too. It is believed that about eight machine guns were firing at ranges between three hundred yards and seven hundred yards. There was no German shelling. The covered nature of the line of advance and its suddenness would account for this.

The machine guns were firing from both sides of the valley. There seemed to be rather more of them to the north (or left side) than on the other. No detachment was made to deal with any of these guns, but I noticed that the strike of one became distinctly unsteady as we came abreast of it. The German must have had uneasy thoughts of lances at his back.

Our pace down the valley was a good sixteen annas, and until we halted our casualties were negligible.

The led horses which returned the same way were badly hammered, losing about fifty men and one hundred and twenty horses.

(2) *What obstacles were there?*

The going was excellent—good spring turf, and only a few shell-holes.

There was nothing to stop the advance until within two hundred yards of the sunken road : hence we came on a single apron of wire with two gaps.

There was a check here as we reduced front. Colonel Turner was killed here and all of Regimental Head-quarters killed or wounded except the Adjutant (myself) and the Head-quarter Signallers.

(3) *What distance did it have to cover?*

From the point where we crossed the British infantry's line to the sunken road is about one and a half miles. I should think that we did it in about five minutes.

(4) *What covering fire was there?*

None of any sort, either during the charge or later in the day.

(5) *What degree of surprise was there?*

Absolute, I should imagine. Our own infantry were astounded when we galloped through them. They cheered us like blazes.

(6) *What was the quality of the Boche?*

Judging by his advance the day before—good. Judging by his action on our appearance—rotten. The moment we began to gallop out of Épéhy we could see Germans running at distances up to a mile away. Only the machine-gunners stood fast : the others rallied on them after we had passed through.

Narrative. At 7 a.m. on 30th November the 2nd Lancers sent off a trench party (from Athies), which with horse-holders amounted to about 85 per cent. of the total strength, to take over (in conjunction with trench parties of the Inniskillings and the 38th Central India Horse) a sub-sector of trenches near Lempire.

At 11 a.m. (?) the Brigade (H.Q. Ennemain) telephoned to say that what remained of the three Regiments was to rendezvous near Estrées en Chausée.

The Brigade moved off about an hour later towards Villers Faucon. After much changing of direction and many halts, the column bivouacked just north-west of St. Emilie. It seemed to consist principally of trumpeters, farriers, and pack-horses. The lances and swords of the trench party were brought along in G.S. wagons.

During the whole of that day no clear information as to what it was all about reached the troops.

We surmised, and correctly so, that the long-promised " G in gap " had come at last—only that the gap was in our line. The trench parties rejoined at about midnight in the pitch dark. They had marched and countermarched all the day, mostly on their feet. The Hun at one point had given them a dose of gas shell, and they were tired, angry, and famished.

There was much confusion in reforming squadrons in the dark. A new Indian M.O. reported his arrival at about this time. Apparently he tried to follow us the next morning and rode straight into the hands of the Boche. His very existance was clean forgotten until the medical authorities inquired about him five days later.

The lance and sword wagons were lost in the night.

At about 4 a.m. Operation Orders came in.

Villers Guislain was to be attacked by the Division at dawn. Our rôle was to make a mounted advance, seize Pigeon and Quail Ravines, and form a defensive flank to the south.

At about 6 a.m. the Mhow Brigade moved to the north-east outskirts of Peizières and halted, dismounted in mass behind a low ridge behind the railway.

Here the Brigade came in for some ·77 shelling, but did not move. Several men and horses were hit. It was unpleasant standing there in mass, but the discipline was good. After about fifteen minutes of it the shelling stopped. The Hun probably thought that we had moved off.

At about 8 a.m. the 2nd Lancers were told off to lead the attack. The sword and lance wagons had just arrived and were not all distributed.

Lances were being thrown to men of the rear squadron as we moved off.

We passed through Épéhy and turning to the left debouched from the village at the level crossing. A hundred yards on we crossed the trenches of our very astonished—and relieved—infantry, who were expecting a German attack at any minute. We then deployed into open column of squadrons at extended distances, each squadron in line of troop columns.

As soon as the leading squadron—Sikhs, Major Knowles—began to gallop, Boche machine guns opened from both sides of the valley. It was Colonel Turner's intention to follow the valley for some way and then turn left-handed over the ridge. The pace soon became an all out gallop and the cracking of machine guns was deafening. For all this there seemed to be few casualties. The Boche had an ideal target, or what most machine-gunners would call an ideal target, but the fact remains that little damage was done, and from that day we feared machine guns little if the going was good and the ground clear of obstacles. Ten months later five machine guns fired at two of our squadrons as we charged them over open ground near Afuleh, and hit five horses. Not a man was touched.

By this time we could see running Germans in every direction. The garrison of Kildare Lane, about two hundred rifles and some machine guns (we captured three of the latter), bolted before we were within five hundred yards of them. About two hundred yards short of Kildare Lane the leading squadron hit a single apron of wire. There were two good gaps in it, but the check was sufficient to give the Hun machine guns in Limerick Post their chance. We were well past them by that time, and they turned their guns back on us. Regimental Head-quarters caught it first.

Colonel Turner was killed and all the Head-quarters group, except the Adjutant and some signallers, were killed or wounded. The two leading squadrons managed to get their horses into Kildare Lane. The remainder of the Regiment, and Captain Moncrieff's Squadron of the Inniskillings and a section of machine guns who had followed us, went in dismounted. The led horses had to return along the valley, and the Boche took full toll of this slower moving body.

The lane was now a mass of men and horses. The upper, or left, end was under heavy machine-gun fire from our left rear, and to our right, just beyond Catelet Copse, an intermittent barrage of H.E. went on all the day. The object of this barrage presumably was to prevent on attack being launched against the flank of the German salient from the direction of the Lempire Road re-entrant.

Immediately on taking Kildare Lane we had found a thick bundle of telephone wire running across it. This was promptly cut through, and so, presumably, all the German posts to our rear were cut off from their Headquarters. This is the only thing which can account for the fact that we were not once shelled during the whole day. Only the Germans in our rear could see us. To our front, rising ground only allowed a field of view of fifty yards or so.

Three separate counter-attacks were made against us.

The first was easily dealt with as the Hun came over the rise in front and was shot down at close range.

The next came from the posts on our left rear. It was dealt with by Major Salkeld with the Rajput Squadron, who went out to meet the Hun with the bayonet.

The Hun was more than twice as strong as Salkeld's Squadron, but would not face cold steel, and went back.

The third attack took the form of a bombing party, which came along some trenches from the direction of Limerick Post. This was met with the same weapon and driven back.

And about 11 a.m. the Central India Horse made a very gallant dismounted attack along the Limerick Post ridge, with the object of coming to our assistance. Three British Officers and many Indian Ranks were killed, and they were forced to return.

At about this time two volunteers were called for to take a duplicate message back to Épéhy. Two men immediately came forward—Sowar Jot Ram, a Jat, and L. D. Govind Singh, a Rahtore of the 28th Cavalry attached to the 2nd Lancers. They started together, but took different routes. Jot Ram was shot down almost at once. Immediately after Govind Singh's horse came down, and we thought that he had been killed too. An hour later, however, he appeared with an answer from the Brigade. He had managed to make his way on foot through the German posts, falling down whenever they fired at him and lying doggo until their attention was attracted elsewhere.

He had started back from the Brigade on another horse, but this too was killed, and he made his way back to us in a similar manner. An hour later another message had to go back, and he again volunteered. This time he galloped straight through the barrage to our right. Half-way through we saw his horse cut clean in two by a direct hit. Again he finished his journey on foot, and then volunteered to return again. The Brigadier, however, thought that he had done enough. This earned Govind Singh the Victoria Cross.

During the morning we had discovered that British infantry were holding the slopes behind Little Priel Farm. At about 4 p.m. the Adjutant managed to get through to them and telephone to the Brigade. He came back with orders that the 2nd Lancers were to withdraw if possible as soon as it became dark.

At sundown the barrage beyond Catelet Copse stopped, and in the hour and a half before moonrise we had slipped out of Kildare Lane and were marching for Épéhy via the Lempire Road, taking our wounded and the body of Colonel Turner with us.

That piercingly cold night we slept in the open behind Épéhy. The next day we returned to our billets at Athies, less about one hundred men and two hundred horses.

Lieutenant Broadway had, when the Regiment reached Kildare Lane, just spared a German officer who held up one hand in token of surrender. When Broadway turned away, this German drew a pistol, held behind his back in his other hand, and shot the unfortunate officer. He was promptly speared with a hog-spear by Major Knowles' orderly.

The foregoing account is probably much fuller than what is required, but gives the events of 1st December as accurately as I can remember them.

We did not know the details of the German success on 30th November till after the battle. There had been indications of a big attack on the Cambrai Salient three days before. The infantry had been " standing to " three nights in expectation and, in the case of the 55th Division at all events, patrols had been sent out every morning at 04.00. The 55th Divisional R.A. had opened on the enemy line in bursts beginning at 05.00. This Division had only two brigades of artillery and was watching 13,000 yards of front, however, and it is easy to realize what this meant.

It had been the idea to open " counter preparation "—in other words, shell likely forming-up places and lines of approach—with the corps, heavy artillery, but this did not come off on the 55th Divisional Front. At 07.00 on the 30th the enemy opened a very heavy bombardment in a thick fog, and attacked after the troops had " stood down," and while they were having breakfast.

The line first went to the north of Villers Guislain and the break spread. There was, bluntly, a panic, and the ill-officered and half-trained troops bolted.

Where there were stout officers and where troops were out of the way of the panic-stricken men, posts hung on, thereby enabling the Guards and cavalry to come up. Many of these posts, however, found themselves attacked from the rear—a particularly disconcerting feature for raw troops.

Owing to the thoroughness with which the Germans had cleared the ground in front of the Hindenburg Line we had had to put batteries right forward in some cases, and these had been overwhelmed in the first rush —there were two batteries of the 12th Division in Villers Guislain, for instance.

As showing how infectious panics are, a certain regular battalion of great name, whose boast it had been that it had not lost a trench the whole war, went off as quick as the rest.

One unfortunate brigadier was run in for " leaving his brigade " when in point of fact his head-quarters were the only people who held out.

It must be remembered that the battalions were very weak and that the troops were all tired. Furthermore, if the dispositions were anything like what they were when we were in the Honnecourt sector in August, it is quite conceivable that anything might have happened, particularly with troops fresh to the line.

It was the 55th Division that subsequently covered itself with glory when the Portuguese broke.

It will be remembered that the enemy received a tremendous hammering on the north of the Cambrai Salient which, to a certain extent, set off our defeat to the south. It was on this side that Lieut.-Colonel Giles, Scinde Horse, G.S.O.I., 2nd Infantry Division, greatly distinguished himself.

CHAPTER XV

WINTER 1917–18 IN THE DEVASTATED AREA.
DEPARTURE FROM FRANCE. THE MOVE TO EGYPT.

THE two Indian Cavalry Divisions returned to their normal area north of the Omignon after the Épéhy Battle.

Brigades began to take over the trench sectors between Pontru and Hargicourt as before.

For the first three weeks of December there was a suppressed state of "wind up" in high places, and brigades in reserve were constantly in a state of readiness at one hour's notice to move. The Lucknow Brigade thus "stood to" for no less than seventy-two hours from the 12th December till the 15th December.

Things had an unpleasant aspect. The Hun was now rushing troops over from his Russian front—for the Russians had made peace.

Our own troops had shown definite symptoms of what is termed "tiredness," and no wonder. The Passchendaele Battle was enough to make any wretched men lose their keenness in attack. A particular feature had been that among a big proportion an uneasy feeling seems to have been caused that they were being slaughtered to no purpose, whereas we simply had to go on attacking in order to prevent the French ratting. If the Boche had turned on the French in the summer of 1917 he would, undoubtedly, have knocked them out, for they had had a series of mutinies in the army. These had to be kept quiet from our men and the world in general. The French had not properly recovered by the winter of 1917.

Our Cambrai offensive had largely failed owing to weariness in our infantry, quite apart from the mishandling of the cavalry.

The Épéhy Battle had now given many furiously to think. That there was a grave falling off in the quality of our infantry was obvious. A certain corps commander is known to have observed that the men were not worth 25 per cent. of those who fought on the Somme.

To add to the trouble, the politicians had so persistently hung up the supply of men that we had had to cut down the number of battalions per division from twelve to nine, and even these were not up to strength.

Thanks to the same gentry, too, we had to take over the line to the south of the Omignon from the French, who had not done a stroke of work on new lines of defence. When the French wanted to rest they rested, quite regardless of the danger it might involve. The discipline of their Army seemed to be such, that if the " Poilus " as a whole did not want to do a thing they didn't, and that was the end of it.

Although we liked the French very much individually, there is no blinking the fact that collectively, both in a military and in a diplomatic sense, as allies they bordered on the impossible. Time after time they let us down badly, even in the middle of a battle, after promising to do something and then going back on it.

Frantic efforts were now made to strengthen our rear lines of defence, and the men were greatly overworked. The Regiment was employed, in the main, on works about Jeancourt. When working parties were up, the men with the horses had a very trying time, each man having as many as six animals on his hands. Sometimes they could not get their boots dry for days on end, as they had to work on wet muddy standings.

In addition, all were extremely badly housed, and it was necessary to run up bivouacs inside the huts.

The men's eyes suffered owing to smoke from the open braziers—the only kind available. The general result was that the sick rate went up higher than it had ever been for the three years we had been in France.

It must not, however, be imagined that the Indian units were one whit worse in this respect than the British, whose sick rate also increased enormously. It had been clearly shown, in the bivouacs of March and April 1917, that provided the Indian trooper was properly clothed and fed he was just as capable of standing exposure as anyone else.

The horses stood the weather wonderfully. They were not absolutely in the open and had overhead cover. They had plenty of rugs, were well fed and not worked hard.

Very severe frosts occurred in January, and lorries could not be used. As the road surfaces were almost a sheet of ice it was a matter of considerable difficulty to move about.

The Regiment was in the line for the last time at the end of this month.

It was, by now, a very different place from the comparative rest cure it had been when we went into it in the summer.

The Boche was getting extremely sensitive, and any undue activity on our part would at once result in his guns opening.

In front was the great Bellenglise dump which he was now preparing, and he was taking no chances with regard to it.

From the high ground about Le Verguier and Ferverques Farm one could see the flares spouting all night with a profusion one had never seen in the summer.

Some Regiments, notably the 2nd Lancers, lost more men this tour in the line than they had lost the whole of the time we had been in the sector.

Only an idiot, or a politician, who preferred to shut his eyes to what he did not want to see could fail to realize that there was dirty work afoot.

Our Brigadier, General Gage, had left us in December, his place being taken by Brig.-General Beatty, 9th Hodson's Horse. His departure was regretted, not merely throughout the Brigade, but throughout the Division. It is not too much to say that there was a pretty general feeling that he had been made the scapegoat of a senior officer.

About a fortnight after we had returned from the Cambrai Battle, the Yorkshire Dragoons (Yeomanry) were sent to the Brigade.

Since the King's Dragoon Guards had left it had been found necessary to detail British officers for many jobs that had been hitherto done by sergeants. In France, where British troops enormously bulked, police work, for instance, jobs with the baggage echelons, and, in battle, much patrol work, particularly liaison patrol work, could be done with British ranks, whereas with Indian they could not be carried out satisfactorily. The detailing of British officers, none too plentiful in Indian regiments, for this type of thing was obviously a waste of power.

With the standard of battle efficiency and fighting capacity now attained by the Indian cavalry in France, there was no question of British troops as "stiffeners" as would have been the case earlier in the War.

At the beginning of February, the Indian Regiments of the 4th Cavalry Division were moved right back to billets near Amiens, preparatory to embarking for Palestine. Jacob's Horse went to Loeuilly, an exceedingly pleasant spot. The inhabitants were very good to the men. This village had had but few troops in it, and had none of the war-worn look of so many in Northern France at this period.

It may seem strange, but the first inkling some of us had that the Indian Cavalry were to leave France was while on leave in England, when we heard it in our clubs.

At Loeuilly Captain Channer rode a wild boar and stuck it. This was the first pigstick we had had in France, though some other regiments had had one or two back in the Crecy area. The French boar is not, however, of the hard fighting brand that his Indian relative is.

The Indian Cavalry left Northern France for Marseilles not much more than a fortnight before the great German offensive was launched.

The Central India Horse and 2nd Lancers were actually in the train at Marseilles when the storm broke. It is understood that they were nearly recalled. Some of the machine-gun squadrons which had, seemingly by error, gone down there were brought back in time and did great work, under appalling conditions of demoralization and confusion.

Jacob's Horse were at the Mont Furon camp in Marseilles for about ten days or so while ships were being assembled. It was very cold, and it rained continually.

Close by was a battalion of Sambos. The hospital was full of these men, frequently minus a foot or hand as a result of frostbite. The medical people told us that the lack of stamina among them was simply astounding. The Sambos had a grievance in that they were not allowed into cafés by the French, as the Senegalais were forbidden to enter them. On Sundays they used to sing hymns all day, the intonation not being exactly of the traditional nigger breakdown type. A suggestion that they should indulge in a few "coon" songs for a change would have been received with some lack of cordiality, it is feared, for they were extremely sensitive with regard to their choral attainments.

Extreme care, moreover, had to be exercised with regard to any allusion to a possible difference in hue of the skin from that of Mr. Atkins.

We left France with very mingled feelings, particularly as, at the moment most of us left, we knew that a tremendous German offensive was about to be launched. We had no great opinion of the then type of infantry soldier in France and fully realized the weakness of our line. Had the troops been like the old Regular, or the men of 1916, things would have been different. As it was, we were astounded at our being withdrawn from the country at such a moment.

In leaving France, we were leaving the front on which everything would be decided, all other fronts being subsidiary.

At the same time, we realized that we had greater scope as cavalry soldiers elsewhere, particularly in Palestine. Some officers doubtless considered that there were greater prospects of advancement on these secondary fronts, for Indian Army officers, serving with Indian troops in France, were, it was thought then, and has been realized since, greatly handicapped in relation to those serving in Mesopotamia or even in India.

There are many officers who went through the heat and burden of the day in both France and Palestine for the whole period of the War only to find that they had been passed over by seemingly innumerable brevets, given sometimes for comparatively short service in either Mesopotamia or India, and for services for which, in France, it was the custom to award a decoration only.

With regard to the men, on actually leaving France they probably looked forward to Palestine. We know, however, that on getting there they wished they were back in France, as they found they were no nearer to India in practice than they had been before, and were far more uncomfortable.

In France, life in the line was certainly more dangerous than on other fronts. Within four miles of the line, one was never clear of shelling and there was always a certain degree of nerve strain. In Palestine there was but little shelling or no strain to speak of.

At the same time in France there were many very compensating advantages. The climate was healthy and feeding excellent. One managed to get numerous periods of rest in beautiful country in comfortable billets. One got a week's leave home about every five months. Furthermore, if one were hit and brought in, one would always be well attended in hospital. On other fronts there was always a bit of uncertainty of what kind of hospital one might get sent to, and the general degree of comfort was pretty sure to be much lower.

In France, again, the general interest was infinitely greater than elsewhere. One knocked up against all kinds and conditions of men, and was always, physically, very fit.

The general consensus of opinion was that it was preferable to have periods of danger and be badly frightened at intervals, than to live in discomfort and in not too good a climate, but be otherwise pretty safe. It was a case of " moderation in all things " really.

The psychology of the Prussian officer who longed for a war is, in many ways, understandable if one appreciates the type of war he imagined he would have, that is to say a war based on 1866 or 1870.

In both these cases victory was easily obtained, but the glory was, nevertheless, very great. The countries he fought in were rich. Billets were good, and living, when some very strenuous operations were not actually taking place, was comfortable and devoid of strain.

Furthermore, the battles fought were comparatively safe affairs as compared with those of the Great War, and a large proportion of even fighting troops were only in danger for a short time and not very often.

There was none of the long-drawn-out pounding and constant danger of this War. In 1870 one never heard of casualties amounting to 75 per cent. of the strength of units, as was by no means unusual in France. We know that the infantry would often consider themselves lucky if they got off with 40 per cent., whereas, in 1870, 20 per cent. would be thought heavy. Finally there was comparatively little mud and monotony.

To most Indian Cavalry officers, France has very pleasant memories on the whole.

War is not all one long dream of horror, as some writers would have one believe. There are many compensations, more particularly in the wonderful comradeship thereby inspired.

In so far as the Indian Cavalry were concerned, however, it must be remembered that it was never really " put through it " as the infantry were. It is true that the Lucknow Brigade in particular was in the line from mid-March 1917 till the end of February 1918, with short intervals of rest, but it was never, except at Cambrai, in a really hot spot. One's views on war are therefore rather apt to be different from those unfortunates who had to spend their days in the Salient.

The policy in France in 1917 as regards the cavalry, more particularly the Indian Cavalry, was that it was not to be subjected to heavy casualties if it could be possibly avoided. The cavalry were the only real seasoned reserve of troops in the country, being all regulars, with an exceptionally fine cadre of officers.

As regards the Indian Cavalry, the bitter experience of the Indian infantry was ever before the authorities with reference to replacement of officers. Three really heavy days' pounding might, quite conceivably, reduce the British Officer cadre to very dangerous proportions. Indian Cavalry, short of British officers, would be of less value, relatively speaking, than Indian infantry as a much higher standard of tactical training is called for.

THE MOVE TO EGYPT

For shipment to Egypt the men were to go by Taranto and the horses direct from Marseilles. The ship carrying the Regiment's horses broke a propeller. A dead horse had been thrown overboard and is said to have fouled it, though this seems a little hard to believe.

The convoy of three ships with its escort of two destroyers had, in consequence, to put into Malta. The horse decks were very hot, and horse sickness broke out soon after harbour was reached.

At first it was thought that the forage was responsible, but subsequent investigations showed that it was septic pneumonia.

The animals were all disembarked, some dying afterwards. In all, however, we lost only thirteen out of six hundred and fifty.

It may be of interest to recall that the old Scinde Irregular Horse lost no fewer than one hundred and sixty horses, ponies and camels out of about eight hundred in the two three-week voyages to Bushire and back in 1857. The heat on the return journey must, however, have been terrible.

A halt of a fortnight had to be made while the horses were recovering.

The men, when they could get away from the horses, and other duties, enjoyed Malta greatly.

On re-embarking the weather was beautiful for the first day, but was very lumpy for the rest of the voyage. The result was that most of the men were very sea-sick. As usual on such occasions, the lesser-afflicted gentry vaunted their prowess over their brethren, and Captain Blacker was informed by one gallant sowar that, such was his courage and physique, that even if the ship's captain got ill he could carry on—a truly modest man.

Another, however, attributed his malaise to the fact that, when rough, the sea gave forth some dreadful vapour which affected him. In order, therefore, to deaden the stench he filled his nostrils with flannelette soaked in rifle oil. In order to still further secure himself against this gas attack he retired to near the engine room and carefully wrapped a blanket round his head.

The rail journey to Taranto from Marseilles took five days, and that from Cherbourg, whence the drafts from England started, ten.

After leaving the French Riviera it was not of great interest, the plain of the Po and the Adriatic coast being far from beautiful.

The contrast between the Italian towns and villages, which were full of young men, and those of France, where there were none, was most marked.

Troop train after troop train of Italian troops moving north was passed. We thought they were going to France. The Italian troops were better turned out than the French and seemed a well-set-up lot of men, though not of such fine physique.

In point of fact the " poilu " of Northern France was a bigger and stronger man than Mr. Atkins. The average French soldier was, probably, a hardier man, being drawn mainly from the peasant class. We know that French troops differed greatly according to the part of France they came from, some being excellent, others far from it. They were far more uneven than British or German. Their discipline, moreover, varied enormously. Speaking generally, it was not good.

British officers on the Italian front gave divergent accounts of the Italian fighting qualities. By far the majority, however, looked upon them in the same light as the French did. The latter were perfectly outspoken and said, " Les Italiens ne valent rien."

On one point, however, all officers seemed agreed, and that was, that the Italian idea of war was oriental in its general lack of organization.

The jawans caused much amusement in the mixed troop trains owing to their getting out to fetch hot water from every engine that happened to stop where the train stopped. A Tommy gibe was: " 'Ullo, Johnny, don't take all the 'ot water out of that there engine, or poor Antonio won't be able to get to the war "—this pleasantry being specially directed when we met an Italian troop train.

A halt, and a very welcome one, was made for the day at Fienza, a small town in Northern Italy. Here we were received with an oration from the Camp Commandant, one of those modest personages we concluded must be an aspirant for Parliamentary honours, if he was not already a member of that august body. In terms which reminded one of an equally modest Viceroy, he informed us that it was extremely fortunate for us that we had found such a man to run a rest camp. Prior to his arrival, he stated, the place was a wilderness, but now no spot brighter could be found in all Italy.

Such was his attention to detail, he continued, that he had desired to obtain bathing drawers for us to wear when bathing in the Adriatic, but owing to the delinquencies of the Ordnance Department, he had been unable to obtain them.

At the conclusion of this exordium, which had lasted some forty minutes and which had been accompanied by gestures such as Lewis Waller, Beerbohm Tree or Harry Tate would have envied, we were treated to a second—from the A.P.M., a hearty young man. The burden of this was a request that the officers and gentlemen of his audience should not get drunk and visit the local brothels.

At this lapse of time, to regular officers, brought up in the strict code of "not sullying the cloth," an oration like this might seem insulting. Nevertheless, some half-dozen of the odd ninety officers on the train paraded drunk that evening when the time for entrainment arrived. None, it is hardly necessary to state, were Indian Cavalry. Furthermore, they were neither K.1 nor good Terriers. They belonged to the category now known as " N.E.T.'s."

We learnt later that this was quite a usual thing, and they were not even placed under arrest.

At the beginning of 1918 it was a hard thing to get convictions by a court-martial against an officer for drunkenness, partly owing to the lack of clear definition of what drunkenness was. It is hard enough to define it at any time. With gentry on the court, who in civil life, apparently regarded it on the principle of " 'e ain't drunk, I saw 'im move," it became doubly so.

It is not known whether the Austrians made any effort to destroy the railway line that skirted the Adriatic. Had they been British or German naval officers, however, it would have been continually smashed up.

As one travelled further south numerous thefts, attributed to the Italian sentries on the line, took place.

The country became most uninteresting.

The Southern Italian we came across was a ridiculous creature, not far removed from the Levantine.

One had often heard it said that Indian troops were not suited to a war in Europe. This remark was primarily based on the experience of the Indian Corps. An analysis of this will, however, reveal that the sepoy did extraordinarily well while he had his British officers, and, very often, when he had not. His failures, as a rule, took place when they had become casualties.

Furthermore, at the period the Indian Corps was in France, the British troops were all extremely good, and the sepoy was always compared with them.

The question is, What would those same Indian regiments have been like later in the War, say in late 1917 or 1918, had they arrived fresh? The quality of both Allied and German troops had deteriorated enormously.

From our own observation we came to the conclusion that they would have been a great success.

There was not the slightest doubt in our minds that good Indian troops, given a large cadre of British officers and N.C.O.'s like the French North African and Senegalais, could go anywhere and fight any enemy.

There were numbers of real French troops who were mediocre, to put things mildly; and Italian likewise.

It must always be remembered that there is war and war, fighting and fighting, and there are Indian troops and Indian troops, most of whom are the salt of the earth, men with whom it is an honour to serve.

Incidentally, one fact became definitely certain, and that was that Indian troops had not the slightest objection to service outside India.

The feeling that they were part of an Imperial Army appealed to them to a certain extent.

The main thing, however, was that they were seeing the world and getting well paid for doing so. The remarks passed by some of the dreadful " Wog " politicians regarding the wickedness of banishing poor Indian soldiers in countries which should be garrisoned by British troops may be regarded as bunkum in the first place and a brand of sedition in the second.

The Indian politician, with anything in common with the Indian soldier races, is yet to be found.

An Army which is condemned to be a local one can never attain the degree of efficiency an Imperial Army can. All of us longed for the latter.

One could not help contrasting the sowar who had served in France with the men who had only been in Mesopotamia and other Oriental countries.

A long train journey in even an Indian first-class carriage is bad enough, but one in an ordinary compartment on a Continental train is infinitely worse. The unfortunate men were six to a compartment, which was full of kit. Sanitary conveniences on the train were non-existent. Many windows were missing—and that in mid-winter with heavy rain and even snow. The halts for a wash or to stretch one's legs were very short, and one could never count on the time-table.

As may be well imagined, every one was delighted to reach even the dirty badly run camp at Taranto.

Most of us were at Taranto when the news of the disaster to the Third and Fifth Armies reached us. Our feelings, mixed as has been said before at leaving France, were now doubly so.

To pretend that anyone would like to be in the battle would be a ridiculous statement—the man who says he likes fighting is either a liar or an eccentric. There is, on the other hand, always a lurking feeling that one would like to take part in great events, despite the risk, and this is what most of us felt. One does hear of men who like active service, which is not necessarily the same thing, particularly in " small wars."

In these latter, however, the danger is but a fleabite as compared to that of a great war, and there is often a great deal of interest to make up for the hardships.

One voyage on a transport is very much like another. In crossing the Mediterranean in early 1918, however, the submarine menace was about at its worst. The ship the writer crossed on, a big P. & O., had some two thousand three hundred men on board, with boat accommodation for about fifteen hundred; the rest were supposed to get on to rafts. The ship was escorted by two Japanese destroyers. The decks were absolutely packed at " boat stations," and it was easy to imagine what might happen if we were torpedoed. An armed guard, commanded by an officer, was on each boat and we were ordered to carry our lifebelts everywhere.

The troops were a miscellaneous collection of drafts for Palestine, and included three hundred jawans, also of different regiments.

The discipline of these latter was everywhere commented on. It would be easy to contrast what it was in 1914, and what it was then. In 1914 it might, and quite probably would have been, as regards a portion of the men anyhow, rather on the lines of " This sahib is not our sahib; he has neither the gift of patronage nor the power of punishment, so we need not bother about him." This objectionable characteristic was by no means a rare one, particularly when dealing with men from the Punjab or Frontier. Hindus were usually more docile. As mentioned earlier, the discipline of Indian cavalry in general was not by any means too good. There were exceptions, of course, but not many. The service was a modification of the old "Irregular Horse" and carried on many of the undesirable characteristics of such formations. By 1917, however, the discipline had become excellent. Furthermore, all eleven Regiments in France had become one Corps—the Indian Cavalry—and a genuine *esprit de corps* as distinct from the original narrow *esprit de régiment* had sprung up. One had only to appeal to this and the men would at once play up, quite regardless of who the officer was.

THE BATTLE HONOURS

THE GREAT WAR

" SOMME, 1916 "	" CAMBRAI, 1917 "
" MORVAL "	" FRANCE AND FLANDERS, 1914–18 "

CHAPTER XVI

EGYPT, TEL EL KEBIR. PALESTINE, THE JORDAN.

1918.

THE eleven Regiments of Indian Cavalry were transported across the Mediterranean without a hitch, and that at a time when submarine torpedoing was almost at its zenith.

One transport, carrying a Yeomanry Regiment, was put down on the way to France. This was this regiment's second experience.

It was most unpleasant to arrive off Alexandria and then find it too late in the day to be admitted to harbour. The ship was then turned round and cruised wildly about till next day.

Some very ugly tales were floating round concerning the sinking of the *Aragon*, which had taken place early in the year as the result of some hitch in closing the gates.

To many of us, Egypt was a step backwards into a secondary theatre of war, and, what was worse, to one closer to India.

It must be remembered that at this period India was regarded by most Indian Army officers serving out of it as some dreadful antediluvian spot, to be avoided at all costs.

Certainly the products of India, in the shape of certain officers and sepoys we came up against in Cairo, and the tales one heard from Indian Army officers, some now in very high positions, who had just left the country, gave much colour to the idea.

EGYPT.

The first concentration area was at Tel el Kebir, a dreary, desolate spot.

Here the horses and saddlery were got together, and the sundry details who had sailed from Marseilles or Taranto assembled.

Tel el Kebir might have been a very fair training area, with a hard gravel gently undulating plain to work on.

It became uncomfortably warm in the middle of the day, but nothing in comparison to India. One could still wear a small cap, though it was uncomfortable.

The horses were gently exercised, which was badly wanted, as they had had no saddles on since the middle of March.

It was of interest to visit Arabi Pasha's entrenchments of 1882, about two or three miles from camp. The trench—for there was only one line —or rather parapet, is still clearly visible as well as the bones of a few dead Egyptians. Grass had evidently been used to revet. The position was a most formidable one to tackle by day, with a tremendous field of fire. It could, of course, be turned. One could easily see why a night advance was made. The ground was well suited to this, there being no obstacle of any sort.

Cairo was only three hours off, and most officers seized the opportunity to visit it.

It was decidedly disappointing, and seemed an inferior spot in every respect.

There were, of course, many places of interest to see. Later on we began to appreciate it, rather on the lines of the disreputable French proverb, "Faute de mieux on couche avec sa femme."

The fat flabby Greeks and other Dagoes disgusted one.

At Cairo we saw a brand of British soldier we had not seen since the Somme—well-set-up, decently officered infantry, some with two or even three service chevrons. Their superiority in class of officers was the most striking thing, quite a number being real officers in the accepted sense of the word, and only a proportion being the third-rate creatures that were then the rule in France.

An item of interest we learnt, was that at the very moment that Mr. Lloyd George was saying there was only one white Division in theatres other than France, there were no fewer than nine in Palestine alone, to say nothing of Salonica.

It was here one realized the extraordinarily small outlook of people on various fronts. The Allies had just received a blow in France which all but brought them to their knees. Mount Kemmel had fallen and another great German blow was known to be impending. In Egypt the normal person seemed totally incapable of realizing the gravity of the situation.

One small feature struck one, and that was that ladies wore evening dress in the hotels, a thing we had not seen since the beginning of the War.

There was, it is understood, a considerable degree of uncertainty as to what formations the Indian Cavalry were to be made into on arrival in Palestine. There was talk of an "All Indian" Division. The disadvantages of such a formation have already been alluded to.

It was, therefore, decided to use the Yeomanry Regiments merely to replace the British Cavalry of the old 4th and 5th Cavalry Divisions.

There was no question of a " stiffener " being required for the purposes of battle. It was a matter of policy.

We and the 29th therefore joined a formation then termed the 8th Mounted Brigade, 1st Mounted Division, later known as the 11th Cavalry Brigade, 4th Cavalry Division. The Middlesex Yeomanry was the British unit.

4TH CAVALRY DIVISION
PALESTINE

Major-General Sir G. de S. Barrow, K.C.M.G., C.B.

10TH CAVALRY BRIGADE.

1/1st Dorset Yeomanry.
2nd Lancers.
38th Central India Horse.
(1/1st Buckinghamshire Yeomanry and 1/1st Berkshire Yeomanry ceased to belong to E.E.F. 19th June 1918.)
10th Cavalry Brigade Signal Troop R.E.
17th Machine Gun Squadron.

11TH CAVALRY BRIGADE.

1/1st County of London Yeomanry (Middlesex).
29th Lancers.
36th Jacob's Horse.
(1/1st City of London Yeomanry, and 1/3rd County of London Yeomanry ceased to belong to E.E.F. 2nd July 1918.)
11th Cavalry Brigade Signal Troop R.E.
21st Machine Gun Squadron.

12TH CAVALRY BRIGADE.

1/1st Staffordshire Yeomanry.
6th Cavalry.
19th Lancers.
(1/1st Lincolnshire Yeomanry, and 1/1st East Riding Yeomanry, ceased to belong to E.E.F. 2nd July 1918.)
12th Cavalry Brigade Signal Troop R.E.
18th Machine Gun Squadron.

CORPS CAVALRY REGIMENT.

1/2nd County of London Yeomanry (ceased to belong to E.E.F. 28th May 1918).

DIVISIONAL TROOPS.

20th Brigade R.H.A.
1/1st Berkshire, Hampshire, Leicestershire Batteries Brigade Ammunition Column.
4th Field Squadron (late No. 6) R.E.
4th Cavalry Division Signal Squadron R.E.
4th Cavalry Divisional Train (Nos. 999–1002 Companies R.A.S.C.).
10th, 11th, 12th Cavalry Brigade Mobile Veterinary Section.

On reorganization, August 1917, the Division joined the Desert Mounted Corps as the Yeomanry Division.

Six Regiments were withdrawn in April 1918 for service as machine-gunners on the Western Front, the vacancies being filled by Indian Cavalry Regiments.

The Division was renamed the 4th Cavalry Division in July 1918, and became the 10th, 11th, 12th Cavalry Brigades respectively.

5TH CAVALRY DIVISION
PALESTINE

Major-General H. J. M. MacAndrew, C.B., D.S.O.

13TH CAVALRY BRIGADE.

1/1st Gloucestershire Yeomanry.
9th Hodson's Horse.
18th Lancers.
(1/1st Warwickshire Yeomanry ceased to belong to E.E.F. 19th June 1918.)
13th Cavalry Brigade Signal Troop R.E.
19th Machine Gun Squadron.

14TH CAVALRY BRIGADE.

1/1st Sherwood Rangers.
20th Deccan Horse.
34th Poona Horse.
14th Cavalry Brigade Signal Troop R.E.
20th Machine Gun Squadron.

15TH (IMPERIAL SERVICE) CAVALRY BRIGADE.

Jodhpore I.S. Lancers.
Mysore I.S. Lancers.
1st Hyderabad I.S. Lancers.
15th Kathiawar I.S. Signal Troop.
I.S. Machine Gun Squadron.

Divisional Troops.

Essex Battery R.H.A.
Brigade Ammunition Column (less 2 Sections).
5th Field Squadron R.E.
5th Cavalry Division Signal Squadron R.E.
5th Cavalry Divisional Train (Nos. 1103, 1044, 1104, 1105 Companies R.A.S.C.).
13th, 14th, 15th I.S. Cavalry Brigade Mobile Veterinary Sections.

The 5th Cavalry Division landed in Egypt March 1918, and was brought up to strength by the inclusion of Yeomanry and Imperial Service Cavalry who had been serving with the E.E.C. Joined the Desert Mounted Corps on 2nd July.

Brigadier-General Claude Rome was the Brigadier and Major-General Barrow (Scinde Horse) the Divisional Commander.

Just before the Sharon operations Brigadier-General Gregory took over the Brigade, General Rome having gone on leave.

The Jodhpore Lancers, who had been brigaded with us in France since April 1917, were shifted to the Imperial Service Cavalry Brigade, 5th Cavalry Division. The Brigadiers who had commanded in Palestine remained on, but the Indian Cavalry officers who had had Brigades in France had to go back to India after wasting a long time hanging about Ismailia and other places on the lines of communication.

A good many staff changes took place, for the Yeomanry staff officers, for the most part inexperienced at any time, were now of less value than ever as they knew nothing of Indian troops. In respect of staffing generally the advent of a number of regular officers proved a godsend in the Desert Corps.

The forward concentration area was Deir el Bela, a few miles south of Gaza.

Regiments marched as far as Kantara and entrained thence. It reflected considerable credit on the horsemastership that the percentage of even minor sorebacks and galls in the three days' march from Tel el Kebir was infinitesimally small, considering the fact that the horses were very soft and fat after their month on board ship and loafing about. It was pretty hot too.

The Indian ranks were extremely sniffy about Egypt, and Kantara especially. They were particularly contemptuous over the Kantara cinema, which they considered, strange to say, greatly inferior to those of "Marsellaise," as they called Marseilles.

PALESTINE.

Deir el Bela was a pleasant spot close to the sea. There was excellent riding country and the bathing was good.

The whole area was an admirable one for any kind of training.

A certain amount of bother was caused by horses getting colic from the sand in their forage. They recovered after a time, but a good many animals died.

Some of us visited Gaza, which was a fairish ride off. One could not help being struck with the strength of the place. It had tremendous observation and a very long open field of fire

We did not know much about the First and Second Battles of Gaza beyond the fact that they had been muddled, almost, if not quite as badly as Loos, which had hitherto been regarded as the worst-fought battle of the British Army.

From accounts of officers who had fought both Germans and Turks, the latter, particularly the Anatolian, was every bit as formidable a man as the Boche individually, provided he was even reasonably fed. The writer also heard this from a German he met in Jerusalem in 1925. This German said the average issue of rations to Turkish soldiers on the Amman front, where he was, was about two days a week and, late on in 1918 even that was uncertain.

As we had heard a good bit of the mounted operations in Palestine we were, not unnaturally, a little curious to contrast the Palestine troops with those of France.

To be perfectly frank, they were not in the same street, and it is not reasonable to suppose they ever could be when one realizes the very severe training the British Cavalry went through before the War. A slightly superior class of man cannot possibly make up for long, detailed and careful grinding in the duties of a soldier.

We very soon found we had nothing whatever to learn from any of the mounted troops in the country, and in dash the sowar from France could show the way to most. There is always a tendency to imagine that actual war experience can make up for training. Provided, however, this training is run on up-to-date lines it has been proved, time and again, that the peace-trained soldier will beat the partially trained man with only war experience.

There is a certain adage concerning Frederick the Great's mules which is applicable.

Although we had had a good bit less actual open war fighting than the Palestine mounted troops, we had had the enormous advantage of some excellent generals to train us behind the line.

PALESTINE.

*The Imperial War Museum.
By kind permission.*

NEAR HEBRON.

*The Imperial War Museum.
By kind permission.*

ENAB.

By the foregoing remarks it is not intended to decry these troops, who had done extremely well.

On seeing them, however, we felt we could have done even better.

Major-General Godwin, M.G. Cavalry in India, who actually commanded a brigade in the Beersheba-Jerusalem operations, and more particularly at Al Mughar and Abu Shusheh, gave his opinion to the writer that Regular troops would have done 75 per cent. better.

A somewhat similar remark might be made with regard to nearly all troops raised in the War. There would, however, be this difference, that the proportionate variation would be much less. It is infinitely harder to train cavalry than any other arm.

General Godwin's opinion, coupled with that of another Brigadier, who was a highly placed staff officer in the Jerusalem operations, is as follows :—

The mounted troops in Palestine were not cavalry. They were fairly well-trained mounted rifles—a very different thing.

They were not as good as the Yeomanry brigaded with British cavalry in France, who had the enormous advantage of being properly disciplined and trained. Many Yeomanry officers, if not most, were wanting in initiative owing to lack of knowledge.

The men were indifferent with their arms. Until regular officers arrived at the beginning of 1917 a good number of minor mishaps owing to ignorance and lack of training occurred.

As the War went on the lack of proper grounding in their work, on the part of the officers, began to affect the training in periods of rest.

The two Colonial Divisions were not altogether satisfactory owing to irregular discipline.

The Higher Command could never be certain that they would do things in the manner desired. They were, on occasion, rather difficult for other troops to work with, owing to their not keeping strictly to their jobs, or by turning up in places or at times which upset calculations.

Sometimes it was uncertain that a job would be done at all if the " Boys " did not want to do it. The result was difficulty in counting on anything with them which required careful calculation.

The main forte of the Colonial formations was the wonderful physique and initiative of the men.

The Horse batteries could in no way compare with regular Horse artillery —it is, indeed, unreasonable to expect that they ever would.

The machine gunners were indifferent.

From the above it may be deduced that had we only had regular cavalry in Palestine in the Beersheba-Jerusalem operations the Turk might have received his *coup de grâce* in 1917.

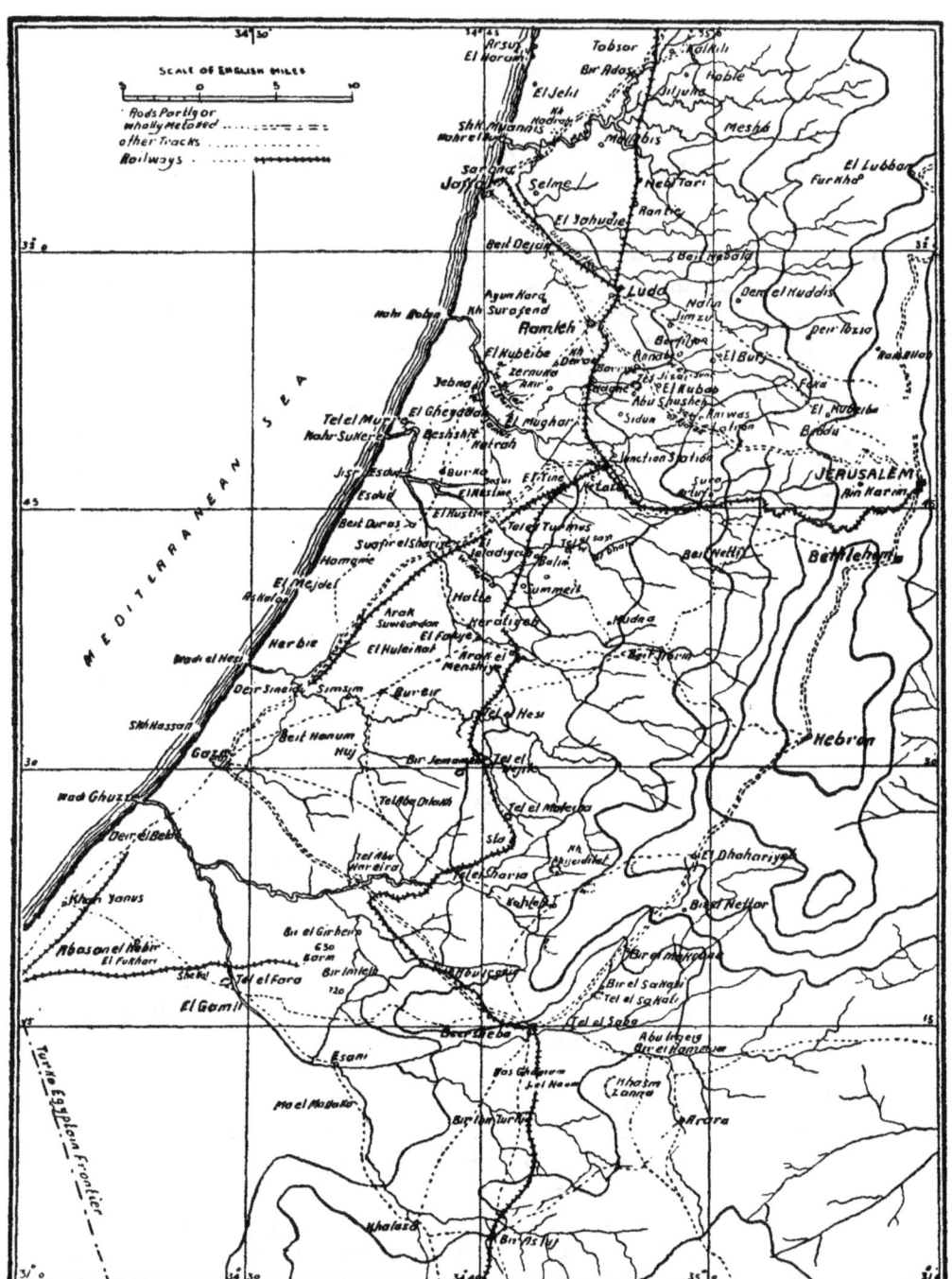

PALESTINE.

While we were concentrating at Deir el Bela, the Es Salt raid took place, and the Yeomanry were pushed down to the Jordan ahead of us. The accounts we heard of this bump-stunt, more particularly of the retirement, or rather bolt, down the mountains, gave one the impression that we had only escaped a very serious disaster by the skin of our teeth.

A brigade of Australian Light Horse, posted in the Jordan Valley so as to secure the mouth of the passes into the mountains against an advance from the north, had yielded ground in a most extraordinary manner, after losing only some seventy men. They had thus lost us eight guns, and the whole existence of the troops up in the mountains had been imperilled.

Though the affair was a tactical failure, it was a strategic success, as it made the Turk so nervous of his communications at Deraa that he extended his line to breaking point.

The departure of the Yeomanry from Bela was noticed by one of our batmen shouting out to a confrère: " 'Ere, Raven (the gentleman's name), come and look at the Scots Greys marchin' out." We then saw an extraordinary procession of Yeoboys riding white donkeys at the tail of their column. They were the officers' batmen. Every Yeomanry officer was allowed one donkey for his kit. These animals became great pets, and amply showed that the term donkey as one indicating stupidity was very far from correct, for their intelligence was astounding. The Indian Cavalry did not have them.

In Egypt we started a regimental mess in contradistinction to squadron messes.

On the 4th May, we marched for the Jordan. The route passed Deir Seneid, Beit Duras, Junction Station, Enab, Talaat el Dumm and Jericho.

As far as Beit Duras the country was practically a desert of hard undulating sand, with water from wells in villages only. These villages occurred only about every six or seven miles. They were, in all cases, surrounded by cactus hedges and were of the mud and rubble variety, as dirty as any Indian village.

The local inhabitants were very few and far between, but were highly unpleasant Arabs—not nearly such fine men in physique as the Buddoo of Mesopotamia.

It was quite easy to see that these villages must have been formidable places to tackle, with the ground all round as bare as a board.

They had a lot of orange trees.

The country in appearance was very similar to that bordering the Baghdad railway towards Nisibin, about thirty miles out of Mosul, but was not nearly so well watered. It was an ideal one for cavalry or artillery —rolling downland with very few obstacles, if any.

At Beit Duras the Zionist villages begin. These in appearance resemble the Prairie towns one sees in the cinema. It is about here that the country gets richer or, rather, less of a desert and the grape area commences.

At the time we passed through, such crops as there were—they were not many—had been cut.

One could not help being struck with the brand of Jew without the hooked nose one encountered, also with the number with ginger hair.

It rained heavily one march in the Philistean Plain and the greater part of the night. Fortunately we had had some excellent bivouac sheets of the German pattern issued to us, and these kept us dry. We carried these on the horse. A pattern of chagul, slung on the side of the horse, and not under the belly as had been the case in India, had also been issued.

At Junction Station we came on the stony area and began to enter the foothills.

At Latrun, about ten miles further on, we definitely entered the mountains and struck the Jerusalem Road. The ground about here, one recollects, was simply yellow with orange peel passing troops had left.

The mountains were terraced in a most extraordinary manner, an aeroplane photo giving the impression of a contoured map. They were almost bare, but here and there one would come on a few olive trees.

The villages passed on this road were prosperous. The houses were well built and, in most cases, quite fit for European habitations. This was accounted for by the pilgrim traffic, there being sundry monasteries and hospices *en route*.

One had a wonderful view from the top of the pass, right over the Philistean Plain and the sand-dune area, to the Mediterranean. El Enab was a pretty bivouac in a deep valley under olives. The ground had, however, been fouled by passing troops. In view of the fact that it was continually used it would seem that a good deal more might have been done to keep the place clean. We were to strike a far fouler spot at Talaat el Dumm (The Samaritans' Hut). From Enab we had to march at night as the Jerusalem-Jericho road was reserved for lorries by day.

The road grew very hilly, and we had to walk and lead the whole way.

Jerusalem was passed in the moonlight and very wonderful it looked, with its battlemented walls.

We passed Gethsemane, a crude garish enclosure with cypress trees and Russian domed shrines, and at Bethel we began to descend.

We saw before us a huge uncanny trough, seemingly bottomless, with mountains behind, on which the brightest star we had ever seen in our lives was beginning to rise. This was the Valley, with Moab behind. The star was Venus, just then at its brightest.

JERUSALEM.
FROM THE JERICHO ROAD.

The Mosque of Omar and the walls of the Holy City are in the centre, and the Valley of Jehoshaphat and the Jewish Cemetery in the foreground.

*The Imperial War Museum.
By kind permission.*

JERICHO.

*The Imperial War Museum.
By kind permission.*

The hills this side were not terraced, and resembled those on the Indian Frontier. The road became steeper and steeper and was about a foot deep in dust. It was, fortunately, enormously wide or it is difficult to see how lorries could have managed it.

This march from Enab to Talaat el Dumm was fatiguing to a degree and very long—in fact, some of us actually fell asleep in our saddles, a thing we had never done before

As one descended, so did one's spirits. Verily the East was upon us.

At Talaat el Dumm one's spirits were about zero. This beauty spot was about on a par with those delectable places like the mouth of the Gomal and Bolan, where every one so loves to pass the summer.

The place was shut in by the normal brand of Frontier hill, bare and brown.

The ground was foul to a degree. Flies simply swarmed. Flies were bad enough anyhere in Palestine, but here they were the limit.

One of us found the biggest and blackest scorpion we had ever seen, under a stone in the mess shelter.

From about 09.00 a continuous stream of lorries in dense clouds of white dust began to pass down to Jericho. At 13.00 they began to go up again, and continued till about 15.30.

Every blade of grass or grain of corn consumed in the Valley had to be carried down there, and as there were usually at least two cavalry divisions down there it can be realized what this meant.

Some of us climbed one of the hills by the bivouac, and a great relief it was to get to the top out of the stuffy sweaty valley. From here the view was very wonderful. We could see the Dead Sea, beautifully blue and cool-looking. The Valley itself was extraordinary to look at, with clouds of dust. One could see nothing of the Jordan. Everything was very hazy and brown coloured.

We left the main road at Talaat el Dumm, and took an old Roman road—one with a gradient of about 1 in 1, it seemed—with an enormously deep nullah on our left. This was the Wady Kelt that ran past Jericho.

We reached the Valley as dawn was breaking and saw a mournful dreary-looking plain, with some green trees and houses ahead, the modern Jericho.

This place was not altogether unlike a dirty variety of Tank or Loralai, with a number of pomegranate trees and vines.

It was a relief to reach it, for the air was fresher. Some Turkish aeroplanes were bombing one of our bivouacs as we passed through. They did a good deal of damage to animals but did not molest us. This bombing was a regular performance for our first week or so. The 'planes flew over, unmolested except from Archies, every morning.

We heard that our airmen had then bombed their aerodrome, which kept them quiet for the rest of our stay. We never saw one of our own 'planes the whole time we were in the Valley. It is understood that air pockets were very bad for flying.

There were some quite good houses in Jericho, hospices for pilgrims, but most were of the ramshackle, tumbledown variety.

We had now struck vegetation the same as one might find in the Punjab or Sind. There were quantities of Ber trees with enormous thorns—the traditional tree from which the " crown of thorns " was made—and big, rather prickly bushes.

It was quite easy to rig up shelter from the sun, which was very powerful, though nothing like an Indian sun. Many Yeoboys went about in small caps though it was mid-May.

The soil was, however, the trying thing, being that soft powdery dust commonly met with on the Frontier. Any move made a positive cloud. With the slightest rain it became greasy.

The appearance of the Valley was like many in Baluchistan, the only difference being that it was covered with bush, some as high as a horse, but most about four feet high. On the Turkish side towards the Dead Sea it became dense in parts.

The hills on either side were, however, much higher. Jerusalem, not more than fifteen miles away direct, was some four thousand feet up, for the Dead Sea is twelve hundred feet below sea-level, and the ground from Jericho falls but gradually in that direction.

The horrors of life in the Valley have been greatly exaggerated.

The flies and dust were the trying things, but in some bivouacs, notably in the Ghoraniyeh Bridgehead, we had little of either.

The mosquitoes were both deadly and annoying in certain portions, notably close to the varying wadys, where there was water. In most other places they did not bother one.

At one or two bivouacs dust devils of enormous size would sweep through, but they were not so formidable as their Mespot brethren. Those one saw outside Baghdad were records. The Hinaidi camp devils were of different layers of colour, in accordance with the incinerators of the camps they passed through, the 7th Dragoon Guards layer—presumably through *esprit de corps* as belonging to the " Black Horse "—was always black.

Possibly the worst feature of the Valley was a curious sense of oppression from being at such a low level below the sea.

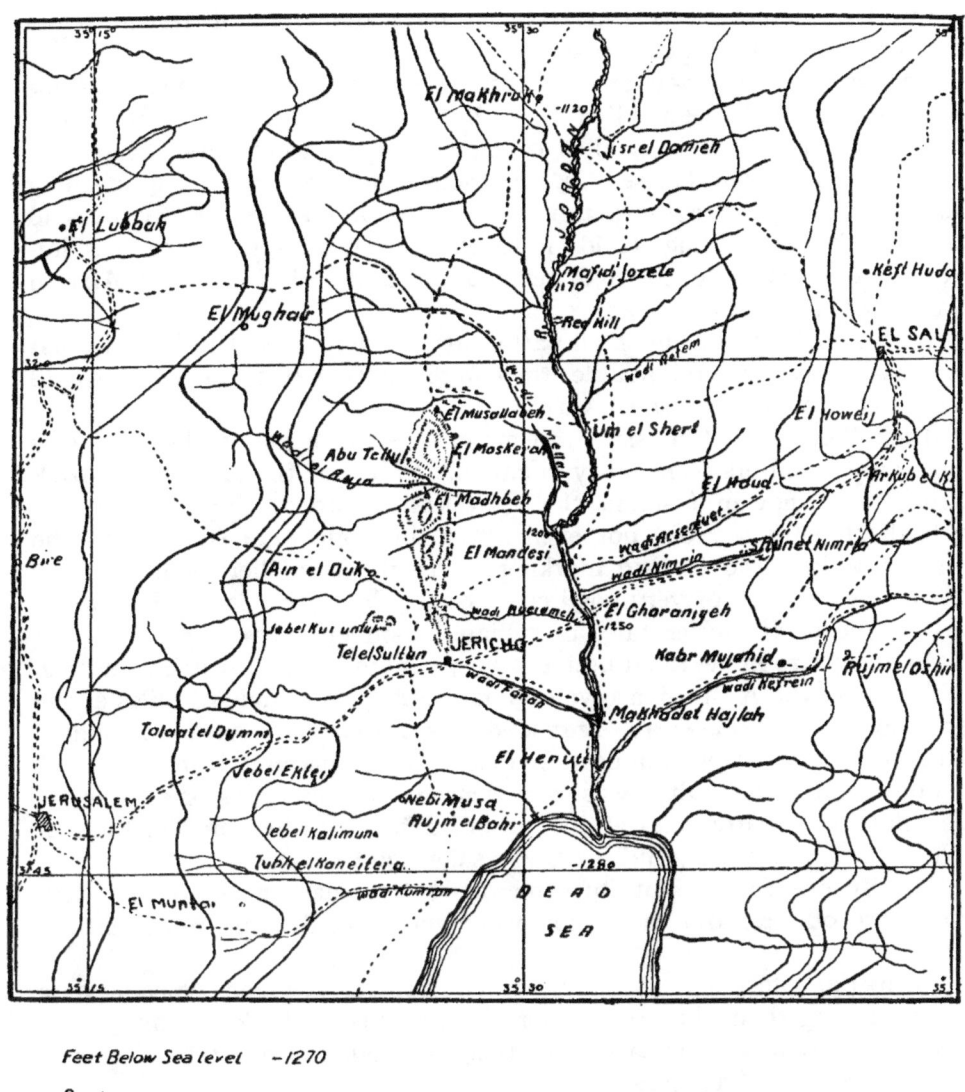

THE RIVER JORDAN.

Our first bivouac was about two or three miles out of Jericho, close to some Australian Light Horse.

This was our first view of the Aussie of Palestine. The stench of some unburied horses, to leeward of them but to windward of us, proclaimed that their notions on disposal of carcasses differed from ours.

The term "Light Horse" is a misnomer, for the men were anything but light. They were quite the finest body of men physically we had seen, the "Tins" being children to them. Their appearance was impressive and distinctly original, reminiscent more of the South African War than of the Great War.

It was obvious that, in small parties at all events, if not in large formations as is quite understandable, they were the real stuff, men you would like to go into a dirty show with.

Their "uniforms" consisted, in many cases, of a pair of breeches and boots only. Gaiters were fairly common. Shirts of the British greyback pattern were not in fashion, the sleeveless, collarless singlet being the garb affected. Many did not even affect this, but were stripped to the waist, a white band of skin marking where the bandolier went.

The men seemed of very good class, better than the infantry in France, and one heard far fewer tales of ruffianism among them.

As one got to know them better, a very genuine liking arose between us.

A visit to the Australian bivouacs on the Auja, a couple of miles above the Ghoraniyeh bridgehead, reminded one rather of a visit to Buffalo Bill's Wild West show, minus the squaws, wigwams and feathers.

Considerable difficulty was experienced in "spotting the orficer." His relations towards the "Boys" seemed to be rather on the lines of "Now, boys, don't spit, and for God's sake don't call me Alf."

Socially one found, not infrequently, better men in the ranks than among the officers, and men, moreover, who seemed to be more natural leaders.

"Imperial officers," as they termed British Regular officers, were popular among them, but there seemed an antipathy to Yeomanry. One noticed a good many indications of this, and remarks made by Colonials since the War tend to confirm it.

The Australian Official History has overstepped the limits in this respect.

On the march down to the Valley some of us had been regaled by Yeomanry officers with tales of indiscipline and ruffianism on the part of the Australians—for the New Zealanders were not included.

Later on some of us heard the Australians giving vent to their notions on the Yeomanry, or more particularly Yeomanry officers. They descanted on the ignorance and lack of interest in their job displayed by the latter. The amount of transport required for Yeomanry messes had astonished them.

The rock-bottom basis of the dislike seemed social, and, between the lines, one gathered that certain Yeoboys, who deemed themselves leaders of society on their own local dungheaps, had patronized the Colonials.

It may have been a coincidence of course, but the first night we doubled the horse guards. The Woordi Major, a confirmed gambler, on hearing the word " double," is supposed to have been unable to resist the temptation to re-double them. In the very early dawn an Australian gentleman was observed undoing the picqueting rope of the Colonel's horse. The conversation that ensued was, however, of a most amicable nature. The jawans explained their point of view in French and Hindustani, mixed with Punjabi, together with the expression " No Order Johnny," which had always made things clear in dealings with Atkins in France. The Aussi replied in Sidneyese, a dialect not dissimilar to that spoken in the neighbourhood of Seven Dials (hence the word dialect), mingled with Arabic picked up in Cairo, the words " Imshi " and " mafeesh " predominating. It is quite probable that he merely wished to satisfy himself that the horse was not lame, some of his comrades having said it was. Quite possibly he merely wished to take the animal outside the lines, give it a feed of carrots, and then bring it back. We know that Australians are very fond of horses.

A story was current to the effect that, in the Es Salt raid, an Aussie colonel, whose regiment had, after an infinity of labour, occupied a position which the Turks had been thought certain to hold but which they had never gone near at all, spotted a turning movement against it by another band of the " Boys."

This kind man was so upset at the thought that these latter would be done out of a fight that he called up one of his squadron commanders and addressed him thus: " Look down there, Joe, at the poor old 20th Light Horse. Won't they be angry if they climb all this way up and then find no Johnny Turk up here? Just you get a few of your boys and fire some shots over their heads—that'll cheer them up."

History does not relate what the 20th Light Horse said.

While on the march down there were one or two indications that things were inclined to be of the *laisser aller* order. The staff work in several particulars was slipshod and lacked the precision of France. From what one heard there is but little doubt that there was a good bit of letting things slide in the Yeomanry, and there were a good many signs, such as their bad turn out and their rather sketchy march discipline, that we were in for a type of war not to be compared with that to which we had been accustomed.

We moved at a walk the whole way from Bela to Jericho and only dismounted to lead when the hills became steep—and this was done on the initiative of C.O.'s.

Speaking with much experience on the subject of long marches with cavalry, the writer has no hesitation in saying that this was absolutely unsound. It was extremely fatiguing both to man and horse. The actual pace at which a march should be carried out necessarily varies with the ground and condition of the horses.

If animals are in very poor condition, the best thing is to lead long distances and trot very short ones.

Our feeding, naturally, did not come up to that of France, for the country was a desert. The only local produce was oranges, and down in the Valley they were hard to get.

The bread was bad, and our vegetables were tinned. When one considers that we had the whole of Egypt at our back, it is surprising that the bread should not have been better. The writer recollects, however, the bad feeding at Kantara later in the year, and if the feeding was bad there it is quite understandable what it would be miles up the line.

CHAPTER XVII

THE JORDAN VALLEY. THE PHILISTEAN PLAIN.

FROM Jericho the Jordan was invisible, flowing as it did in a trough about one hundred or one hundred and fifty feet below the Valley floor. It was distant about four miles, the plain in between being almost open and very good going for movement across the Valley, though interrupted by astonishingly deep nullahs for movement up or down it. These nullahs had usually dense vegetation and quite big trees in them, simply swarming with mosquitoes—most of them anopheles of the worst kind.

They were most formidable obstacles.

We took over the outposts, in the sector outside the Ghoraniyeh bridgehead, on the 17th May.

This was a far pleasanter spot than our dusty bivouac and life was distinctly more interesting.

The bridgehead was held by the Imperial Service Infantry Brigade. The Jordan is a most disappointing stream, not much bigger than many canals in India. Only two pontoons were required to span it.

Owing to the heat haze and dust it must have been difficult for the Turks to see the bridge properly even from El Haud, the hill which dominated the whole Valley, and on which they had an observation post. Regular shrapnelling of this bridge on French lines would have made it an extremely unpleasant spot.

There was dense jhow jungle on either side of the river for some two hundred to three hundred yards, and the banks were sheer about five or six feet above water-level. Difficulties of bridging were primarily due to this jungle. The steep banks rendered swimming horses impossible.

The Turk had bombed bivouacs during our first few days in the Valley, but for some reason did absolutely nothing to the horse lines in the bridgehead, where he would have obtained a fine bag, either by bomb-dropping or machine-gunning, particularly had he elected to appear at times when crowds of horses were watering. In connection with watering, some quite unnecessary casualties occurred from Turk shelling. It was not as though there was only one spot where it was necessary to water. With very little trouble on the part of the brigade staff officers plenty could have been made available.

As said before, the work of junior staffs left much to be desired.

One feature noticed with regard to many troops, other than Regular, was that they seemed far more inclined to tolerate, quite possibly through ignorance, things which Regular Commanding Officers would very soon cry out about.

The writer can recall one or two rather ridiculous " come downs " of swelled-headed young staff officers, when confronted by irate regular C.O.'s who knew what was what.

There was, both in France and Palestine, on many occasions, far too little care taken to see that unnecessary casualties to horses did not occur. In 1918 it will be remembered that, in France, severe measures had to be taken to see that horses had adequate or even reasonable protection against aerial bombing.

The fronts of the Ghoraniyeh and Auja bridgeheads were watched by mounted picquets on the same lines as taught before the War.

Picquets averaged thirty men, including telephonists, and were about a mile, possibly under, from the wire of the bridgehead works. This distance seems small, but there was a belt of bush in front in which it would have been too risky for them to have been posted.

On the other side of this bush were high crops which the Turks used to go down and cut. On our side of the Jordan there were few if any crops.

The actual distance to the foothills from the bridgehead was from three and a half to four miles, and these foothills represented the Turk outpost line.

Our patrols would ride through this bush at irregular intervals, and constantly bumped Turkish parties, either cutting crops or laying up for our men. In most cases these Turks were on foot, but in one or two instances mounted combats took place. The average strength of these patrols was four men, and this worked very well.

Almost every day some encounter took place, usually, but by no means always, turning to our advantage. The sowar showed up brilliantly, and opened the eyes of all other mounted troops to what they could do.

These affairs had an enormous moral effect on the men, which stood them in good stead when the final drive took place.

It was the Indian Cavalry who imported the, to the Turk, highly objectionable practice of charging him at sight. The latter had never been treated in this manner before, and in two definite instances in which Jacob's Horse patrols were concerned, successes were obtained which, had there

THE RIVER JORDAN.—GHORANIYEH BRIDGEHEAD, NEAR JERICHO.

The Imperial War Museum. By kind permission.

*The Imperial War Museum.
By kind permission.*

MOUNT OF TEMPTATION, NEAR JERICHO.
(The Head-quarters of the 4th Cavalry Division were situated in the clump of trees in the centre.)

been any hesitation, would have resulted in serious casualties. In three cases out of four the Turk would throw up his hands.

In our first week in the bridgehead, Jacob's Horse took more prisoners than had been taken since the British had gone down into the Valley, not, of course, including the Amman and Es Salt raids.

There were, incidentally, a good many traces of these raids still left in front of us.

British corpses still lay at the mouth of the Wady Nimrin and there were numerous small dumps of bully beef and biscuit out in "No Man's Land."

The prisoners were, for the most part, rather miserable specimens, badly fed but very fairly well clothed. Not many were genuine Turks, but included a mixture of Arabs, Syrians and miscellaneous creatures. Some were almost starving.

The contrast between them and the big, hefty, red-faced and almost Boche-looking soldiery one can now see at Smyrna and Constantinople was such that one would hardly imagine that we were fighting the same people. The Turkish soldier evidently varied as much, if not more than, the Italian or French.

One thing noticeable in Palestine was that there was never the slightest rancour against the Turk. It is, in the writer's opinion, a very rare thing to ever find an officer who has had dealings with them, who will not say he both likes and admires them.

The Turkish artillery, posted apparently in the Wady Nimrin inside the foothills, would shell picquets, if they bunched, as well as formed bodies coming within range. Extraordinarily little damage was done, however.

Certain Brigade Head-quarters, notably one under the Mount of Temptation, caught it badly and lost a good many horses.

Divisional Head-quarters right back at Jericho were shelled by a gun, said to be eighteen miles away, known as Jericho Jane, but little damage was done.

There was none of the tremendous gunfire of France and the Turk was too far off to machine-gun. Provided one kept within a mile of the Jordan one could hack ride, with impunity, for a stretch of about three or four miles up or down stream, the chief danger being the excessive zeal, or rather infernal stupidity, of some of our own posts who might fire on one.

The trough in which the Jordan flowed at Ghoraniyeh varied in width on the Turkish side from about one hundred yards to four hundred, and movement along it could be easily concealed. The defences were on the edge of the clay cliffs which formed the fringes of the trough and the position was a strong one. The general effect when viewed from the river was of a series of clay hills. From the Turkish side, however, it was very hard to see anything. At the same time, had the Turks even two batteries of 5.9's well provided with ammunition tried shelling by sudden crashes, the bridgehead with the number of horses in it, would have been a most unpleasant spot and some dreadful stampede would have occurred. He did but little more than put over a breakfast ration of a dozen shells. He could have done more harm by saving up this ration for a week and giving us a burst of gunfire when we had been lulled into fancied security.

Although the Turk artillery demanded respect, the art of using it in the best manner was apparently unknown. In August, certainly, he became more active, but concentrated his hates more towards the bivouacs north of Jericho, but even then in not the most deadly manner. A number of gunners with the Turks were Austrian and it might have been thought that they would have made the Turk wise. It will, however, be remembered that it was not until the British went down to the Italian front that any really high-class artillery work was done and the Austrians in Palestine had evidently not had the lessons passed on to them.

On one occasion we brought a couple of 60-pounders to shell the Turk O.P. on El Haud, the hill eight thousand yards off which overlooked the bridgehead and the whole valley. They effected nothing. A light Turk gun commenced retaliating and killed six infantry sepoys who were suffering from undue curiosity and standing close by—rather a humiliating experience.

It must be confessed that to us, straight out from France and accustomed to extreme precision, as well as to regarding the Boche with great respect, things in the bridgehead struck one as being somewhat casual. There was emphatically the idea " they are only Turks and we need not bother." As a school for war it was by no means the best.

A combat took place with some Turks, at the end of our first tour in the bridgehead, which caused a good deal of amusement on account of the colossal noise of the firing and the total absence of casualties on either side. Our Pathan squadron under Lieutenant Vosper had been sent out to recover a ford over the Wadi Rame about three miles south-east of the bridgehead from which the Turks had ejected the Yeomanry. It advanced at the gallop with great éclat until the prickly bushes stopped the horses. The squadron then advanced with the bayonet and recovered the post under a very heavy fire indeed, both of rifle and machine gun. It is true it was hard to see the men advancing through the bush, but we were, none the less, amazed at there being no casualties.

On relief from the bridgehead we moved to a very pretty vineyard, Ain Hujla, about three miles south-east of Jericho. The place was owned by Greek monks, who also ran two monasteries at Kasr el Yahud. This was quite a good bivouac, shady and cool. The eternal flies were, nevertheless, always with us, and in a nullah close by mosquitoes swarmed. We were, however, clear of dust. The Regiment had the task of watching the right bank of the Jordan between the Ghoraniyeh bridgehead and the Dead Sea. The only two possible points of passage were at Makhadet Hajla and El Henu. It was at the former place we had originally crossed when moving up for the Amman raid. The river was full from snow water, and both "fords" were about sixteen feet deep.

Makhadet Hajla is the traditional point where John the Baptist baptized converts. If it were anything like the depth it was when we were there it must have been a most thorough baptism, for the banks were sheer, and about four feet above the water.

Mosquitoes simply swarmed at these passages, and doubtless it was they who first infected the men with that deadly malaria which proved such a scourge in the great advance of September. One squadron was responsible for each passage, keeping the minimum number of men by the river so as to avoid the mosquitoes, which were, in point of fact, a good deal more dangerous than the Turk.

At Makhadet Hajla there was a rickety raft and we had a dismounted standing patrol across the river.

Patrols moved at irregular intervals between our squadrons and Dead Sea Post about four miles off and the Ghoraniyeh bridgehead, up the right bank.

Dead Sea Post was held by the infantry. It was a pleasant spot but dull. There was always a breeze, and the flies, mosquitoes and dust were not in nearly the same strength as in other parts. There were some motorboats manned by bluejackets. The petty officer in command of one boat had just arrived from the Iceland patrol, as a change of air. Bathing in the Dead Sea was a curious experience, as the water was so extraordinarily heavy. It was extremely good for boils, sores or any skin affections and doubtless the prophet Elisha's instructions to Naaman were really to bathe in the Dead Sea and not the Jordan which had no healing properties. One's bathing clothes absolutely stood up stiff as though they had been starched while drying after a bathe.

The Greek monk at Ain Hajla was one of those cheerful characters one would so like to take out to dine in Paris or London if one wanted to enjoy oneself. He gave us a bottle of wine—at a price. The mess president was weak enough to pay for it—and even the regimental sweepers appeared incapable of drinking it. In the course of a particularly jovial conversation, connected chiefly with death and pestilence, he informed us that no man had been known to come out of a summer in the Valley alive. A recently joined second-lieutenant at once wrote out an application for appointment as 20th Corps Commander, the residence of that officer on the Mount of Olives, some four thousand feet above us, having taken his fancy.

There were a certain number of pig in the jungle bordering the Jordan and an inventive medico liaised with the machine gunners for a drive. The pig were to be driven across a barrage of two machine guns. The affair succeeded in bagging three squeakers.

Some muddy fish were caught which proved a most welcome addition to our very indifferent rations.

There was a considerable difficulty about transport on our first arrival in the Valley, and it was a difficult matter to feed the mass of horses and men down there. The Valley itself produced nothing and every blade of grass even had to come down by lorry. This grass—if it could be described as such—was Indian.

It can, therefore, be easily understood that one did not live as well as one did in France.

One of the earliest crises that arose was a whisky famine, or rather a famine for any kind of alcoholic stimulant. In the relaxing climate of the Jordan one needed a pick-me-up. One individual considered a bit of liaison work with the infantry and other units in the bridgehead might do good service generally. He was affably received, but was merely given tea and condensed milk.

Driven desperate, he proceeded on what he considered an absolutely certain draw—the Australians. This time he was still more affably received but merely received black strong tea minus milk and sugar. It was a terrible shock!

A particularly tantalizing feature in the Jordan was the number of sisi and chicker about—huge coveys of them. In our early days, however, no one had any cartridges.

The interior of the monastery El Yahud was worth visiting. The most extraordinary pictures adorned the walls of the chapel. In particular, one of Elijah going up to heaven in a chariot on top of a dust devil was singularly impressive. Of a truth Christianity, as both practised and preached, in Palestine was barbaric.

The Regiment only remained at Ain Hajla a week, when it was relieved and proceeded to a most unpleasant bivouac north of Jericho on the Wadi Neuieme. Here flies, dust and mosquitoes were at their best and it was very hot.

On the 15th June a divisional reconnaissance in force to the foothills on the east border of the Valley to the south of the Wadi Nimrin was made from the Ghoraniyeh bridgehead and from a bridge made at El Henu.

The Regiment reached the foothills and the reconnaissance established the fact that the Turk outposts extended right down to the Dead Sea. It, in all probability, also kept the Turk alarmed of another raid on Amman.

At the beginning of July the Regiment returned to the bridgehead.

On the 4th a very fine piece of work was done by Jemadar Dur Khan, Scinde Horse. A body of Turks had been in the habit of annoying our left picquet on the Shunet Nimrin track by sniping it at night. Dur Khan took out thirty men, and while on his way to his lying-up position, was suddenly fired on at close range. He promptly charged with the bayonet. Owing to the darkness and bush most of the enemy succeeded in getting away, but he nevertheless bagged three prisoners. This officer subsequently greatly distinguished himself in the famous rearguard action of the Scinde Horse outside Hillah, on the occasion of the Manchester Column disaster at the outbreak of the Arab Rebellion in 1920.

In mid-July the Division moved back to the Philistean Plain for a change of air, much needed, for the sick rate was increasing greatly. The health of the British troops was getting serious, as many of the men were somewhat run down before going into the Valley.

It was a great relief to get clear of the place, for life, even on outpost, was boring to a degree.

The climate at Jerusalem, two thousand eight hundred feet above sea-level, was delightful, but it was rather hot in the Philistean Plain by day, though the nights were very pleasant.

For some reason, presumably transport difficulties, no reinforcements had been sent to units in the Valley, with the result that, what with sickness and other casualties, units were rather diminished. There were some two thousand five hundred men waiting at Kantara to reinforce thirteen regiments.

The casualties in patrol affairs had been very slight—only some three men and two horses a week. Considering that the patrols came under fire practically every day and sometimes twice, it will be seen that small bodies of horse moving fast in loose order are not very vulnerable, even if under fire from very close ranges as these were. It is true that in rifle shooting the Turk had nothing to throw up his hat over, but our experiences against the Boche in early 1917 had been the same—and these were very good troops.

Some officers visited Jerusalem. It was an interesting place for a day or two with an excellent climate. The only religious building for which one had the least respect was the Mosque of Omar, a really beautiful edifice, built on the site of the old Temple. The Church of the Holy Sepulchre disgusted one, though in a measure most interesting. The feuds of the various creeds describing themselves as Christian had to be placated by Mussulman Police.

The Jews' wailing place was interesting.

Jewish school children were marched down to kiss the stone foundations of the old Temple. Their "wailing" was assisted by cuffs on the head from their pedagogues.

A visit to the Church of the Holy Sepulchre was marred by howling bands of priests conducting services and pestering for alms in every one of the numberless side chapels.

In July, some cases of desertion among Pathans occurred in the Indian Cavalry. These were the first that had ever taken place in the War. They were not confined to Trans-Border men entirely, as one or two from the Vale of Peshawar had gone off as well. Jacob's Horse had none, though at this period the composition of the Regiment was about one-third Pathan, one-third Sikh and the rest a mixture of Tiwanas, Awans and Derajatis. As a consequence it had been decided to return all Trans-Border men to the Base, for certain infantry units, of great repute before the War, had had numerous and serious cases of desertion from among them.

The writer was at Kantara when the men arrived there. While the conduct of the men from Jacob's Horse was excellent, that of men from other regiments gave serious grounds for anxiety. They appeared to be on the verge of mutiny and care was taken to see they had neither ammunition nor rifles.

The grievance of most of the men appeared to be that they thought they had been unfairly dealt with.

Thanks, however, to the admirable conduct of the two Jacob's Horse Indian Officers, Ressaldar Abu Khan and Jemadar Khan Shirin, both Adam Khel Afridis, the whole were brought to reason very soon. This was a very great tribute to these officers, and, as every one at the Depot said, to the tone and discipline of Jacob's Horse.

The Regiment had, it is not too much to say, the name of being disciplined above the average, despite its being composed of men who were normally of the most turbulent character of any recruited in India. Any officer who has had dealings with the extremely jungly gentleman of the Derajat will bear out the latter part of this statement.

On reaching the Philistean Plain the Regiment camped a few miles from Yebnah. It was near Yebnah, it will be remembered, that Napoleon had only escaped capture by the skin of his teeth in 1798. The country was a first-class one for training in cavalry work. Not far away were Al Mughar and Abu Shusheh, where the Yeomanry had carried out the two most successful mounted attacks of the War, and a couple of tactical rides under General Barrow, who had commanded the Yeomanry Division at the time, were held on the sites. The Regiment furnished a squadron for demonstration purposes at the Desert Corps School at Richon, a Zionist colony founded by the Rothschilds.

This was a school, primarily, for Australian and New Zealand officers promoted from the ranks, but young Yeomanry and Indian Cavalry officers also went there. The Colonial officers were very genuine men, and were extremely well liked by our young officers.

At Richon there were the second largest wine vats in the world. The Palestine wine is coarse and, of itself, not particularly palatable. It is exported in large quantities to Bordeaux for blending with French wines.

The Jewish inhabitants of this part of the country were, at the time, pleasant enough.

It was later on they began to be objectionable, the Arab even being preferable.

Not far away from the Regiment's Camp was Ludd (ancient Lydda), the traditional home of St. George and the Dragon.

Reinforcements at last arrived from Kantara, and badly needed they were too as the horses greatly outnumbered the men.

These reinforcements had just been put through a refresher course of Individual Training at Kantara, under a scheme which had just been started under the writer. Yeomanry reinforcements had been included for training purposes but not for administration.

The experience was an interesting one, for one gained an insight into the extraordinarily backward state of training in India.

The men from Depots were, in almost every case, undeveloped, slipshod and badly turned out. Those from regiments were better, but were by no means the equal of the men from France. When one returned to India after the Armistice one got an inkling of the type of work done in many cavalry Depots, which amply explained things.

It had always been the custom to leave at the Depot, individuals not wanted at the Front, together with a few drill instructors and usually indifferent instructors at that.

In wars where the unit had only been absent a few months at the outside, as was the normal thing, the evil result was not so great, for casualties were, as a rule, negligible.

When, however, it came to a Great War, things were very different. One wanted really smart good men to get a move on with the new drafts. The writer was greatly struck in talking to French officers on this point in 1914. They fully realized its importance, and took care to see that drill instructors received their full share of decorations and rewards. One had heard a good bit about the French soldier being fed on *gloire* and thirsting for battle, but from what the writer observed, they were under no illusions in this respect, and stated, bluntly, that a soldier was doing his job just as much training men behind the line as up in front.

In many ways the French seemed to have a far greater idea of *la grande guerre* than we had at that time.

One definite lesson was learnt from Kantara experience, and that was that all Indian Officers and N.C.O.'s must have a thorough grounding in elementary recruit instruction, particularly in making men work smartly. Pre-War Indian Cavalry officers can testify to the almost complete inability of the average Indian Officer or N.C.O. in this respect. Although there were some two thousand three hundred Indian Cavalry reinforcements at Kantara for a long time, it was with the utmost difficulty some half-dozen instructors could be found in the whole lot. One of these, Dafadar Mahomed Niwaz, Scinde Horse, had been the spot instructor at the Imperial School at Zeitoun. He afterwards greatly distinguished himself in the Arab Rebellion, rising from Dafadar to Ressaldar in four months.

A rather absurd incident occurred when the Kantara Depot guard was turning out to the Base Commandant, a late Adjutant of the Grenadier Guards who always took the keenest interest in the Indian Cavalry. The trumpeter's effort at sounding was so horrible as to cause us to investigate the matter. With some diffidence the man thus explained the disaster:

" I was eating my food when I heard ' Guard Turn Out.' I ran out and fell in very smartly indeed. The Dafadar said, ' Carry Lance ' before I could swallow all my chupatti. I attempted to sound with some bits still in my mouth but they blew down the trumpet and I have had great difficulty in clearing the pipe."

" The Guardsman who dropped it " has its parallel in " The trumpeter who stopped it."

The smartness and turn-out of the Indian cavalry guard at Kantara was frequently commented on.

It had been the intention to rearm all sabre regiments in the Division with the lance, but time did not permit before the great advance.

Jacob's Horse remained, therefore, a sabre unit.

The lances were, however, received at Damascus. In the frequent patrol combats that occurred in the Valley there were but few recorded instances of a Turk being sabred as he either surrendered when charged, or got under a bush where he could not be reached.

There had been no fewer than seventy speared in patrol fights alone by the 4th Cavalry Division.

As the number of sabre units exceeded the lancer units, the figures are significant—for there was no reason to suppose that the sabre units were any less dashing.

The lance, held a little below the point of balance, gave an additional reach of a yard over the sword, and the moral effect seemed paralysing.

So far as mounted fighting is concerned, the lance is, without question, the better weapon.

The armament of the horse soldier is, however, a matter of compromise between the respective demands of fire and shock. Where shock will bulk, the lance is the weapon, but where fire will, the sabre.

The type of enemy and the country one is working in must also be considered. Thus, it was found that in the flat open country of Mesopotamia, it was so hard to approach without being seen miles off that the prospects of successful shock were not great.

The Arab was too elusive, and the Turk had too great fire power as a rule.

There is not the slightest reason why good cavalry should not be equally capable of using both.

To pretend that any very high degree of training, in either the lance or the thrusting sword, is essential, is to ignore facts, for the Yeomanry had killed large numbers of Turks at Al Mughar and Abu Shusheh with the sword.

No man in his senses could claim that they were highly skilled as swordsmen.

One squadron of the Scinde Horse, very short of swords, afterwards killed a number of Arabs at Kufa without difficulty. These swords had only been received some few weeks before and there had been no time to train the men in their use at all. The thrusting sword requires but little else than to be held out straight and it will go through with very little impetus. The cutting sword requires considerably more practice, in order to cut with the edge leading and, above all, to avoid cutting the horse.

Many senior officers can recall old horses minus a ear, the result of some misdirected effort on the part of its rider with a sharp sword. Some can recall the wicked words uttered by indignant C.O.'s on hearing of the catastrophe.

So far as the lance is concerned, the chief danger is sticking it into one's neighbours, but it is significant that the men of Jacob's Horse were more efficient with it after little or no training, than they had been with the sword. Furthermore, in Damascus, the people frequently spoke of their dread of the lance.

Speaking generally, training in almost any form of *arme blanche* is primarily to give confidence and strength. In practice, in war there is seldom if ever any actual "fence." The majority of men bayoneted will, on investigation, prove to have been more or less helpless at the time.

The maxim, "Thrice armed is he who has his quarrel just, but four times he who gets his blow in first," is singularly applicable.

In mid-August, the Division returned to the Valley.

The Regiment went into the bridgehead and stayed there until the 11th of September, when the concentration for the great advance began.

Turkish patrols seemed more active than before and a number of encounters took place.

On the 20th August, Jemadar Ataullah and seven I.O.R.'s met twenty Turks, scattered about in groups under bushes, with two machine guns. He charged, sabring two and capturing one. On being fired at from the foothills and seeing the approach of a Turkish troop he withdrew. He had two horses killed and one wounded.

On the 26th Dafadar Maluk Khan was heavily fired on by a similar body of Turks in the very early dawn. His horse, and that of another man, was shot. With great gallantry, Sowars Ursula Khan and Zargun Shah carried off the dafadar, and a man who was wounded, on their own horses, all under a close and heavy fire.

The following day a troop under Ressaldar Iltaf Hussein, in the very early dawn, came upon a number of Turks with a couple of machine guns. The Ressaldar promptly charged, but his horse was shot within twenty yards of the enemy machine gun. He was last seen firing his revolver at Turks who were closing in on all sides. Sowar Zarghun Shah, mentioned above, sabred two Turks, but his horse was also shot and the man was last seen shouting instructions to his comrades.

As the troop was greatly outnumbered it was impossible to rescue them. This affair was rather an expensive one, as we lost one I.O. missing, three men believed killed and two wounded, together with two horses. The scrub and bush made lying up for our patrols a comparatively easy affair, though, on the other hand, it facilitated a concealed approach for us.

In the afternoon, a party, carrying a Red Cross flag, was sent out to bring in the bodies. The Turks had hitherto always been very good in this respect, but this time they fired on it.

The party pushed on to the scene of action. Both Iltaf Hussein and Zargun Shah had been removed, which probably indicated they had been wounded, but the body of Rahim Khan was found quite close up to the position, while a pile of cartridge cases, evidently fired from a machine gun, were within five yards of Iltaf Hussein's horse.

The firing on the Red Cross would seem to have been justifiable in this instance as a warning that the Turks did not want us hanging about. No one was hit as a result of it.

Iltaf Hussein was traced to Damascus, but not beyond. He must have died of wounds. He was a very fine officer and a good football player. He had, like many other Pathans in the Regiment, been educated at the Kohat Mission School.

Incidentally we had had no cases of mutilation of bodies when we were in the Valley. They had, however, occurred on other parts of the line.

It is more than doubtful if the genuine Anatolian Turk did the mutilating. It was more probably the work of Arabs or Circassians.

About midnight, the 31st August, the enemy made a small attack against a picquet of the Regiment west of a hut known as Jacob's House. They were driven off. This was the last encounter of the Regiment prior to the Battle of Sharon.

As stated previously, the casualties in the patrol actions as regards proportion of men to horses worked out very much the same.

In the nine actions in which they occurred we had nine men killed, six wounded, ten horses killed and four wounded.

These were spread over sixty-six days and it is safe to say a patrol came under fire at least every second day.

About this period a wonderful formation came down to the Valley. It consisted of a much mixed brigade of Sambos, Zionist Jews and Cape Boys. The last named were a very fine lot indeed.

It is not known whether the Ikey Mos, who adorned the Royal Fusiliers with their presence, adopted the motto of that famous corps. That by which they were more generally known, however, was " No advance without security."

The preparations now being made for the great advance were mainly directed to keeping the enemy in the dark as to the impending blow on the Sharon side.

It was of particular importance to keep any thinning off of the mounted troops on the Jordan flank hidden from the enemy.

The measures to this end were both amusing and interesting.

Lines of dummy horses were erected. As air reconnaissances showed that sacks filled with brushwood threw equally good shadows they were afterwards used instead.

Horse teams dragging bushes about created dust where it was normally to be seen.

Tents were left standing and special parties detailed to light fires or create the impression that they were occupied.

Finally the Sambos, Ikey Mos and Cape Boys were kept marching backwards and forwards between Talaat El Dumm and Jericho so as to give the impression that troops were coming down to the Valley. The return march to Talaat El Dumm was always carried out at night.

CHAPTER XVIII

THE GREAT ADVANCE. THE BATTLE OF SHARON. MEGIDDO.

ON the evening of the 11th September the Regiment turned its back on the Valley for the last time. It marched in Brigade to Talaat el Dumm, the 10th (formerly Mhow) Cavalry Brigade joining the column at Jericho.

This was nineteen miles.

The next night the march was continued to El Enab, twenty miles. Both of these marches were extremely fatiguing, the first being appallingly dusty in addition.

Ramleh was reached early on the morning of the 17th. Little rest was possible all that day as surplus stores were being dumped.

All great-coats, extra picqueting gear, and spare blankets were left behind.

Every man was to carry one day's iron and two days' emergency rations. Twenty-one pounds of corn were to be carried on the horse and one day's grain in the "A" echelon limber wagons.

The actual weight carried by the horse thus worked out to much the same as that normally carried, viz., about seventeen stone. The extra grain was carried in sandbags across the front arch of the saddle.

After a tiring day the march was continued to Yazur, near Jaffa, where the troops remained until 04.15 on the morning of the 12th, when the final move to the assembly for the Sharon Battle was made.

There were enormous orange groves at Yazur and concealment from aeroplanes was a comparatively easy matter.

These night marches were all more or less fatiguing, although the actual average distance covered worked out to only about fourteen miles per night for five nights.

It must, however, be remembered that the pace at night is almost always slow, or, if it is not slow, it is irregular. Horses, moreover, require watering and feeding the following day. One's rest, therefore, is broken continually. With the infantry this is not the case. The rank and file, as well as most officers, can rest pretty well the whole time.

As the marches to follow were the greatest ever executed by large form-

*The Imperial War Museum.
By kind permission.*

THE JORDAN VALLEY—A TYPICAL STRETCH OF COUNTRY.

THE RIVER AUJA.
(One of two pontoon bridges over which the 4th Cavalry Division crossed.)

19th September, 1918.

*The Imperial War Museum.
By kind permission.*

ations of cavalry, and were carried out with astonishingly small waste in horseflesh, it may be as well to state the condition both men and animals were in before the start.

The men of the 4th Cavalry Division were somewhat run down owing to their long stay in the Valley. There had been a good many cases of fever. The British troops, in particular, were not very fit.

The 5th Cavalry Division had been out of the Valley some time when the advance started and had had time to pull together.

The horses were in nothing approaching the condition they were in in France—it had been rather depressing to see how they had steadily fallen off owing to their indifferent feeding. They had not had hard work, fortunately, and had had lots of water.

The animals were of a good stamp, though not so good as those now in regiments in India. There was a great mixture of breed among them. The bulk were Walers, with a few English and American horses thrown in. The pack-horses were coarser than the others, and it has been argued that the greater proportion of casualties among them was in a measure due to this. The most probable explanation, however, lies in the dead weight they had to carry and to the impossibility of easing them when men dismounted to lead or for very short halts.

The plan of operations was given out at Yazur, viz. :—

On the morning of the 19th September, the infantry were to break through on the Sharon Plain and wheel north-east on Tul Keram. The 4th and 5th Cavalry Divisions, followed by the Australian Division, were to pass through the gap in their rear.

The mounted troops were to cross the Mount Carmel Range dividing the Plain of Sharon from the Vale of Esdraelon and seize, firstly, El Afule, the junction of the lines running from Nablus to Haifa and Damascus, and, secondly, Beisan, in the Jordan Valley, thus severing the lines-of-communication of the Turkish 7th and 8th Armies and their means of retreat by the Valley.

The 4th Cavalry Division was to cross via the Musmus Pass and the 5th Cavalry Division by a track in the hills a few miles further to the west.

The Australian Division, less one brigade which was to be with the XXI. Corps, was to follow through the Musmus Pass.

It was an open secret that the two Indian Cavalry Divisions had been placed in front, as cavalry, trained to " ride in," were wanted.

The Australian Division had just been armed with swords and would, doubtless, have " ridden in " just as well as anyone else, but their senior officers, it is understood, were not altogether united as regards abandoning the " mounted rifle " idea.

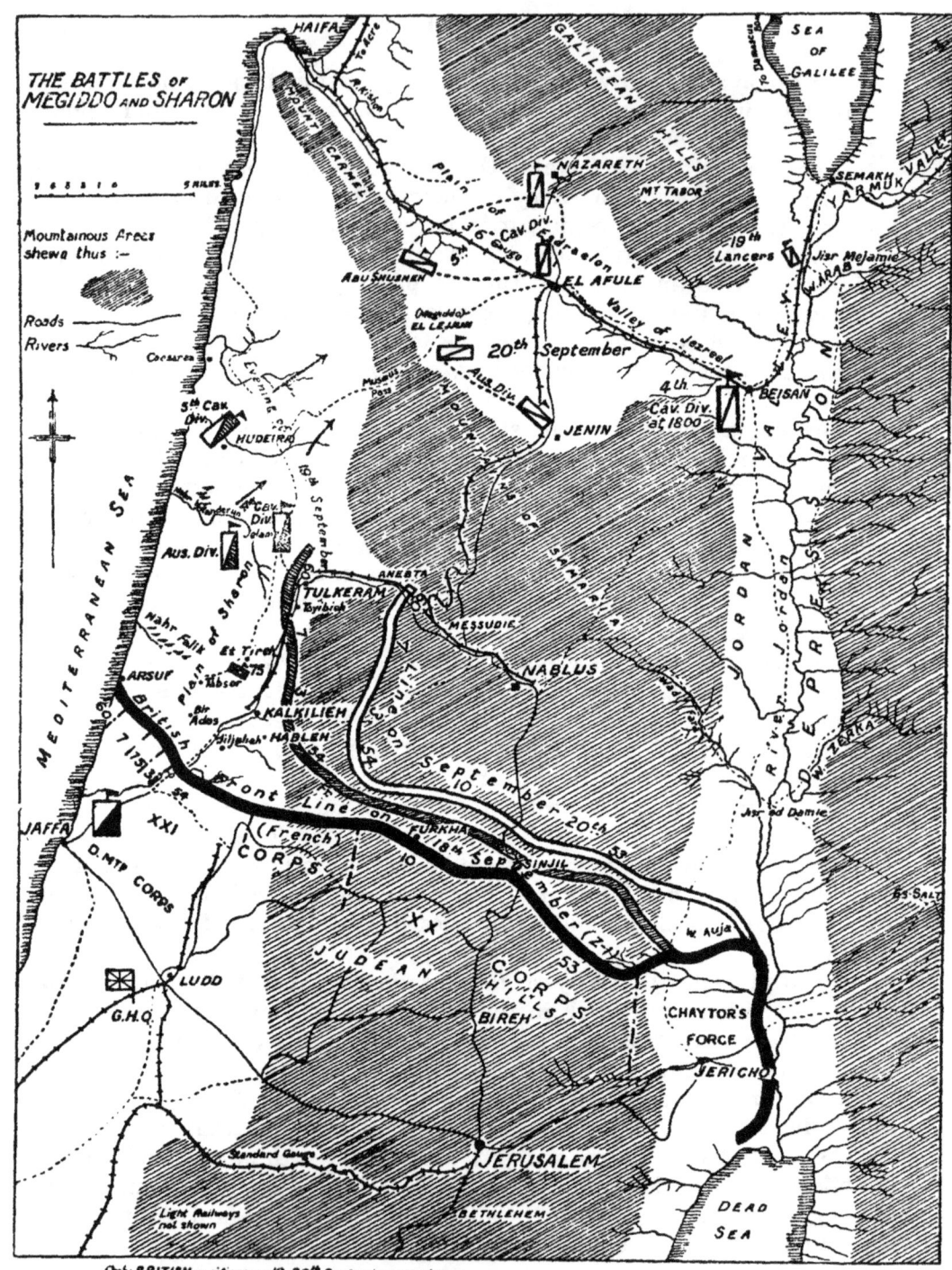

The Anzac Division, for some inscrutable reason, persisted in the " mounted rifle " notion, and was therefore detailed for operations about Amman.

There had been discussion with regard to the assembly positions for the cavalry.

The orders were that on no account was it to be ahead of the line of the heavy artillery—some batteries being as much as five thousand yards behind our front-line wire.

The argument put forward by the XXI. Corps Commander was that the presence of cavalry among infantry making an attack would be an impediment.

Above all, there was danger of the fire of the batteries being masked.

Urgent representations by most able cavalry officers that such a danger could be obviated by good staff work were overridden. Only five weeks before, at the Battle of Amiens on 8th August, it had been clearly demonstrated that cavalry could, quite well, assemble well forward among the infantry without either getting in the way or masking batteries. The fatal results of having cavalry too far back had been shown at Cambrai, where the delay imposed had enabled the enemy to bring up fresh troops.

In the case of the Sheria Battle of 7th November 1917, the time lost in getting the mounted troops through had enabled the Turks to form rear-guards.

Experience in France had, moreover, shown that the word " go " for the cavalry had to come from a *cavalry* commander well forward and in close touch with the leading infantry. This lesson had been emphasized in many of the tactical rides held in Palestine prior to the Sharon Battle.

In the case of this battle, however, the permission for the cavalry to move was to come from the XXI. Corps.

In view of the serious consequences that might ensue should the Turk have time to either bring up fresh troops, form rear-guards, or man the passes in the Mount Carmel Range, Major-General Barrow (Scinde Horse), Commanding 4th Cavalry Division, went so far as to imperil his career by ignoring these orders.

A letter explaining the situation runs as follows :—

Copy of letter from Lieut.-General Sir G. de S. Barrow, regarding the point of assembly of the 4th Cavalry Division at Battle of Sharon, 19th September 1918.

" It is true that the XXI. Corps orders prohibited the advance of the cavalry until all the infantry had cleared the front. I knew this order would not do from my point of view, and I also knew that it would be quite possible for the cavalry to pass through the infantry without impeding it.

There was just one difficulty, and that was the existence of a large marshy track in front of my line of advance, shown on the map and reported to be impassable for cavalry. There was a risk that this would seriously hamper my advance; however, finding my arguments of no avail, I decided to disregard the Corps orders.

I attached myself to General Fane's * head-quarters, and the moment the route was reported clear we went through the gap. It was more good luck than anything that brought the head of the column through the gap just at the very moment we were able to pass through, although I think the work of my staff deserves great credit.

There was not a single hitch. My orders, given me verbally by General Allenby, were that on no account was I to become involved in any fighting at this period of operations. Had we dashed through on the very heels of the infantry as they went for the first trench, we should certainly not have been able to avoid fighting. I think this question has already been gone into fully in " The Cavalry Journal."

The reason the 5th Cavalry Division was able to get a start of us was that they were right on the coast and were able to move by a track under cover of the cliffs, which protected them from the Turkish fire.

It had always been recognized by General Head-quarters that this Division would get a good start, and the original plan had been for me to follow the 5th Cavalry Division.

Lord Allenby, however, agreed to my strong protestations and allowed me to take my own line. I never saw the XXI. Commander on the morning of the advance."

At 04.15 on the 19th September, Jacob's Horse left bivouac at Yazur for the point of assembly in the 7th (Meerut) Divisional area. This was reached at 07.00. Lieutenant Watkins and a squadron had been sent on ahead as a pumping party for the horses of the 4th Cavalry Division. As the Regiment was for vanguard the wisdom of detailing a squadron from it seems questionable.

In France this job, as well as making the cavalry track, would have been done by the 10 per cent. reinforcements. In Palestine, for some reason, apparently supply, these men were right back at Kantara.

The cavalry track was made by details from other units in the Division, It must be understood that this was child's play to the work that would have to be done in France. Neither the trenches nor the wire were in any way comparable.

The infantry gained their objectives by 06.30, meeting with hardly any

* Commanding 7th (Meerut) Division.

resistance. The Turk was absolutely surprised and swept off his feet. The speed with which the whole of the subsequent operations were conducted had an enormous amount to do with the huge success. The Turk, once settled down, is a dangerous man, and the best method of dealing with him is to rush him and keep him moving.

At that hour the 5th Cavalry Division, advancing under the cliffs by the sea, passed through the line. It was shelled by some of our ships, but the casualties were light.

Time now had to be allowed for the 60th Division, which was on the extreme left, to swing north-east on Tul Keram.

The 7th Division on its right also began to swing. By the time the 4th Cavalry Division began to pass through, or rather behind, the latter, the battle in these parts was over, though its roar could be heard to the east.

Jacob's Horse, as vanguard to the 4th Cavalry Division, moved off at 08.30.

The head of the Division cleared our front-line wire at 08.58, its order of march being the 11th, 10th, and 12th Cavalry Brigades.

The Turkish defences were in no way as formidable or as complicated as German and the difficulty in traversing them was not great.

The Regiment passed through the rear elements of our infantry, then moving north-east.

On clearing them the advance was pushed at a steady walk and trot, no notice being taken of the numerous Turkish stragglers encountered on the way. These latter had no desire for anything but surrender. There was no opposition and only a few ill-aimed shells flew over from time to time.

The instructions were clear that the advance was not to be held up by enemy on the flanks if they could be avoided. The seizure of El Afule was to dominate everything.

The going was good, over the gently rolling Sharon Plain.

The first objective was Kakon, where the Turks had a rear line of defence, distant some eighteen miles from the rendezvous and twenty-three from bivouac. This was to be reached by evening.

The Regiment covered a wide front as vanguard. The advanced squadron was fired on from some trenches near Zeleffe, north of the Nahr Iskanderuneh.

Another squadron, immediately despatched round by the right, charged and the Turks threw up the sponge. Some one hundred and fifteen prisoners were taken.

The Regiment reached Tel el Dhrur about 16.00. This is four miles north of Kakon. It watered and fed here, less two squadrons detached about a mile and a half to the right and left fronts.

The 10th Brigade then took over advanced guard.

About eighty stragglers were captured in this neighbourhood, poor miserable creatures with no desire to fight.

In the meanwhile the 12th Brigade occupied Kerkur after very slight opposition.

The detached squadrons were called in, but that commanded by Lieutenant Watkins found all the water finished.

It was, by now, getting dusk and it was possible to see a light or fire near a village that looked about a mile or so off. The squadron was, accordingly, directed to try its luck there. The distance must have been nearer four miles and the inhabitants had to be "persuaded" at the revolver-point before they would allow water to be drawn from the well.

It took a very long time to water. On moving back to where the Regiment had been, it was found that the column had moved off without leaving a trace. It was dark and tracks ran in all sorts of directions.

Finally the squadron stumbled on the tail of the Division. Not a sound could be heard of the move of this big column a hundred yards off.

Jacob's Horse had moved off at 21.15, after a halt of about five and a half hours.

The Division was to move through the Musmus Pass, the 5th Cavalry Division being some way off to the left. A serious hitch now occurred.

Proper arrangements to reconnoitre the entrance had not been made, with the result that, although the vanguard regiment of the 10th Cavalry Brigade—the 2nd Lancers—moved on it correctly, the remainder of the Brigade went astray, one regiment of the 11th Cavalry Brigade following it.

General Barrow arrived on the scene in his car at this juncture and spotted the mistake.

He at once detailed the 12th Brigade (in France the old Sialkot Brigade) to push on in the right direction and our own to follow it. The 10th was then to join in in rear.

Some armoured cars pushed ahead of the cavalry and proved of the greatest value in reconnoitring the very tricky gorge the pass was found to be. Nevertheless, a delay of two hours had occurred, and this might have been very serious.

Had the company the 2nd Lancers found sitting round a fire on the northern exit of the pass, succeeded in manning it there might have been the greatest difficulty in driving them out.

The two hours, however, enabled people to get a bit of a rest and every one stretched themselves out on the ground—some slept in a manner which did not show many signs of ever waking.

Had it been very dark there would have been some risk of tired men

THE BATTLE OF SHARON—THE COMMENCEMENT OF THE ADVANCE.

19th September, 1918.

*The Imperial War Museum.
By kind permission.*

VIEW OVER MEGIDDO TO THE ESDRAELON VALLEY.

20th September, 1918.

*The Imperial War Museum.
By kind permission.*

being left behind. Fortunately the moon had risen soon after the head had gone astray. This enabled the 10th Cavalry Brigade to retrace its steps across country.

The 2nd Lancers debouched from the north end of the pass at about 03.00, when they found the Turks, who were absolutely surprised and surrendered at once. The 2nd pushed on, still ignorant that the brigade in rear had gone astray.

On approaching Megiddo their advanced scouts were fired on. A brilliant mounted action followed, with the result that a whole battalion surrendered. This battalion was an L. of C. unit hastily ordered up to man the Musmus Pass.

Jacob's Horse reached the north end of the pass about 07.30. It watered and fed at Lejjun.

Here Colonel Green, who had commanded the Regiment since November 1915, was directed to take over the 10th Cavalry Brigade, Major Nixon temporarily taking over the Regiment.

While at this place a number of Turkish mounted men rode up, evidently unaware of our presence. They were charged by a squadron of the 29th and some one hundred and fifty prisoners were taken with no loss to ourselves.

The Esdraelon Plain is flat, but rather cut up with watercourses. The going is bad owing to black cotton soil and high thistles. In their Megiddo attack the 2nd Lancers had been lucky in finding a patch less full of holes than most.

Jacob's Horse marched again at 09.30 and reached El Afule at 11.30. Everything here was quiet. There had been a mild skirmish on the vanguard (2nd Lancers) approaching the place, and an enemy aeroplane even came down thinking all was safe. Some lorries also drove in under the same impression. This gives some idea of the absolute surprise our rapid advance had caused.

El Afule was, in a way, interesting as it was an aerodrome and wireless station. It was also a railway junction with some supply trains waiting there.

There were a number of German wireless operators and aerodrome mechanics, who surrendered without putting up a fight.

The wireless installation, incidentally, had been put out of action by our aereal bombardment that had preceded our offensive.

The supply trains were tapped and both men and horses had good feeds. Lucky officers found some bottles of champagne.

There was no sign of any approach of the Turkish main bodies from the Nablus direction.

It will be remembered that the Australian Brigade that moved southeast from Lejjun on Jenin in the afternoon captured some Germans who had not the foggiest idea that British cavalry had been only twelve miles to the north of them since 09.00 that morning.

At 14.00, after two and a half hour's rest, Jacob's Horse marched, in Division, on Beisan.

The 10th Cavalry Brigade again furnished the advanced guard, with the Dorset Yeomanry as vanguard.

The 19th Lancers remained at El Afule until 19.00 so as to hand the place over to the 5th Cavalry Division. It then moved off to seize the railway bridge over the Jordan at Jisr Mejamie.

The bridge was reached by dawn the next morning, after a very difficult march across almost impassable country. The Regiment had by then covered some eighty miles in the fifty hours that had elapsed since it had left the Selmeh orange groves.

The official despatch states the 5th Cavalry Division occupied El Afule before the 4th. This is incorrect.

As the advanced guard of the 4th Cavalry Division had to push ahead fast, so as to secure Beisan as soon as possible, it found its progress impeded by covering a wide front. Its commander therefore decided to risk it and move the bulk of the brigade by the main road. It became necessary, therefore, for the troops following to put out flank guards.

On entering the Vale of Jezreel the right flank guard of the 11th Cavalry Brigade, furnished by Jacob's Horse, came upon some huts that had evidently been passed by the flankers of the advanced guard without being searched. On looking inside, the jawans found them full of Germans, who were mostly asleep.

The latter were so absolutely surprised that they surrendered without a word. It was curious to see parties of a dozen or so come across with only one or two men as escort. They were exceedingly fine troops, well equipped and well turned out.

Had they not been surprised they might have made themselves exceedingly nasty.

The Vale of Jezreel is not unlike the Miranshah Valley, the hills on either side being of the same type. Beisan was reached at 20.00 (20th September), every one, as may be imagined, extremely tired.

No opposition had been met on the advanced guard entering the place, and there was still no sign of the Turkish forces to the south.

*The Imperial War Museum.
By kind permission.*

THE RIVER JORDAN AT JISR MEJAMIE.

THE VALLEY OF JEZREEL AND MOUNT GILBOA.
(Convoy of Turkish Prisoners.)

The Imperial War Museum.
By kind permission.

CHAPTER XIX

BEISAN.

WITHIN thirty-six hours of zero the encirclement of the Turkish armies west of the Jordan was complete.

The 4th Cavalry Division was about Beisan, the 5th Cavalry Division about El Afule, Nazareth and Abu Shusheh, and the Australian Division at Lejjun and Jenin. All bolt holes except via the Hedjaz Railway, were stopped, and the Turks, for the most part, were quite unaware of the fact.

There were no signs of their main bodies moving north as yet, though air reports showed them to be in full retreat.

It was not until the next day that stragglers began to appear.

The map distance from the Selmeh orange groves was sixty-eight miles. The 10th Cavalry Brigade, which had been on advanced guard since El Afule, had done this distance in thirty-five hours, and our Brigade in forty.

Many patrols must have covered over eighty miles, and detached squadrons some seventy-five.

The 10th Cavalry Brigade lost fifteen horses all told. Jacob's Horse, who had done a great amount of extra work after passing through the enemy line, lost four horses, and the 29th Lancers one. The 10th and 11th Cavalry Brigades had had only two full nights' rest since leaving the Valley on the 11th September, nine nights before, and must have covered some one hundred and fifty miles in that period. They had had no rest at all the last three nights. When one bears in mind that neither horses nor men were in too hard condition at the start, it may reasonably be claimed that these marches were a feat of arms which will take its place for ever as an example of the capacity of cavalry for sustained movement.

The fact must always be borne in mind that it is one thing to march long distances in small bodies, but quite another to do so in large formations, particularly if the march is along a dusty road. The conditions for watering, feeding and off-saddling become greatly complicated as a rule, and, if the marches are at night, the pace is often uneven. The difference is, more often than not, forgotten and comparisons are made with marches of squadrons, or even patrols.

The small loss in horses testifies to the excellence of the march discipline and to the degree of horsemastership attained.

The length of the marches have certainly been equalled, both in this and in previous wars, but hardly, if ever, with such small loss in horses.

With regard to casualties it is not unusual to hear it stated that they are inevitable if exceptional exertions are called for. This point of view is not uncommon among officers with but little knowledge of the horse, and its capacity, if only it has a fair chance of being conditioned prior to the operations intended.

A man does not enter for a prize fight unless he is fit, and it is no more reasonable to expect horses to march enormous distances if they are not.

If one analyses wastage, it will, not infrequently, be found that ignorance of officers ordering out the cavalry has more to do with it than bad horsemastership in the cavalry itself. The case of Sordet's Cavalry Corps, in August 1914, was an exception, for the French horsemastership was abominable, and there was no reason why the animals should not have been fit at the very outbreak of the War.

We have, on the other hand, the historic example of Pope overworking his cavalry in a quite unnecessary manner in the Second Bull Run campaign, with the result that they could do nothing when the supreme effort was required. In South Africa it was a pretty generally known fact that many of the failures were due to trying to work with large numbers of badly mounted men, the majority of whom, moreover, knew nothing about horses, in preference to a more limited number well mounted and who understood them.

In the post-war Army ignorance of animal management is far greater than ever it was before, owing to the advent of the motor-bicycle. It would, therefore, seem advisable to introduce this as a subject for promotion examinations. In reference to horsemastership, acrimonious arguments arise from time to time with regard to the weight to be carried. Experience has, however, shown that under certain conditions it pays better to march regular troops heavily loaded than light, and that the horse is capable of carrying great weights a long distance if march discipline is good.

On the other hand, if the march discipline is bad, casualties will be heavy, even with animals lightly loaded. An historic example is that of the German and French cavalries of 1870, when the German weight in marching order were nearly a stone heavier than the French. Their discipline being infinitely better, their horse casualties were far lower.

In connection with horse rations, it is a matter for consideration whether it would not be as well to have certain feeds reserved by the supply service for special operations, on the lines of a man's iron ration.

Bulk for bulk and weight for weight it is obvious that good oats and hay are worth more than equivalent weights of any other feed.

At the period of operations in Palestine now under review, however, shipping was scarce, and India was the quickest place to get things from.

From a financial point of view, it would appear penny wise and pound foolish to underfeed horses worth, landed in the theatre of war, some £100 each.

In Palestine the Army was fortunate in having a Commander-in-Chief who was himself a cavalry soldier. The proportion of cavalry officers commanding formations other than the Desert Corps was also very high. Under these circumstances it would only be reasonable to expect that the mounted troops would be ably handled. On a certain other front, from what one is able to gather from cavalry officers who took part in the operations, there is reason to doubt whether, even at the best of times, the higher direction of the cavalry was remarkable for its skill, and on this front there was not one solitary officer in a really big position who was a cavalry soldier.

There was one or two extraordinary examples of its misuse, notably a case where a retreat became necessary and where the cavalry brigade was not employed to cover the retirement, despite the fact that it had hardly been engaged, and the infantry had been very badly hammered.

The proportion of horse casualties was, on one or two occasions, extremely high considering the distances covered. In one definite instance, this was due to the senior officer responsible despatching the cavalry on a mission the brigadier, an officer now occupying a high position, had warned him could only result in heavy wastage with no adequate gain. This wastage, moreover, might, and did actually, prejudice subsequent operations.

The senior officer, like quite a proportion of others in high positions on this front, had not had a thorough apprenticeship with men and animals. His tendency, as with the others, was to regard them much as machines, to be ordered about without regard to food, sleep or rest.

According to many, much of the early failure in this theatre was due to too high a proportion of this type of officer.

It would seem, however, that the cavalry commanders were, in the first two years or so, mediocre men. This, coupled with the fact that there is reason to doubt whether the higher direction was all it might have been, gave the cavalry a bad name.

A bad cavalry, given a resolute and sound direction, will do better than a good cavalry indifferently directed by the higher command.

The Napoleonic cavalry, as such, were not one whit better than the Prussian or Austrian, but had the enormous advantage of a genius as commander-in-chief.

The night of our arrival (20–21 September) passed quietly at Beisan. The outposts were furnished by the 10th Cavalry Brigade, so the Regiment secured a much-needed rest.

Numerous Turkish stragglers trickled in from the south and were made prisoners. From them it was gathered that the Turkish command was as yet unaware that the British had occupied the place.

Beisan was not an important centre on the enemy lines-of-communication in so far as being a supply centre or aerodrome.

There were practically no enemy troops there at all. It was on a low ridge and was a very strong position, provided there were enough troops to hold it, almost from any direction. There was a very fine Turkish police barrack there and a lot of water.

Mosquitoes, however, swarmed—some, judging from the accounts of veracious sufferers from their voracious attentions, as large as Handley Page bombing planes. It was here the final seeds of the deadly malaria which broke out about ten days later, just before entering Damascus, were laid—for mosquito nets had all been left behind.

Rations had now run short and the supply columns had not come up. With some difficulty, chiefly by means of requisition, supplies were got together by the evening of the 21st September. This day a large number of enemy stragglers came in from the south and west. Aeroplane reports showed that very large forces were retiring on the Nablus Road. At dusk the outpost troop of the Dorset Yeomanry, some two miles to the south, reported a large body of enemy troops with motor-cars advancing.

A small bridge in our outpost line had been removed so as to stop cars coming in.

At about 20.00 on the 21st September the enemy cars came up to our outposts, but were fired on. Bickering began along the outposts till about 21.00, when more determined attacks began.

A fight in the moonlight developed, in which a troop of the Central India Horse charged. The attack came to an end, one hundred and eighty prisoners surrendering.

In the meantime the R.H.A. battery shelled the Nablus Road and prevented the huge Turk rabble supporting the advanced party.

The main body of the division in Beisan was unaffected by this fighting.

On the morning of the 22nd the balance of the advance party which had attacked the outposts came in and surrendered. They numbered some three hundred. Four motor-cars containing staff officers, mostly German, also came in.

The country to the south of Beisan was found to be strewn with thousands

MEJDAH—CAPTURED TURKISH CONVOY.

20th September, 1918.

The Imperial War Museum. By kind permission.

*The Imperial War Museum.
By kind permission.*

TURKISH PRISONERS AT BEISAN.

22nd September, 1918.

(The Commander of the Turkish 16th Division, wearing white arm band, is seated on the right.)

of rifles, machine guns by the score, boxes, papers, and equipment of every description.

Prisoners, amounting to some four thousand, with some motor-lorries and numberless horse transport wagons, had passed through the outposts by nightfall of the 22nd September, the poor creatures streaming in in batches of three hundred to six hundred, many mounted on horses, ponies, or mules.

One of the German staff officers gave a harrowing description of the appalling state of demoralization of the Turks on the retreat from Nablus.

Our bombing planes had given them no peace by day or night—the bright moon had helped in this—and they were short of food and water. He said they had heard some cavalry had come to Beisan, but they had no idea that such a large formation as a division was there and hoped to brush them aside.

The German officers had tried to pull the Turks together, so as to cut their way through, but the latter had no stomach for the fight, which was not altogether surprising, considering their fatigue, thirst and general feeling of helplessness on account of the general lack of arrangement to counter our aeroplanes. No attempt seems to have been made to get machine guns or any form of fire to bear on the latter, which had a very easy task of bombing the helpless crowd.

On the afternoon of the 22nd September Jacob's Horse took over the Jisr Esh Sheikh Hussein crossing over the Jordan to the east of Beisan and the valley as far as the Moab Hills.

The bridge dates back to the Saracens.

The Regiment had, however, to send two troops off to escort prisoners to Ef Afule.

During the night some three hundred and fifty Turks straggled in to it.

With regard to escorting prisoners a somewhat embarrassing incident occurred to an Indian officer who happened to be commanding a troop detailed to escort prisoners back from the Abu Naj fight, which took place the following day (23rd September). While *en route* the officer saw a strong body of infantry approaching him from the enemy direction and heard someone hailing him in French. He rode over and found a company of German Jägers, fully armed and in good fettle, who said they were fed up and intended to surrender as soon as they reached Beisan. They refused to give up their arms as they said the Arabs might scupper them. Further on some Turkish mounted men were met, who had no intention of surrendering. The Boche officer told them to go away, which they did after some parley. On approaching Beisan the Jägers refused to follow the same route as the rest of the prisoners, saying they knew a better one. They outnumbered the Indian officer's party by about five to one and were far too strong to be taken on by him, so he had no alternative but to let them go the way they wanted to after detailing some jawans to watch them, and guarding the other prisoners with the balance.

The German, however, kept his word and marched in and surrendered as he had promised.

Quite a proportion of the German officer prisoners were decent fellows, approaching our ideas of gentlemen. There were, however, one or two horrid brutes among them, cads of the worst order, though Prussians of noble birth.

The term *noblesse oblige* does not by any means necessarily hold water in Prussia. In other parts of Germany it does seem to, to a great extent.

These officer prisoners persisted in the idea that we had landed at Haifa and would not believe that we had marched round.

The German soldiery were a very fine lot of men, every bit as good as good British.

The 1st Line Transport wagons, which had not been seen since leaving the Selmeh orange groves, arrived at Beisan on the afternoon of the 23rd inst., after our Brigade had moved south to the Abu Naj operations. Their arrival was very welcome, as we were down to bed-rock in the ration line.

BEISAN—CAMP OF TURKISH PRISONERS.
September, 1918.

The Imperial War Museum. By kind permission.

*The Imperial War Museum.
By kind permission.*

THE FIRST TRAIN RUN BY BRITISH TROOPS INTO BEISAN.
(The train and engine were captured at Afule.)

CHAPTER XX

THE ACTION OF ABU NAJ.

BY the night of the 22–23rd September, air reports, coupled with prisoners' statements, showed that the Turks were now beginning to approach the fords of the Jordan south of Beisan.

The 11th Cavalry Brigade was accordingly ordered south to intercept them. For some reason no Horse Battery was directed to accompany it. The Jordan in these parts does not flow in such a deep trough as further south, and the hills are closer in on the Moab side, particularly near Abu Naj, some six miles to the south of Beisan. Here they were not much more than a half to three-quarters of a mile from the left bank.

There is a quantity of bush on both sides of the river, but this is particularly dense to the north of Abu Naj, where it thins out and where the valley begins to widen to the east.

The ground on the right bank is mostly good going, while on the left there are a good many nullahs for the first five or six miles.

The Middlesex Yeomanry and 29th moved down the right bank and Jacob's Horse down the left.

Jacob's Horse had had to leave two troops behind at the Jisr Esh Sheikh Hussein passage, and had two troops escorting prisoners back to El Afule. It was thus short of a whole squadron. Taking into account various casualties and duties its strength was not much more than about one hundred and eighty all told.

Although it was possible to communicate at intervals by helio across the river, it was not possible to see fully what was happening on the other side owing to the bush. All one could see definitely was clouds of dust.

A little way short of Abu Naj, the advanced guard squadron, under Lieutenant Stroud, which had just cleared the bush area, encountered some two thousand Turks, supported by about thirty machine guns, as it turned out afterwards, moving north. This was about 08.00 hours.

Heavy rifle and machine-gun fire from the direction of the right bank about the same time proclaimed that the 29th and Middlesex Yeomanry were also engaged.

As yet no guns had come into action.

The squadron fell back some four hundred yards and took up a position in a nullah roughly about the edge of the bush.

The supporting squadron came up on its left, and with its assistance the enemy's advance was held up.

Owing to the scrub it was very hard to get much idea either of what was in front or of the ground, and the heavy hostile machine-gun fire made movement extremely difficult.

It was possible to see the dust made by the 29th across the river, but no more, and one could helio to Brigade Head-quarters. It was evident, however, that without artillery to help, or some strong enfilading fire from across the river, it was hopeless to try and advance.

On the right the Jordan and its broken banks impeded movement, while the foothills were not much more than half a mile off on the left.

Captain Braithwaite, with one sabre troop and one Hotchkiss troop, was sent off to get a footing in these hills, so as to enfilade the hostile line.

He unfortunately went too far, and was almost surrounded by a big party of Germans. Only some four or five men of the two troops arrived back that afternoon. Three or four, minus their clothes and equipment, straggled in next day, and four or five rejoined at Damascus, having been made prisoners. The rest, including Braithwaite and Jemadar Attaulla Khan, a very fine Indian officer, were killed. The prisoners were well treated, all things considering.

The Turks made a further effort to advance. This was, however, frustrated by our fire. A helio message was sent to Brigade Head-quarters asking for artillery support, as the Turkish advance seemed so half-hearted as to indicate the possibility of our getting forward should it be forthcoming.

Shortly after this the Hants Battery, which had been hastily despatched from Beisan, came into action on the right bank of the river.

It engaged the Turks fronting Jacob's Horse. A few rounds had been fired when a hostile 5·9 battery, hitherto silent, opened on it. We could see its heavy shells bursting right in the middle of our guns, temporarily silencing them. For some extraordinary reason no casualties were inflicted on the personnel, though the guns themselves were splintered all over with fragments.

The few shells the Hants Battery had fired had, however, shaken the Turks. A troop of the Regiment, under Jemadar Amar Singh, had, at the same time, worked its way forward, dismounted, by the broken ground by the Jordan, and succeeded in surprising some machine guns manned by Germans. It captured no fewer than six.

A mounted patrol of "B" Squadron found a mound to our left front unoccupied. This was promptly seized and the Regiment was enabled to work forward a bit.

By 14.20 the 29th on the right bank succeeded in closing in to the river. The enemy were now under a very heavy rifle and machine-gun fire and began to fall back rapidly.

A squadron of the 29th, under Captain Rice, after crossing the river by a ford, which must have been some five feet deep, joined Jacob's Horse about 16.00.

With its assistance the advance was pushed as fast as the ground admitted, for a succession of formidable nullahs, in which the Turks had taken up their first position, had to be crossed. It was as well that no attempt had been made to charge, for disaster would have inevitably resulted on ground like this.

About three hundred prisoners, including one hundred Germans, together with ten machine guns, fell into the hands of the Regiment. The 5·9 battery was found abandoned next day about two miles from where we had been held up. There were no signs of any fighting in its neighbourhood. How the Germans ever got it across the Jordan astonished us.

The ford it went over by was four and a half feet deep with very steep banks.

While Jacob's Horse had been thus engaged the 29th had met with great success. The Regiment had moved down as advanced guard to the rest of the brigade.

Its vanguard squadron found itself hung up about level with Jacob's Horse. It was reinforced by two squadrons under Captain Jackson. A strong Turkish column was then found to be crossing the river by the Abu Naj ford, covered by a rear-guard.

Leaving two squadrons to engage the enemy frontally and towards the river, Jackson, taking the three lance troops of the third squadron, worked round the enemy's left (our right) flank. He found himself well located for the delivery of a charge and he seized the chance. It proved a brilliant success, nearly a thousand prisoners, a divisional commander, and eighteen machine guns being taken. A good deal was undoubtedly due to the enemy being taken up with the rest of the Regiment.

The Turk was, it must be admitted, not particularly desirous of fighting. At the same time, had we contented ourselves with merely a fire fight, it is practically certain that most of the enemy would have got away. As it was, Jackson's success enabled the other squadrons to close in on the Jordan and open fire on the enemy opposing Jacob's Horse, with the result we know.

The 11th Cavalry Brigade made a bag of nearly four thousand prisoners this day, and inflicted very heavy loss with rifle and machine-gun fire on the enemy. A number of Turks, however, escaped into the hills to the east of the Jordan. They were in a state of complete demoralization and would be valueless for fighting purposes for a very long time—probably months.

The day having been very hot, the advance was stopped about three miles south of the AbuNaj ford. The Brigade then returned and bivouacked beside it.

At 06.30 next day (24th September) the Brigade received orders to push further south, via the east bank of the Jordan, with the object of mopping up fugitives between Beisan and Jisr ed Damieh, about twenty-five miles to the south. The Anzac Division was at the last-named place.

It was, however, necessary to draw rations before moving, and it was not until 11.30 that the 29th and Middlesex Yeomanry marched, the former on the right and the latter on the left bank. Jacob's Horse was not ready by that hour and received orders from the Brigade staff (contrary to the wishes of the Brigadier as it turned out) to complete rationing first.

Very shortly after starting the Brigade found itself engaged with the enemy, who were debouching from the foothills to the west and crossing the river. On hearing the firing Jacob's Horse at once inquired if it was to march or not. Orders were received (contrary, again, to the knowledge of the Brigadier) for the Regiment to stay where it was. The result was that it did not start until 14.00 Having gone some seven miles it came upon the Middlesex Yeomanry, took up a position covering their left and detached a squadron to round up prisoners under the foothills.

The total bag of the 11th Cavalry Brigade was again some four thousand prisoners, all poor miserable creatures only too glad to have done with fighting.

It is safe to say the dominating feeling of all ranks was pity for the poor fellows. As said before, there was never any rancour or hatred for the Turk. A patrol despatched from the 29th did a remarkable feat. It had orders to get into touch with the XX. Cavalry Corps, who were known to be approaching from the Nablus direction. Lieutenant King, the commander, led it clean through the Turkish army and joined up with the Worcestershire Yeomanry, as ordered. This gives some idea of the state of demoralization the Turks were in.

As the horses were now getting pretty exhausted, and as it was known that much hard work was still in store for them, it was decided to recall the Brigade to Beisan, which it reached the next evening (25th September).

With the exception of the casualties in Jacob's Horse, the Brigade losses in the three days to the south of Beisan were astonishingly low, though the proportion of officer and Indian officer casualties was very high. The 29th, for instance, lost one British officer (Captain Wright) and three Indian officers to fourteen men all told.

CHAPTER XXI

THE ADVANCE ON DAMASCUS, FALL OF DAMASCUS. END OF THE GREAT WAR. THE RETURN TO INDIA.
1918–1921

AS the Turks west of the Jordan had now been completely shattered, the only troops left to deal with were those about Amman. Information had come in that they were now falling back. The general disorganization of the enemy signal service had, doubtless, caused this army to hang on in its position for a dangerously long period.

It is quite probable that it had no idea that we were at Beisan in such strength.

The Desert Corps was now to pursue to Damascus and occupy that city.

The 4th Cavalry Division was to endeavour to intercept the enemy about Deraa, while the Australian and 5th Cavalry Divisions were to move on Damascus via the route north of Lake Tiberias.

The 10th Cavalry Brigade had been sent to the railway bridge at Jisr Mejamie on the 25th September, where it joined up with one of its units, the Central India Horse, which had been there since the 23rd. This Brigade was ordered to move on Irbid on the morning of the 26th, and get into touch with Feisul's Arabs.

The remainder of the Division was to leave Beisan the same day and follow by the same route.

The 10th Cavalry Brigade was thus a day's march ahead.

The 11th Cavalry Brigade was in rear of the Division, and the Jacob's Horse only reached Jisr Mejamie at 18.30, when it went on outpost.

On the 27th September the Division reached Irbid. The country was extremely rough and covered with boulders, so much so that to move out of a walk was a matter of the utmost difficulty.

The horses were dropping shoes continually, and the farriers had their hands full. By some amazing feats of driving, thirty lorries followed the Division.

The 10th Cavalry Brigade had now moved on Deraa, but we saw the dead horses of the fight that had taken place at Irbid the day previously.

In this a squadron of the 2nd Lancers had struck a snag and had lost over half its strength.

Owing to the difficulties of the road the 10th Cavalry Brigade had become badly strung out, and the 2nd, who were advanced guard, had pushed further ahead of the Brigade than may, perhaps, have been quite warrantable. Anxiety to seize the water supply in Irbid before dark had been the primary, and possibly justifiable, reason.

On approaching the place the leading patrol was fired on. As judged from the weight of the fire the village did not appear to be strongly held.

It was, therefore, decided to charge it without further ado.

One squadron, under Captain Vaughan, attempted this, but found the going so bad that a rapid advance was not possible. A very heavy fire from Turks in and about the houses at once opened. Just short of the village was a very steep slope the horses could not negotiate. The result was a costly repulse. Captain Vaughan was wounded in the knee, the doctor attending him, one Captain Morris, next attending him over six years later for trouble that had just broken out in the same place as a result of a pig-sticking accident—rather a coincidence.

The effect of the bold effort was, however, to cause the Turks to stream out, though this was not known at the time. According to inhabitants there were some three thousand or four thousand in the neighbourhood and inside the village.

The chief point for speculation is as to whether a more detailed reconnaissance should not have been made. It was, however, getting dark and time pressed. Furthermore, the Turks had hitherto proved so susceptible to a cavalry charge that the likelihood of their making a stand, in their then state of moral, did not seem very great.

The fight was rather a disconnected affair. The Brigadier (Lieut.-Colonel Green, Jacob's Horse) had had his hands full in the earlier stages of the march keeping the column and its transport together. The distance which the 2nd Lancers were ahead made it imperative to take particular steps to see that the balance of the Brigade was well in hand to meet a attack from any direction in the difficult and tricky country we were traversing. He had, in consequence, been unable to get as far forward in the early stages of the fight as he could have wished.

The 10th Cavalry Brigade had another combat at Er Remte the following day. The Turks did not put up much of a fight. As the Brigade was not so strung out, the commander was able to get well forward this time and work in a well co-ordinated action.

On the 28th the Division, less the 10th Cavalry Brigade which moved to Deraa, marched to Mezerib, turning north at Er Remte.

Here we first met elements of the Sherifian army—scallywags mounted on camels, of whom the jawans were very justly suspicious.

The 10th Cavalry Brigade occupied Deraa without opposition this day. The place was in a general state of confusion, having been very heavily bombed by our aeroplanes. The Arabs were looting in every direction. There was a hospital train in the station full of Turk wounded. Our Arab allies proceeded to pull the poor fellows out and murder them in cold blood, their varying sheikhs and commanders not making the slightest effort to check them. General Barrow happened to arrive and at once put a guard over the train. This, of course, had to be removed when the Brigade marched again, and there is but little doubt that all the wounded we could not get away were foully done to death.

The conduct of the Arabs at Deraa infuriated British and Indian alike. With much further provocation it was quite on the cards that they would have been shot on sight.

After leaving Irbid the country improved and it was possible to move rather faster along the track, though the ground on either side was still very stony.

For the rest of the way to Damascus it was most uninteresting, a bare stony plateau with huge patches of lava cropping out, very trying for the horses' feet.

A few, but astonishingly few, of the weedier animals began to drop out. The pack-horses suffered most.

In the better disciplined units the casualties were considerably lower than in the others.

Those jawans whose horses had foundered took Turkish ponies and followed as best they could. It must be confessed that the average appearance of these gentry did not give much indication of smartness or regularity, particularly when the Derajati got going. The Bashi-Bazouk of fiction would have found his match here all right.

At Mezerib there was, at last, plenty of water, the headwaters of the Yarmuk. There was, also, a certain amount of grazing.

Some miserable Turk stragglers were picked up on the way, many of them were wounded. They stood every chance of being scuppered by Arabs if we did not protect them.

On the 29th September the march was resumed to Dilli, or Ezra, a station on the Damascus–Hedjaz Railway, Jacob's Horse leading. The Arab scallywags were on our right—and the farther they were off the happier we were.

About midday the leading squadron was treacherously fired upon by villagers at Sheikh Miskin. It promptly charged, killing some fifteen or twenty of these vermin, for they were nothing else. It was with difficulty that the men could be restrained from killing more.

One miscreant clung round the neck of Lieutenant Vosper's horse, trying

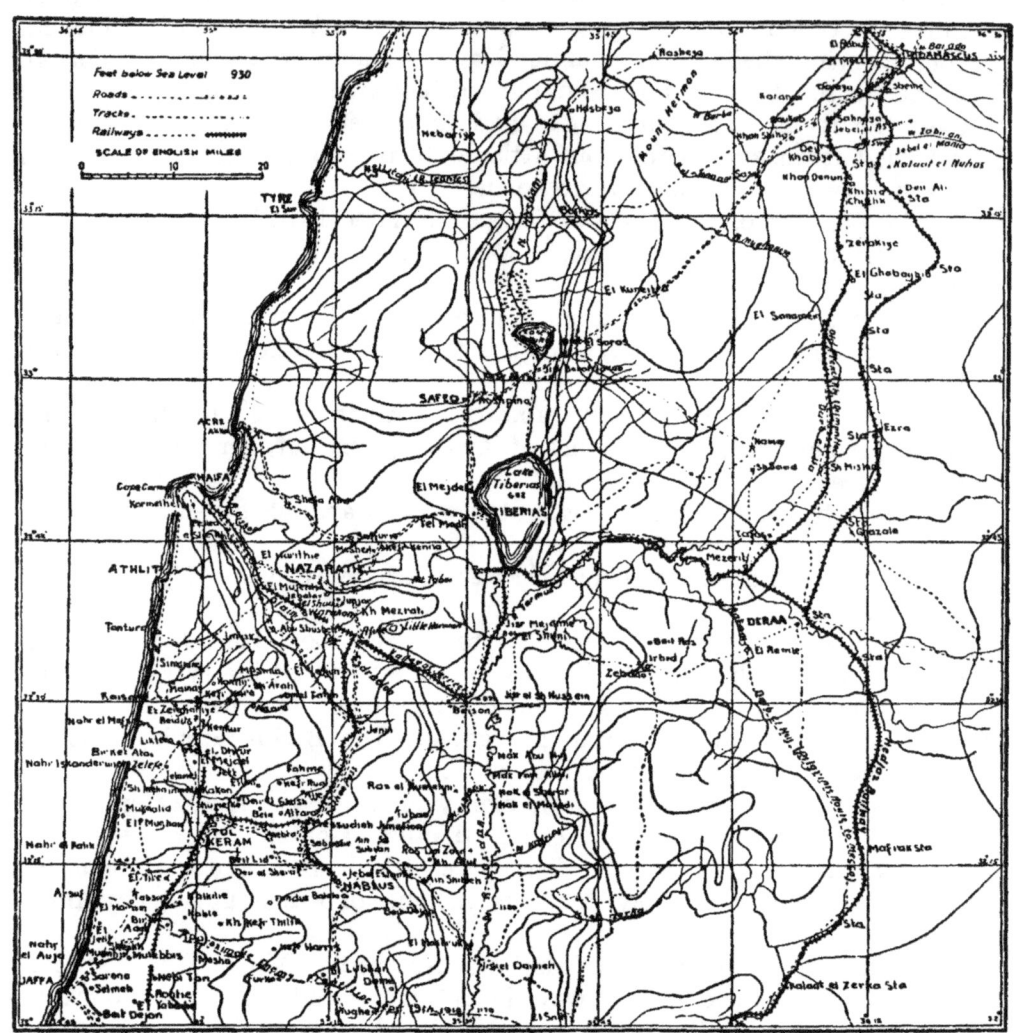

THE ADVANCE TO DAMASCUS.
September, 1918.

to evade a well-merited sabre thrust. The horse, rider and Arab fell into a deep canal full of water. The Arab received his deserts and Vosper and his horse were only pulled out with much difficulty.

The mentality of certain British writers who sought to palliate the conduct of the Arabs was about on a par with those who backed up Sinn Fein Irish who murdered British officers in their beds.

It may be urged that Turks and Arabs massacring each other was the normal thing.

From the point of view of British officers who have had dealings with both, however, there is but little doubt that the Turk is the first gentleman throughout the Middle East, and the Arabs deserved all they got.

There was good water at Ezra, the water coming from an old Roman aqueduct. It seems curious that there should have been Roman remains as far east as this, but there were some at Amman, and it is known that Romans were for a time at Tel Afar and Sinjar, west of Mosul.

At nightfall news was received that a large column of Turks had retreated into Damascus that afternoon. It was believed to have a strong rearguard at Kiswe, some twenty-five miles north. The 4th Cavalry Division had thus failed to cut the enemy off.

The Australians and 5th Cavalry Division were this day at Kuneitra, some fifteen or twenty miles to the north-west of us, having advanced by the north of Lake Tiberias. It was known that the enemy had a strong force in position south of Sasa, between them and Damascus. These two divisions, however, made a night advance with a view to reaching the city, which was thirty-seven miles off, by next morning.

This did not meet with much success, largely owing to difficulties of ground, and we came into contact with patrols from the 14th Cavalry Brigade, 5th Cavalry Division, next evening (30th September).

This day the 4th Cavalry Division had marched with Kiswe as objective. Our Brigade led, watering at Ghabaghib and Zedakie about midday.

Shortly afterwards, information came in that the Turks were in position on the high ground north and north-east of Khiara Chiflik and Khan Denun, about three and a half miles short of Kiswe. Pushing on, the Brigade came into contact with the enemy on this line and was shelled from the high ground.

Jacob's Horse was directed against the Turk left, crossing the old railway not far from Khiara Chiflik.

It reached the foothills of Jebel el Mania, but it was too late to do anything. Our guns had shelled the enemy as he was falling back through the pass where the railway ran.

The Brigade bivouacked at Khan Denun.

The casualties were negligible with one exception, and that was Captain O'Connor, 29th Lancers, who had his leg blown off by a shell. This was extraordinarily bad luck, for this proved to be the last fight of the War.

By now the stony surface of the ground had made the horses so footsore that they could hardly work up a trot.

During the earlier part of the night a glare, often so bright as to light up the whole country, came from the Damascus direction. The Turks were burning dumps preparatory to evacuating the city.

We had heard our guns going all the day off to our left front where the Australians and 5th Cavalry Division were. We learnt subsequently that we had been engaged with Turks who had been headed back towards us by the 14th Cavalry Brigade.

It was this day that an Australian Brigade, together with the Regiment Mixte de Cavalerie had succeeded in getting astride of the Damascus—Beirut Road over the Barada Gorge and cut off a large column of Turks.

The gorge is similar to the Bolan at the Quetta end, and the hills on either side are of the normal Indian Frontier type, though with easier slopes.

At the moment of arrival of the Australians, the road and railway were blocked with a mass of fugitives moving west. The opening of fire resulted in a terrible panic and most of the enemy column broke back into Damascus.

Two railway trains, absolutely packed with people, were captured.

The next day the 3rd Australian Light Horse Brigade succeeded in gaining the Homs Road, north of Damascus. The result was the whole of the Turks in the city were trapped, thirteen thousand prisoners being taken.

The 4th Cavalry Division bivouacked to the south-west of Damascus, about the El Kuneitra Road, which was the easiest line for lorries to come up by.

It remained here till the 6th October, when it moved towards Baalbek.

Since leaving the Jordan on the 11th September, Jacob's Horse and the 29th Lancers had covered over three hundred miles in nineteen days, by map distances. It will be realized that many horses like those on escorts or on patrol must have covered considerably more.

The only complete rest during the whole period was the day at Beisan, and even then it must be borne in mind that orders, plans and odd duties interrupted one.

The average weight carried by horses was about seventeen stone—probably more, and the country passed through was stony for the most part, and, practically everywhere, very barren.

Nevertheless the 36th loss in horses from exhaustion did not exceed forty out of five hundred. The 29th lost fifty-seven animals, including battle casualties. In the 10th Cavalry Brigade the total loss in horses had been

DAMASCUS.

October, 1918.

The Imperial War Museum. By kind permission.

*The Imperial War Museum.
By kind permission.*

**THE RIVER JORDAN.
SARACEN BRIDGE AT JISR MEJAMIE.**

THE JISR MEJAMIE–IRBID ROAD.

Motor lorries had to cross the bridge, and when it collapsed, they were dragged across the stream bed. Thirty lorries, with supplies, followed the 4th Cavalry Division to Damascus, over seventy to one hundred miles of roadless country.

ARAB LEVIES NEAR PALMYRA.

1918.

two hundred and thirty, of which ninety-one had been battle casualties.

The percentage of sore-backs was extraordinarily low—practically infinitesimal.

It will be seen, therefore, that the standard of horsemastership was a very high one.

The 5th Cavalry Division in the pursuit to Aleppo, a distance of five hundred miles from the Selmeh orange groves, lost only 21 per cent. of its horses in thirty-seven days' marching and fighting.

The greatest known cavalry pursuit heretofore had been that by Murat after Jena, when he marched four hundred and twenty-five miles in twenty-three days. His loss in horses was, however, enormous and the percentage of sore-backs colossal. From our own experience of French horsemastership we can quite well picture the state of affairs. His pursuit was, in addition, through a rich country and he was able to get remounts *en route* from the inhabitants.

On arrival south of Damascus a terrible epidemic of malaria and influenza decimated the 4th Cavalry Division.

The consequence was, it was unable to follow up the 5th Cavalry Division in its move on Aleppo.

The late strenuous operations, with the consequent exhaustion combined with indifferent food, had rendered all ranks very susceptible to such form of disease, particularly after their long sojourn in the Jordan, which had taken it out of every one.

The last five days about Beisan had an added effect.

The 5th Cavalry Division had been fortunate in having had a good rest in the Philistean Plain before the advance started. It did not, moreover, go down to Beisan where the malarial germs got their first grip. The 4th Cavalry Division, on the other hand, started with everything against it from a preparatory point of view.

The epidemic raged for about a fortnight before any appreciable diminution could be noticed.

Men fell sick on the march as well as in bivouac.

The death-rate was high, being in the 10th Cavalry Brigade 10 per cent. of admissions to hospital.

Among others, occurred that of Major Carpendale, Jacob's Horse, who had been in every action since the Regiment landed in France in 1914, also that of an I.A.R. officer with the 29th Lancers well known for his gallantry, named Follett.

The British troops suffered more severely than the Indian. The former had been in Palestine for about three years, however, and had not had the advantages of good living in a good European climate like most of the jawans.

The medical officers absolutely excelled themselves in their devoted efforts. Not only did they have to deal with our own people, but with the miserable Turks, who were also dying in every direction from dysentery, malaria, and influenza. The Syrian and other doctors who had been in the Turk hospitals in Damascus had been ordered to quit before we reached the place, and we found houses full of sick who had been there some weeks.

By the time the Division reached Baalbek, the Division had evacuated three thousand six hundred cases, of whom four hundred died. The percentage of sick must have thus approached nearly 80 per cent.—an enormous proportion.

The Middlesex Yeomanry were down to twenty-six officers and men, while Jacob's Horse had an average of twenty-five men per squadron only.

The difficulty in looking after the horses can be imagined and we had to have numbers of Turk prisoners to help.

Among people who deserved enormous credit for hard work were the lorry drivers. The whole of the Desert Corps was dependent on their efforts for rationing many miles ahead of railhead and over bad roads.

The unfortunate men would arrive half dead from fatigue, and many accidents occurred owing to their dropping to sleep at the wheel.

The Division had left Selmeh with one iron ration and two days' special emergency ration per man, and twenty-one pounds of grain per horse, all carried on the horse.

In addition, one day's grain per horse had been carried on the 1st Line Transport limbered wagons.

On leaving Beisan the above scale was again made good, but it was not till the 3rd October that any further rations were issued from the supply column. Resort had to be made to requisition and to use of Turkish supply dumps. There were a good many sheep and goats about, but supply was a matter of great difficulty.

On the 2nd October a representative detachment of the Desert Corps, consisting of one composite squadron from each regiment in the three divisions present and one battery from each division, marched through Damascus. The populace must have been greatly impressed by this immense procession of mounted troops and guns, but the men in the ranks could see little either of the spectators or the city, by reason of the dense clouds of dust raised by the column.

On the 6th October the Division left the neighbourhood of Damascus for the Baalbek area. It moved through the Barada Gorge, where the stench of corpses and carcasses was overpowering—the result of the Australians intercepting a Turkish column on the 30th September.

A violent storm, lasting several hours, burst as soon as bivouac was reached and lasted the greater part of the night. This did not improve matters as regards the malaria outbreak, which was by then almost at its height.

Next day the Brigade moved on to Khan Meizelun, some 3,500 feet above sea-level.

It was now getting chilly at nights, especially at a height like this.

On the 14th October the Division moved to Shtora (3,000 feet), in the Ryak Valley.

This was magnificent, very fertile, and with many fruit trees. It was also a great grain-growing area. There were many wine factories at Shtora. The slopes of the Lebanon were covered with vineyards. The Anti-Lebanon, that is the range on the Damascus side of the valley, are pretty bare and resemble the Indian Frontier.

At Shtora the surplus horses were left behind. They far outnumbered the men and it was with the utmost difficulty that they could be moved about. One man was leading five horses in Jacob's Horse, and the British units had to drive animals like herds.

Baalbek was reached on the 16th October. There was a copious water supply and a lot of tibben (bhoosa) was obtainable in the neighbourhood. The ruins here are magnificent.

The sun was hot, but the nights were cool.

In November it became very cold, with bitter winds.

A supply of warm clothing, brought up from Beirout, arrived none too soon.

The 11th Cavalry Brigade was sent to Damascus at the end of October, where it remained the winter.

The initial idea was that we should be billeted in the city. This, however, proved impossible owing to the vermin in every house. Despite every effort to clean the floor and walls, bugs would drop down on one in the night.

Damascus is a disappointing city. Its chief peculiarity lies in the extent of its covered-in bazaars, the roofs being of corrugated iron. These bazaars are certainly picturesque, but do not compare with those of Stamboul.

One sees a great diversity of races in the streets.

The pictures of stately sheikhs and beautiful ladies wearing yashmaks one reads of, are chiefly the realm of fiction, for the tarbush-wearing Syrian is the most common.

The most interesting building is the Great Mosque, an enormous place. It is one of the few edifices where both Christian and Mussulman services were held under the same roof for a very long period, one-half of the building being reserved for the Christians and the other for Mohammedans.

The city has trams and electric light and most of its buildings are rather of the variety one will see in certain small towns on the Riviera. There is not the slightest resemblance to anything Indian, beyond the dirt and bad smells.

Most beautiful gardens surround the place, but most of the country outside is bare and stony, not unlike the Frontier.

The standard of civilization is, however, very much higher than in India. There is little of beauty inside the city, and the interest chiefly lies in the different types of humanity one sees.

The place it most resembles is Mosul.

As a result of the vermin, the Brigade camped a few miles outside the town, on a very stony plain.

The Great War, so far as the 4th Cavalry Division was concerned, was ended.

The 5th Cavalry Division carried on the pursuit to Aleppo, where, to our great regret, our old friend Hyler Holden, commanding the Jodhpore Lancers, was killed.

Lieut.-Colonel Lance, 19th Lancers, was sent to take over the temporary command in October 1918, and only relinquished just before Jacob's Horse returned to India two years later.

Thus ended the Great War. Not only had the Scinde Horse fully maintained the traditions of John Jacob, but had added to them. The First Regiment, the 35th, was soon to show its mettle in the Arab Rebellion in Mesopotamia, particularly in the affair known as " The Manchester Column Disaster," a debacle that threw as much strain on the Indian soldier, in all probability, as any in which he has ever taken part since the British went to India.

This statement may appear too sweeping. The writer, however, has studied the military history of India since the days of Clive with considerable care, and is acquainted with the details of disasters like Monson's Retreat, Kabul, and Maiwand. There were circumstances connected with this affair that had occurred in none of them.

After the Armistice

The two years following the Armistice were spent in various places in Syria and Palestine.

As regards Syria, things, just before we left, were getting somewhat tricky owing to the unpopularity of the French, who were taking over the mandate.

In Palestine the Regiment was chiefly at Sarona and Tiberias.

It was not until early 1921 that Jacob's Horse returned to India.

*The Imperial War Museum.
By kind permission.*

BEIRUT.
(Indian Cavalry camp on the Seashore.)

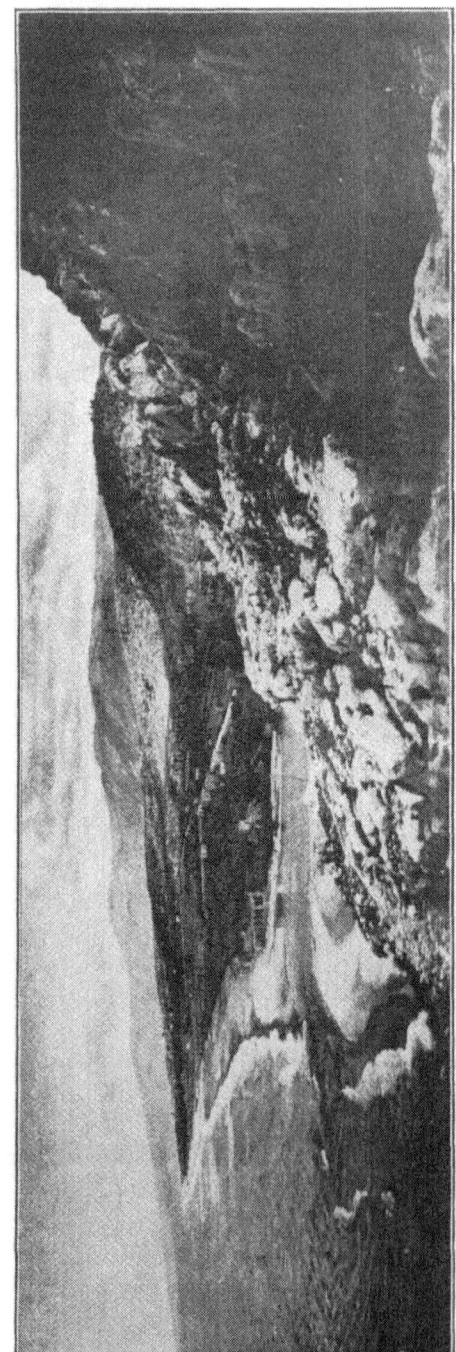

*The Imperial War Museum.
By kind permission.*

BEIRUT.
(The Coast to the North and the mouth of the Dog River.)

It has often been asked whether bringing Indian troops into close contact with the lower classes of European had an adverse effect on our prestige in India. The answer is that the men were just as capable as the Britisher of distinguishing between good and bad, and no evil has resulted.

The Indian officers were quite able to see that the " temporary gent " type of officer was not the normal sahib. Our men, moreover, could tell whether the British troops they happened to be alongside were of good or mediocre quality.

They marked down the Guards at once as being above the rest.

Another question often put has been : " Which race of Indian soldier did best in the War ? " Speaking of the classes enlisted in the Indian Cavalry the answer is an easy one.

It depended, first of all, on the commander of the moment, and, secondly, on the discipline and training of the men. The race question did not come in.

We know that, on fronts other than France, certain cavalry regiments of inferior discipline did extremely badly, despite the fact that the class composition was identical with that of other units which were well disciplined and doing brilliantly.

It is to be clearly understood that a " thruster " suddenly placed in command of troops in a bad state of discipline and given no chance of wheeling them into line might find himself badly let down. We know that such instances happened. Given time, however, and the backing of a strong general, there would be no reason whatever why even the worst of cavalry regiments should not be welded into shape, without change in the actual class composition. With the infantry, it was not the same, for there were certain classes recruited whom it would never have been possible to hammer into real fighting material.

The notion, generally accepted before the War, that the only soldier worth having was to be found in the Punjab or to the north of it was the outcome of the Mutiny and Second Afghan War, and was, in the main, owing to the fact that the best type of officer usually tried to get into units recruiting there. In the Great War, however, it was shown that the hitherto despised Mahratta was just as good a man as any.

To have made this statement before 1914 would have been to incur ridicule.

One would like to hear the remarks of some old Indian Army officer who had retired before the war had he listened to a discussion the writer heard, at the end of the Arab Rebellion in 1921, as to whether a certain Mahratta or a certain Sikh Battalion was not the finest in the country, bar none.

The Sikh Battalion was, and is, justly known as one of the spot regiments of the whole Indian Army.

One has occasionally heard it pointed out that such and such a unit, not particularly remarkable for its discipline or high standard of training, did extremely well. This may have been the case. The point is, however, that with discipline and hard training it would have done even better. Furthermore, it is pretty certain that such a unit, if subjected to a prolonged strain, would fall off infinitely quicker than others which had been kept well up to the mark. There was a certain unit in France which was, as compared with the others, rather scallywag.

It certainly "got there" in the sense that it always displayed great gallantry in action. It always, or nearly always, lost more men, however, in doing so than the other Indian unit in its Brigade, which was far better disciplined. Furthermore, it was apt to be erratic in its work and, as a result, not an easy unit to work with.

We know that the Guards Division in France went further, lost fewer, relatively to the work done, and was always more reliable than any other in the country, and this was due to the tremendous spirit and discipline of the Guards. Precisely the same thing is applicable to the Indian soldier.

THE BATTLE HONOURS

THE GREAT WAR

"Megiddo"	"Damascus"
"Sharon"	"Palestine, 1918"

*The Imperial War Museum.
By kind permission.*

BRIDGE OVER THE DOG RIVER.

**MAJOR-GENERAL SIR G. de S. BARROW AND STAFF.
4th CAVALRY DIVISION.
BEIRUT.**

1919.

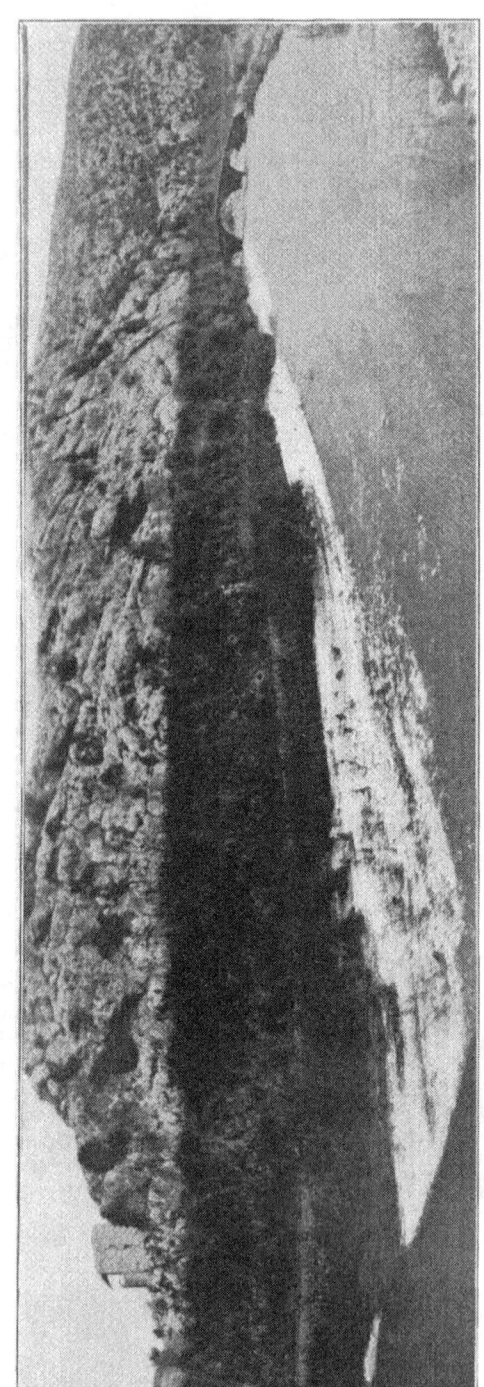

THE DOG RIVER.
(About ten miles north of Beirut on the Tripoli Road.)

*The Imperial War Museum.
By kind permission.*

CHAPTER XXII

THE 35TH SCINDE HORSE.

1914-1920

SERVICE IN INDIA DURING THE GREAT WAR.
ORDERED TO MESOPOTAMIA.

WHILE Jacob's Horse had been winning glory in France and Palestine, its sister Regiment had been having a hard time in India, but without glory.

The lot of Internal Security units in that country was by no means an enviable one, particularly for Regimental Head-quarters. They were used, in the main, as feeders for the units on service, as well as for the formation of new units.

In the years 1914, 1915, until early 1916, the 35th were at Dera Ismail Khan, with two squadrons at Tank. Raiders were not abnormally busy at this period, but the Tank detachment was in a perimeter camp for the whole time. Life under such conditions, with the heat, dust, flies and absence of privacy can soon make life merely an existence if long protracted. In mounted units the presence of horses makes things still more unpleasant.

A move to Jubbulpore in 1916 was, in consequence, a very welcome and deserved change, for the Regiment had been at Dera Ismail Khan since early 1912.

Numerous drafts were sent off to France, not all to Jacob's Horse unfortunately.

They were composed of the very pick of the Regiment. Although this greatly benefited the units reinforced, it is doubtful whether it was an altogether sound move for a great war that was to last a long time. It must, however, be remembered that in 1914 an extraordinary notion prevailed that all would be over by Christmas. It was, therefore, more or less natural for units that thought of things as they should have, to bleed themselves in this manner.

The effect of the measure, nevertheless, was to seriously handicap the Regiment when it began to expand. It is, in any case, not by any means a certainty that reinforcements from outside will receive altogether fair treatment in Indian units, unless the British officers take steps to make it clear that there is to be no nonsense as regards treating them any differently from their own men.

It is doubtful if the average Indian officer has the sense of fair play sufficiently developed to guarantee absolute equality of treatment. In Jacob's Horse this measure was taken from the very start. As to whether it was in all other units to which the Regiment sent reinforcements, is another matter.

To detail one's best men wholesale for drafts is, therefore, in many cases, very liable to lead to a number not pulling their weight as well as if they were kept behind.

The principle to work on would appear to be "A fair average sample," but no bad men should be included. From certain occurrences in France, there is reason to suppose that one or two regiments in India seized the opportunity to unload their rag, tag and bobtail on those overseas.

Things in the 35th ran smoothly enough until the beginning of 1917. Although there were no fewer than seven officers in France in 1914 and 1915, there were enough to carry on in India. Furthermore, the I.A.R. officers who joined in those years were of excellent quality and learnt their jobs very quickly. The Regiment, above all, was fairly well concentrated. In 1917, however, all the trained I.A.R. officers were sent overseas and the Regular officers began to be heavily drawn on. Squadrons were detached at Calcutta, Lucknow, and, for a time, at Arrah. There was an enormous increase in the amount of administrative work, particularly in relationship to accounts. A fifth squadron, and shortly after a sixth, was raised. This sixth squadron went off to form part of the 42nd Cavalry, a newly raised regiment, disbanded in 1919.

The "general post" of officers, and a deterioration of class in the newly joined ones, together with the sudden expansion in strength of the rank and file, soon began to make things very difficult. The detached squadrons absorbed all the most experienced officers, and the result was that the commanding officer and adjutant soon found themselves doing not merely their ordinary jobs, but those of accounts officer, quartermaster and mess-president as well. The clerical establishment was swamped with work and bad clerks complicated things at once. Leave was difficult to get and there were many officers in India who had not had a month clear of hot weather or rains since 1913. The strain thrown on these unfortunates is apt to be forgotten, and but little sympathy is sometimes extended to individuals who only got on service to some minor front late in the war.

Numbers of officers in India were in the position that they were absolutely indispensable in the country. Many had their healths permanently ruined thereby, and some died.

Among the latter category was the unfortunate Colonel da Costa, who died in October 1918. Incidentally, as showing the methods of the Indian Government, his unfortunate widow was, at first, only allowed a pension on the ordinary scale, the representation that the death was due to overwork not having any effect. Later on the matter was remedied.

The writer was directed to proceed to India and take over temporary command, which he did on 20th December 1918. Colonel Lukin, 9th Hodson's Horse, was appointed substantive commandant, but did not join until two days before the Regiment proceeded to Mesopotamia, in March 1920, and then left it again in July.

To one who had been continuously on service since 8th August 1914, a return to India was a curious experience. It was stepping back almost to the days of the South African War, and soldiering was hopelessly behind-hand in its larger aspect. Military stations were full of freshly raised units. The only officers of real military experience were the commanding officers, assisted, possibly, by a second in command. The generals were all either "dug outs," or men who had been more or less failures on various fronts. Neither category tended to efficiency as regards higher training, and nearly all their time was taken up in administration.

There had been a distinct advance in recruit training in all units and there were numerous schools for N.C.O.'s which did good work. On the other hand, musketry was extraordinarily bad and accounted for many of the mishaps that subsequently occurred on the Frontier. In the cavalry, where it had always been indifferent, it might now be said to have been non-existent.

Tactical training was puerile, to put things mildly, and some of the remarks one heard at pow-wows were almost banal. One was not surprised at hearing of some truly wonderful performances that took place in the Afghan War a few weeks later.

The ignorance of the power of the machine gun, and of fire generally, was simply amazing, and it was quite easy to understand why certain officers had received bowler hats.

To watch the infantry carrying out an attack was enough to make one tremble. Fire and movement was a sealed book, and no attempt was made to make use of the unit's own fire power. As regards cavalry, the prevailing notion appeared to be that they should be employed as mounted infantry. Shock action was regarded askance, even by brigadiers who had served in the cavalry. These officers, however, dated back to South Africa.

The Regiment had, at the end of 1918, five squadrons, one mounted on country-bred ponies and specially intended for Internal Security in India only. These ponies were extremely good and certainly surprised one.

The strength was about eleven hundred and fifty, with a number of absentees without leave. In this respect the infantry were far worse off, some having as many as fifty or sixty away.

The British officers were nearly all men who had joined up during the war and were of first-class material, only requiring moulding and training. Many had seen a good deal of war, though this was no guarantee that they knew anything of tactics and field work. The weakness lay in the Indian officers and N.C.O.'s, though there were a few really good men among the former. The N.C.O.'s were indifferent owing to the heavy drafts that had gone overseas having drained the best material. There were, however, two towers of strength, the Ressaldar Major, Mahomed Azim, and the head clerk, Jemadar Sangat Singh. Thanks to these two officers, things had been kept on their legs at very critical periods. A number of men had now begun to rejoin from overseas, particularly from Jacob's Horse, and it was largely due to these that the Regiment made the name it did in the Arab Rebellion.

At the beginning of 1919 demobilization began, and the opportunity was at once seized for weeding out undesirables. The men back from overseas had mostly served under the writer, either in Jacob's Horse or at Kantara, and were persuaded to stay on. The fifth squadron was broken up. Hardly had the demobilization finished when the Afghan War broke out and we mobilized again. The men from overseas were at once promoted and things really began to improve. The difficulty was with the British officers. There was a constant "general post" with the regulars, and the detachments absorbed the only ones available. To give some idea of the manner the Regiment was strewn about, we had, in April 1919, one squadron at Calcutta, one at Bombay, one at Lucknow and one at Jubbulpore, together with large detachments with Remount Depots at Bangalore and Sehore—a distribution that would have pleased the heart of the military brains in Mesopotamia at that period. There was a great deal of sedition flying about India, and the Punjab Rebellion was on. The squadron at Bombay had been urgently despatched there for riots engineered by Ghandi. By mischance this individual just escaped scuppering by the squadron—an event which, had it materialized, would have saved much trouble later on. We had two men very badly knocked about by rioters owing to their horses coming down, but the squadron had the satisfaction of getting its own back well.

British officers were being steadily demobilized the whole year, and by the beginning of 1920 the only officers left were those who intended taking permanent commissions. The constant changes had made things very difficult and the burden of work at regimental head-quarters had fallen upon Captain Bird and Lieutenant Colquhoun.

In December 1919, orders were received for Palestine in relief of Jacob's Horse. To our disgust these were changed for Mesopotamia.

The greatest difficulty was experienced in ascertaining what to arrange for in the move there. We were not going on service, but on relief, and most varied tales were heard of the state of affairs in the country. We heard, correctly it may be stated, that British units were, in some instances, taking out full-dress uniforms and mess plate.

General Head-quarters at Baghdad had even allowed wives and families to go out to the country, and everything tended to show that the conditions were pretty well the same as in India. General Haldane's views on the family question can be seen in his book. That some outcry did not occur may be attributed to the fact that the British public was absolutely war weary and took but little interest in anything except getting back to peace. The Irish situation was not even bothering them seriously. The only popular shriek was the expense of Mesopotamia. It would seem that the Baghdad authorities were in luck.

Fortunately, we only arranged to take out mess furniture of a semi-permanent kind suitable for standing camps, and things like dhurris and cheap china. We brought out, of course, camp kit, and good stuff at that. Nearly the whole of this last " went west " in the Manchester Column disaster and we could get no compensation for it as the authorities were anxious not to hurt the delicate feelings of the Arab Government that was being established at the time the matter was brought up.

Certain married officers, however, brought out stuff with a view to their wives joining them later on. Although this did not get lost, it was badly damaged in subsequent moves. One officer had his full dress uniform badly damaged.

The great difficulty was mess servants, for none would leave India. After much trouble we got some scallywags at Bombay, men rather of the class one would find in the Institutes of a British unit. Their wages were exorbitant and there was always one man drunk. Fortunately, there was a followers' depot in Mesopotamia for the provision of servants, and this fixed us up with some who were slightly better and cheaper.

The most serious question was that of British officers. The only experienced officers present with the Regiment were Colonel Lukin, the writer and Captain Bird. The pre-war regular officers, having had no leave since the beginning of the war, were all at home. The whole of the rest were very young and untrained. A good man had to be left at the Depot, so Captain Bird was selected. No fewer than five officers (Captain Hudson, Lieutenants Geddes and Marten, Second-Lieutenants Aspinall and Robinson) joined a week before proceeding overseas. As Colonel Lukin only joined two days before sailing, it worked down to the writer being the only officer present who knew anything about the Regiment at all.

It was well off as regards Indian ranks, particularly in the Pathan and Sikh squadrons, and there was a big proportion, both of Indian officers and N.C.O.'s, who had served in France.

Although an enormous amount of work had been put in in the past year, it is doubtful if the standard of mounted work was up to that of regiments trained in France, largely owing to the manner in which the Regiment had been strewn about and owing to the almost complete inexperience of most of the British officers.

In one point, however, the training was a good bit higher, and that was in footwork, particularly in fire discipline and control. The men were really smart on their feet and their discipline had improved enormously owing to a daily foot parade with British officers present—for without their presence any smart work in Indian Cavalry is usually out of the question. Subsequent results in the Rebellion showed that this labour had paid, hands down. The fire discipline of the men proved excellent, and our guards and sentries were very different from those of the normal Indian cavalry of before the war.

Speaking with considerable experience of pulling together troops in a poor state of both discipline and training, the writer cannot lay too much stress on the importance of really smart footwork. Its introduction was revolutionary and met with no inconsiderable amount of opposition, particularly from senior officers, but it paid, as said before, hands down. The psychology of the Indian soldier does not differ from that of the British in this respect, and we know that those British units that go in tremendously for spit and polish are the ones that did best in the war.

With regard to the moral effect of a number of men who had been in France, it is regrettable but none the less true that strict veracity does not appear to have been their forte. According to their own accounts (one gathers) they sometimes ate Boches by the handful. The result, however, was to inspire violent ambition among the less travelled, and in the subsequent fighting some of the greatest thrusters we had were men who had not before seen a shot fired.

The following officers accompanied the Regiment to Mesopotamia :—

Lieut.-Colonel Lukin, Major Maunsell, Captains Hudson and Nokes, Lieutenants Geddes and Marten, Second-Lieutenants Bott, Mmd. Ayub, Aspinall and Robinson.

CHAPTER XXIII

MESOPOTAMIA.

FROM INDIA. DIWANIYAH. HINAIDI.

1920

THE Regiment, minus horses, left Jubbulpore on 17th March 1920. As indicating the bond of union existing in the Corps, it marched out of barracks to its last campaign as the old 1st Sind Horse under an archway containing the Koran. The Sikhs stated straight out that there was only one God for all, and that so long as a man was a good man, the particular creed to which he belonged was immaterial. In this connection, similar instances occurred after the amalgamation of the 35th and 36th Horse, when the writer, as Commandant of the Regiment, laid the foundation-stone of the new Mohammedan mosque and opened the Sikh Gurdwara, both of which we had built as War Memorials to the fallen of the Great War and Arab Rebellion. On each occasion British officers and their wives, Mussulmans, Sikhs and Hindus were present.

Thus does the tone of a good regiment rise above differences of race and creed.

We had the ship to ourselves and one could study the jawans at their ease on board, in a manner which had not been possible on previous transports.

The Pathans had a Marasi piper, an excellent performer, specially enlisted for service. Normally the recruitment of Marasis is undesirable, but in this case the man pulled his weight—every ounce—in the dull hot weather that preceded the Rebellion. The Sikhs had a rival show, in the shape of a beauty chorus, selected seemingly for extreme hairiness of person combined with very nasal voices. They had, furthermore, an instrument of torture described as a "harmoonyum." The Pathans won, however, when the weather became a bit lumpy, for the beauty chorus and the "harmoonyum" became strangely silent, whereas the dol and sernai were at it hard the whole time.

Mesopotamia proved to be very much what one expected, and did not differ materially in beauty of scenery from our old friend the "Pat" between Jacobabad and Sibi. Basra also had a kind of resemblance to Sukkur and

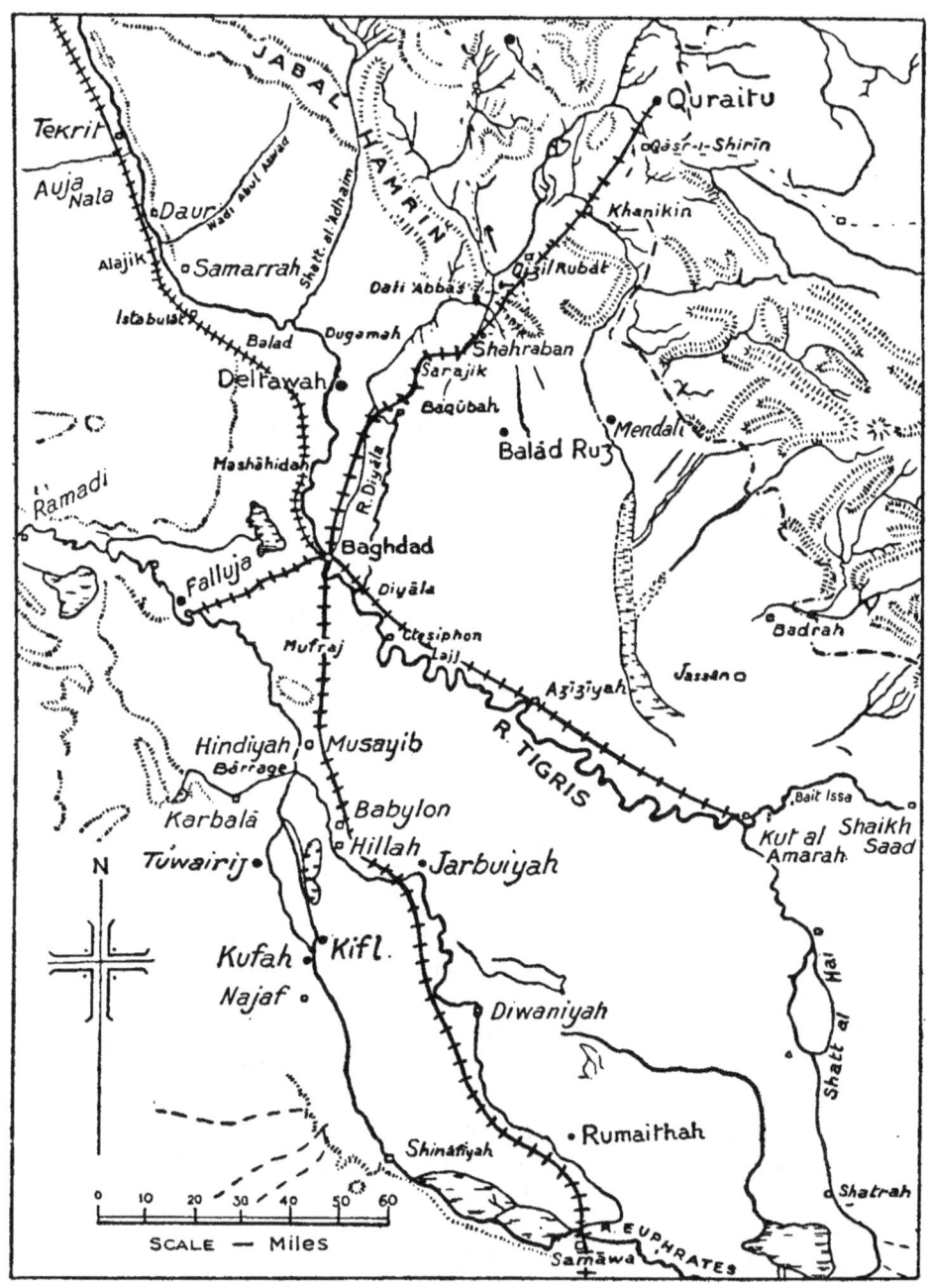

LOWER MESOPOTAMIA.

one or two other places one had seen on the Indus. It was still comparatively cool and pleasant at night and in the early morning, though it got unpleasantly hot in the sun in the middle of the day.

At the period we arrived in the country, the Army was suffering from a too rapid demobilization. A number of the most experienced regular officers, both on the staff and in the Administrative Services, had left the country, and many of those who remained, as judged from the state of things, were second-class men at the best of times. Some seemed third or fourth class.

The good temporary officers appeared, almost to a man, to have departed, for "temporary gents," and bad ones at that, swarmed, particularly in jobs where they could, in the old Indian parlance, "shake the pagoda tree." There is good reason for supposing that supervision, over these latter had been, for some time past, by no means what it might have been, even allowing for difficulties of movement, climate and shortage of personnel. We have General Haldane's statement, "the extent to which peculation was carried on almost defies belief," and regular officers who went to that country in early 1920 will thoroughly endorse it. One could almost feel the miasma of lethargy, apathy and corruption that pervaded the whole country. It will be remembered that certain letters to *The Morning Post, Pioneer*, and other newspapers of repute commented on the state of things.

The staff work at Basra was indifferent. Having arrived at a camp somewhere in the wilderness we were practically marooned there. The telephone was out of order when we arrived, and as we were not provided with a list of calls, was of extremely little value when it did work, for the gentleman at the exchange, evidently a "Wog" of sorts, knew nothing and could do nothing. We had no means of getting about beyond our flat feet, and it was getting too hot to do much walking after nine in the morning when the sundry offices were supposed to open. No effort had been made to provide us with a map or diagram showing us where important places like Ordnance, Supplies or Hospitals were.

The result was, having wandered about for what seemed hours looking for places, one would arrive, not infrequently, when they had closed down for the day. In this connection most offices seemed to shut for good about midday, and it was impossible to find the individual sought for.

There was ample evidence that the supervision of senior officers was sketchy, and, in some cases, nil.

We were unable to obtain mineral waters even. Right up country in out-of-the-way places there was never any difficulty in doing this. We had, in consequence, to go to a private firm selling Schweppe's at twelve annas a bottle. There could have been no possible greater contrast between the manner in which Basra was run in early 1920 and that of July 1921. On the latter occasion the staff officers were excellent, and, although the temperature ran up to 129 and 130 on three of the ten days we were there, we were infinitely more comfortable than in 1920. Early in that year the attitude of most staff and administrative officers on the lines of communication, together, it was whispered, with a goodly proportion of General Head-quarters, seemed first of all to serve themselves; second, in order to keep their jobs, the general; third and last, the troops. In other words, a complete reversal of the code preached at the Staff Colleges.

The 37th Lancers, one of our old local regiments, had also arrived at Basra about the same time as ourselves. There were a certain number of men in it who had served under the writer in Jacob's Horse, whom it was very pleasant to see again.

We learnt that we were to go to Diwaniyah, a small town on the Hillah branch of the Euphrates, to relieve the 22nd Cavalry, the 37th going to Ahwaz in Persia.

The arrangements for entrainment were typically Mesopotamian. There was an enormous jumble of trucks at the station and no one to tell us which lot to get into. The R.T.O. who, on decently run fronts would have been there, was presumably, and in accordance with the customs of the Mespot lines of communication, quaffing beer with brother temporary gents and, quite probably, with sergeants.

We got into what appeared to be a train as it had some first- and second-class compartments on it. About two minutes before the hour for departure a dusky gentleman told us we were on the wrong train.

The Colonel refused to shift—and we won.

DIWANIYAH

Our arrival at Diwaniyah was typical of many of our subsequent moves by rail, in that the " movements " branch of the staff seemed to ignore the necessity of warning authorities of the arrival of troops. The result would be, as on this occasion, that no preparations would be made for one's reception at the destination.

As trains would arrive sometimes in the very hottest time of the day, and as the stations had, almost invariably, neither water nor shade, the hardship inflicted on the men can be imagined. In this instance an officer of the 22nd Cavalry happened to be going out shooting and passed by the station. The stationmaster casually told him we were arriving in an hour. This was the first and only notification that we were coming, although we had left Basra fifteen hours before. Wiring ahead was not, however, any guarantee that much notice would be taken of it at the other end, particularly if one was arriving at Baghdad, where the staff responsible for the reception of troops was about on a par with the Basra gang. In all our many moves through Baghdad by rail, only once did an officer meet the train and assist with transport or orders. Movements at Baghdad, it may be said, were greatly complicated by the distance apart of the stations—some seven miles between Baghdad Right Bank and Hinaidi on the left, and by the distance between various camps.

When leaving the country we took the precaution of always sending one of our own officers ahead to arrange something—experience had shown that even in 1921 one could not trust the local staff at Baghdad. In 1920, however, we had the disadvantage of having been only schooled in France, Palestine and India.

Diwaniyah is the usual small Arab town fringing the river. Some of the houses were quite good. The British officers were in the old Turkish fort —a mud building like Frontier forts with much the same accommodation. The men were in E.P. tents close by.

There is a good bit of cultivation in the neighbourhood with sundry very deep water canals, which have high banks and sheer sides, only passable at a few points. There are a few palms close to the town, but otherwise the country is " miles and miles of blink all," as Mr. Atkins put it. In the winter the place would have been quite a good station. There was lots of sport and some of the best snipe and duck shooting in the world. One could get, in addition, very good jackal hunting with long dogs, and polo of sorts. The dead flat country made training rather a difficulty.

When we arrived, however, it was getting very hot after about 10.00 in the morning.

There were a good many other British officers of varying categories there: Railway, Levies, Public Works, and Political. Nearly the whole of these were below the average type of Sahib one meets in India, and one or two were frequently drunk. On seeing them one could understand the Arab not thinking much of us. The Political Officer had his wife with him and some of the married officers of the 22nd had had theirs as well.

There were sundry British soldiers running things like ice machines, mineral-water machines and rations. They were undisciplined and usually a nuisance, though one had to have them as there was no one else to do the work until our men had learnt it. The constant calls on the British units to supply men for this type of job militated seriously against their efficiency and made them very short-handed. All things considered, our rations were by no means too bad considering the country produced but little. We got ice and mineral waters. The difficulty was fresh vegetables and we could not even get potatoes in a few weeks' time. All potatoes came from India. There was a good canteen at Hillah, fifty miles off, though it took a long time to get there, the train being very slow. The only troops in the place were two squadrons of the 22nd and a platoon of the 114th Mahrattas guarding Turkish prisoners. As to why we had Turkish prisoners eighteen months after the Armistice baffled one. It was cruel, and their feed cost an enormous amount. These prisoners were supposed to work on one of the canals. In practice they mooched about much as British labour corps in France did.

Cavalry regiments in Mesopotamia all had machine-gun sections, a fact quite unknown in India.

The result was we had no trained personnel whatever, and it was not until the Rebellion was more or less finished that our men became skilled gunners. The transport we took over was limber wagon. There were no G.S. wagons.

The 22nd, wise through bitter experience, had accumulated a simply enormous stock of Ordnance stores, about enough to equip two regiments. We, unfortunately, accustomed to France, Palestine and even India, thought it our duty to return such stuff as we did not think we should want. The result was fatal. Once back in Ordnance, indents or urgent letters were so much waste paper in so far as getting anything out was concerned. We heard that the members of the department spent their time quarrelling among themselves as to whether the Indian Service should be top dogs or the British. It was positively infuriating to go round some stores and see stuff the unfortunate troops were crying out for, lying in heaps, sometimes rotting.

The only method of getting things from Ordnance was to despatch an officer, with the necessary transport, to the particular section in which the article lay. At Baghdad there seemed to be innumerable sections, some on one side of the Tigris and some on the other, sometimes several miles apart.

The attitude of by far the majority of the warrant-officer type towards officers was free and easy. This was owing to the normal junior officer of the period being much of his own class. If a young officer did not appreciate the honour and showed a disposition to be " stand-offish " he would, in all probability, be obstructed—and the capacity for obstruction of the lower middle- and lower-class Britisher is remarkable. Vitally essential equipment like Hotchkiss rifles, pack saddlery and water gear would be held up regardless of the fact that the unit might be under orders for a column. In one peculiarly futile case we could get no farriers' tools, although squadrons were under orders for stony country towards Mosul. There was ample stuff to supply ten times the number demanded.

We had been at Diwaniyah about a week when the new G.O.C.-in-C., Lieut.-General Sir Aylmer Haldane, visited the place on his first tour of inspection. He had only landed in the country a few days before we had.

He commented on the manner in which troops were strewn about the country in squadrons and companies, on, apparently, the lines of police rather than soldiers. At that time he was under the impression that our rule was popular. We had thought so too, and it was rather a shock to hear from the 22nd Cavalry that it was not the case.

The astounding distribution was based, it seems, on the old Turkish system. The authorities, however, failed to appreciate the fact that while the Turks sought to divide the tribes, our system tended to unite them. Furthermore, the notion that our rule might not be exactly popular, and might even be more unpopular than that of the wicked Turk, was too ridiculous to be considered. An extraordinary feature in Mesopotamia was that although troops were strewn all over the place by companies and squadrons, there were no local defence schemes for cases of emergency.

We were ordered to make one out at once. On getting down to it it was an eye-opener. The Political Officer himself doubted our popularity. His estimate of possible numbers up against us in time of trouble was about two thousand, with an unknown number of rifles. It must be remembered that the battlefields south of Kut were only some sixty miles to the east, and there must have been arms and ammunition galore to be had merely for the picking up.

The General Staff furnished us with no intelligence whatever, everything being based on the Political Officer. To show how inaccurate this was, within three months the best part of ten thousand tribesmen concentrated on Rumeitha, some fifty miles to the south and in the same political division.

The maps were so inaccurate as to be almost a danger—and this was eighteen months after the Armistice.

If we were to hang on to Diwaniyah, the nearest place whence help would come would be from Hillah, fifty miles away to the north. There was supposed to be a brigade there, but it consisted, in point of fact, of one weak British battalion, all recruits, one Indian battalion and a battery, but no cavalry. The rest of it was strewn about the country like the proverbial peas on a drum. The first thing that occurred to one was to wonder where a relief force would be collected from.

Between ourselves and Hillah was a single line of railway with sundry bridges, all certain to be destroyed as soon as trouble began. The Hillah branch of the Euphrates was unnavigable and the country on either side only desert. We had seven days' rations for men and three for horses, with little or nothing to supplement this amount locally.

Furthermore, the railway was the far side of the river from the fort, in which all the stores were. The perimeter of both was far too great for us to watch.

There were many other complicating items such as the probable attitude of the levies and local inhabitants, for the latter were Sunni Mussulmans, while the country Arab is a Shiah.

Tales were, by now, floating down about the fighting qualities of the Arabs encountered on the Upper Euphrates, and they were not encouraging. The Mesopotamian Arab is an extraordinarily fine man physically and there were many indications that, whatever our experience had hitherto been, he might prove a tough enough customer if there was sufficient incentive for loot. In the past we had plenty of seasoned troops, and they were not strewn all over the country. The attitude of the 17th Division, nevertheless, was that they were rabbits and not to be bothered about. It is understood that General Head-quarters and the Division rather came to loggerheads on this point.

Frankly, one may have been pessimistic, but on going into these details one did not like the look of things and thought that the best thing to do would be to break through to Hillah as soon as things got nasty.

A significant and disturbing feature with regard to every service in the country in which some form of graft was possible, was the manner in which one so often saw junior temporary officers, warrant-officers and N.C.O.'s fitted out with carpets and trophies which must have cost far beyond what their pay could ever have allowed. It made one think. One has often pondered over the certain corruption of " Wog " rule uncontrolled by good British officials, but it is doubtful if it could be very much more corrupt than that of bad-class European.

It was not for nothing that the Duke of Wellington observed: "Only the better-class Englishman is fit to hold the King's commission."

A further unpleasant feature was the extremely poor quality of the British troops. Units consisted merely of half-disciplined, pale-faced boys who were always going sick.

From much study of previous campaigns in which British and Indian troops have taken part, it seems doubtful whether the latter have ever had less stiffening than in 1920.

Things have now changed, or a state of *tête monté* might have resulted, with serious consequences.

It became extremely hot after the first week in April, though it was pleasant enough until about nine in the morning. After that it usually blew, either down or up the Euphrates, and there was nearly always more or less of a dust-storm. The nights were quite pleasant. In Mesopotamia, indeed, they are, as compared with India, always fairly cool. There were few or none of those stifling nights one experienced at Jacobabad or in the Derajat. The sand-flies, however, were a positive pest unless one smeared oneself with a disgusting concoction called "Vermigelli," which made one look as if one had dabbed curry powder over one.

Hinaidi

On the 22nd April, the Pathan and Sikh squadrons, under the writer, without horses, proceeded to join the 7th Cavalry Brigade at Hinaidi, a desert spot, yclept a "cantonment," about seven miles out of Baghdad, about a mile from the left bank of the Tigris. We were, at that time, destined for the Upper Euphrates about Anah, in relief of the two squadrons of the 22nd that were still up there. This was subsequently changed and we remained on at Hinaidi.

There was the normal muddle on arrival at the Right Bank station at Baghdad. There was no one to meet the train, and not one of us knew anything at all of the local geography. We had arrived at about nine in the morning and had great difficulty in getting hold of the staff captain of the 7th Cavalry Brigade on the telephone. This, as usual, was in indifferent working order, but we gathered that he had only just learnt that we were arriving at all, and that through a telegram we had sent off regimentally. The "movements" branch had told the brigade nothing. No camp was prepared, and all this had to be done by a detachment of the Guides Cavalry who worked hard all day long pitching tents for us.

After hanging about for two or three hours, one squadron embarked on a steamer. The Inland Water Transport officer then sent it to the wrong landing-place, with the result that the transport had gone to another some four miles off. He nearly sent the second squadron to a third place, but we attracted the skipper's attention in time. Thanks to the abominable staff work, our unfortunate men were exposed to a roasting sun for hours and only came into camp by dark.

The matter was reported. It is, however, doubtful if the report got far. There was an attitude of apathy among most senior officers who had been in the country some time, and many seemed in a terror of making complaints. Things only began to get right when a number of officers who had served in France and other properly run fronts began to turn up. Thanks to these men, things became fairly satisfactory by the end of the year.

Hinaidi Cantonment had been "laid out" by a man who "thought big." A full account of it can be seen in Sir Aylmer Haldane's book. It was a wonderful testimony to the great brains that had ordered things military in Mesopotamia in the last year or so. To have placed the mounted units in the neighbourhood of either the Tigris or Diala was too simple a plan. They were, accordingly, located two miles from either. By this means, the Electrical and Mechanical Service who were responsible for the pumping, could come to loggerheads with the Military Works Service who dug the open channels from which horses were watered. It is rumoured that the former accused the latter of trying to make the fluid flow uphill. At any rate, the camp where we were, incidentally the best part of three miles from the pumping station, was continually short of water other than that from a small one-inch pipe which, with difficulty, supplied the men. The waste of power in using open channels can be appreciated. The result was we had to send horses to the Diala. This meant at least eight miles' trek every day and the best part of four hours taken up in watering alone.

It was small wonder that the wretched sowars were delighted to get shut of such a place.

The 7th Cavalry Brigade—where the other brigades were is not known—was commanded by Brigadier-General Young, 10th Lancers. It consisted of our old friends the King's Dragoon Guards, the 7th Dragoon Guards and "A" Battery R.H.A., "The Chestnut Troop." The British cavalry units were much under strength and the men were, like all the British troops of the period, young recruits. They were still in the very elementary stages of learning to ride. Thanks, also, to the introduction of a system of education in algebra, Shakespeare and similar useful subjects for men who have to earn their living with their hands, their time was diverted from the tasks experience had hitherto shown essential to soldiering. Their officers continually complained of the impossible job they had, to combine both education and recruit instruction.

The King's Dragoon Guards had not one single man who had been with us in France, the 7th only two or three, and "A" Battery was much the same. The officers were all men who had been through the War, and the two British cavalry regiments were extremely fortunate in having had very small battle casualties. The wives and families were also at Hinaidi. With the exception of one or two mud barracks the whole were in E.P. tents and were as comfortable as could be expected in such a country. Among the British troops the percentage of men suffering from sand-fly fever was very high in the hot-weather months.

In so far as we were concerned, we were far more comfortable than one would be in a camp on the Indian Frontier. The soil, though in appearance like the Indian "pat," has far more clay in it and is not nearly so dusty. Our camp was almost entirely free of flies, though, owing to litter having been put down to make a race-course near brigade head-quarters, there were a good many there.

The horses were kept well away from both officers and men and the arrangements for disposal of litter were excellent. There was a canteen fairly close and we could get any amount of light Japanese beer. The men's rations were good, and had it not been for the watering of horses and complete absence of any shade outside their tents they would have been pretty happy.

The horse feed, although sufficient in quantity for those in good condition, was of very poor quality. It was extremely difficult to get animals which were run down fattened up. The grass was bad—all Indian. The grain was filthy. The grass could hardly be helped, but the dirty and poor grain could have been. It was obviously false economy to run the risk of losing valuable horses to save a few annas—and we did lose them.

Badly administered though Mesopotamia was, there is no blinking the fact that troops out there were far better fed after 1916 than had ever been the case on the Indian Frontier before the War.

As one has heard officers grouse at the conditions of the Afghan War, it may not be amiss to remind them of what the normal pre-war conditions on the Indian Frontier were, particularly of those under which the Scinde Horse served. In the first place officers drew no rations. They had to fend for themselves. Unless there were British troops about, one's food in the hot weather was usually of the poorest quality and ice was often unprocurable. On outposts, bread was not to be had, and one lived on indigestible chupattis. Vegetables and potatoes could not be obtained. Many an officer has had only rice, onions, tough chicken or goat and tinned stores to live on for long periods together. There were no canteens, and tinned stores cost a fortune. Furthermore, one had to pay for one's transport. The tentage was confined to 80-lb. tents at the largest, and often not even them. In many places, and intensely hot ones at that, there were no punkahs, as there was no one to pull them. In native cavalry units there were herds of followers, and the sanitary discipline was almost always indifferent. As one was hugger-mugger with horses, mules and vile-smelling camels, there were, not infrequently, flies in abundance.

Finally, the hospital conditions were primitive, to put things mildly. The men's hospital at Fort Sandeman in 1900 was worse than a barn owing to the inhuman parsimony of the Indian Government.

The two squadrons of the 22nd Cavalry, under Major Montagu Smith, Scinde Horse, who had served with that Regiment since 1917, arrived at Hinaidi about the end of April and we took over from them. Their horses were all in poor condition, and one squadron was so bad as to have its animals thrown out of work till the end of June, and even then were not right.

The absence of shade and the constant difficulty over watering did not help things, and a number had to be shot. Many horses were suffering from laminitis, as the effect of long hard marching over the dead soil of the country without shoes.

A little green stuff was obtained from the Government Grass Farm, but was not sufficient to effect anything. Had more been obtainable there is but little doubt that the horses would have pulled together very quickly. We had a somewhat similar experience the following April at Mosul. In this month there is excellent grazing in places. Mesopotamia, it may be as well to state, is a healthier country than by far the larger portion of India. Men, horses and dogs will get fit extremely quickly if the amenities of civilization are obtainable.

In mid-May the King's Dragoon Guards, 7th Dragoon Guards and "A" Battery R.H.A. (less one section) went up to Karind, the so-called hill station in Persian territory. A satirical poem, based on the "Charge of the Light Brigade" appeared in *Truth* apropos this camp and the money spent on it.

The "mass of manœuvre" now left at Baghdad appeared to amount to our two squadrons, the section of "A" Battery, and about a battalion of indifferent Indian infantry who were at Daurah, on the far side of the Tigris. All were the best part of seven miles out of the city. There were mechanical transport, ordnance and supply depots strewn about promiscuously in every direction on the outskirts. Hardly anyone knew where they were owing to the difficulty of getting a car to take one round to reconnoitre. One did not feel tempted to ride fifteen miles in the appalling heat.

About mid-June the 45th Sikhs were brought down from up country to Hinaidi.

There were fourteen thousand Turkish prisoners in Mesopotamia, of whom a very large number were about Baghdad. Theoretically, they were employed on laying out the boulevards of the modern Babylon that Hinaidi was seemingly destined to become. In practice they spent their time smoking and talking. We had some working for us levelling the ground, which was full of holes. They were extremely nice men, and one felt very sorry for them. They were shipped out of the country when the Rebellion was at its height, greatly to the relief of the G.O.C.-in-C., to whom they were a sore embarrassment. They were eventually sent direct from Basra to Constantinople. On crossing to their villages in Anatolia they were promptly made soldiers again, to oust the hated and despised Greek from Turkish territory—which they did to some effect.

At the beginning of June, Regimental Head-quarters and "A" and "D" Squadrons arrived from Diwaniyah, where they had been relieved by the 37th. We did not, however, have the Regiment together for long, for trouble broke out on the lines of communication between Shergat and Mosul and some convoys had been scuppered. "A" and "C" Squadrons (Sikh and Derejat), with Major Montagu Smith, Captain Hudson and Second-Lieutenant Aspinall, went up there. These squadrons formed part of sundry columns from time to time.

Two days after " C " Squadron arrived at Quaiyarah, one of our patrols accompanying the daily convoy spotted a band of raiders close to the place. The squadron at once moved out and engaged them. A running fight took place, the enemy covering a very wide front in small groups, all mounted. The ground here is rather broken and favoured them greatly. Nevertheless, although greatly outnumbered, the squadron pushed them back. Second-Lieutenant Aspinall had his horse hit and Jemadar Bhagat Singh was slightly wounded.

Although at Hinaidi one heard of petty fights on the Mosul lines of communication and about Tel Afar, there was absolutely no indication given to the troops of the possibility of any trouble beyond riots in Baghdad. There was not an inkling in the 7th Cavalry Brigade office even. The civil authorities, on the other hand, had repeatedly warned General Head-quarters that a rebellion was imminent, and it is related that the Acting Civil Commissioner, on being called up on the telephone by some one telling him of the rising at Rumeitha, merely observed, " Oh, well, it has come at last." The civil authorities were in no way surprised.

Towards the end of June some shots were fired at some men of the 45th Sikhs near Hinaidi. This indicated that things were not normal, but not much notice was taken of it.

The dominating idea in every one's mind was to get through the hot weather as comfortably as the extremely uncomfortable circumstances permitted. We had, by then, got the British officers into the mud barracks the King's Dragoon Guards had quitted, and these were infinitely preferable to E.P. tents. Some of the rooms were supposed to be fitted out with electric fans. Such fans as there were, however, revolved at about one mile per hour and were about fifteen feet from the ground.

The heat out of the sun, provided the hot wind could be kept out, was nothing like as great as corresponding temperatures would make it in India, and in a good house would not be thought very much of. With the same amenities of civilization, indeed, a hot weather at Baghdad would not compare to one in Rajputana. The men's lines were nearly a mile away, and were just on the fringe of the track of the most enormous dust devils one had ever seen. We were, for some reason, clear of this track, and one method of killing time was to speculate and bet on which of our men's tents would be hit. In this pastime, however, we were deprived of that ineffable pleasure it always is to see some brother officer's tent soar into the air, for this particular form of glee is not applicable when it comes to one's men. In some respects it resembled watching a battery being shelled in France, with the enormous fountain of black smoke and earth of the last shell, coupled with the horrible scream of its successor.

Perhaps the worst feature of Hinaidi was the deadly boredom.

All work practically ceased at 09.00, as the sun became so powerful that it was impossible to do any parade work or stables after that hour. There were no trees at all and absolutely no shade.

Owing to the distance of the lines away it would come very hard on the N.C.O.'s to give them sand-table or other exercises in our quarters.

In an Indian hot weather the time of officers is well occupied up till lunch owing to the amount of administration that has to be attended to. In Mesopotamia, there was little or none, and the only breaks in the day were the arrival of the ice at about midday, which signified a cold shandy gaff, lunch and tea. It was seldom cool enough to go out before 17.30.

There were sundry "stand to's" in June, and towards the end of the month we had to go into Baghdad to patrol the streets. There was strong anti-British propaganda flying round. Major Connop had then joined the Regiment. Thanks to our having been seven miles out of the place we did not know much of its geography as regards the side streets, and this might have been a serious matter.

The Police attached to us knew neither English nor Hindustani, and it was very difficult to carry on.

A situation that might have precipitated the Rebellion occurred near Kadhimain, the sacred mosque outside Baghdad. A patrol of a dozen men under Jemadar Mahomed Niwaz, the P.T. instructor of Kantara, met a mob of several hundreds in a highly excited state against anything British. The situation, as reported by the Police Inspector, was delicate in the extreme. Thanks, however, to the coolness and presence of mind of the jemadar, the mob was quietened and very serious trouble averted. We were well looked after by the 17th Division and would have welcomed permanent duty in Baghdad. Some of the officers messed with the R.A.M.C. in a Jewish Hospital that had been taken over by the military. This was quite comfortable, though the sand-flies on the roof at night were simply awful. A rich Jewboy had built the place, and this gentleman had no intention of letting his memory fade away, for he had announced the fact on an enormous marble slab in no less than three different languages.

Among other preparations for the Rebellion it would seem that the leaders had made attempts to tamper with Mussulman troops, and many units were under suspicion, some justly.

Under Government arrangements, parties of sepoys had gone on pilgrimages to Najaf and Karbala, and there is strong reason to suppose that the men had been approached while on them, but by no means necessarily with success from the agitator's point of view. It must, at the same time, be remarked that with Indian troops, religion is occasionally apt to loom in the foreground when the conditions of service are not to their liking. We know that Baghdad was a singularly holy place in early 1916 when rations were short and the fighting hard, and Mesopotamia in the hot weather is never a nice country. The fact remains that in most regiments the attitude of Mussulman troops was watched with a certain degree of anxiety in the early phases of the Rebellion. In our own case, we know that our Indian officers fought shy of a certain other unit, that was frequently located in the same place with us, as they said they were not to be wholly trusted. As regards our own men, we had been rather struck with the attitude of some of our Pathans at Hinaidi when they were asked if they wanted to go on a pilgrimage.

Their reply rather reminded us of the unspeakable dictum of Mr. Atkins on the subject of church parades, and the subject was dropped.

One is cynical enough to imagine that the probable reason was that these men were Sunnis and regarded Shiah shrines much on the same lines as a full-blooded Orangeman would regard an R.C. church. It must, however, be remembered that a large proportion of our Pathan N.C.O.'s were men who had been in France and Palestine, and some had been to Mecca. They were pretty tough-headed gentry and were not going to waste their hard-earned pay on making uncomfortable journeys in the hot weather. One man was so irreverent as to describe some of the people they would come across on pilgrimages as only fit for the fate of Sodom and Gomorrah, and there is but little doubt that numbers of inhabitants of holy places belong to this category. Some men of the other squadrons duly went, but did not show many signs of wanting to go again, and by mid-June there were no candidates at all.

Trouble in Indian regiments on religious matters will usually be found due to two things: first, some defect in the running of the unit which has led to discontent, either in whole or in part, and second, to not enough work being done, whereby time becomes available for intrigue—and intrigue is the very breath of life to some classes. A happy, well-disciplined regiment that works hard will withstand the strongest propaganda, whether racial or religious.

It is significant that those units in the Punjab in April 1919, in which the men were kept hard at it, there was no trouble whatever.

As leave was open and as there were no indications of trouble, the writer and Lieutenant Marten took advantage of the fact. There were, at that time, many officers who had had no leave in England for as much as seven or eight years. While waiting for a ship at Basra news was received of the isolation of Rumeitha. In those days, however, there were no illusions on the subject of giving up leave to go on service—four and a half years of a great war were enough to cure that.

CHAPTER XXIV

THE 35TH SCINDE HORSE.
THE ARAB REBELLION.
1920–1921.

THE OUTBREAK OF THE REBELLION.
THE MANCHESTER COLUMN DISASTER. OPERATIONS ROUND HILLAH.

1920

THE OUTBREAK

THE Rebellion proper may be said to have broken out on the 3rd July, when a small force of the 99th Infantry and the 114th Mahrattas, numbering about three hundred and fifty all told, was shut up in Rumeitha, a small town on the Hillah branch of the Euphrates about thirty-five miles south of Diwaniyah.

There were very many causes leading to it. The primary reasons were, however, first, our withdrawal of so many troops from the country. The Arab believes what he sees and understands but little beyond force. Second, we had taken, lying down, an ejectment from Deir el Zor, on the Upper Euphrates, some months before, and had made no attempt to re-establish ourselves there. Third, our administration was unpopular—some say even more so than that of the Turk.

The immediate cause was the arrest of a Sheikh near Rumeitha for not paying back a loan which was greatly overdue. There are yarns of a breach of faith on our part, the Sheikh having been induced to come into Rumeitha on the understanding that nothing would happen, and then being arrested.

This was the Arab idea on the subject, and caustic comments by British officers besieged in Rumeitha show there was something behind it.

The small detachments of troops that had been sent there found themselves invested with only a few days' rations. It was only by means of raids into the bazaar that they were supplemented. A relief column, consisting of a squadron of the 37th from Diwaniyah, the 45th Sikhs and a couple of guns, attempted to get through on the 7th July. The enemy was found to be in great strength, strongly posted behind a bund with a boggy patch of ground in front, which held up the assault. As the casualties were very heavy owing to the absolutely open ground, Colonel McVean, the column commander, very wisely determined to retire. He estimated the enemy at anything between three thousand and five thousand. A dust-storm fortunately enabled him to get back about a mile before the enemy spotted it. The casualties had amounted to no less than two hundred and fifteen out of about nine hundred present. It was, later on, estimated that there were nearer nine thousand than five thousand Arabs engaged. The next attempt was made with two squadrons of the 37th, two batteries and four battalions, which one would, as judged from Indian and Afghan experiences, have imagined enough to hammer almost any force of irregulars. On the 19th July this column found the enemy on the same position as before. The attack failed to dislodge the enemy, who counter-attacked our right battalion, but got severely punished in doing so.

The force was cut off from water in the river on its left flank as the enemy had occupied the far banks. A fifth battalion, the 10th Gurkhas, who had just "marched to the cannon" from Imam Hamza, was directed to cross and clear the enemy away. This attempt also failed. The British troops were in a state of collapse owing to heat and the Indians not much better. The situation was almost desperate. Fortunately a train arrived next morning with water and ammunition, which had been running short. The 10th Gurkhas also succeeded in getting over the river. The enemy was then found to have evacuated the position, and Rumeitha was relieved. The hostile entrenchments were most skilfully constructed, and there was every evidence of Turkish trained officers running the enemy.

The casualties in the relief column had amounted to nearly two hundred.

The Rumeitha garrison had lost no fewer than one hundred and forty-eight out of five hundred, including non-combatants. It had been shut up for sixteen days and only had four days' half rations left. A general massacre would have inevitably occurred had they not been relieved.

On the 22nd July the force began to withdraw to Diwaniyah, and for a brief space the column was in great danger owing to Arabs taking advantage of a dust-storm to rush the rear-guard.

The Scinde Horse, less "A" and "C" Squadrons, marched from Hinaidi on the 15th July, for Hillah. Captain Knox had just rejoined from leave and went to his own Pathan squadron ("B").

The following officers accompanied the Regiment :—Colonel Lukin, Major Connop, Captain Knox, Lieutenants Bott, Geddes, Robinson and Mmd Ayub.

There had been the usual difficulty in getting stores out of the Baghdad

Ordnance, and the Regiment had not managed to complete its equipment when it left.

All ranks were only too delighted to get clear of the Hinaidi dust heap.

At Hillah there was a pretty fair " wind up " and there was a good bit of confusion, for " Rumcol " (the Rumeitha relief column) was assembling to the south near Imam Hamza.

On the 19th, " B " Squadron entrained for Diwaniyah, but, having gone a certain distance, the train was recalled, reaching Hillah next day.

On the 20th July, the Manchester Regiment, less one company at Diwaniyah, and its machine-gun section which was with " Rumcol," arrived from Tekrit. It, in common with all other British units, was full of half-trained recruits, town-bred men, not physically fit for the appallingly trying conditions of heat and exposure that prevailed.

In Mesopotamia there was no shade, and any previous attempts at hot-weather fighting had invariably led to heavy casualties from heat stroke, even when the troops were fairly old soldiers. Failure to appreciate this fact was responsible, to a great extent, for the disaster that took place four days later.

The troops now in Hillah were :—

>   Scinde Horse, H.Q. and two squadrons.
>   39th Battery R.F.A.
>   Sappers and Miners, one company.
>   2nd Manchester Regiment (less one company and M.G.'s).
>   32nd Pioneers, one company.

There were dumps, hospitals and various depots in the place, which was, to a great extent, a base for the relief of Rumeitha. General Haldane tells us that too large a proportion of stores had been concentrated forward at Diwaniyah, which complicated things enormously, and eventually led to the abandonment of something like a million sterling worth.

All around Hillah, up stream and down stream, there is a belt of date palms and mud wall enclosures to a distance of about half a mile from the river. A number of branch irrigation canals also strike off in the neighbourhood. The place, therefore, was not strong defensively owing to the ease with which it could be approached under cover. The attitude of the townspeople was peaceful outwardly, but officers, who marched out on the fatal 23rd of July, only saw scowling faces the whole way through the streets. The country Arabs, for twenty miles around, had shown no signs of trouble, but about Kifl, twenty-two miles to the south-west, there was known to be a hostile concentration. Furthermore, Kufah, thirty-seven miles in the same direction, had actually been invested, with a garrison of two companies of the 108th Infantry, on the 21st.

News that Rumeitha had been relieved had just come in, and the tales of the fighting to the south certainly belied the yarns before current that the Arab was not a formidable opponent.

The manner in which he had tampered with the railway, at times and at places which were most inconvenient for us, his method of controlling the water channels, and his amazing capacity to concentrate large numbers of men seemingly out of nowhere, had become apparent. The intense heat had shown the limitations of our forces, particularly of the young British troops, who had been almost " hors de combat " on occasions.

On the 21st July Colonel Lukin took over command of the troops at Hillah as the senior officer on the spot. He never rejoined the Regiment, which was commanded by Major Connop, until Major Landon came out from leave in October. There had been a good many changes in command in the last few days. Troops were expected at Hillah from Diwaniyah daily now that Rumeitha had been relieved.

The Manchester Column Disaster

On the 23rd July the Political Officer at Hillah urgently represented to Colonel Lukin the necessity of "showing the flag" in the Kifl direction. This was agreed to, and approval of the movement was received from the divisional general at Diwaniyah. The column, however, was not to go farther than six miles down the Kifl Road. Information from Political sources indicated water at the halting-place, but no military reconnaissance was sent out to confirm it.

The troops composing the column were as follows :—

> Scinde Horse (less two squadrons), under Major Connop.
> 39th Battery R.F.A.
> 2nd Manchester Regiment (less one company).
> 32nd Pioneers, one company.
> 24th Combined Field Ambulance.

The commander was a brevet-lieut.-colonel of the Manchesters, his own C.O. commanding the battalion, an arrangement which complicated things greatly.

The only troops to remain in Hillah were the Sapper and Miner company. In view of the serious consequences that might ensue if trouble broke out in the town this garrison was totally inadequate, even admitting the possibility of troops arriving very shortly. The constant interruptions on the railway made movements of troops by train very uncertain.

The country towards Kifl is of the ordinary flat Mesopotamian type but with numerous dry water channels. Most of these are formidable obstacles and quite unjumpable by a horse. There are no trees, and there is only a certain amount of low scrub here and there, just sufficient to hide a man lying down at night. For the most part, however, the country is quite bare.

The Kifl track was unmetalled and ill defined, crossing the various irrigation channels by narrow bridges.

No opposition was anticipated on the march out. The column marched at 16.00 the same day (23rd). This meant that the unfortunate young British troops were knocking about in the sun at least an hour before, and that at a temperature of something like 117 degrees in the shade—and there was no shade. Some one hundred and fifty A.T. carts, with tentage and stores, accompanied the column. Despite this amount of transport, no special arrangements for water beyond the ordinary battalion water carts was made. The Scinde Horse, however, carried both water bottles and chaguls as their normal marching order, a factor that saved many unfortunate infantry soldiers in the rout the next day.

On arrival at bivouac after a most fatiguing march it was found that the only water available was from a railway tank, sufficient for the men, but quite inadequate for animals. The latter, therefore, remained unwatered that night as it was not considered prudent to send them far afield in the growing darkness.

It may be as well to state here that the only soldier of any experience in Arab warfare in the whole column was Major Connop and he, on his own initiative, continually took measures not thought of elsewhere. He did not like the look of things at all, nor did the battery commander.

The British infantry had reached bivouac in a state of great exhaustion through the heat and dust. The medical officer reported they were unfit to march for another twenty-four hours. This was passed on to Hillah (authority, The History of the Manchester Regiment). Despite this, the commandant at Hillah, just after midnight, ordered the column to march next day to the Rustumiyah Canal, about seven miles farther out.

The Political Officer had persuaded Colonel Lukin to push the column on with a view to striking a blow to discourage a rising on the part of the neighbouring tribes, who were, it was said, at present perfectly friendly.

As to what was to be expected from young infantry soldiers in a state of exhaustion is hard to conceive.

Water having been found some distance from bivouac, the animals were given a drink, but, owing to the sides of the canal being sheer, great delay occurred, and it was not until 09.30 that the column again marched. The state of affairs can be imagined.

The heat was intense, but there was a high wind and almost a duststorm, which eased things slightly.

The information this day was that opposition was likely as Arab scouts had been seen at various crossing-places.

The Arab villagers passed on the march seemed perfectly peaceful, and the force reached the new bivouac without encounter of any sort about midday.

The unfortunate British infantry were, however, almost in a state of collapse and a number of heat cases had occurred.

No perimeter camp was formed.

Two troops of the Scinde Horse were despatched as standing patrols on the Kifl Road and on the light railway leading to that place respectively.

They were to take up positions about a mile from camp.

In the meantime the force settled down and made itself as comfortable as the great heat permitted. Tents were pitched, and every one prepared for an afternoon sleep.

Lorries had arrived from Hillah with ice and rations. There were then two days' rations in hand with the column.

The question now arises as to whether the cavalry should have been pushed on or not.

Reliable information indicated the presence of the enemy some seven miles farther on about Kifl early that morning. The advanced scouts of the Scinde Horse had seen nothing, however, by noon within three miles of camp.

The force was in no condition to advance farther as a whole should the enemy be encountered some distance off.

Should the enemy advance it was extremely unlikely that he would care to leave the force behind him and push on to Hillah, for, although he has no lines of communication in the proper sense of the word, the Arab is as sensitive as any other irregular of his line of retreat. There was no certainty, from his point of view, that the clans between the force and Hillah would join in when they knew there was an unbeaten British column still in the neighbourhood.

If it were the original intention of the British to engage the enemy, whatever his strength, should he advance, it would seem that all that was required was sufficient warning to enable troops to " stand to " in case of attack. At first sight, this would have appeared to have been the intention, and the dispositions of the cavalry were adequate to this end.

If it were the intention to advance next day and engage the enemy, sufficient time would have been available for reconnaissance if the cavalry were pushed ahead early in the morning. Despatching them on a reconnaissance in the evening would have meant their going out some six or seven miles, probably having at least a skirmish, and returning the same evening. Judging from previous Mesopotamian experience there was quite a reasonable chance of their finding some difficulty in getting back, and the exhausted infantry might have had to move out to help them in.

With regard to a withdrawal to Hillah, from the condition of the infantry it was certain that they could not move till the evening, say, 18.00. It was essential, again, in view of their condition, that the move be unmolested. In order to guarantee this a protective reconnaissance despatched about 16.00 would have been called for to ensure there being no large bodies of the enemy in the neighbourhood. This reconnaissance need not have been pushed farther out than, say, three miles from camp.

The original intention, however, would appear to have been to remain in position, and under these circumstances the cavalry dispositions sufficed.

A Political Officer with the column had asked for a squadron to escort him to interview a sheikh a mile or two from camp at 16.00.

This squadron was in the act of saddling up when an orderly from one of the advanced troops galloped in with the report that Arabs were tearing up and destroying the rails and culverts on the Kifl light railway.

This was followed up by another from the troop on the road reporting a mass of Arabs coming down it. Shortly after this a wounded man and then both troops came in, reporting some thousands of Arabs advancing.

Soon a force, estimated at two thousand mounted and dismounted, with banners, came into view about two thousand five hundred yards off. The gunner telephonists at this juncture were endeavouring to get into touch with Hillah by attaching their instruments to the telegraph line. Hence a considerable delay occurred in getting the guns into action.

Their shooting, when it did begin, was good, and the enemy began to work round the flanks.

The ground round the camp had irrigation canals at about four hundred to eight hundred yards distance. In front was the Rustumiyah Canal, six feet deep, twenty feet wide, with banks six feet high, with some water in it. The branch canals were for the most part dry, but were formidable obstacles, being quite unjumpable.

For some six miles towards Hillah was the same type of intersected country, the canals being all dry. It was, therefore, admirably suited to Arab tactics, giving covered lines of approach to the road in every direction.

The Arab advance was very slow directly in front, and it was not until about 18.30 that sniping into the flanks had begun.

In the meantime, however, the Political Officers had represented to the column commander that the country in his rear would be up, and reminded him of the weak garrison left in Hillah, where all the dumps were. It was impressed on him that there might be great difficulty in getting back should the enemy block the road. The fact that fresh troops were expected in Hillah that day was apparently either forgotten, or the numbers arriving were considered insufficient to hold it by the Force Commander.

Anyhow, the decision was come to to fall back at once, leaving the camp standing.

The Manchesters were to furnish the advance and flank guards, together with two guns.

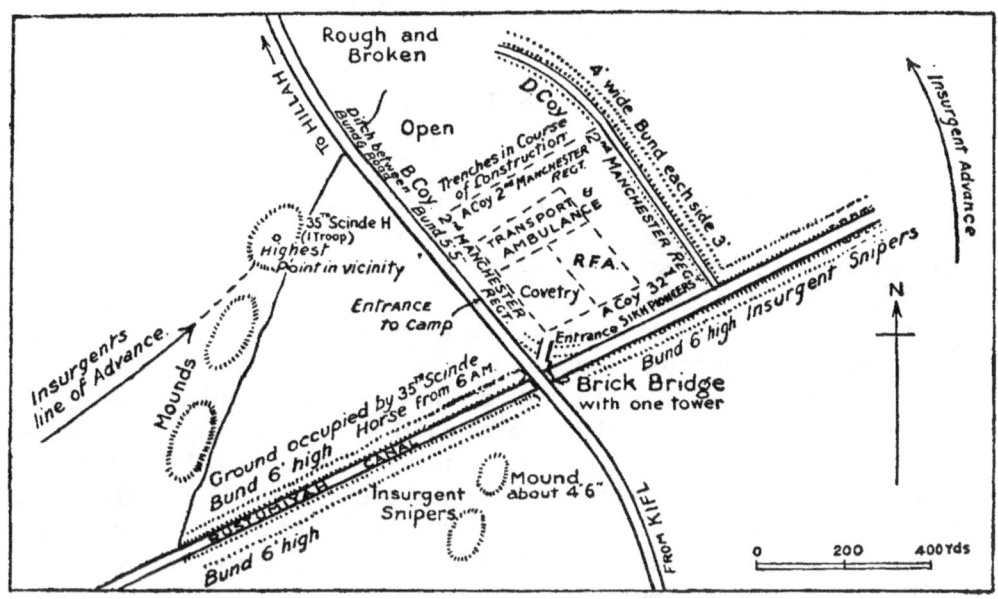

CAMP OF THE MANCHESTER COLUMN.
24th July, 1920.

The battery, the Scinde Horse less two squadrons, and the company of the 32nd Pioneers formed the rear-guard.

The Manchesters moved off at about 19.45. There was then a certain amount of sniping into the flanks, the flanks of the rear-guard being most seriously involved. These were "B" Squadron (Captain Knox) and "D" Squadron (Lieutenant Geddes) of the Scinde Horse on the right and left respectively.

The pressure on our right increased, and eventually it became necessary to reinforce "B" Squadron with two Vickers guns (Second-Lieutenant Robinson). This squadron had great difficulty in holding its ground while the transport began to get on the move.

The latter was in a state of hopeless confusion.

The commencement of sniping and the sudden appearance of the enemy had started a panic among the drabis and followers.

Mule carts and mules were stampeding in every direction. Loose horses, led by a white pony, careered wildly up and down the track where the unfortunate Manchesters were endeavouring to march.

The dust and approaching darkness added to the terror, which was shortly afterwards intensified by large bodies of Arabs entering the camp.

About then, also, a burst of heavy and continuous firing ahead announced that the Manchesters were fighting their way out.

The column had with it some one hundred and fifty A.T. carts, and it may well be imagined how difficult it was to get these on the move along the narrow ill-defined track by which the force had advanced.

The danger was intensified by carts upsetting at the narrow passages over the irrigation canals.

By the time all the transport which there was any hope of getting clear had moved off, it was high time for the rear-guard to be moving, for it was obvious that the force stood every chance of being cut in two.

Accordingly " D " Squadron, on the left, was ordered to withdraw It had to draw swords to clear the camp, which was then full of Arabs. It was just at this juncture that the battery opened on the camp with fuse zero at a range of about one hundred and fifty yards, and it was by the greatest good fortune that the squadron did not run on top of the guns.

Ressaldar Major Mahomed Azim, Scinde Horse, had, in the meantime, been endeavouring to rally the fugitives and collect men to clear the Arabs from the flanks of the guns. He had shown the greatest gallantry and coolness when he was hit in the stomach and died shortly after.

By now the Arabs had come within eighty yards of the guns and it became a question of getting them away.

In order to do so, Major Connop and a troop of " D " Squadron charged and gained sufficient air space for them to limber up and move off.

The squadron on our right, " B," had the greatest difficulty in hanging on while this withdrawal was in progress, but succeeded in getting clear, when a further body of Arabs was encountered advancing from the north, i.e., from the Hillah direction. These were charged by " B " Squadron and cleared away. It is probable that these were from villages close to the route.

The troops actually present then were the two squadrons Scinde Horse, the 39th Battery and the remains of the Pioneer Company, which had been badly cut up.

The congestion and confusion on the track made movements of the guns a matter of great difficulty. It was necessary to manhandle A.T. cart after A.T. cart off it and to clear every bridge encountered.

It was, by now, dark, though there was a moon, occasionally obscured by clouds.

The retirement was conducted in this manner for some three miles, squadrons retiring as far as was possible alternately by bounds of some four hundred yards each.

About this point, however, a gun apparently mistook the track, and upset in one of the irrigation canals.

This necessitated a halt of some duration and the Scinde Horse and battery were completely surrounded.

It was only found possible to remove the sights and breech block, the gunners displaying most extraordinary coolness and *sangfroid*.

Numerous stragglers had been picked up, some stripped naked, and many only wearing a pair of shorts, and minus boots, shirt or head-dress.

The casualties at this point among horses were very heavy, but, extraordinary to relate, those among the men were comparatively light.

The fighting had become so close that the only hope was a bayonet charge, which was delivered by "B" Squadron with great dash. This gave air space for the remainder to mount, and cover "B" Squadron's withdrawal.

The guns were duly extricated and the ground, fortunately, became more open and mounted action more possible.

"B" Squadron, led by Captain Knox, seized the opportunity to charge and a considerable air space was gained, but Knox was wounded. Shortly afterwards he again led a charge, but once more was hit, and Ressaldar Dur Khan then took over the squadron, Lieutenant Bott, the squadron officer, having been badly wounded shortly before while trying to steady the transport.

The ressaldar led the squadron to two more charges a couple of miles or so farther on.

By now it was evident that the villagers *en route* had begun to join in, for there was a steady increase of the hostile strength for the first four miles or so of the retirement. The pressure then began to relax somewhat, thanks both to the repeated charges made by the Scinde Horse and to the steadiness of the battery.

The tribesmen had, furthermore, commenced to devote their attentions to plundering the overturned carts which could not be moved.

The charges did not inflict many actual casualties, as the mounted element of the enemy invariably bolted, while the dismounted men lay down in depressions and ditches where they could not be seen in the dark.

They had, however, the effect of making him cautious and unwilling to face open ground where he could be sabred.

The staunchness of the sowars was beyond all praise, for it must be remembered that, with the demoralization and darkness, there was every opportunity for frightened or faint-hearted men to sneak off and join the fugitives.

After the seventh mile the pursuit had petered out, which was most fortunate as ammunition was almost exhausted and more than half the horses had become casualties.

It was subsequently estimated that some five thousand tribesmen were engaged in all.

The two squadrons and the battery reached Hillah at 05.30 next morning, after a retreat of sixteen miles under the most difficult and trying conditions. Some of the men had been in action since 16.00 the previous afternoon, and that at the height of the hot weather. The head of the column had arrived some two or three hours before. The principle in " small wars " of the main body keeping pace with the rear-guard had thus been violated and the column had run the risk of being permanently cut in two. That this did not occur was, in the main, due to the Arabs being taken up looting, very much as had occurred at Maiwand.

The British infantry, from heat, thirst and exhaustion, were in a desperate plight. One can quite well picture the state of affairs with seasoned troops, but with men but little better than recruits it was infinitely worse. It says much, however, for many that, when picked up by the battery wagons or mounted on the sowars' horses, they resolutely clung on to their rifles—a point which impressed the Scinde Horse troopers greatly.

As may be imagined, the casualties were extremely heavy, amounting to nearly four hundred out of the column's total strength of some eleven hundred. The Manchesters lost close on two hundred and eighty alone and, of these, only some seventy were recovered from the Arabs later on, nearly all the rest being killed.

A number of the men had gone astray where the track made a bend near Birs Nimrud and actually wandered back towards the Hindiyah or Western branch of the Euphrates, where they were either murdered or captured.

The gunners lost one gun and one wagon, together with very many horses.

Of the one hundred and fifty A.T. carts that went out, only some thirty arrived back.

The two squadrons of the Scinde Horse were comparatively lucky as regards loss in men, the total amounting to forty-seven, including followers. The killed, including missing who never rejoined, numbered twenty-two.

Among these, unfortunately, was Ressaldar Major Mahomed Azim, one of the ablest and finest Indian officers the writer has had the honour of serving with. Captain Knox, Lieutenant Bott and one Indian officer and seventeen men were wounded. Lieutenant Bott died in hospital. He was a great loss, being a capable and exceedingly cheery young officer, well liked by every one.

Eventually eight of the missing were handed over by the Arabs, by whom they had been made prisoners. The casualties in horses were extremely heavy and amounted to one hundred, not including a good many who were only slightly wounded.

Every British officer had two horses shot under him, and Major Connop had three. Among these were some very valuable polo ponies. Quite two-thirds of the men were, by the end, fighting on foot, as loose horses were stampeding in every direction.

The whole of the mess stores, amounting to some Rs 1,200 in value, all tents and all officers' and men's kits were lost, People had to carry on in the clothes they stood up in for some days after, and it was thanks to the hospitality of the 108th Infantry, in particular, that life was made bearable.

A point worth noting was that Major Connop was the only pre-war regular officer, and the only two others who had been with the Regiment any length of time, Captain Knox and Lieutenant Bott, were wounded early in the fight. The remaining young officers had only joined at the beginning of March.

At the subsequent court-of-inquiry the column commander stated that had it not been for the Scinde Horse the casualties would have been very much heavier than they were. As the unfortunate officer was fighting for his career as a soldier, to have made such a remark indicates that he was a very great gentleman.

Some of the stragglers who reached Hillah had wonderful escapes. A couple of the men of the Manchesters succeeded in getting away by throwing down money and bolting while the Arabs were looking for it. Certain Sikhs and Hindus claimed to be Mussulmans and thus got clear. One Hindu in hospital with Captain Knox, on being asked how he got away, grinned and showed him his top-knot cut off, saying, " Jab Buddoo log nazdik aya main ek dum Mussulman bangya." Most of the Hindus who got in followed his example.

These gentry, at all events, had determined to avoid the fate of the martyrs.

The mess dafadar, Sadik Shah, distinguished himself greatly in trying to save the mess, bayoneting two and shooting three Arabs. In subsequent operations he continually volunteered for patrol work and always showed up well. When the mess servants were sick he not infrequently did the cooking.

Captain Knox and Lieutenant Robinson were awarded the Military Cross, Ressaldar Dur Khan a bar to the Indian Order of Merit he had gained at the Ghoraniyeh Bridgehead on the Jordan, and Jemadar Mahomed Niwaz and two I.O.R.'s the Indian Distinguished Service Medal. Major Connop, being the senior officer present, was obviously unable to submit his own name, and it was not for some time that his admirable conduct was made known.

A most cordial relationship between the Manchester Regiment and ourselves has always existed since this miserable affair.

Thus ended the third great rear-guard fight in the history of the Scinde Horse. In the first, Clibborn's disaster at the Nuffosk Pass in the abortive effort to relieve Kahun in 1838, the regiment had lost 70 per cent. in men and 85 per cent. in horses, but had enabled the remains of the force to reach the plains.

At Maiwand, in 1880, the Third Scinde Horse had, by its charge at the end of the day, saved the 1st Bombay Grenadiers from utter destruction.

The Kifl rear-guard was in accordance with the regimental tradition.

From a cavalry point of view the following are the salient lessons:

(1) Troops must be physically fit to be able to work in very hot weather.

(2) The supreme value of discipline and steadiness, particularly in a night retirement such as this, where the chances for faint-hearted or badly trained men to fade away are unbounded.

(3) A night retirement across intersected country when in close contact with irregulars can only lead to heavy casualties, and may, more probably, lead to disaster.

(4) The value of the countercharge, either mounted or dismounted.

(5) The importance of prompt rallying.

(6) In close fighting of this description, Vickers guns and Hotchkiss rifles have great limitations, owing to the delay in loading them up when the time to retire arrives. Steady, carefully controlled rifle fire was found to be the most effective.

(7) The moral effect of arming cavalry with the bayonet, which rendered a countercharge on foot more than mere bluff. It was found, later on, that it added greatly to the men's *morale* when in close country or villages, when the sowars had several small bayonet encounters.

(8) The enormous value of cavalry in Arab warfare. Without cavalry the infantry would have been almost helpless.

It is of interest to speculate on what the Air Force could have done under the circumstances. It is reasonable to suppose that, if there had been a large Air Force, the Arab would have had some knowledge of its limitations and acted accordingly. In the first place, the Arab force would have remained very scattered until nightfall, when it would have been immune. Warning of the Arab approach might certainly have been brought in sooner, but it seems probable that the force would have been attacked just the same, closer to Hillah, as the Arab was infinitely more mobile and would have been encouraged by the retirement. In the night fighting aeroplanes would have been more a menace than a help.

Similarly, armoured cars might have brought in news of the Arab approach, provided—and this proviso is an important one—no damage was done to the route by which they had to come back. At night the armoured cars could have done little or nothing, especially as so many bridges were blocked. A L.A.M. car falling into a canal by a bridge might have completely blocked the route for anything in its rear.

It is hard to understand what the Air Force alone could do should similar circumstances arise.

Operations round Hillah

While the column was out, the detached company of the Manchester Regiment had rejoined from Diwaniyah. This was sent out, on lorries, for a short distance to help in the stragglers. On the 25th also, just after the return of the column, the 32nd Lancers (less two squadrons), the 8th Rajputs and one hundred and fifty rifles of the 108th Infantry arrived. In the evening the Royal Irish Rifles came in by train from Diwaniyah. The place thus received reinforcements in the very nick of time. Some Arab levies had done very useful work helping in stragglers.

From all accounts, however, there was muddle and confusion in the place, which only ceased when Major-General Leslie arrived from Diwaniyah. The debacle to the column had been reported to Baghdad " in clear," with the result that it became common property, with the normal exaggerations that accompany tales of disaster.

Our two squadrons had gone back to their old bivouac and were trying to snatch a little rest when they were ordered to shift elsewhere to shorten the line. This measure was probably necessary enough, but was very trying on exhausted men. Though tired, the jawans were full of fight and were greatly cheered by the complimentary remarks made to them by other units. Hillah was quiet this day, though there were now symptoms of unrest in the town itself.

At 08.00 on the 26th a troop under Second-Lieutenant Mmd Ayub was posted on the bund to the north-west of Hillah, where the Tuwairij Road crossed it. The remainder of the Regiment refitted and drew horses from Remounts. By now the tribesmen had approached Hillah, and a patrol under Jemadar Mmd Niwaz was fired on. The following day the two squadrons were posted on the bund. There was a good deal of desultory fire, but no casualties resulted. The 8th Rajputs relieved us. They were attacked there, but it was a half-hearted effort.

Jemadar Mmd Niwaz again went on a reconnaissance to the north-west of the bund. He came under a heavy fire and had a couple of men hit.

Reconnaissances were sent out by the Regiment daily, though not to any great distance. News was received of the complete evacuation of Diwaniyah on the 30th, the troops, accompanied by an enormous railway train, moving back north. On this date the Regiment shifted bivouac to the left bank of the river.

On the night of the 31st July–1st August a big attack was made on Hillah, first of all on the north-west front—a half-hearted affair—but later on a more serious one on the south-west front. Some Arabs succeeded in penetrating into the southern portion of the town, but were ejected by the 8th Rajputs. Some one hundred and fifty corpses were found the next day. The Regiment was unaffected by the fighting.

On the 2nd August the 32nd and ourselves were under orders to move out by night and burn the Arab villages to the north-west of the town, but the orders were cancelled.

On the 4th August the whole of the cavalry were ordered to be ready to ride to Jarbuiyah, an important railway bridge some fifteen miles south-east of Hillah on the Diwaniyah line. It had been anticipated by the 17th Division apparently, that "Rumcol," which was now approaching Jarbuiyah, would be opposed there. General Head-quarters at Baghdad, however, cancelled the order, a good deal to the relief of the cavalry, who felt that they would only be launched into the midst of overwhelming numbers of tribesmen. Incidentally, General Head-quarters and the 17th Division do not seem to have seen exactly eye to eye as regards the fighting qualities of the Arabs. The Division was prone to underrate them, according to G.H.Q.—and according, also, to a number of officers who had to do the actual fighting.

On the 6th our two squadrons reconnoitred to the east of Hillah. Considerable opposition was met with, the enemy being estimated at some two thousand. We had three men and six horses hit.

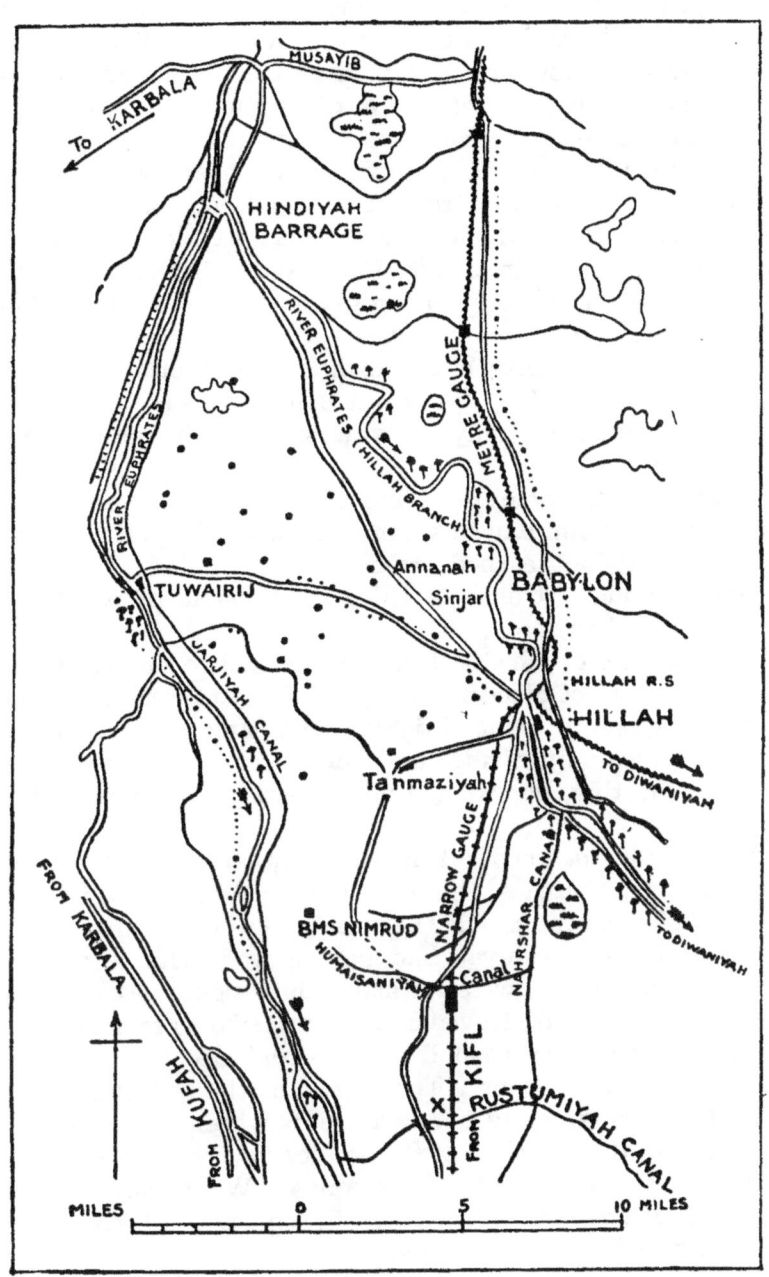

OPERATIONS ROUND HILLAH.

The affair, had there been any bungling, might have proved a very nasty one. The difficulty in coping with Arabs is the extraordinary manner they seem to appear from nowhere, and their mobility. On this occasion the steadiness of the men and the manner in which they were handled by Major Connop was admirable. Eye-witnesses commented greatly on this.

A particular maxim adopted, with the greatest care, was "after the section the troop, and after the troop, the squadron," and, by this means, mishaps to small parties, which, if continued, may lead to weakening of moral, were obviated. Patrols were but seldom allowed more than eight hundred yards away from a supporting troop, and a troop but seldom more than twelve hundred from its squadron.

The railway to the north of Hillah had been continually smashed up and was, by the end of July, quite out of use, as were all the telegraph lines, communication being only by wireless. Hillah was isolated for the next three weeks.

On the 8th a small force, including all the cavalry in Hillah, together with a construction train, moved south to bring in the 51st Brigade portion of "Rumcol," which had reached Jarbuiyah. The G.O.C.-in-C. was anxious to concentrate as many troops in Hillah as possible preparatory to despatching columns elsewhere.

Lieutenant Crichton, 5th Cavalry, was attached to the Regiment for the day as we were short of officers. The 32nd Lancers were advanced guard, and our "B" Squadron, under Crichton, left flank guard. The squadron drove some insurgents off a ridge and burnt some grass huts. There was a good deal of shooting, but we had no casualties. We returned to Hillah at midnight.

The 51st Brigade portion of "Rumcol" duly came in, the remainder halting at the Birmanah marshes, ten miles south-east of Hillah, in order to get the line finished for the trains. By next day the whole column had come in.

The retreat from Diwaniyah had been a wonderful feat. The trains accompanying the column were an astounding sight, nearly a mile long. The railway had been so destroyed and the material so removed that it had been continually necessary to pull up rails and sleepers from behind the train, and relay them in front. The labour in the appalling heat can be imagined. The average daily temperature had been 107 degrees, and the troops had been in the full glare of the sun for twelve hours daily for eleven days. The only shade was that of the trains. Water had to be carried in the trucks and rationed out. The rate of progress had been at an average of five and a half miles a day only.

Considering the conditions, the number of sick had been very small, which speaks well for the endurance of the troops. Nearly the whole of these were Indian, only the gunners and a few odds and ends like signals being British.

On the 10th the Regiment acted as escort to a railway construction party and met with a good deal of opposition. Under cover of guns, it drove out a few insurgents and burnt the village of Janyumah, returning to bivouac at 20.20.

As Kufah was known to be well rationed up and in no need of immediate relief the G.O.C.-in-C. had determined to secure the Hindiyah Barrage, sixteen miles north-west of Hillah, and the town of Musayib, which lies some eight miles farther up the river. Both these places are important points of passage over the Euphrates.

By holding the Hindiyah Barrage, moreover, it would become possible to control the flow of water down either the Hindiyah or the Hillah branches of the river, and thereby either put pressure on tribes in certain districts or assist our own columns to move without the danger of their water supply being cut off.

In the meantime, also, it would become possible to reopen railway communication between Hillah and Baghdad, in order to facilitate the accumulation of supplies and a bridging train at the former place, preparatory to the relief of Kufah. The Euphrates at Kufah is, incidentally, some two hundred and fifty yards wide.

Two columns, accordingly, were ordered out from Hillah on the 10th and 11th August, under Brigadier-General Walker and Lieut.-Colonel Scott respectively. The first column was directed on Musayib, which it duly occupied on the 12th, after some opposition, our old friends the Manchesters showing that they had not been affected by their bitter experience with us. On the 13th, this column captured the Hindiyah Barrage, after leaving the 8th Rajputs to garrison Musayib.

The second column, consisting of our two squadrons, one section 18 prs., one section 4·5 Howitzers, 99th Infantry and 10th Gurkhas moved north along the line of the railway. A number of blockhouses were constructed and the line was repaired. All villages in the vicinity of the road were destroyed, after slight opposition.

On the 12th the Regiment was ordered to burn the village of Mahomed Effendi. " D " Squadron (Lieutenant Geddes), in advance, met with strong opposition. The squadron advanced, dismounted, with the bayonet, into the date palm groves, while the Vickers guns (Second-Lieutenant Robinson) searched the village and trees. Meanwhile, Ressaldar Dur Khan, with two and a half troops of " B," galloped the north-west side of the place. The village was burnt, two hundred and fifty sheep and goats captured and some fifteen to twenty Arabs killed or wounded. It was a very-well-run affair, combining fire and movement, both mounted and dismounted, admirably.

Time after time, in these minor affairs, the possession of the bayonet enormously enhanced the men's keenness to attack.

The column only advanced some three miles this day and two the next, which gives some idea of the manner in which the railway had been torn up.

On the 14th Dafadar Taj Mahomed (our ginger-headed friend of before Croissilles) with one troop engaged two hundred insurgents as right flank guard. He kept them busy and after an hour's bickering they made off.

This day Khan Mahawil, twelve miles north of Hillah, was reached. A post was constructed here and a small garrison left.

The next day was a halt, but for the following week the column was engaged on punitive measures between the railway and the Euphrates towards Musayib in conjunction with General Walker's column, which was quite close.

The first train for three weeks down to Hillah from Baghdad ran on the 19th, the line north of Khan Mahawil having been restored by a small column from the north. On the 23rd and 24th both Walker's Column and "Scotcol" returned to Hillah, having destroyed no fewer than thirty-three mud villages which had contained insurgents.

The weather, while the columns had been out, had been even hotter than before.

In the meantime, Hillah had been heavily attacked on its southern face. The 45th Sikhs heavily punished the enemy, who effected nothing.

It may be of interest to state that, since the first attempt to relieve Rumeitha, the 45th Sikhs had lost no fewer than two hundred and thirty men.

The possession of the Hindiyah Barrage was now made use of to put pressure on the tribes by cutting off their water, and blockhouses were erected at many points controlling branch canals.

Lieutenant Mahomed Ayub was wounded shortly after our return, and his horse, a valuable polo pony which had escaped the Manchester debacle, was killed. On the 26th a column was despatched south from Hillah to bring in the garrison from Jarbuiyah post. The Regiment did not form part.

The G.O.C.-in-C. saw no prospect of being able to operate far south of Hillah for some time, and the detachment was rather a danger and was doing no good for the present.

The column duly returned on the 29th August.

CHAPTER XXV

NORTH-EAST OF BAGHDAD.

MEANWHILE the G.O.C.-in-C. had resolved to shift troops from Hillah to the north-east of Baghdad.

There had been some unrest on the Persian lines of communication. We had, it will be remembered, a largish force right up towards the Caspian, and railway communication from Baqubah onwards had been interrupted since the 9th August.

A small column, under Colonel Young, sent out to quieten things, had met with a mishap on a night march, owing to the Indian infantry getting the wind up and starting a panic among the pack mules of the mountain battery. The natural consequence was that by the 25th August nearly all the tribes north of the Diala were implicated. Thanks, however, to the energetic action of Colonel Lakin, commanding the Persian lines of communication, trouble did not extend beyond the border. The married families up at Karind were pretty safe, as they had plenty of supplies and about ten hundred British troops as a guard, but a very extended rising might also imperil them.

Under these circumstances the G.O.C.-in-C. had resolved to let operations about Hillah hang fire for the present, and pacify the country in the Persian direction.

In consequence, a big transfer of troops from Hillah was made. Our two squadrons entrained on the 29th, arriving at Baghdad West the same evening. Greatly to the surprise of the British officers, they were met by a staff officer from G.H.Q., who had actually arranged for transport to Hinaidi station, seven miles off, on the left bank. This was a new departure, and indicated that, at last, some effort was being made to stir the staff officers up to study the comfort of the troops instead of their own. At Hinaidi the squadrons entrained at 05.00 on the 30th for Baqubah, where they arrived early on the 31st. The actual mileage from Hillah to Baghdad and from Baghdad to Baqubah is sixty and thirty-five respectively. The rate of travel was not, therefore, exactly that of the "Flying Scotsman."

For the next five days there was nothing doing, as troops were concentrating at Baqubah. Brigadier-General Coningham was to command the new column.

The men's clothes were now almost in rags. There had not been enough stuff at Hillah to replace them, and there were no dumps at Baqubah. The Baghdad Ordnance certainly showed signs of being less obstructionist, but there was difficulty in getting stores sent out in time.

The men had started operations in "shirt sleeves." This kit is not suitable for officers owing to the absence of pockets.

Lieutenant Marten, who had gone off on leave just at the outbreak of the Rebellion, rejoined at Baqubah.

A very welcome feature at this place had been the find of a quantity of fresh fruit and vegetables not far from camp.

By the 5th September the column was assembled. It was composed as follows :—

>32nd Lancers (less two squadrons).
>Scinde Horse (ditto).
>Two Field Batteries.
>15th Sikhs.
>45th Sikhs.
>99th Infantry.
>10th Gurkhas.
>Bridging Train (one section).

On the 6th the column advanced up the left bank of the Diala, accompanied by a train, as the railway line was not badly damaged.

The march was uneventful, but at the halting-place, Abu Hawah, the watering parties were heavily sniped. The Regiment was lucky and had no casualties, but other units had.

The following day Abu Jisrah was reached with no opposition.

The column now began to traverse much more interesting country, cultivation being very plentiful and water easy to come by.

On the 8th, between Abu Jisrah and Shahroban, about six hundred insurgents were encountered who were holding the Marut Canal. These, evidently thinking they had only a small force up against them, began advancing from their position with some boldness. No sooner, however, had our main body come in sight than they began to hesitate, and the 32nd, galloping forward, crossed the bridge, routed a portion of the force, and turned the flank of the remainder, who withdrew in haste.

Camp was at Muqdad. The ground about was very marshy and pig and snipe abounded.

The next day Sharaban was entered without opposition. The column was met by salaaming dignitaries, who professed great friendship for the British, and imparted the information that the hostile tribes had only just left the town by the northern gate, having battened on the inhabitants for some time. The last part of their statement was pretty true.

It was at Sharaban that, three weeks before, a small colony of English, with a lady, had been isolated in the old Turkish barracks, together with a few Arab and Kurd levies. The Arab levies nearly all deserted, but some of Kurdish origin remained faithful. During a pause in the fighting, there had been a parley and things might have gone off satisfactorily, when the Kurdish levies, who failed to appreciate the situation, opened fire, and the enemy resumed their attack. The Arabs succeeded in entering the barracks and the whole garrison, except one British soldier who was badly wounded, was cut to pieces. Mrs. Buchanan, the English lady, was taken care of by a petty sheikh in Sharaban. Both she and the wounded British soldier were now handed over. Seemingly neither had been maltreated.

A fine of rifles was levied on the town and about one hundred and seventy were brought in. The tribes had used the place as a dump and had left many tents behind, which, alone, were valued at some 60,000 to 70,000 rupees.

The houses of certain notables who had taken a prominent part in the Rebellion were also burnt. There was an abundant supply of beautiful grapes, which the inhabitants were ordered to bring in. The column halted at Sharaban for the 10th. On the night of 9/10th, however, an attack had been made on the post at Abu Jisrah in our rear, which demonstrated the necessity for erecting blockhouses at intervals along the line before the withdrawal of the married families at Karind could take place.

The force, accordingly, marched back to Abu Jisrah, "B" Squadron, with the 45th Sikhs, halting at Muqdad. In three days no fewer than forty-five blockhouses were constructed between Abu Hawa and the Balad Ruz Canal.

After the departure of the column, the tribesmen poured into Sharaban and proceeded to loot it. A Political Officer, Captain Lloyd, who had been prisoner with the Arabs for nearly a month, rode in on the 11th. He had been well treated.

The back of the Rebellion in these parts was now broken.

On the 13th the whole column had returned to Sharaban, and on the 14th marched to Table Mountain, where the Diala passes through the Jebel Hamrin. This range, in this neighbourhood, is of no great height.

The river here is a beautiful sight, the water being very deep and clear, with any number of fish.

Bombing succeeded in getting a good bag—but for the infantry only, as we had no bombs.

On the 15th September junction was effected with a column from the Karind direction.

Brigadier-General G. Beatty, who had commanded the Lucknow Cavalry Brigade after Épéhy in France, now took over from General Coningham, who was going south, as he had been given command of a column for the relief of Samawah, about ninety miles south of Hillah.

While at Table Mountain, the Regiment constructed works to defend the regulators at the heads of the many canals that take off near here. This was with a view to putting pressure on the tribes if necessary.

On the 17th, " D " Squadron returned to Sharaban, being followed on the 20th by " B." The march was then resumed to Baqubah, which was reached on the 22nd. This day the first train with families from Karind reached Baghdad. These families were then passed down by train to Kut and thence by river to Basra. G.H.Q. must have been only too delighted to have got shut of them.

Some ten miles to the north of Baqubah lies the small town of Deltawah, a place which, for long, had been the haunt of sedition mongers and a centre of disturbances.

A column under General Beatty was sent out on the 24th September, with the view to re-establishment of order. It was composed as follows :—

      Scinde Horse (less two squadrons).
      Two Field Batteries (less three sections).
      9th Coy. Sappers and Miners.
      15th Sikhs.
      119th Infantry (less two companies).

Deltawah is situated in a dense forest of palm trees. About one and a half miles to the south-west of the town there is a wide and deep canal full of water, the only point of passage being the bridge.

The Regiment was advanced guard, moving off at 04.50. The first objective was the bridge. There was slight opposition on the march, but this was duly secured. The enemy attempted to come out and attack, but this was prevented by Ressaldar Dur Khan (" B " Squadron), with two Vickers guns and his Hotchkiss rifles.

The next job was to protect the flank of the infantry as they swung round to attack the enemy in the village. " D " Squadron accordingly passed through " B " so as to get into position to effect this, " B " then rallying. " D " Squadron, after advancing about twelve hundred yards came under a heavy fire from its front. Fire also opened from two small villages in its rear, which had been clear when the advanced patrols had ridden through. They were in date palm groves, and it would have been easy to miss men lying up. A troop, under Dafadar Ali Khan, cleared one by a dismounted advance with the bayonet. Hotchkiss and Vickers fire dealt with the enemy and our infantry were enabled to enter the town almost unopposed.

Punitive measures were taken in the town, and, on the 26th, "D" Squadron and the 15th Sikhs went out and burnt Abu Tamar.

There was a notorious brigand whose village, Qurnabit by name, was about four miles out of Baqubah on the left bank of the Diala. This individual had been the scourge of the countryside for the last two years, and had all the pleasant habits peculiar to this type of local hero. It was, accordingly, decided to round him up. "B" Squadron, with the M.G. section, went into Baqubah to work with the 45 Sikhs on the left bank of the Diala, while "D" and the 15th Sikhs were to close the bolt holes on the right bank. The attempt was made in the early hours of the 28th September. The ground was greatly cut up with irrigation cuts and gardens, and the greatest difficulty was experienced in getting the M.G. pack animals along.

The operation worked out extremely well, but was just too late, and Mr. Abdika was seen streaking across the desert on a swift horse. He was heavily fired on, but managed to get away. It would seem that it might have been as well to have left the pack animals behind on this occasion—but it is always easy to be wise after the event. It has often been a moot point altogether as to whether the Hotchkiss rifle and Vickers will really pull their weight if there is a very great deal of movement, particularly at night. When things are not rushed they are, undoubtedly, of enormous value, though it was found that they simply devoured ammunition.

Qurnabit was thoroughly searched, but only a few carpets and sewing machines were found. The 45th Sikhs bayoneted a few Arabs, but otherwise not much damage was done.

General Beatty's column returned to Baqubah, leaving a couple of companies at Deltawah.

The general situation in the country now, was that the railway and country to the north-east of Baghdad was pretty well quietened. A few troops could look after it. Hillah was safe, and a small column operating to the east of the place had pacified the area. Blockhouses had been constructed along the railway, and our control over the water at the Hindiyah Barrage was making things uncomfortable for the tribes. On the other hand, both Kufah and Samawa were invested and the Rebellion was still formidable in their neighbourhood.

The G.O.C.-in-C. now determined on the relief of Kufah, and a transfer of troops from the north-east of Baghdad began.

The Regiment marched from Baqubah on the 29th September, reaching

Khirr Depot, Baghdad, on the 1st October. Here General Haldane presented medals to Second-Lieutenant Robinson, Ressaldar Dur Khan and Jemadar Mahomed Niwaz. He spoke most highly regarding the conduct of the Regiment.

Major Landon, D.S.O., joined and took over command from Major Connop.

The state of the men's clothing and of equipment in general, as a result of the hard and constant knocking about in the last two and a half months was now serious. The Baghdad Ordnance, however, showed signs of having had ginger well applied and it was possible to get something done, though not enough. There were many indications that the various subordinates had begun to be put in their places, and the off-hand " I'm just as good as you " attitude had ceased. It must be remembered that a number of senior regular officers, who had served on decently run fronts, had, by now, arrived in the country, and we know that some of second-class administrative personnel had received very rude shocks.

The nights were now getting cold, though the sun was still very powerful.

On the 4th October the Regiment left Baghdad for Hillah, forming part of a small column with the 10th Gurkhas, under Lieut.-Colonel Scott.

On the first day's march to Mahmoudiyeh the enemy appeared on the right flank and eventually attacked the rear-guard, which consisted of " D " Squadron, following it up to about a couple of miles from camp. They wounded one man and one horse. These affairs were, when the ground was open, always at some pretty long range like eleven hundred yards. Particular care, however, had to be taken to see that parties did not get isolated and that nothing was rushed in such a manner as to cause unsteadiness. A retirement at a gallop, unless to some well-defined point, was always a thing to be guarded against.

The fire discipline, furthermore, had to be good, and no uncontrolled wild bursts of fire, as were common in some units when an Arab appeared, were allowed. The Regiment, indeed, was universally commented on for its steadiness and high training. These were the results of hard work in India, combined with good leading. One might add that the good leading was the outcome of confidence, also the result of hard work and study.

The march was resumed the following day to the Musayib Canal, which was reached without incident, and the next evening Hillah was entered.

The railway line all the way down had blockhouses along it. In some cases these were held by armed Labour Corps, who did the job quite well.

There were a number of tribesmen round Hillah still, despite the large garrison, and there was a constant regular sniping at night, sometimes even by day. The amount of cover around favoured the enemy.

The preparations for the relief of Kufah were by now pretty well finished.

MESOPOTAMIA.

DIWANIYAH.

TEL AFAR.

NAJAF.

HILLAH.

CHAPTER XXVI
THE RELIEF OF KUFAH.

KUFAH stands on the right bank of the Kufah or western loop of the Hindiyah branch of the Euphrates, and has the normal surroundings of date palms and gardens. It is about thirty-seven miles south-west of Hillah.

Its main historical interest lies in the fact that 'Ali, the founder of the Shiah sect, was assassinated there in A.D. 661. 'Ali was actually buried at Najaf, some seven miles to the south-west and in the desert. The story is that, as 'Ali requested while dying, his body was tied to a camel which was free to wander and graze where it wanted. Where the camel lay down was to be the burial place.

The rival holy city to Najaf is Karbala, some forty miles to the north.

Kufah had been invested on the 21st July, two days before the Manchester Column went out. The garrison consisted of two companies of the 108th Infantry, who, fortunately, had plenty of rations. These two companies had only just been concentrated in time. Previous to this they had been strewn about in the normal fashion peculiar to Mesopotamia before the Rebellion, and it was only through treating with the tribesmen that one detachment entered at all.

At the time the relief columns started operations the place had been besieged for two and a half months. With the example of Kut before him, however, the commander carefully refrained from calling out for instant relief, in order to guarantee that when it did come there should be no failure through lack of preparation.

The G.O.C.-in-C. was desirous of making as great a show of force as possible about Hillah. The arrival of reinforcements from India enabled this to be done without dangerously denuding other parts of the country.

Two strong mixed brigade columns, the 53rd and 55th, as they were termed, were formed under Brigadier-Generals Sanders and Walker respectively. The first column was to act towards Tuwairij, some twelve miles west by north of Hillah, and the second to relieve Kufah.

Our two squadrons belonged to the latter, which was composed as follows:—

> Scinde Horse (less two squadrons).
> 37th Lancers (less two squadrons).
> Three Field Batteries.

One Pack Battery.
Sappers and Miners (two companies).
2nd Manchester Regiment.
2nd Royal Irish Rifles.
8th Rajputs.
87th Punjabis.
1/116th Mahrattas.
108th Infantry (less two companies in Kufah).
1/32nd Pioneers.

A preliminary operation was necessary, both to guarantee that the approach march on Kifl should not be affected by the water being cut off, as there were certain grounds for supposing had been the case when the unfortunate Manchester Column went out, and to obtain a subsidiary line of supply by a navigable canal. This canal is called the Nahr Shah, and takes off about two and a half miles below Hillah. From it branch canals cross the Kifl Road at intervals and supply it with water.

On the 7th, accordingly, the infantry and guns made a sweep down both sides of the river, through the date palm groves, erecting blockhouses at intervals outside them and securing the canal. The opposition was strong, as the tribes seemed confident of their ability to prevent us relieving Kufah. The hostile strength was estimated at some three thousand five hundred. There was some pretty close fighting, but the enemy got severely handled and we effected our object after losing about one hundred and twenty. The Regiment did not take part in this affair.

The action had the effect of making the resistance in our advance on Kufah comparatively slight.

On the 11th October the troops of the Tuwairij and Kufah columns, being now assembled, carried out operations to clear the flanks of the subsequent lines of advance.

The 53rd Brigade column destroyed sundry villages on the north-eastern flank of the Tuwairij Road. The 55th Brigade column moved on Tahmaziyah about four miles west of Hillah. The cavalry, under Major Landon, consisting of the Scinde Horse (less two squadrons) and the 37th Lancers (less two squadrons) operated on the left flank of the Brigade advanced guard.

The enemy were encountered on a bund to the east of Tahmaziyah. Their flank was turned by " B " Squadron (Lieutenant Marten), and the cavalry reached its allotted objective. Our machine guns found some good targets at the retiring enemy.

About noon the Brigade resumed its advance and the cavalry was given the task of burning three villages. This was duly effected, and camp at Tahmaziyah was reached about 18.00. The operations of the 55th Brigade this day thus cleared the left flank of the 53rd Brigade as well as the right flank of the Kifl Road. On the 12th, each column began its main advance. The 53rd Brigade, after a good bit of opposition, pushed through to Tuwairij, just in time to save the bridge of boats over the Euphrates, to which the enemy had set fire. It was estimated that some two hundred Arabs were killed. As a result of the occupation of Tuwairij the submission of Karbala, about ten miles to the west, became imminent.

The 55th Brigade returned towards Hillah and then moved down the Kifl Road.

A portion of this column, it should be stated, was already working down the Nahr Shah Canal, about three miles away on the eastern flank of the road. Boats with supplies were brought down this and it was blockhoused at intervals.

The rôle of the cavalry this day was the distant protection of our right flank. The 37th were the leading regiment. The enemy was encountered on the Humaisaniyah Canal, eight miles from Hillah, with a few men ahead on an old disused channel with a deep ditch in front of a bank some twenty feet high. The 37th galloped the latter and brought their machine guns into action against the Humaisaniyah Canal. The Scinde Horse, working farther round to the right, crossed the old channel and secured a position enfilading the enemy on the canal. The 87th Punjabis, who had been held up, were now enabled to advance, supported by our guns which had come into action at six hundred yards range. The column bivouacked that night on the canal.

On the 13th the column advanced to the scene of the Manchester Column camp on the Rustumiyah Canal without incident. The mournful relics of the disaster strewed the whole route.

On the 14th October a body of six hundred insurgents, who held the canal bank north-east of Kifl, was disposed of by the 116th Mahrattas and the town was entered. The cavalry again operated on the right flank. The Nahr Shah Canal, it will be understood, protected the left, and the column that moved along it now joined the main one. An attempt was made to ferry the Manchesters across the Euphrates, but the river was too wide. It was, moreover, running like a mill-race. Consequently all the bridging material which had been intended for Tuwairij had to be despatched to Kifl on the 15th, reaching the place after an eighteen-mile march. A bridge was completed within two and a half hours after arrival.

This day the Scinde Horse operated to the south of Kifl. "B" Squadron managed to surprise a group of the enemy on an island and effected some good work with their Hotchkiss rifles. In the afternoon the cavalry crossed the river by the pontoon bridge and bivouacked with the 15th Sikhs on the right bank.

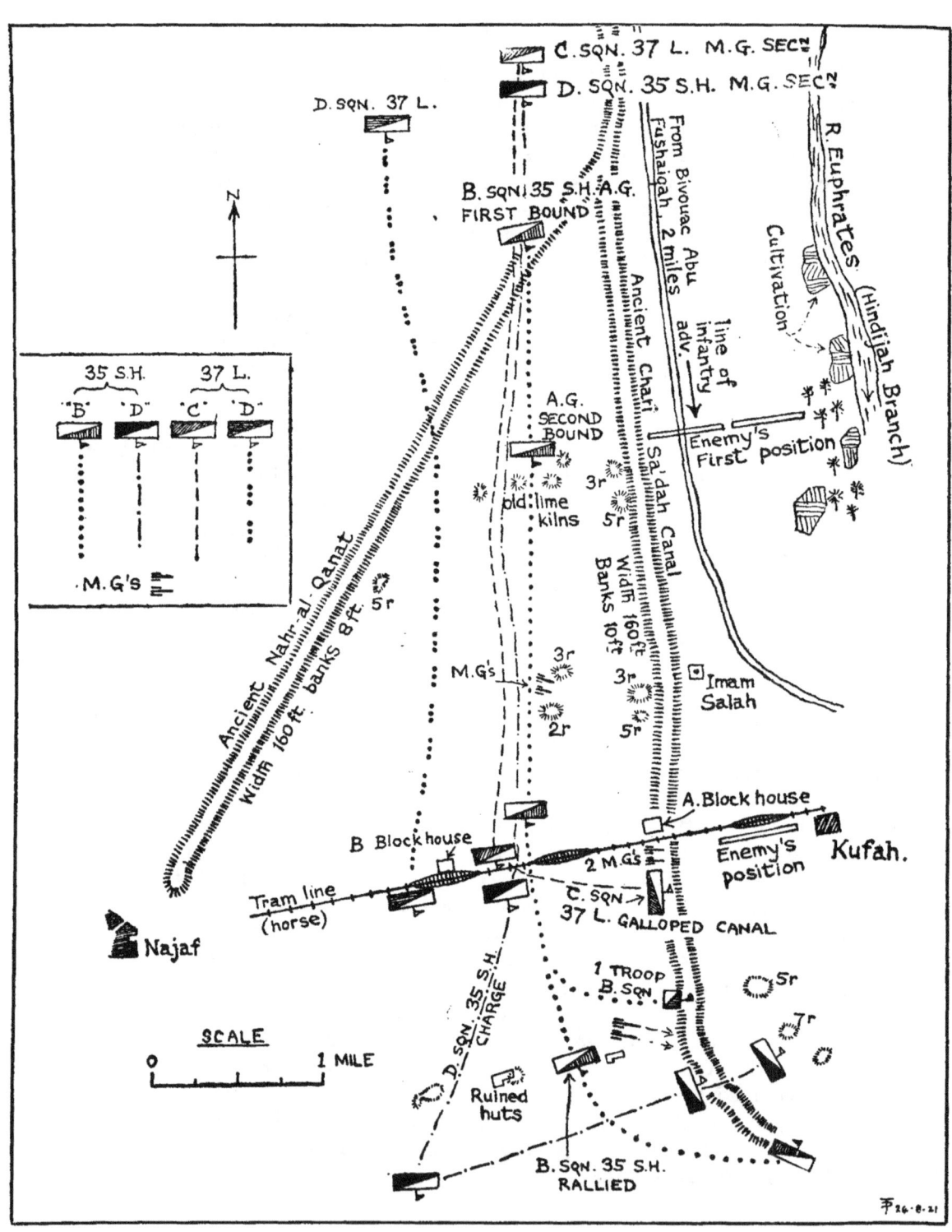

THE ACTION AT KUFAH.
17th October, 1920.

On the 16th October this detachment moved out early as far as the edge of the desert where the Karbala-Najaf Road runs. The rest of the column crossed and moved on Abu Fushaiqah, about seven miles north of Kufah. The cavalry were in advance. A squadron of the 37th, and Major Landon, reconnoitred to within a couple of miles of Kufah. Little opposition was met, but considerable numbers of enemy were seen close to the place.

Both banks of the Euphrates were cultivated, and, for three miles north of Kufah, were densely covered with date palm groves. On the right bank these did not extend more than a mile from the river, beyond which was hard open desert, devoid of all obstacles to movement and excellent going. There were some old ruined canal embankments such as are to be found all over the country, important pivots of manœuvre.

In Mesopotamia all camps by the river are liable to be sniped from the opposite bank if this is not picqueted. On the far side of the stream from Abu Fushaiqah some mahelas were moored to the bank. Volunteers were called for to bring them over. A number of the Scinde Horse and 37th at once came forward. After a hard swim the boats were secured. This was a dangerous service, for there was no guarantee that the men, on approaching the other side, would not be scuppered. A strong picquet of the 15th Sikhs was then ferried over and occupied some houses. Thanks to this the night was not disturbed by sniping, though a dust-storm of considerable violence blew and kept every one awake.

The operations for the following day envisaged a direct advance on Kufah, parallel to the river, on the part of the infantry and guns, while the cavalry moved about a couple of miles out in the desert. Their objective was the crossing over the ancient Chari Sadah Canal by the Kufah-Najaf tramway. This was a possible line of retreat of the enemy. Furthermore, the cavalry would be in a position to protect the force from interference from the Najaf direction.

Major Landon, Scinde Horse, commanded the group cavalry, and Majors Connop and Stewart the Scinde Horse and 37th Lancer wings respectively. The day proved to be extremely hot for the time of year, though nothing, of course, to what it had been before.

A very early start was made so as to guarantee the cavalry reaching the objective before the enemy had bolted. There were about seven miles to cover. In fighting irregulars there is always the danger of a premature " turn " frightening them away before the infantry have time to close and get a butcher's bill out of them. In this particular case the Arabs by the Euphrates could not have been much in the know about the cavalry being in their rear owing to the palm groves and cover. Furthermore, the enemy had not, hitherto, shown much disposition to clear out prior to a " turn " developing. The relief of Kufah, again, was in this instance of more importance than a heavy tribal casualty list, for the garrison was, by now, pretty short of food.

The cavalry advanced with "B" Squadron, Scinde Horse (Lieutenant Marten), as advanced guard, and "D" Squadron, 37th Lancers, as right flank guard.

"D" Squadron and machine-gun section, Scinde Horse, and "C" Squadron and machine-gun section, 37th Lancers, formed the main body. On reaching the Nahr al Qanat, about three miles north of Kufah, the enemy were seen in position, their left flank on the Chari Sadah Canal and their right on the Euphrates.

The advanced guard pushed on at a trot to an underfeature, consisting of mounds surrounding an old lime-kiln, about opposite the enemy left, and came under fire from the Chari Sadah and some small mounds, "5R" and "3R," to the immediate west of it. Fire also opened from the Nahr al Qanat on the right front.

The advance, however, was continued at a trot without replying, until about opposite Imam Salah, where six machine guns were dropped to engage the Chari Sadah. The enemy fire had been at about six hundred to seven hundred yards range, but had done hardly any damage.

The advanced guard now began to gallop, and, on approaching the tramline, saw and charged about one hundred and fifty of the enemy who were moving on Najaf in small groups. It then rallied at a line of ruined huts about a mile and a quarter south of the tram-line.

A certain amount of fire was coming from the Chari Sadah, which was apparently held in some strength, and the huts furnished a little cover. Ressaldar Dur Khan, with a troop of the advanced guard and a Hotchkiss, now galloped a point on this canal, and opened fire on the surprised enemy, who furnished an excellent target.

Meanwhile "D" Squadron, Scinde Horse (Lieutenant Geddes), from the main body, was directed by Major Connop on to further groups of the enemy in a south-west direction.

The squadron formed line and charged, rallying to the south-west of the line of ruined huts after sabring some twenty-five of the enemy. Some machine guns had taken up a position at the huts, and the squadron, having rallied, galloped the Chari Sadah covered by their fire. It was now able to bring a heavy fire on the disorganized enemy to the east of the canal. Prior to its advance there had been an attempt at a counter-attack from the Chari Sadah, but Dur Khan's fire, coupled with "D" Squadron's advance, effectually prevented it.

The former advanced guard ("B" Squadron) had extended "D's"

right on the canal and was able to open on the enemy who was now in full retreat towards the date palms to the south of Kufah. The Scinde Horse machine guns also came into action and the enemy could be seen dropping where our fire caught them. One of our Hotchkiss rifles inflicted casualties at eighteen hundred yards range. While the Scinde Horse was engaged as above, " C " Squadron, 37th Lancers (Major Forster), who had followed " D " of the Scinde Horse, found small parties of the enemy passing along the tram-line in rear of " D " Squadron towards Najaf.

These were either lanced, or dispersed by rifle fire. There was still a fairly heavy fire from the Chari Sadah, as well as a few odd shots from the right, or western flank. The last were easily disposed of by the flank guard squadron (" D " Squadron, 37th). " C " Squadron accordingly galloped the Chari Sadah, followed by two machine guns, and occupied a position on the left of the Scinde Horse. The squadron found itself enfilading a cutting in which the tram-line runs at a range of about twelve hundred yards. Many of the enemy were only about six hundred yards off. Heavy casualties were inflicted and the enemy fled towards Kufah town, which place the infantry were now approaching.

By 09.30 the garrison of Kufah was relieved after ninety days' investment.

Lessons

(a) Rapid movement secured practical immunity from enemy fire. The total of our casualties amounted to one man and six horses wounded only.

(b) The rapidity of the advance seemed to paralyse the enemy and prevented any initiative on his part.

(c) The enemy plan was evidently that of successive retirements to Kufah itself, and indicated Turkish trained officers. The push by cavalry at his flanks evidently unsettled him.

(d) The sword and lance had great moral effect, not merely on the enemy, but on our own men. The straight sword abundantly proved its value as a formidable weapon. The Scinde Horse, incidentally, were very short of swords, and the men without them borrowed scabbards from their comrades and beat the enemy on the heads with them.

(e) The Hotchkiss rifles proved of great value as pivots. They always had a great moral effect, their chief disadvantage being the manner they ate up ammunition.

The horses, it may be stated, were all on the fine side through hard work, but stood the long and rapid advance (two-and-a-half-miles' trot and four miles' gallop) extremely well. General Walker, the column commander, was most complimentary over this affair, and the Scinde Horse were specially mentioned in despatches.

CHAPTER XXVII

THE COLUMN TO MENDALI. MOSUL. BELED SINJAR. RETURN TO INDIA.

THE G.O.C.-in-C., in order to show the tribes that British troops could reach them in every quarter of the country, and to guarantee that the British power was made manifest, now arranged that columns should move into out-of-the-way areas where the Turks had never penetrated. In many cases this meant that troops had to be supplied by small country boats pushed up numerous side canals and over marshes where the water was only a few inches deep.

Troops from the 55th Brigade had much of this type of work, but the Regiment did not accompany them.

As regards the surrender of rifles, there were very complicating factors, quite apart from the difficulty in getting them in. There were certain clans inhabiting border regions, for instance, who simply had to be left some arms for their own protection. There were all sorts of other categories, like semi-nomad tribes, tribes that had assisted to quell the Rebellion, and tribes that had remained neutral, who each demanded different treatment. Furthermore, if it were known that a general disarmament was contemplated, there was a possibility of the Rebellion spreading beyond its present limits. The method was, therefore, adopted of inflicting fines on guilty tribes that practically amounted to the deprivation of all serviceable arms and ammunition. Where these were not forthcoming by specified dates, demands would be enhanced and punitive action would follow. In lieu of an unpaid residue, sums considerably exceeding the market value of the articles would be accepted.

As a result of this policy some sixty-three thousand rifles, of which twenty-one thousand were modern weapons, were handed in. Nevertheless, as showing the impossibility of disarming completely, within a year of the end of the Rebellion an enormous number of new arms had come in.

The wing marched from Kufah on the 10th November, reaching Hillah on the 11th.

On the 13th it entrained for Baghdad to form part of a column under Brigadier-General Young to visit the country about Balad-Ruz.

The 14th was spent at Baghdad re-equipping, which was, by now, a desperate necessity as the men's clothes were almost indecent. The anguish of one officer, a well-known sartorial authority to whose views General Smith-Dorrien is reported to have bowed down, is described as having been pitiable when our ragged objects appeared before him. It has been stated, perhaps libellously, that his sole consolation was to gaze on his own boots (by Peall of Jermyn Street) and his own breeches (by Hammond of Oxford Street).

On the 15th November, the wing joined the column at Hinaidi and marched to Cassels Post on the Diala. The column was composed as under :—

"F" Battery, R.H.A.
Field Troop, Sappers and Miners.
7th Dragoon Guards.
8th Hussars.
32nd Lancers (less three squadrons).
Scinde Horse (less two squadrons).

Its task was to " show the flag " and pacify the country about Balad-Ruz and Mendali, which lies to the south of the Baqubah-Shahraban railway line. Mendali is fifty miles due east of Baqubah.

On the 20th the column reached Mendali after a thirty-two-mile march in very cold weather, bivouacking after dark. The British troops were still more or less in the recruit stage, but could now ride a little.

In one of the regiments, however, there was an order that no horse was to be saddled in full marching order without three men to do the job—a very wise and necessary measure with young soldiers, for a horse hastily or badly saddled up may easily gall.

The next two days were spent in collecting rifles and giving out terms to the inhabitants. Some houses in the town whose owners had been prominent rebels were also burnt. On the 27th the brigade returned to Balad-Ruz, and on the 29th two squadrons of the 7th Dragoon Guards and the Scinde Horse moved south of the place collecting rifles. The cold was very severe and an early start was always a difficulty owing to the numbed state of the men's hands for saddling up.

After a couple of days at Balad-Ruz the column returned to Hinaidi, the last march in being of thirty-five miles from Baqubah.

One heard many comments on the contrast between the precise manner previous columns had been handled, and the casual way things were carried on on this occasion. On many sides the opinion was given that it was just as well that nothing serious happened. The arrival at Mendali in the dark after a very long march might have been most unpleasant, for the country was very broken and it was absolutely fresh ground. A mounted column in the dark is always pretty helpless, and a bivouac full of horses, which is suddenly fired into, might easily become a shambles through a stampede. The only thing to be said was that the column looked an enormous one and might have frightened any bolder spirits off touching it. The Arab at this stage, moreover, had begun to learn our strength.

A point to which attention might be drawn was the state of the medical service at that time. As compared with anything pre-war, the administrative methods were excellent, but it is doubtful if the actual doctoring with Indian units was anything like as good. Indian units had temporary " Indian " doctors attached. In some cases these men were fairly good. In others they were useless. We had, in our own case, definite instances of men who were either wounded or badly hurt, refusing to go to hospital for fear that they might get into the doctor's clutches and be maltreated. They said they would carry on until they got a chance of being looked at by some selected doctor, who usually happened to be a sahib. The permanent I.M.S. doctors were and are all better men. A number of the temporary doctors were seemingly but little more than apothecaries in Presidency towns, men with a low code of honour professionally and as callous of suffering as is usual among Indians.

Officers who were on famine or plague duty in the old days can recall the objectionable, corrupt creatures who ran many of the dispensaries, and some of these " doctors " were but little, if anything, better.

Mosul

The wing remained at Hinaidi until the 22nd December, when " D " Squadron entrained for Shergat, Head-quarters and " B " following on the 26th. Captain Kennedy and Lieutenants Husband and Fraser joined the Regiment on the 23rd. The two last named were demobilized officers who had served with Indian units during the War and who now had rejoined, under the War Office, for service in Mesopotamia. Husband was a good machine gunner who had been with the 5th Cavalry. " D " Squadron remained at Shergat, but Head-quarters and " B " passed on through to Mosul. We were to relieve the 11th Lancers.

The march on from Shergat was in heavy rain, and the going was very bad owing to the mud, for there is no metalled road. After heavy rain the convoys would be held up, by order, so as to prevent the track becoming impassable, but we were urgently wanted north and would not seriously affect the route as we only had our limbered wagons.

The Sikh squadron, which had been away from the Regiment since June, was passed at Quaiyarah, where it had been almost all the time. Our old Baluchistan friends, the 106th Pioneers, were here.

From Shergat to Mosul the country is quite different from the flat monotonous plain, with mounds and old canals, one sees nearer Baghdad. It is gently undulating ground, a little stony in places, and in this respect is far more interesting. In April and May it is fairly green. There is only one tree the whole way until about three miles out of Mosul, and that was a scraggly Ber tree. The date palms cease below Samarra.

Near Shergat there was still the debris of the battle that had brought about the surrender of the 6th Turkish Army owing to Cassel's Brigade getting in rear and blocking its retreat.

Just below the place is the site of the old Assyrian city of Asshur, but one could not understand anything from visiting the ruins. The houses had, seemingly, been largely built of the soft alabaster marble that is found round Mosul, and it is said that the plan of construction of houses in Mosul now is precisely the same as it was in those days.

The country on the right bank of the Tigris is almost uninhabited the whole way, though raiders on our convoys came from the desert to the west. A squadron of the 11th Lancers had caught it rather in the neck near Quaiyarah just prior to "C" Squadron going there. It had been attacked by overwhelming numbers of mounted men and lost its Hotchkiss rifles. These raiders must have come from some immense distance.

It was at Hadraniyah, the first march out from Shergat, that Cassels had crossed the Tigris and seized the ruins of the ancient town. From these it is possible to see for miles. These ruins, in common with those of Nimrud and Nineveh, are merely four huge embankments in a parallelogram shape enclosing the old city.

At Quaiyarah the ground exudes pitch. There is a rough and ready kind of factory which is said to manufacture oil. As to whether it does is doubtful.

"C" Squadron had a jawan whose job it was to be special instructor in burning this sort of oily pitch for the langar. He was "the dirtiest man wot ever I see'd" with the possible exception of a Sikh squadron langri in Jacob's Horse. This last-named character was supposed to be a really high-class chef. Doubtless the fact that he simply exuded ghee at every pore made his culinary efforts greatly appreciated by the Khalsa. In France we often discussed taking him to England and getting him a job at a popular restaurant where he would hand round the curry, so as to add to the real Oriental air that dish always inspires. Had the guests there only seen and smelt him we felt certain that his fortune would have been made.

There are always some duck near Quaiyarah, and ten miles off, on the other side of the Tigris, there was quite good black partridge and quail shooting.

There were, however, too many guns and the country was soon shot out.

Both at Hadra and Hamam Ali were small posts held by the 106th Hazaras. Beyond one or two mud huts there are no villages the whole way between Shergat and Mosul, and only very little cultivation. At Hamam Ali there are sulphur and hot-water springs running into the Tigris.

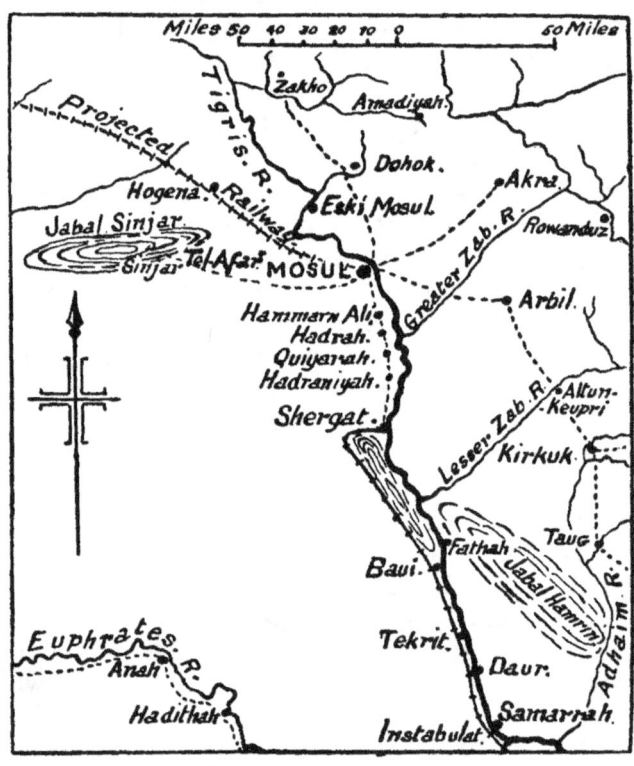

UPPER MESOPOTAMIA.

All posts on the river had to send in daily reports as to the height of the water, for a flood in Mesopotamia might affect country as much as one hundred miles south.

Short of Mosul there is some pretty rough country, and one could still see the debris of German lorries that had fallen over an embankment.

Mosul itself is an interesting town, both as regards inhabitants and as regards buildings. It differs completely from Baghdad or any town to the south. It is " The Middle East."

One saw there people of races one would never see elsewhere—Chaldæans,

Kurds, Assyrians, together with Arabs, Jews and Armenians. The place is full of Christian churches, Nestorian, Jacobæan, Syrian, Chaldæan and Roman Catholic. The Turk was a very tolerant man as regards religions until European nations began to stir up the Christian sects to intrigue, when he naturally got fed up with them. This anti-Christian action only dates back about one hundred and twenty years. Certain of the Christian sects are chronically drunk; a Chaldæan village, Tel Kaif, some fifteen miles north of Mosul, with a gaudy church, was remarkable in this respect. Here, one day, some of the inhabitants, for our especial benefit, changed their very picturesque costumes for clothes they had had in America, and spoke Yankee.

The Nestorian Christian Church had, at one time, extended as far east as Pekin and as far south as Malabar, where there are still Nestorian Christians. A monk actually made a pilgrimage from Pekin to France, where he met Edward I, King of England—which was " some " pilgrimage.

We were billeted in some houses on the northern ramparts of Mosul, on a bluff on the right bank overlooking Nineveh. The latter place was a quadrangular town, some three miles by two miles, surrounded by simply enormous ramparts, which are now like railway embankments.

Inside there are two colossal mounds, the southern (the Tomb of Jonah) being the site of the palaces of Sargon, Sennacherib and Esarhaddon, dating from about B.C. 800, and the northern, the palaces of Ashur-Bani-pal, dating from B.C. 700. It was from the northern mound that Layard excavated such wonderful treasures in 1852.

Our billets were clean but appallingly cold, having no woodwork at all in them. All door- and window-frames and all shelves in Mosul are made of soft alabaster, which one can cut out with a knife. The buildings were all made of rubble stone with poor cement. Certain of the head-quarters were in extremely nice houses built round a courtyard with a fountain in the middle and with nice alabaster carvings.

Our billets were formerly the store-rooms of the German mechanical transport. The mess of the East Yorkshire Regiment, about half a mile off, had been the German officers' mess. It had some interesting German pictures, taken out of their comic papers evidently, but extremely well copied. There was one picture from an English artist, Bateman, representing a man undergoing medical examination, also well copied. The most interesting thing of all, however, was a " tree," on the lines of a genealogical tree, showing where the M.T. company had been and ending up with a query. The company had started from Berlin, passing through Vienna and Constantinople, and passing down to Kut, after visiting Hamadan and Teheran—an itinerary to be proud of.

The country round Mosul is rolling downland, like Palestine. It is excellent cavalry and artillery country, though the going is, in places, very stony. The Kurdish mountains, the outspurs of which come down to within about fifteen miles of the place, were all snow covered. It was bitterly cold, with sleet or drizzle such as one would get anywhere in winter at Home.

We were very well fed, and had first-class butter and cream from the Government dairy. We started a mess farmyard with geese, ducks and chickens, which flourished amazingly and were every bit as fine as British. There was a slight difficulty over green vegetables.

Firewood for the town was floated down the Tigris in big rafts from the Kurdish hills. A good deal of trade was also brought down this way, the rafts being made more buoyant by mussocks. It is understood that the Turks had carried their heavy stores and ammunition down to their armies in this fashion.

The horses we took over from the 11th were in poor condition owing to much hard work, and owing to poor rations and no green stuff. The animals were out in the open and were not warmly enough rugged. They had been clipped, which was, in the writer's opinion, a mistake under the circumstances. The ethics of clipping are primarily connected with the pace animals are likely to work at, and the shelter they get from cold. If they do not do very fast work, and it is impossible to clothe them warmly, it is better to leave them unclipped.

The 11th had handed over some chestnuts, evidently sired by the same stallion on their stud farm, for they all had the same markings. Incidentally the 11th stud farm is about the only silladar cavalry farm that seems to have done anything further than feather the nests of native officers.

The Scinde Horse were scattered about all over the country in the most extraordinary and exasperating manner. " D " Squadron was at Shergat, the railhead, " C " at Quaiyarah, " A " at Tel Afar, forty miles to the west of Mosul, and only " B " and Head-quarters at Mosul. A troop of " C " had also to go to Zakkho, a post in the Kurdish hills directly fronting a Turkish post, which was on the far side of a river. The detachments were all with small bodies of infantry. Had things gone wrong south of Baghdad, however, we should have been properly in the soup and many detachments would have been scuppered.

At the time we arrived at Mosul there was a certain amount of excitement to the attitude of the Turkish Nationalist party. The 8th Hussars had been pushed up there, and we had a brigade of infantry and three batteries as well.

Some trenches had been dug about a couple of miles out of the town on the Nisibin Road, astride the Baghdad railway. This last consisted merely of the cuttings and embankments, but no metalling.

When it is remembered that the unfortunate Turk had been utterly and absolutely knocked out two years before, and that Allied troops had been in Constantinople and elsewhere since the Armistice, it is a little hard to imagine that the danger of a Turk advance on Mosul can have been very great. Strange things, however, had been happening in that country, and Mr. Lloyd George must be credited with having applied the spur which caused the re-birth of the Turkish nation, though this was the last thing that politician desired. The landing of the Greek troops at Smyrna, with a backing of British warships, was the thing that did the trick. It may be as well to state that, within one hour of the landing, and in full view of our helpless and disgusted naval officers, the Greeks perpetrated the most abominable atrocities on some unfortunate Turks who had been bluffed into a surrender. Every decent-minded Turk, seeing that the national existence was now in peril, rallied to the Nationalist flag, which had now been raised by that great man, Mustapha Kemal.

The Turks were fully under the impression that the British were behind the Greeks, and had good grounds for being incensed with us. They had, moreover, a strong French backing. This last was probably the basic cause of the threat to Mosul.

On Saturdays, when the weather was fine, the Jews of Mosul used to come and sit on the ramparts near our lines. They wore Oriental and very picturesque clothes, and the older men were fine dignified old fellows. The Mosul Jew, incidentally, considers himself superior to the Baghdadi, as coming from Samaria originally, when Sargon took the inhabitants off to Nineveh in B.C. 712. They were, strictly speaking, Israelites and not Jews.

The Baghdad Jews had been taken to Babylon in B.C. 586. They hailed from Jerusalem and were proper Jews.

On Sundays the Chaldæan Christians used to follow the Jews' example, with this difference, however, that they used to sit in circles round some arrack bottles and drink. In the case of both Jews and Christians, the women sat by themselves in separate groups. There was a monastery about four miles away called Ma Michael, which used to be a favourite Chaldæan picnic place, and they used to drive back, all hopelessly drunk and singing at the tops of their voices. There were some graves of British soldiers near this monastery who had been Kut prisoners employed on digging the railway. There was much evidence to show that many of the Christians had done a good deal to help our prisoners.

On the 20th December 1920 the writer was appointed Commandant, but, owing to shortage of shipping, could not join before mid-February. Colonel

Lukin had gone home in September, but had left the Regiment in July. There had thus been one of those unsatisfactory breaks for some months when there was no Commandant.

News was received at this time that we were to amalgamate with our old Second Regiment, Jacob's Horse. It is always a sad thing breaking up a Regiment, but particularly old regiments that had a great name. Fortunately our two units were very closely allied. The 36th had been well served by the 35th during the Great War, and it was largely due to these same men, who had had a very fine finish put on their training and discipline in the 36th, that the 35th had shown up so brilliantly in Mesopotamia. Amalgamation would, at the same time, inevitably mean that a number of good officers and men would have to go, but the matter was accepted in the right spirit.

1921

We put in a tremendous lot of field firing near Mosul, and the men became pretty useful. One day the Vickers were firing at a hole in a cliff when, during a pause in the firing, an enormous jackal ran out. The animal was not hurt, which was extraordinary, for the strike of the bullets was right down the entrance,

Although the country close in to Mosul and on the Kurdistan side had been well mapped, that towards Tel Afar and Nisibin had only just been surveyed, and extremely little was known about it. The 11th Lancers had been over a certain amount, but there had been no systematized collection of information. As it was of importance to get to know something of it, we applied to be allowed to go out for a few days and look round. We first visited a place called Jirin, about twenty miles to the south of Mosul on the fringe of the desert and an important junction point on the route from Tel Afar to Quaiyarah. There was quite a respectable amount of cultivation and water, together with a number of small mud villages, all bearing a great similarity to those of Baluchistan. The country is treeless, and carts can go all over it.

In mid-April the writer was directed to take out a small column to visit Sinjar, the capital of the Yezidis, lying about eighty miles due west of Mosul, at the foot of the Beled Sinjar.

This is a ridge springing direct out of the Jezirah, the area between the Tigris and Euphrates, and rising to some four thousand feet. The ridge is some forty miles long and only about four deep. We had a company of the 52nd Sikhs and a couple of 18 prs. The march was extremely pleasant. We passed through Tel Afar, an interesting place for a day, but not longer. The water in this place, like a great deal of that in Baluchistan or Persia, was brilliantly clear and sparkling, but was disgusting to drink, being full of salts. The country, in April, is pleasantly green and there is excellent grazing in parts, usually near the sites of old villages. It is gradually rolling downland, good hard going and admirable for cavalry or artillery. Armoured cars could work over a good bit of it even. The Jezirah is covered with the remains of old villages and towns. It must, in days long gone by, have been extremely fertile as judged by the number of these mounds. It was not watered by irrigation as was the case in the flat Mesopotamian plain, for the country is too undulating. There is, however, always a good deal of rain in the winter months. We heard that there was plenty of water of sorts, which the wandering Arab lives on. We passed an enormous caravan of the Shammar Arabs, migrating north. These were real out and out desert people, One or two of the men, when they stripped, bore the most extraordinary resemblance to the Baluch, and, in particular, to one or two of the Baluch we had in the Regiment. On passing any Arab camps the people would, almost invariably, offer one curded goat and sheep's milk, on the lines of the Biblical writer's " She brought forth butter in a lordly dish."

Both at Tel Afar and Beled Sinjar it is possible to trace buildings of different epochs, some of the stonework going back to Assyrian days.

The Yezidis are a very mysterious people, neither Arab, Kurd, Turk nor Christian. They prohibit all mention of Satan and are particularly careful to propitiate him. Their worship has something to do with the sun, and a theory has been advanced that they are the actual descendants of the original Assyrians of Assyria. Their maliks have a curious way of doing their head-dress which causes them to look, in profile, like the old Assyrian sculptures. They do not wear the Arab horsehair ring round their heads, but a tall kullah and turban.

They were extremely friendly, and delighted to see us. They are not a martial people, and probably owe their existence to their being able to escape up their mountain when threatened. They had been very good in refusing to give up some Armenian refugees to the Turks, but the poor people suffered severely from the subsequent retaliation.

The writer and some of the other officers climbed the mountain—three and a half hours of the hardest and roughest ascent we had known. It was well worth it. There are many traces of quite respectably cultivated ground right up on the top and on the slopes, together with olives and fruit trees. From the summit one can see miles and miles over the Jezirah, both to north and south. On clear days it is said that Nisibin can be seen.

There was a curious little shrine on top with a number of tiny hammocks made of string and rag, each with a pebble in. They were put there by women wishing to become mothers.

After leaving Sinjar we visited a point on the Baghdad railway called Hogena, some fifty miles from Mosul. It was an interesting example of German thoroughness. The station was partially built, but was to be a kind of blockhouse with a deep well. The cuttings and embankments of the railway were all made and only the bridges wanted completion. These last had the stones ready in many cases.

The German lorry road, unmetalled, showed up the excellence of their march discipline and care in driving. It was almost as straight as a railway with the tracks of the lorries like sunken lines. It is believed we were the very first British troops, except some armoured cars, who had ever been so far north as this. We then visited Eski Mosul, a very fertile place on the Tigris. The Arabs were greatly startled to see us. The country about Hogena is well watered, and with quiet and steady rule might become pretty fertile. There had, however, been feuds and bloodshed from time immemorial, and there was no population to work on the soil. The Arab is not addicted to overwork as a cultivator, and, in any case, there had never been much incentive to cultivate anything beyond immediate needs. At the time we were out it was extremely pretty and green, the Kurdistan mountains being covered with snow. The weather was also very pleasant, though a little hot about midday. This was at the end of April. There was but little game about, though there were large flocks of sandgrouse.

We thoroughly reported on the country and routes, in a systematized manner that had never been done before, and our reports would come in very useful in case of necessity.

As a good bit of the country passed over meant hard work for flanking patrols, we worked on the picqueting system, the picquets moving along the track with the advanced guard and branching off. This worked extremely well and made the passage of the long baggage column far more secure than a flank guard moving over broken ground. Where thought necessary we dropped Vickers guns to watch tricky places.

A party of officers and N.C.O.'s of the 8th Hussars accompanied us to learn the lie of the land and study our methods. They took the greatest interest in things, and we received an unsolicited chit from them in hearing one sergeant say to another, " These 'ere Scinde 'orse, they knows this kind of war, don't they ? Just look 'ow they use their Vickers and 'otchkiss." We had, there is no doubt whatever, attained a very high standard in field work.

The crops about Mosul are harvested in May, and the women gleaning have a curious custom of running up to the passer-by waving bunches of corn and receiving a small gift of bakhshish in return. To be lucky the present should be in silver.

There is plenty of good grazing available just now, though by the end of the month the sun has usually roasted the grass all up to brown tinder. The Mosul polo tournament came off soon after our return. We went as far as the semi-finals, the 8th Hussars, Head-quarters Squadron, being the winners. The ponies, or rather horses, were a somewhat mixed lot, some being regular hairies, especially the gunners' animals and some really high class ponies. We were able to buy a few of these last.

At the beginning of June, greatly to our astonishment, we learnt that we were to leave the country, as the garrison was being cut down, and on the 15th June we marched for Shergat, which we reached five days later, entraining thence to Baghdad. There were a number of Russian refugees in Baghdad then, people who had come down when the Bolsheviks occupied the Caspian ports. Some of the officers were very nice fellows, but there were many very bad people as well.

We were extremely well looked after at Baghdad, and the " blighters in barns " attitude towards the troops which had seemingly existed at the beginning of 1920 with a portion of General Head-quarters, had completely ceased.

It was very hot, but at Kut it was infinitely worse, as a roasting wind blew all day and every day. We were hung up at Kut for four or five days owing to a shortage in steamers.

We arrived at Basra on the 1st July, having lost a man overboard on the way. No trace of the poor fellow's body was seen although we searched for a long time. Going downstream through the Narrows was rather like " cannoning off the cush," for one goes down bumping against one bank and then against the other.

We were a fortnight at Basra in E.P. tents, just outside the palm-tree area fortunately, or it would have been absolutely stifling. The temperature ran up to 129 degrees twice, and 130 once while we were there. Fortunately it cooled down at night, and one could even have a sheet over one. The Base staff had been completely changed since March 1920, and we were extremely well looked after.

On the 15th July the Regiment embarked for its last voyage. We had four heat cases in the first day. Two of these were due to the gluttonous habits of the soldiery wanting hot food in the middle of the day. When the squadron commander was summoned there was a fire enough to roast three oxen at a hundred yards' range. A couple of Sikhs who had been unable to resist the odour of ghee had gone to help the langris, and were laid out, breathing stertorously. By dint of copious buckets of water, itself pretty hot, application of ice and fanning, the idiots recovered. The other two cases occurred later in the day, but were not very serious.

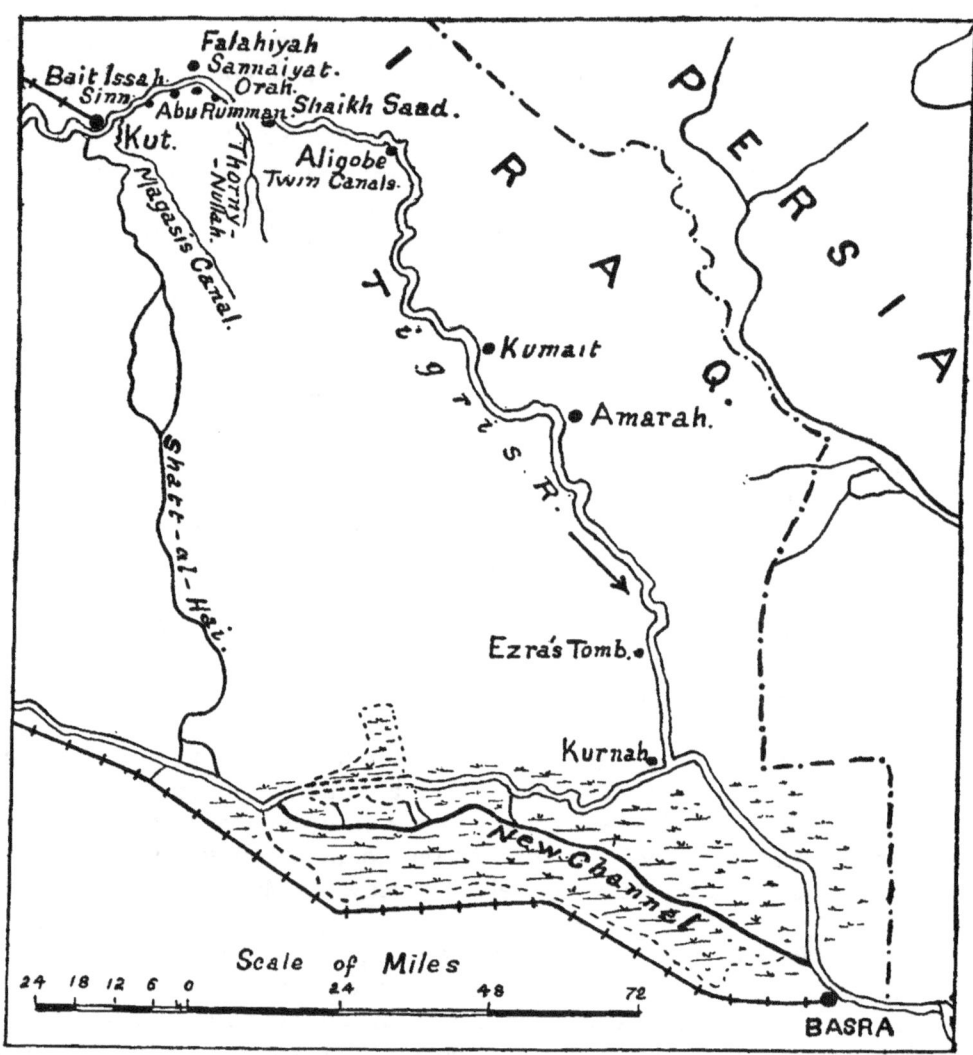

THE RIVER TIGRIS—KUT–BASRA.

All horses had been left behind at Basra. There was a scheme to sell them to the Greek Army, which fortunately did not materialize as the poor beasts would have been maltreated.

Some five thousand animals were shot at Basra alone, as being too expensive to keep. It was the best way out of the difficulty.

The ship we were on board was a British India boat, and was unsuitable for carrying troops. The ship's officers however, like all B.I. officers, were good fellows and most obliging.

It is appallingly hot in the Persian Gulf at this time of year, but is much more humid than the Red Sea.

The decks always had a damp look. The water is extremely phosphorescent, far more so than anywhere we had yet seen.

The rains had broken when we reached Bombay, and the railway carriages the men were in on the journey up to Jubbulpore leaked like sieves, with the result that every one arrived soaked.

The days following our arrival were rather sad ones, for they meant the breaking up of the Regiment for good. There was this point, however, as a consolation. General Haldane had sent us a most complimentary message on our record in Mesopotamia, and we had many evidences that our services out there had been well appreciated in all quarters. The records of both the 35th and 36th Horse since 1914 showed that the tone of the days of John Jacob had been thoroughly maintained.

Jacob's Horse were at Jubbulpore on our return, and the writer was transferred to command it preparatory to the amalgamation. The measure was a sound one and enabled both units to come together in the smoothest possible manner. The conditions for this were extremely favourable, as he knew both regiments well, and within three months or so of the official date of amalgamation the new regiment was absolutely one.

Farewell Message to the 35th Scinde Horse on leaving Mesopotamia in June 1921.

"On leaving Mesopotamia, after nearly eighteen months' service in that country, I wish to place on record my appreciation of the good service rendered by the 35th Scinde Horse.

"The circumstances which prevailed last summer prevented my employing the Regiment as a whole at any time, but two squadrons constantly formed that part of the several columns engaged, and of the other two, one squadron either took its turn with these columns or was employed in the Mosul Villayet.

"The squadrons which shared in the unfortunate incident between Hillah and Kifl did their best, under exceptionally trying conditions, to cover the retreat of the column and fought with great gallantry so as to ensure the withdrawal of the guns.

"When with the column working between Hillah and Baghdad, and again in the Diala operations, the Regiment did useful service. Lastly it shared in the operations for the Relief of Kufah when, by a wide turning movement it cut the Kifl-Najaf Road, charged the insurgents, and inflicted on them heavy casualties.

"I congratulate the Regiment on its fine record while in this country."

(Sd.) A. HALDANE, Lieut.-General
Commanding-in-Chief, M.E.F.

GENERAL HEAD-QUARTERS,
    BAGHDAD,
      20th June 1921.

THE BATTLE HONOURS

"KIFL"
"IRAQ, 1920"

The Goldsmiths and Silversmiths Co., London.

"FRANCE AND FLANDERS."

1914—1918.

The
Goldsmiths
and
Silversmiths
Co.,
London.

"MESOPOTAMIA."

1920—1921.

CHAPTER XXVIII

AMALGAMATION

OF

THE 35TH SCINDE HORSE AND THE 36TH JACOB'S HORSE.

1921–1922

THE 35th and 36th Horse amalgamated on the 1st November 1921, with the writer as commandant.

On the 1st January 1922 the Regiment had the honour of having H.R.H. The Prince of Wales appointed Colonel-in-Chief, and at the end of the month acted as his escort on his visit to Nagpur.

There was a very large surplus of British officers who had to be disposed of, but the terms on which they left the Regiment were generous.

As regards the Indian ranks, the new regiment had only about thirty per cent. each from the old regiments, as the so-called Derajat squadrons ceased to exist, Mussulman Rajputs being substituted. Most of the surplus men took their discharge, being allowed good terms. Some went off to other regiments, but not a large number.

The nucleus of the Mussulman Rajputs were for the most part from the 21st Cavalry and the Central India Horse, and included some excellent Indian officers. Taken on the whole, however, it was found to pay better to bring in new recruits and train them ourselves.

We parted with the Derajat, or rather, mixed Derajat, and Punjabi Mussulman squadrons with mingled feelings, particularly as regards the Derajat element pure and simple. This class requires very careful recruitment, for the men are of very variable value, and it by no means signifies that because a man is a relative of some big notable that he is worth anything. Very frequently he is not, and there were a number of useless men who managed to get into the service. There was often considerable difficulty in getting good Indian officers and N.C.O.'s, and, without them, the men were troublesome, slovenly and a nuisance.

The new class, mainly for this reason, is the better, for it produces quite a number of really good Indian officers and N.C.O.'s.

With the amalgamation, the whole organization of the Indian cavalry was brought up to date, for before the War it was not on the same lines as the British cavalry.

There were now three squadrons and the Head-quarters Squadron, instead of the four squadrons hitherto. The Head-quarters Squadron had a machine-gun section and a signal troop. The other three had three sabre troops and a Hotchkiss troop.

The silladar system, to the relief of every officer of the Scinde Horse who

St. George.
The Patron Saint of Cavalry.

had experienced it, was abolished and the Regiment became " regular " in every sense of the word. The horses and equipment became uniformly good, as the state of the regimental funds did not influence quality and type.

We were freed from the herds of undisciplined syces and scallywags who always accompanied the silladar units. Above all, both men and horses were fed by Government, and we were thus rid of the bunnias who corrupted the Indian officers, robbed the men, and conspired to starve the horses and mules. For petty war the silladar system may have answered, but it broke down, as most thinking officers foresaw it would, the moment a great war began.

The anxiety of all British officers to make the new regiment a success, and the fact that the writer knew both units well, facilitated things greatly.

Numbers of men of the 35th had served for a long period in the 36th and all had been very happy together, and as only the pick of the two regiments remained it was easy to get a high standard from the start.

The community of tradition of the two old regiments, who had always been the greatest friends, was also of assistance.

In the officers' mess, a number of trophies and pictures dating back for many years in the history of the Scinde Horse enabled parties of the Indian ranks to be given ocular demonstration of the unity of the Corps. The mess was thus used on the lines of the "salle d'honneur" of a French regiment. These demonstrations and lectures were of particular value to the men who came from outside units. Care was taken to avoid any collection of the men of an old unit into any one troop, and they were all mixed up in their own squadrons in such a manner as to prevent any old "die hards" not joining in the common union. It is believed that this policy had not always been observed in certain other Indian units, and we know that it was not in the case of the British cavalry on their amalgamation. The consequence was that the men of the old regiments often kept up their differences.

The policy in the Scinde Horse mixed the men up so much in their troops and sections that such aloofness would be impossible, and a system of inter-troop competitions was introduced to further harden the amalgam. There is but little doubt that the high tone set by John Jacob, Merewether, Malcolm and Green in the old days had an enormous amount to do with enabling the regiments to withstand the strain of over sixty years' service in Sind and Baluchistan, and the tone in the new corps shows every sign of being no whit behind.

"MAN DIES, BUT THE REGIMENT LIVES."

THE TITLES OF THE REGIMENT

The various titles of both The 35th Scinde Horse and The 36th Jacob's Horse, from the dates of formation, 1839 and 1846 respectively, including the amalgamation of the two units in 1921, are detailed on page xx.

APPENDICES

I—X

    I   Brigadier-General John Jacob, C.B.
   II   Commandants of The Regiment.
  III   Nominal Roll of Officers.
  IV   Officers—The Great War.
    V   Casualties.
  VI   Honours and Awards.
 VII   An Historical Précis.
VIII   A Relic of Sir Charles Napier.
  IX   Correspondence—Masnières.
   X   The Silladar System.

APPENDIX I

BRIGADIER-GENERAL JOHN JACOB, C.B.

1812–1858.

JOHN JACOB was born on the 11th January 1812. He was the fifth son of the Reverend Stephen Long Jacob, vicar of Woolavington, Somerset. All the schooling he had was received from his father, who, being a man of small means, taught his own boys.

On obtaining his cadetship, he went straight to Addiscombe, the military college of the Honourable East India Company. In January 1828, at the age of sixteen, he received his commission as a lieutenant in the Bombay Artillery, and the same month sailed for India, never to return. For thirty years he was to serve, and so absorbed did he become in his work that he never once took furlough during the whole period.

After landing at Bombay, he passed seven uneventful years at regimental duty.

He was, one gathers, a shy man, and had a stutter, and there is reason to suppose that he found mess life, or its equivalent in those days, somewhat irksome. He was of a studious disposition, well-read and clever above the average run of officers of the day, and his position was quite understandable. In particular, he was a student of Oriental languages, though he consistently avoided the required tests that were subsequently introduced for officers in the Company's service. In the " Records of The Scinde Irregular Horse " can be seen some quite entertaining correspondence on this subject. By the time he became a lieutenant, after more than eight years' service be it noted, he was a proficient linguist in Hindi and Persian.

At the outbreak of The First Afghan War, 1838, he was ordered, with his battery, to join the Army of the Indus, then assembling under Sir John Keane. Landing at Karachi, he accompanied the Bombay Column as far as Sukkur, where he was left behind in charge of a detachment of European soldiers, for the most part the dregs and wastrels of the army. The Baluch had harried the lines of communication of Keane's army without ceasing and, despite the intense heat, the authorities decided to attempt punitive measures. Jacob was accordingly charged with organizing a scratch battery from these elements. Having selected some forty of the least ineligible, he was ordered to march, during the latter part of June, 1838, to Shikarpore, about thirty miles from Sukkur. His guns were sent by canal.

The temperature ran up to 130 degrees in the shade, and, although the detachment marched only at night, no fewer than sixteen men out of forty died. This experience decided the authorities to await the cold weather before attempting further operations.

Early in October, however, a fresh expedition under Billamore was organized with orders to proceed to Kutchee and operate against the hill tribes on the north-eastern flank of our line of communications to the foot of the Bolan. This was to consist entirely of Indian troops.

Jacob was again charged with improvising a battery, to be drawn by bullocks and familiarly termed "the beef train." He selected his men chiefly from the 5th Bombay Infantry, all Mahrattas, and turned out many of the original nucleus on account of their giving trouble in caste matters.

The desert was crossed, and Shahpur, a desolate spot in the wilderness about thirty-five miles from the present Jacobabad, was duly reached without difficulty. On arrival at Phooljee, the next march, however, the hovels were all ablaze and the tribesmen had fled to the hills, which at this point are not more than two or three miles off. The only method of coping with the robbers was with mounted men, and, as the levies accompanying the force proved valueless, The Scinde Irregular Horse, which had just been raised at Hyderabad, Scinde, under Lieutenant Clarke, were marched up. Here begins Jacob's connection with the Regiment, although it was not until three years later that he joined it.

At that time the hill country to the east of Phooljee was quite unknown to Europeans and, although surveyed, but little is known of it even at the present day.

The expedition duly entered the hills and penetrated as far as the two tribal strongholds of Deyra and Kahun. Two severe actions with the Boogtis were fought and, in the second, very heavy loss was inflicted. The Scinde Horse distinguished itself greatly on this occasion, its commander, Clarke, killing four of the enemy single-handed. Much of the success of the expedition was, however, due to the energy and resource of John Jacob, who, with extempore pioneers, got his guns over the mountain tracks. The moral effect of this on the tribes was immense, for they had not deemed such a thing possible.

The force returned to Phooljee after an absence of three and a half months, when it was broken up, and Jacob returned to his normal duty with a battery at Hyderabad.

His work as a surveyor, and the experience gained by this expedition, was all thrown away as no proper records were kept, with the result that, six years later, when Sir Charles Napier determined to punish the Boogtis for a second time, his expedition started in almost as complete ignorance of the country and tribes as did that of Billamore.

Little has been heard of Billamore's Hill Campaign, as events in Afghanistan dwarfed everything. Had, however, it occurred at some other period it would undoubtedly have created some stir.

While Jacob was at Hyderabad, he met Outram, who was then Political Agent in Scinde.

The Government was anxious to find a land route from Hyderabad into Kathiawar via Nuggar Pakur, as it did not care to be entirely dependent on the sea route from Bombay to Karachi. The task was a dangerous one, both owing to the expanse of desert, and to the unsettled state of the country. Outram selected Jacob for the task, which was successfully accomplished, only three tribesmen accompanying the latter. For this, Jacob received the thanks of the Bombay Government.

In 1841 it was decided to augment the strength of The Scinde Horse, and Jacob was offered, and accepted, the vacant command. He was, at the same time, placed in charge of the Kutchee Frontier, then in a most disturbed condition owing to our reverses in Afghanistan. The aggressive policy he inaugurated soon quietened things, and in October 1842 England's army crossed from the mouth of the Bolan on its way back to India. For the first time in its march from Kandahar, it was not harried by marauders.

So successful was Jacob that Outram, in an official letter, dated the 19th October 1843, writes: "For the first time in the memory of man, Kutchee and Upper Scinde have been, for a whole year, entirely free from the irruption of hill tribes, by which the villages were annually destroyed, lives and property sacrificed, and the whole country kept in a state of fear."

Orders were now received that Khanghur (Jacobabad) was to be permanently garrisoned by The Scinde Horse. It was then a collection of mud huts round a well or two, a few bauble trees and tamarisk bushes being the only vegetation about.

At the end of November 1842 Jacob was ordered to march his Corps to Sukkur to join the army of Sir Charles Napier, then assembling for the conquest of Scinde. The detail of Meeanee, Hyderabad, and other operations has already been given in the Regimental History. Jacob was rewarded for his services by being appointed Honorary A.D.C. to the Governor-General.

Sir Charles Napier at this period was on most friendly terms with Jacob, and, in his letters to him, frequently refers to The Scinde Horse as "my old advanced guard." Possibly based on this, the trumpet call, for all three regiments of the Corps, was that of the advanced guard, preceded by the number of "G" of the Regiment. The present amalgamated Regiment has the plain "advanced guard" call of the "'forties" with no "G's." The mess call, on the other hand, is that of Jacob's old unit, the Bombay Artillery.

In 1844 Jacob took his regiment north to accompany Sir Charles Napier in his expedition into the Boogti Hills, but remained in the Kutchee plain. A most flattering order was published with regard to the capture of Shahpur by Jacob, ending with the words, "Another laurel leaf has been added to the rich wreath of The Scinde Horse." In April 1845 Jacob and the Regiment returned to Hyderabad.

About this period there was some acrimony between Outram and Napier over the treatment of the Mirs of Scinde. Jacob sided with the former and a coolness sprang up between Sir Charles and himself, which was accentuated by what Jacob considered, and which undoubtedly were, exaggerations by Sir

William Napier in his " History of the Conquest of Scinde " as regards the feats of the General. Jacob was a man of strong opinions and had but little hesitation in letting them be known. Jacob had submitted proposals for doubling the Corps by raising a second regiment. This was acceded to, and the unit commonly known as Jacob's Horse, or The 2nd Scinde Horse, was raised. Jacob claimed to command both regiments, a claim the authorities at first refused as being against all precedent, but to which they finally yielded—a proof of the high estimation he already enjoyed. In this instance the Governor-General observed that " he had been induced, in this single instance, to depart from precedence, out of regard to Captain Jacob's reputation and services." In January 1847 came the turning point in Jacob's career, for the whole of the Scinde Frontier, from the Punjab to Shahpur in Kutchee, with headquarters at Khangur, was placed under his orders. The country, at this period, was in a state of chaos, murder and rapine were rife, and no man's life was safe. His vigorous régime restored order, but it was hard and trying work. In his own words, " Our first year on the border was of enormous bodily labour. With only a single regiment on the Frontier, we had, literally, to lie down to rest with boots and sword on, for many months together." The country is abominable enough even now. What it must have been before rest-houses, punkahs, ice, and other amenities of civilization were introduced can be imagined.

All this time Jacob was busily engaged in organizing and equipping his regiments, and the thoroughness in which this was done was the admiration of everyone who saw them. There were only four executive British officers in the two units, which numbered sixteen hundred sabres and watched a line some hundred and ninety miles long. As these officers had to be constantly on the move, even in the hottest weather, the strain was enormous.

As the pay of the sowars amounted to thirty rupees a month only, from which they had to feed their horses and provide their own food, clothing and equipment, it was not unnatural that murmurings arose when the constant hard work led to extra expense. Jacob sympathized greatly with his men and endeavoured to get the matter righted. The Treasury, however, would do nothing. Meanwhile, as a sop, Jacob asked that the Corps should be changed to " Scinde Silladar Light Cavalry—a distinction, I may say with honest pride and without presumption, we have honestly earned." The Indian Government, in their munificence, finding this cost nothing, granted the request.

In the hot weather of 1848, troubles in the Punjab came to a head, and Jacob was ordered to despatch five hundred sabres to join the Army of the Indus. He wished to proceed in command himself, but his services on the border were too valuable to allow him to be spared. He thus missed The Second Sikh War and the Siege of Multan and the Battle of Gujerat. Owing, moreover, to the weakening of the strength of his troops on the Frontier, his work was enormously increased. While keeping down marauding with a strong hand, Jacob devoted himself with the utmost energy to the administration of the extensive district in his charge. He succeeded in disarming every man who was not a Government servant. Bridges and roads, amounting to over six hundred miles, were constructed, canals were excavated, and a large area which had hitherto been absolute desert was thereby brought under cultivation.

His survey pillars, some twenty feet high, can be seen in many directions in the country round Jacobabad to this day.

The Governor-General named Khangur "Jacobabad" in his honour and the notification of the Post Office to this effect can be seen in the "Records of The Scinde Irregular Horse.' Jacobabad has now no fewer than fourteen thousand inhabitants. Its trees and the "lay out" of the cantonments will compare favourably with any station in India, though the bungalows and lines are now all derelict, the place having been abandoned as a military station—to the regret of but few officers who have been stationed there.

One reads constantly in Jacob's writings of the importance of truth and honesty in dealings with Indians, and repeated stress is laid on having none but English gentlemen in command of Indian troops. He was strongly opposed to having British non-commissioned officers in sepoy units, as was the custom in the old Bengal Army. It must, however, be remembered that the British soldier class of his period was by no means drawn from the best elements of our nation, and the conditions of soldiering did not tend to elevate the man in the ranks. Experience of The Great War showed that really good British N.C.O.'s—men who were Nature's gentlemen—were of enormous value with the Indian soldier. By September 1850 Jacob received the C.B.—a somewhat deferred honour—for his services at Meeanee seven years before.

In the East India Company's service, the C.B. was, in those days, regarded as a very great honour.

Jacob was a man extremely susceptible to any criticism, and regarded with some apprehension the advent of an inspecting officer of regular cavalry. This officer, however, instead of decrying, was most eulogistic of what he saw.

As there had always been much trouble owing to marauders escaping into the territory of the Khan of Khelat, where they could not be pursued, Jacob was charged with negotiating a treaty with this prince to enable us to do so. This was effected in 1854, and the measure greatly added to the quietness of the country.

The same year he wrote a letter, advocating the occupation of Quetta as a British outpost, a measure that was taken thirty years later. In 1856, after eight years on the Frontier, he was appointed Acting Commissioner of Scinde at Karachi. He had just been promoted brevet-colonel and nominated A.D.C. to the Queen, in recognition of his services.

The same year he submitted a plan for a canal, giving full details of the work and probable cost, to run from Kusmore into the Kutchee plain between Sibi and Jacobabad. It is understood that the Sukkur Barrage now under construction contemplates a canal in much the same direction, that is, some sixty years after Jacob's letter. Towards the end of 1856, war with Persia was declared, and Jacob was appointed to the command of the irregular horse accompanying it. The First Scinde Horse formed part. Sudden disturbances at Khelat detained both him and the Regiment, and it was not until the latter part of February that he landed at Bushire, where a garrison of three thousand was to be retained.

To Jacob's mortification, he found he was to be left at the base in command. The campaign ended abruptly. When one considers what kind of a fighting man the Persian is, this is not to be wondered at. The grandiloquent accounts of certain of the petty skirmishes described as " battles " in this campaign make the reader smile.

A month later The Mutiny broke out, but Jacob was detained at Bushire until the evacuation was complete.

Four months later he landed at Bombay, where a sore disappointment awaited him. The Governor-General had previously approved of his appointment to command the Army of Central India then assembling, but, on landing, he received a letter stating that it had been found impossible to wait, and the command had, therefore, to be given to Sir Hugh Rose.

Jacob accordingly went back to his old duties on the Frontier, but found the work greatly increased. The long strain was beginning to tell and, for the first time in his life, his strength was beginning to fail him.

In late 1857 it was decided to raise a third regiment of Scinde Horse, an infantry battalion and a mountain battery. The battalion and battery were each named after Jacob.

The battalion was armed with a double-barrelled muzzle-loading rifle, sighted to two thousand yards, with bead foresights and beautifully made by Swinborne & Co. It can be seen in The Scinde Horse Mess, The Royal United Service Institution Museum, and at certain Schools of Musketry. The British troops of the period were armed either with the Brown Bess or with the Minié rifle only, and this fact, doubtless, led to some hesitation on the part of the authorities.

On the parade ground at Jacobabad can be seen rifle butts, the last butt more than two thousand yards from the Residency, from the roof of which Jacob used to shoot when experimenting for this weapon.

This rifle is still highly prized by the Brahui and Baluch, both for its strength and accuracy, which is said to exceed that of the Martini Henri.

In addition to being a soldier and administrator, Jacob was a skilled mechanic.

In the Residency at Jacobabad can be seen a wonderful clock he made, showing the different phases of the moon. The pendulum is a cannon ball fired from an enemy gun at Multan. Holtztapfell, of the Haymarket, who saw some of his work, said he could have made his fortune as a skilled workman.

He made numerous experiments at Jacobabad with rifled cannon, made in his own workshops. He was, in addition, a writer of no small repute. " The views and opinions of John Jacob " give many admirable hints as regards dealings with Indians. Certain extracts gave considerable offence, and some letters written to the papers in 1852, as regards the state of discipline, or rather indiscipline, of the pampered Bengal sepoy, brought him into trouble with the authorities. His views on the relationship between the British officers of the Bengal Army and their men are also of great interest.

By the end of 1858 Jacob was worn out, and on the 6th December he died, aged forty-seven only, to the inexpressible grief of the officers of his staff, his old native officers of The Scinde Horse, and of the Baluch chiefs who were standing by his bedside to the last.

He was buried the next day, the Baluch, who thronged to his funeral, comforting themselves that, as his body had been committed to their soil, his spirit would remain to watch over them. His name is held in reverence among them, as that of a being more than mortal. A disastrous flood, due to the Indus overflowing its banks, some years later, stopped short at his grave. This was pointed to as an indication of his power, even when dead.

The last of the old native officers of The Scinde Horse present at Jacob's death, one Ressaldar Major Imam Khan, died at Jacobabad in 1899, aged ninety-two. He had joined the Regiment on its first formation and had fought at Meeanee, Hyderabad, Multan, and Gujerat. The whole of the British and Indian officers of the Regiment, including the writer, regardless of creed, were present at his burial, a most unusual thing in Indian affairs of this sort.

There were at Jacobabad in this year still a few old pensioners who had served under him. One old pensioned native officer would turn out at the annual durbar of the Commissioner in Scinde in the faded olive-green uniform, with its handsome silver lacing and red Mahratta tied pagari of The Scinde Horse of the late " 'seventies."

Summary.

1812	. .	Born at Woolavington, Somerset.
1828	. .	Gazetted Second-Lieutenant, Bombay Artillery.
1836	. .	Promoted Lieutenant.
1843	. .	Promoted Captain.
		Appointed Honorary A.D.C. to the Governor-General.
1847	. .	Promoted Major.
1850	. .	Awarded the C.B.
1855	. .	Promoted Lieutenant-Colonel.
1856	. .	Promoted Colonel.
		Appointed A.D.C. to H.M. The Queen.
		Acting-Commissioner of Scinde.
		Promoted Brigadier-General.
1858	. .	Died at Jacobabad.

The illustration, facing page one of this volume, is taken from a portrait (*circa* 1856) in possession of The Royal United Service Institution, London.

APPENDIX II

COMMANDANTS OF THE REGIMENT

The 35th Scinde Horse.

Rank.	Name.	Date. From.	Date. To.
Captain	W. Ward	1839	1840
Captain	W. F. Curtis	1840	1842
Lt.-Col.	J. Jacob	1843	1856
Major	W. L. Merewether	1857	1858
Major	G. W. Macauley	1859	1869
Major	J. Gordon	1870	—
Major	C. A. Lock	1871	—
Lt.-Col.	W. R. Alexander	1872	1878
Lt.-Col.	R. V. Malden	1879	1884
Lt.-Col.	W. H. J. Stopford	1885	1888
Lt.-Col.	M. James	1889	1893
Colonel	G. F. Francis	1894	1901
Lt.-Col.	C. E. Peirse	1902	1905
Lt.-Col.	F. W. G. Wadeson	1906	1912
Lt.-Col.	Sir George de S. Barrow, C.B., K.C.M.G.	1912	1915
Lt.-Col.	Sir John Shea, K.C.B., K.C.M.G.	1916	1916
Lt.-Col.	O. M. J. da Costa	1917	1918
Lt.-Col.	R. C. W. Lukin	1918	1920
Lt.-Col.	E. B. Maunsell	1920	1921

COMMANDANTS OF THE REGIMENT

The 36th Jacob's Horse.

Rank.	Name.	Date. From.	Date. To.
Lt.-Col.	J. Jacob	1846	1856
Major	W. L. Merewether	1857	—
Major	M. S. Green	1854	—
Major	J. H. B. Dennis	1865	1868
Major	W. A. Dick	1868	1871
Captain	J. F. Forbes	1871	1878
Lt.-Col.	M. M. Carpendale	1878	1885
Major	A. M. Hogg	1885	1892
Lt.-Col.	C. A. de N. Lucas	1893	1894
Lt.-Col.	E. L. P. Monteith	1894	1900
Lt.-Col.	R. W. Sherard	1901	1907
Lt.-Col.	C. M. Cartwright	1908	1912
Lt.-Col.	R. E. Roome	1913	1915
Lt.-Col.	W. C. K. Green, C.M.G., D.S.O.	1916	1921

3rd Scinde Horse.

Rank.	Name.	Date. From.	Date. To.
Lieut.	Briggs, W. L.		
Major	Malcolmson, J. H. P.		
Major	Thomas, H. R. D.		

P.W.O. 14th Scinde Horse.

Colonel-in-Chief:

H.R.H. The Prince of Wales.

Colonel:

Lieut.-General Sir G. de S. Barrow, K.C.B., K.C.M.G.

Rank.	Name.	Date. From.	Date. To.
Lt.-Col.	E. B. Maunsell	1921	1924
Lt.-Col.	H. R. Dyer, D.S.O.	1924	—

APPENDIX III

OFFICERS.

1st Sind Horse.
5th Bombay Cavalry.
35th Scinde Horse.

Nominal Roll of Officers who Served in the above Regiment from the Date of its being Raised (1839).

Rank and Name.		Rank and Name.	
Capt.	Abbott, F.	Lieut.	Campbell, R.
Lieut.	Alexander	Lieut.	Carmichael
Lt.-Col.	Alexander	Asst. Surg.	Carnegie
Lieut.	Alexander	Lieut.	Carpendale, M.
2nd Lt.	Alexander, C. G.	Surgeon	Carruther, C. M.
2nd Lt.	Alexander, F. G.	Lieut.	Carter
Lieut.	Aspinall, W. B.	Lieut.	Carthew Yorstoun, M. C.
2nd Lt.	Aucutt, W.	2nd Lt.	Charriol, P.
Asst. Surg.	Banks	Lieut.	Cheyne, A. Y.
Capt.	Barber, C. H., I.M.S.	Lieut.	Clarke, W. H.
Lt.-Col.	Barrow, G. de S.	Surgeon	Clogery, M. C.
Lieut.	Barrow, R. L.	2nd Lt.	Cobham, H. W.
2nd Lt.	Barton, J. W.	Lieut.	Codrington
Lieut.	Bateman Johnson	2nd Lt.	Collis, N. S.
2nd Lt.	Bell, W. B.	2nd Lt.	Colquhoun, G. T.
Lieut.	Benn, R. A. E.	Capt.	Connop, H. E.
Lieut.	Benwell, R. L.	Asst. Surg.	Cooke
Capt.	Bird, R. J.	Surgeon	Cooper
Lieut.	Booth, E. R. C.	Ensign	Coulson, G.
2nd Lt.	Bott, F. G.	Surgeon	Cox, J. H. R.
2nd Lt.	Bowles, W. E.	Asst. Surg.	Cruikshank, M.
Lieut.	Brett, J. A.	Lieut.	Curtis
Lieut.	Briggs, W. L.	Lieut.	Da Costa, O. M. J.
Lieut.	Brown, J. A.	2nd Lt.	Dalley, R. P.
Asst. Surg.	Burn	Cornet	Daniell, R. H.
2nd Lt.	Cameron, E. G.	Asst. Surg.	Daubeny, J.
Asst. Surg.	Campbell	2nd Lt.	Dean, J. N.

OFFICERS

Rank and Name.		Rank and Name.	
Lt.-Col.	Dick	Lieut.	Hughes, W. H. F.
Lieut.	Dickenson	Lieut.	Hutchinson, F. H. G.
2nd Lt.	Digby, E.	2nd Lt.	Jacob, G. W. B.
Lieut.	Domvile, J. R. C.	Capt.	James, M.
2nd Lt.	Donald, C. D.	Lieut.	John Jacob
Lieut.	Dore, A. M.	2nd Lt.	Jones, H. C.
2nd Lt.	Douvetil, P. V.	2nd Lt.	Kennedy, E. E.
2nd Lt.	Drummond, I. G.	Lieut.	Kettlewell, A. M.
Lieut.	Dyer, H. R.	Lieut.	King, E.
Surgeon	Dyson, T. E.	Surgeon	Kirtekar, H. R.
2nd Lt.	Engeldow, G.	Capt.	Knox, J. H. A.
2nd Lt.	Evennett, H. C.	2nd Lt.	Lambert, D. de G.
Lieut.	Fagan	2nd Lt.	Landon, C. R. H. P.
Lieut.	FitzGerald, R.	Lieut.	Leith
2nd Lt.	FitzPatrick, G. O. C.	2nd Lt.	Leslie
2nd Lt.	Flood, F. W. S.	2nd Lt.	Lewis, A. G.
Lieut.	Forbes	Surgeon	Lewis, C. H.
2nd Lt.	Foreman, F. C.	2nd Lt.	Lloyd, J. T.
Lieut.	Francis, G. F.	2nd Lt.	Lloyd Williams
2nd Lt.	Gahan, J.	Major	Loch, C. A.
Capt.	Geddes, T. J. R.	Asst. Surg.	Lowry, J. R. C.
Asst. Surg.	Gilbert	Lieut.	Lucas.
Lieut.	Giles, E. D.	Cornet	Lucas, C. A.
Lieut.	Giles, G. D.	2nd Lt.	Lucas, C. A.
2nd Lt.	Gillespie, J. K.	Lieut.	Macauley, G. W.
2nd Lt.	Godfrey, F.	Asst. Surg.	MacDougal
Lieut.	Gordon, G. S.	Lieut.	MacGeorge, H. K.
Lieut.	Gordon, J. E.	2nd Lt.	Mackay, D. H.
Capt.	Grant, E.	Lieut.	Mainwaring
Lieut.	Grant, R.	Ensign	Malcolm, G.
Lieut.	Green, M. S.	Lieut.	Malden, R. V.
Lieut.	Green, W. H. R.	Lieut.	Marten, E. C.
Capt.	Hagger, R. L., I.M.S.	Lieut.	Mathews, W. H.
Lieut.	Harrison, C. H.	2nd Lt.	Maunsell, E. B.
2nd Lt.	Harrison, H. S.	Asst. Surg.	McDougall
Major	Hartigan, A. E. S.	Asst. Surg.	McCloghry
2nd Lt.	Hartigan, K. L. S.	2nd Lt.	McGlashon
Lieut.	Hervey	Lieut.	McNair, A. L.
Lieut.	Hislop, A. F.	2nd Lt.	Mecleery, H. W. F.
Lieut.	Hocken, C. A. F.	2nd Lt.	Medwell, P. R.
Lieut.	Hogg	Lieut.	Merewether, W. L.
Surgeon	Holy, J.	Surgeon	Milne, A.
Asst. Surg.	Howell, J. A.	Lieut.	Micholetts

Rank and Name.		Rank and Name.	
Surgeon	Mistri, K. H.	2nd Lt.	Rivett Carnac, J.
2nd Lt.	Mitchell, M.	2nd Lt.	Robinson, W. E. D.
2nd Lt.	Montagu Smith, E.	Lieut.	Rooke, B. P. S.
Lieut.	Monteith, E. V. P.	2nd Lt.	Rorison, W. M.
2nd Lt.	Morrell, H. G.	Lieut.	Russell
2nd Lt.	Morrison, C. C.	Lieut.	Sale, C. F.
Lieut.	Myers, C. B.	Surgeon	Schneider, C. V.
2nd Lt.	Napier Fold, G. S.	Lt.-Col.	Shea, J. S. M., D.S.O.
Surgeon	Nariman	Capt.	Sheeky
2nd Lt.	Newnham, W. F.	Lieut.	Sherard, R. W.
2nd Lt.	Nicholl, C. K.	Lieut.	Simonds, J. N.
Capt.	Nokes, G. B. I.	Capt.	Slade Baker
Lieut.	Oldfield, T. A. R. F.	Capt.	Smith, C. D. N.
Lieut.	Owen, E. O.	Capt.	Southey, H. H.
2nd Lt.	Palmer, A. R. B.	Lieut.	Stanley
2nd Lt.	Palmes, W. T.	Capt.	Stevens, G. S.
Asst. Surg.	Pelly, Lewis	Capt.	Stevenson
Asst. Surg.	Pelly, S. M.	Surgeon	Stevenson, H. W.
Major	Phillips, J.	Capt.	Stewart, A. M.
Lieut.	Pickard, B. De H.	2nd Lt.	Stewart, A. W.
Lieut.	Pierse, C. E.	Major	Stopford, W. R. J.
Lieut.	Playfair	Surgeon	Street, H. W. F.
Lieut.	Pollard, J. H.	Lieut.	Thompson, J. P.
Lieut.	Purvis, H. I. E.	Major	Wadeson, F. W. G.
Lieut.	Reid	Capt.	Ward
Lieut.	Reynolds, E. S.	2nd Lt.	Webster, F. G.
2nd Lt.	Richardson	2nd Lt.	Wills, H. G.
2nd Lt.	Rilley Irwing	2nd Lt.	Ziman, S. N.

OFFICERS.

2ND SIND HORSE.
6TH BOMBAY CAVALRY.
36TH JACOB'S HORSE.

NOMINAL ROLL OF OFFICERS WHO SERVED IN THE ABOVE REGIMENT FROM THE DATE OF ITS BEING RAISED (1846).

Rank and Name.		Rank and Name.	
Lieut.	Abbey, W. B. T.	2nd Lt.	Channer, K. F.
Capt.	Abbott, F.	Lieut.	Chubb, W. B.
Lieut.	Abbott, F.	Surgeon	Clogery, Mc.
Lieut.	Alexander, C. H.	Asst. Surg.	Cockell
Capt.	Alexander, F. G.	Lieut.	Codrington
Lieut.	Allardice, H.	Ensign	Collier, J. A.
2nd Lt.	Allen, F. J.	Asst. Surg.	Cook
Lieut.	Alpen, I. M. S.	Surgeon	Copper
Lieut.	Anderson, R. F. B.	Lieut.	Cotton, H. J.
Lieut.	Aplin	Lieut.	Croften, R. M.
Surgeon	Barry	2nd Lt.	Dallas, D. A. G.
Surgeon	Bartholomeusz	Asst. Surg.	Dann
2nd Lt.	Beatty, R. G.	2nd Lt.	Davidson, H. M.
2nd Lt.	Bennet	Major	Dennis, J. H.
Lieut.	Binney, A. J. M.	Major	Dick, W. A.
2nd Lt.	Blacker, W. F.	2nd Lt.	Dormer, E. J.
2nd Lt.	Blakeney, E. C. W.	2nd Lt.	Douglas, D.
Asst. Surg.	Bond, P.	Asst. Surg.	Ellis, T.
2nd Lt.	Braithwaite, P. P.	2nd Lt.	Emerson, D. B.
Lieut.	Briggs, W. L.	Lieut.	Fagan, E. A.
Capt.	Butler	2nd Lt.	Faithful, R. G.
2nd Lt.	Cahusac, C. F.	Lieut.	Farquhar, F. R.
Lieut.	Caiger, A. C. E.	2nd Lt.	Flynn, T. F. A.
Lieut.	Campbell	Lieut.	Forbes, J. F.
Lieut.	Campbell, E. P.	Lieut.	Forteath, A. M.
2nd Lt.	Carpendale, F. M.	2nd Lt.	Foster, T. D.
Lieut.	Carpendale, M. M.	Lieut.	Fraser
Capt.	Carter, R. M.	2nd Lt.	Fry, G. C.
Lieut.	Cartwright, C. M.	Lieut.	Gavin, G. F. A.

APPENDIX III

Rank and Name.		Rank and Name.	
Lieut.	Geoghegan	2nd Lt.	Leith, R. D. T.
Capt.	Geytes, W. Le.	Lieut.	Lightbody.
Asst. Surg.	Glass, A. P.	Lieut.	Lincoln, C. H.
Lieut.	Gordon, J. E.	Lieut.	Loch, W.
2nd Lt.	Gordon Kidd, A. L.	Capt.	Lucas, C. A.
Lieut.	Gostling, D. E.	Lieut.	Lucas, H. F.
Lieut.	Grantham	Lieut.	Lucas, H. F. E.
Capt.	Grantham, C. F.	Capt.	Lunham
Capt.	Graves, J.	Lieut.	MacGeorge, H. K.
Lieut.	Green, H. R.	Lieut.	Mackenzie, D. G.
Lieut.	Green, M.	Capt.	Mahon, B., D.S.O., M.C.
Capt.	Green, W. G. K.	Ensign	Maitland
Lieut.	Griffith	Lieut.	Maitland, P. J.
Lieut.	Hagger, R. L.	Lieut.	Malcolm
2nd Lt.	Harrison, A. W.	Lieut.	Malden, R. V.
Lieut.	Harrison, C. H.	2nd Lt.	Maltby, F. B.
Lieut.	Hartigan, A. E. S.	Lieut.	Martin, H.
Lieut.	Hartigan, E. R.	Lieut.	Mathew, C. T.
Lieut.	Hay, C.	Lieut.	McVean, N. N. G. C., I.M.S.
Lieut.	Haye, De La		
Lieut.	Hogg, A. M.	Lieut.	Menzies, V. G.
Lieut.	Hogg, H. C.	Lieut.	Merewether, W. L.
Lieut.	Hope, T.	Lieut.	Mesurier, E. le
Lieut.	Hossack, I. F.	Surgeon	Miller, R.
2nd Lt.	Howell, G. C. L.	Lieut.	Monteith, A. M.
Surgeon	Hudson, C. T.	Capt.	Monteith, E. V. P.
Lieut.	Hudson, W. H.	Lieut.	Monteith, J.
Capt.	Jacob, J.	Capt.	Moor, R. N.
Capt.	James, M.	2nd Lt.	Morrell, H. G.
Surgeon	Jennings	Capt.	Munro, E. B., I.M.S.
2nd Lt.	Johnson, T. F.	Lieut.	Newnham, W. F.
2nd Lt.	Jones, A. N. G.	2nd Lt.	Nixon, E. M.
Lieut.	Keightley.	2nd Lt.	Ogley, E. F.
2nd Lt.	Keightley, M. F.	Major	Oldfield
Lieut.	Kettlewell, A. W.	2nd Lt.	Owen Jones, R. D.
2nd Lt.	Kidd, J. G.	Lieut.	Paddon, S. S. W.
Lieut.	King, E.	2nd Lt.	Parnell, M. E.
Lieut.	Knight, A. B.	Lieut.	Phadke, S. K., I.M.S.
Asst. Surg.	Lalar, J.	Surgeon	Pherson, Mac, I.M.S.
Lt.-Col.	Lance, F. F.	Lieut.	Phillips, A. M.
2nd Lt.	Landale, H. R.	Lieut.	Pollard, I. H.
Asst. Surg.	Lawry.	Lieut.	Pont, L. V.
Lieut.	Leech	Lieut.	Price, J. R.

OFFICERS

Rank and Name.		Rank and Name.	
Lieut.	Reid, A.	2nd Lt.	Stroud, G. M.
Lieut.	Reid, C. L.	Capt.	Thomas
Lieut.	Reynolds, R.	Lieut.	Trevor, Naylor H.
Lieut.	Robertson, I.	Capt.	Trollope, T. J.
Capt.	Robinson, J. E. M.	Lieut.	Vigors, T. M.
2nd Lt.	Roome, R. E.	2nd Lt.	Vosper, E. E.
Surgeon	Rustam Ji Byramjee	Lieut.	Wadeson
Lieut.	Seacome	Asst. Surg.	Wakefield, H.
Lieut.	Seton	2nd Lt.	Waldron, E. N. E.
Lieut.	Sherard, R. W.	Lieut.	Waller, B. C.
Major	Sherard, R. W.	2nd Lt.	Watkins, F. W. S.
2nd Lt.	Sherman, D. H.	Lieut.	Whately, W.
Capt.	Shettle, F. B., I.M.S.	Surgeon	Whitcombe, E. O. R.
Capt.	Smith, G.	Lieut.	Willans
2nd Lt.	Smith, M. H.	2nd Lt.	Wood, A. E. F.
Capt.	Stevens, G. S.		

3RD SCINDE HORSE.

NOMINAL ROLL OF OFFICERS WHO SERVED IN THE ABOVE REGIMENT.

Briggs, W. L.
Burroughs, G. E. E.

Campbell, R. L.
Asst. Surg. Colson, E.
Coulson, G. J.

Dickinson, W.
Asst. Surg. Duckering, S.

Gavin, G. F. A.
Gordon, J. E.

Hogg, H. C.

Asst. Surg. Lawrence, E. A.
Loch, W.

Malcolmson, J. H. P.

Malden, R. V.
Maitland, P. J.
McNeill, H. B.
McNair, A. L.
Minchin, H. D. M.
Monteith, A. M.
Monteith, E. V. P.

Peat, W. S.

Reynolds, E. S.
Reynolds, W.

Sherard, R. W.
Smith, E. D. M.

Thomas, H. R. D.

Asst. Surg. Wakefield, H.

APPENDIX IV

OFFICERS.

36TH JACOB'S HORSE.

NOMINAL ROLL OF BRITISH OFFICERS WHO SERVED WITH THE REGIMENT DURING THE GREAT WAR, 1914–1918.

Rank and Name.		Date of joining.	Remarks.
Lt.-Col.	R. E. Roome		Sick leave 21.11.15. Vacated Command 18.2.16.
Major	C. H. Alexander		Sick leave 4.1.15.
,,	E. A. Fagan		Transferred to Liverpool Regt. 7.11.15. Wounded July 1917.
,,	W. G. K. Green	Proceeded to France with Regiment in October, 1914.	Temporary Comdt. 21.11.15. Temporary Brig.-General 20.9.18.
Captain	H. M. Davidson		To Depot October 1917.
,,	F. R. Farquhar		Wounded 18.3.1917, Croissille. Wounded 1.12.1917, Cambrai.
,,	A. N. Gavin Jones		Transferred to Infantry, November, 1915.
,,	H. Allardice		Adjutant. Appointed Staff Captain Sialkot Cav. Bde. 4.7.1915. Killed in action 2.7.1916.
,,	M. M. Carpendale		Died in Hospital in October 1918 at Damascus.
Lieut.	C. F. Cahusac		Rejoined from 3rd Hussars 24.12.14. Proceeded Mesopotamia 8.2.16.
,,	M. E. Parnell		Killed in action 1.12.1917 at Épéhy.
,,	W. F. Blacker		—

OFFICERS—THE GREAT WAR

Rank	and Name.	Date of joining.	Remarks.
Lieut.	R. D. Owen Jones. .	Proceeded to France in Oct. 1914	Wounded Festubert January 1915. Accidentally killed 5.1.1916.
Captain	A. C. Munro, I.M.S. .	ditto	Proceeded India 7.10.16.
Lieut.	W. T. Allen (23rd Cav.)	4.1.15	Wounded January 1915. Proceeded India.
Captain	D. S. Stewart (17th Cav.)	29.1.15	Proceeded India February 1915.
Lieut.	R. A. Addington, The Honble. (27th L. Cav.)	31.1.15	Proceeded India November 1915.
Captain	C. H. Kirkwood (23rd Cavalry)	17.2.15	Transferred Ammunition Column 17.3.24.
,,	E. B. Maunsell (35th S.H.)	3.4.15	Gassed near Pontru 31.10.17. Proceeded India December 1918.
2nd Lt.	A. L. Gordon Kidd, I.A.R.O.	5.4.15	Joined R.F.C. in England on 8.11.15. Killed.
Captain	J. F. M. Robinson (West Riding Yeomanry)	15.4.15	Rejoined Yeomanry August 1915.
,,	T. I. Trollope (Lincolnshire Yeomanry)	15.4.15	Rejoined Yeomanry August 1915. Killed en route to Egypt.
Lieut.	I. Robertson (Scottish Horse)	15.4.15	Rejoined Yeomanry August 1915.
2nd Lt.	E. N. E. Waldron, I.A.R.O.	29.4.15	Transferred to R.F.C. 3.7.16.
Lieut.	C. L. Reid, I.A.R.O. .	30.7.15	Sick September 1915, did not rejoin.
2nd Lt.	A. W. Harrison, I.A.R.O.	30.8.15	—
,,	F. B. Maltby, I.A.R.O.	20.9.15	—
,,	P. P. Braithwaite, I.A.R.O.	13.10.15	Killed in action Abu Naj, 21.9.18.
,,	H. R. Landale, I.A.R.O.	13.10.15	—
Lieut.	W. Chubb, I.A.R.O. .	24.10.15	—
Captain	J. N. Simonds (35th S.H.)	25.11.15	To M.G. Corps, August 1916.
2nd Lt.	E. F. Ogley, I.A.R.O. .	1.12.15	—
Captain	A. M. Forteath . .	31.12.15	To 41st Cav. July 1918.
,,	J. Graves, I.V., I.A.R.O.	4.1.16	Died of wounds, Bullecourt, April 1917.
Ty. 2nd Lt.	R. G. Faithfull . . .	2.2.16	To M.G. Corps 19.12.16.

APPENDIX IV

Rank and Name.		Date of joining.	Remarks.
2nd Lt.	J. G. Kidd	2.2.16	To R.F.C. 7.7.16.
,,	D. B. Emerson, I.A.R.O.	11.3.16	To Sappers and Miners, June 1918.
,,	A. E. F. Wood, I.A.R.O.	26.5.16	To 28th Light Cav., March 1918.
Lieut.	K. F. Channer	7.6.16	Evacuated sick, July 1918.
,,	D. A. G. Dallas	28.7.16	Wounded, Croissilles, 18.3.17, did not rejoin.
2nd Lt.	G. C. L. Howell, I.C.S., I.A.R.O.	8.8.16	Gassed, Beaumont Hamel, November 1916. To M.G. Corps 28.8.16.
,,	M. H. Smith, I.A.R.O.	24.10.16	—
,,	T. F. Johnson, I.A.R.O.	2.12.16	—
,,	G. C. Fry	19.4.17	—
,,	F. J. Allen	19.4.17	—
Lieut.	De La Haye	29.4.17	—
2nd Lt.	G. M. Stroud	10.9.17	—
,,	F. W. S. Watkins	18.9.17	—
,,	M. F. Keightley	18.9.17	—
Lieut.	S. K. Phadke I.M.S.	23.9.17	—
2nd Lt.	E. E. Vosper	2.10.17	—
,,	T. F. A. Flynn	11.10.17	—
,,	E. C. W. Blakeney	11.10.17	Died at Karachi in February 1919.
,,	E. J. Dormer	11.10.17	—
Lieut.	A. B. Knight	31.12.17	—
Captain	V. H. S. Smith (32nd Lancers)	31.12.17	—
Lieut.	B. C. Waller	8.1.18	—
Major	E. M. Nixon	1.6.18	—
Lieut.-Col.	F. Lance (19th Lancers)	1.10.18	—

APPENDIX V

CASUALTIES

36TH JACOB'S HORSE—THE GREAT WAR.

	B.O.'s.	I.O.'s.	I.O.R.'s.	Total.	Horses.	Remarks.
FESTUBERT, January 1915.						†Lieut. Owen Jones. *Jemadar. Sham Singh. Some 225 men were affected with trench feet, out of 300.
Killed . .	—	1*	6	7	—	
Wounded . .	1†	—	12	13	—	
Missing . .	—	—	—	—	—	
Total . .	1	1	18	20	—	
YPRES, June 1916.						
Wounded . .	—	—	3	3	—	
ERVILLERS–CROISSILLES, March 1917.						*Jemadar Abdul Samad. †Captain Farquhar, Dallas; Ressdr. Mohd Nur.
Killed . .	—	1*	5	6	7	
Wounded . .	2†	1†	18	21	11	
Missing . .	—	—	2	2	10	
Total . .	2	2	25	29	28	
BULLECOURT, April 1917.						*Captain Graves.
Killed . .	1*	—	1	2	—	
Wounded . .	—	—	16	16	—	
Missing . .	—	—	1	1	—	
Total . .	1	—	18	19	—	
CAMBRAI, December 1917.						*Captain Parnell, Ressdr. Maqbul Shah, Jemdr. Ganesha Singh, Jemdr. Umar Khan. †Capt. Farquhar, Ressdr. Bishan Singh.
Killed . .	1*	3*	10	14	—	
Wounded . .	1†	1†	23	25	—	
Total . .	2	4	33	39	—	
JORDAN (PATROL ACTIONS), June to September 1918.						*Ressdr. Iltaf Hussain Shah.
Killed . .	—	1*	8	9	10	
Wounded . .	—	—	6	6	4	
Total . .	—	1	14	15	14	

	B.O.'s	I.O.'s	I.O.R's	Total	Horses	Remarks
	\multicolumn{5}{c}{ABU NAJ, September, 1918.}		
Killed	1	2	6	9	—	Capt. Braithwaite. Jemadar. Atta Ullah. Jemadar. Sultan Ahmed. (Two complete troops were lost.)
Wounded	—	—	6	6	—	
Missing	—	—	15	15	—	
Total	1	2	27	30	—	

AGGREGATES

KILLED.

	B.O.'s	I.O.'s	I.O.R.'s	Total
Festubert	—	1	6	7
Authuille	—	1	1	2
Ervillers	—	1	5	6
Bullecourt	1	—	1	2
Cambrai	1	3	10	14
Jordan	—	1	8	9
Abu Naj	1	2	14	17
Total	3	9	45	57

Accidentally killed, Captain Owen Jones.

WOUNDED.

	B.O.'s	I.O.'s	I.O.R.'s	Total
Festubert	1	—	12	13
Ypres	—	—	3	3
Authuille	—	—	2	2
Ervillers	2	1	18	21
Bullecourt	—	—	16	16
Cambrai	1	1	23	25
Jordan	—	—	6	6
Abu Naj	—	—	6	6
Total	4	2	86	92

Gassed, Major Maunsell.
    ,,   Lieutenant T. C. G. Howell.

The list is not complete. In addition to the above there was a number of casualties from time to time on working parties and in the line.

CASUALTIES.

35TH SCINDE HORSE—THE ARAB REBELLION.

	B.O.'s.	I.O.'s.	I.O.R.'s.	Followers.	Horses.
Killed	—	1*	22	—	100
Wounded	2†	1	17	—	—
Missing (recovered) .	—	—	5	3	—
Total	2	2	44	3	100

    * Captain Knox.   Ressaldar Major Mmd. Azim.
    † 2nd Lt. Bott died of wounds.   Jemadar Khan Makhmad.

SUNDRY ACTIONS.

	B.O.'s	I.O.'s.	I.O.R.'s	Followers.	Horses.
Killed	—	—	—	—	6
Wounded	2*	1†	14	—	16
Total	2	1	14	—	22

    { * 2nd Lt. Mmd. Ayub.   † Jemadar Bhagat Singh.
      2nd Lt. Robinson.

Total : Killed . . 23   Horses (incomplete) . . 122
        Wounded . 37
                 60

With the exception of one I.O. casualty, the whole of the above occurred in the two squadrons engaged in the suppression of the Rebellion.

APPENDIX VI

HONOURS AND AWARDS.

Officers and Other Ranks
35th Scinde Horse.

(The list is not complete.)

The Great War.

Lieut.-Colonel G. de S. Barrow. Promotion to Major-General. K.C.B., K.C.M.G.
Bt. Lieut.-Colonel J. Shea, D.S.O. Promotion to Major-General. K.C.M.G., C.B.
Lieut.-Colonel Hocken. Promotion to Colonel. C.B.
Captain E. D. Giles. Brevet Lieut.-Colonel. C.M.G., D.S.O.
Captain H. R. Dyer. D.S.O.
Captain J. P. Thompson. O.B.E.
Captain E. E. Kennedy. M.C.
Captain Landon. D.S.O.
Captain E. B. Maunsell. Despatches.
Captain H. E. Connop. Despatches.
Ressaldar Major Mahomed Azin. Order of British India.
The honours for the Indian Ranks in The Great War are included in The Jacob's Horse list.

The Arab Rebellion.

(The list is not complete.)

Major H. E. Connop	D.S.O.
Captain J. H. Knox	M.C.
2nd Lieut. W. E. D. Robinson	M.C.
Ressaldar Dur Khan, I.O.M.	I.O.M. (1st Class) I.D.S.M.
Jemadar Mmd. Niwaz	I.D.S.M.
Defadar Ali Khan	I.D.S.M.
Driver Suraj Bhan	I.D.S.M.
Trumpet Major Latif Beg	I.M.S.M.
Dafadar Ishar Singh	I.M.S.M.
Jemadar Admed Khan	I.M.S.M.
Jemadar Khan Makhmad	I.M.S.M.
Ressaldar Abdul Karim	Despatches
Major Landon, D.S.O.	Despatches

HONOURS AND AWARDS.
36TH JACOB'S HORSE.
THE GREAT WAR.

Regtl. No.	Rank.	Name.	Decoration.	Date.
2723	Dfr.	Said Hassan	Croix de Guerre	15.11.14
	Risaldar Major	Mohd Nasir Khan	Mentioned in Despatches	15.11.15
	Lieut.-Colonel	E. A. Fagan	,, ,,	15.11.15
	,, ,,	E. A. Fagan	D.S.O.	16.9.16
	,, ,,	W. G. K. Green	Mentioned in Despatches	16.9.16
	Ressaidar	Mohd Noor Khan	I.O.M. 2nd Class	16.6.16
3136	Dfr.	Hardit Singh	,, ,,	16.11.16
615	K.D.	Sahib Singh	I.D.S.M.	,,
2143	,,	Abdul Khaliq	,,	,,
3562	Dfr.	Dalip Singh 35th	,,	,,
2896	Sowar	Hazrat Shah	,,	,,
2786	Dfr.	Haji Ahmed Khan	I.O.M. 2nd Class	,,
	Captain	F. R. Farquhar	Military Cross	19.3.17
	Risaldar	Sadiq Mohd Khan	I.O.M. 2nd Class	,,
	Jemadar	Alam Sher Khan 37th	,,	,,
2767	L.D.	Saleh Mohamed	I.D.S.M.	,,
	Lieutenant	E. F. Ogley	Military Cross	11.4.17
	Jemadar	Wazir Singh	I.O.M. 2nd Class	,,
	,,	Bahadur Singh	I.D.S.M.	3.6.17
	,,	Maqbul Shah	,,	,,
2504	Dfr.	Hazara Singh	I.M.S.M.	,,
1845	K.D.	Mukand Singh	,,	,,
1961	,,	Mehar Khan	,,	,,
2312	Dfr.	Nawab Khan	,,	,,
	Risaldar	Sadiq Mohd	Order of B.I.	30.8.18
2715	Dfr.	Haq Nawaz	I.M.S.M.	,,
2069	K.D.	Sarfraz Khan	,,	,,
1296	,,	Gurmukh Singh	,,	,,
2293	,,	Ghulam Sarwar	,,	,,
3241	Sowar	Hassan Khan	,,	,,

APPENDIX VI

Regtl. No.	Rank.	Name.	Decoration.	Date.
114	A.L.D.	Sajawal Khan	I.M.S.M.	30.8.18
2136	Farrier	Bashir Khan	,,	,,
2274	Dfr.	Shah Baz Khan	,,	,,
3150	Sowar	Lala Jan	I.D.S.M.	,,
3115	L.D.	Dan Singh 37th	,,	,,
	Risaldar	Mohd Wazir Khan	I.O.M. 2nd Class	,,
3122	A.L.D.	Arsala Khan	I.D.S.M.	15.2.19
	Jemadar	Amar Singh	I.O.M. 2nd Class	,,
3176	K.D.	Jan Mohamed	I.D.S.M.	,,
3174	A.L.D.	Khanan Khan	,,	,,
	Jemadar	Atta Ullah Khan	I.O.M. 2nd Class	20.8.18
	Captain	W. F. Blacker	Military Cross	1.1.19
	Major	M. M. Carpendale	Mentioned in Despatches	23.10.18
	Captain	P. P. Braithwaite	,, ,,	,,
	Risaldar	Mohd Wazir Khan	,, ,,	,,
	Ty. Brig.-Gen.	W. G. K. Green	Bt. Lieut.-Colonel	1.1.19
	Lieut.-Colonel	F. F. Lance	,, ,,	,,
	,, ,,	F. F. Lance	Order of Nile	13.3.19
	Brig.-General	E. A. Fagan	Mentioned in Despatches	8.1.19
	,,	W. G. K. Green	,, ,,	,,
2744	Dfr.	Fazal Karim 37th	I.M.S.M.	3.6.17
1126	K.D.	Adalat Khan 23rd	,,	,,
	Risaldar Major	Bagga Singh	Order of B.I. 2nd Class	17.4.17
2890	Dfr.	Latif Shah	I.M.S.M.	15.9.17
1293	Naik	Hussain Mohd R.H.A.	,,	,,
2581	K.D.	Allah Dad	,,	,,
2291	Dfr.	Ghulam Muhammad	,,	,,
3070	,,	Sohbat Khan 35th	,,	,,
2472	Sowar	Latif Ahmed	,,	,,
	Jemadar	Wazir Singh	I.O.M. 1st Class	,,
2727	Dfr.	Inzar Gul	I.D.S.M.	20.11.17
	Ty. Brig.-Gen.	E. A. Fagan	C.M.G.	1.1.18
	,, ,,	W. G. K. Green	Mentioned in Despatches	1.1.18
	,, ,,	W. G. K. Green	D.S.O.	3.1.18
	Major	A. N. G. Jones	Mentioned in Despatches	1.1.18
	,,	A. N. G. Jones	D.S.O.	4.1.18
1048	S.A.S.	Parma Nand Misra	I.D.S.M.	,,
2453	Dfr.	Jahan Khan	,,	,,
3046	L.D.	Akram Khan	,,	,,
1734	Sowar	Astabud Din	,,	,,
3414	,,	Fateh Khan	,,	,,

HONOURS AND AWARDS

Regtl. No.	Rank.	Name.	Decoration.	Date.
	Jemadar	Kartar Singh	Croix de Guerre	4.2.18
	Captain	W. F. Blacker	Mentioned in Despatches	7.4.18
2813	Dfr.	Hardit Singh	I.D.S.M.	11.7.18
	Risaldar	Khan Mohamed Khan	I.O.M. 2nd Class	20.5.18
	Jemadar	Dur Khan 35/36th	,, ,,	4.7.18
2921	A.L.D.	Rahim Khan	I.D.S.M.	,,
3027	Sowar	Pai Wali	,,	,,
	Captain	C. F. Cahusac	D.S.O.	
	,,	C. F. Cahusac	O.B.E.	
	,,	B. Mahon	D.S.O., M.C.	

Summary.

C.M.G.	1
D.S.O.	4
M.C.	3
I.O.M. 1st Class	1
I.O.M. 2nd Class	11
I.D.S.M.	20
I.M.S.M.	20
O.B.I.	2
Foreign Decorations	4
Mentions	11
Brevets	2

APPENDIX VII

HISTORY OF P.W.O. THE SCINDE HORSE.

Précis hung in every Barrack Room (with Urdu and Gurmukhi translations)

1. What is the Name of this Regiment?
   The SCINDE HORSE.
2. Who is the Colonel-in-Chief?
   The PRINCE OF WALES.
3. Who is the Prince of Wales?
   The son of The KING GEORGE, EMPEROR OF INDIA.
4. Why was he made Colonel-in-Chief?
   Because the old 35th and 36th Horse did great deeds in THE WAR and in MESOPOTAMIA.
5. Who is the second Colonel?
   GENERAL BARROW.
6. Who is he?
   He is a former Commanding Officer who did great things in THE GREAT WAR and who is now a big general.
7. When was this Regiment raised?
   In 1838.
8. What for?
   To keep the Baluch quiet.
9. What is the first great battle in which the Regiment took part?
   MEEANEE.
10. What did the Regiment do that day?
    It charged the Baluch and won the battle.
11. Who was in Command of the Regiment?
    JOHN JACOB.
12. What was the second great battle?
    HYDERABAD.
13. What did the Regiment do that day?
    It again charged.
14. How long was JOHN JACOB Colonel of The SCINDE HORSE?
    Sixteen years, during which the Regiment became famous in Hindustan.

15. What did the Regiment do at GUJRAT?
    It charged some Afghan Cavalry and routed them.
16. What did the Regiment do in THE MUTINY?
    It remained true to its salt and helped the Sirdar suppress it in CENTRAL INDIA.
17. Where did the Regiment do most of its good work?
    On the SCINDE FRONTIER, near Jacobabad.
18. What kind of work was it?
    Very hard work patrolling and fighting Baluch raiders, in which many Sirdars and Non-Commissioned Officers showed great bravery.
19. Who was Jemadar DURGA SINGH?
    He was a very brave Sirdar who charged an overwhelming number of Baluch with his patrol and got killed. The Baluch call the place where he died DURGA KUSHTA in admiration for his courage.
20. What did the Regiment do at KHUSHK i NAKHUD?
    Two Squadrons at Saddlery Inspection were surprised but they put their saddlery together and charged 1,500 Afghans and killed a large number.
21. What happened at MAIWAND?
    The Regiment sat on its horses under fire for five hours without moving, losing many men and horses. It nevertheless charged and saved an infantry battalion from destruction.
22. What did the Regiment do in THE GREAT WAR?
    It went to FRANCE in 1914 and remained there till 1918, when it went to PALESTINE.
23. What was the first occasion when the Regiment went into action?
    At FESTUBERT in January 1915 it went into trenches full of water and had a very hard time owing to the cold.
24. What was the first great battle the Regiment was at?
    At YPRES in the beginning of 1915.
25. What was the next great battle?
    The SOMME in September 1916.
26. At what battle did the Indian Cavalry particularly distinguish themselves in FRANCE?
    At CAMBRAI.
27. What happened at CAMBRAI?
    The Indian Cavalry made many valiant attacks and prevented the Germans advancing.
28. What else besides fighting did the Regiment do?
    It dug many trenches and put up wire and was thus very useful.
29. Did the Regiment go into the trenches much?
    Yes, all 1917 the Regiment was in the Line.

30. Where did the Regiment go to after FRANCE?
    To PALESTINE.
31. Who did it fight against out there?
    Against the Turks.
32. Where was it most of the time?
    Down in the JORDAN VALLEY.
33. What kind of work was it?
    Outpost work with a lot of patrolling.
34. What was the great battle the Regiment took part in?
    The Battle of SHARON.
35. What did the Regiment do?
    It led the advance through the Turk Lines.
36. What did the Division do that day?
    It marched seventy miles and got behind the whole Turk Army.
37. What did the Turks do?
    They all surrendered.
38. How many prisoners did the British Army take?
    Over 80,000.
39. What big city did the Regiment go to?
    To DAMASCUS.
40. What did the Regiment do in MESOPOTAMIA?
    It went there in 1920 and left in 1921.
41. Was there any fighting?
    Yes, very heavy fighting with the Arabs.
42. What did the Regiment do in its first engagement?
    It saved a battery by its steadiness in a night retirement from near KIFL to HILLAH.
43. What was the next big engagement?
    At KUFAH, where the Regiment charged some Arabs.
44. What did the Commander-in-Chief say of the Regiment?
    He specially mentioned its gallantry and was very pleased with it.

"MAN DIES, BUT THE REGIMENT LIVES"

Jubbulpore,
Dated, 6.11.23.

E. B. MAUNSELL, Lt.-Col.
Commanding
P.W.O. The Scinde Horse.

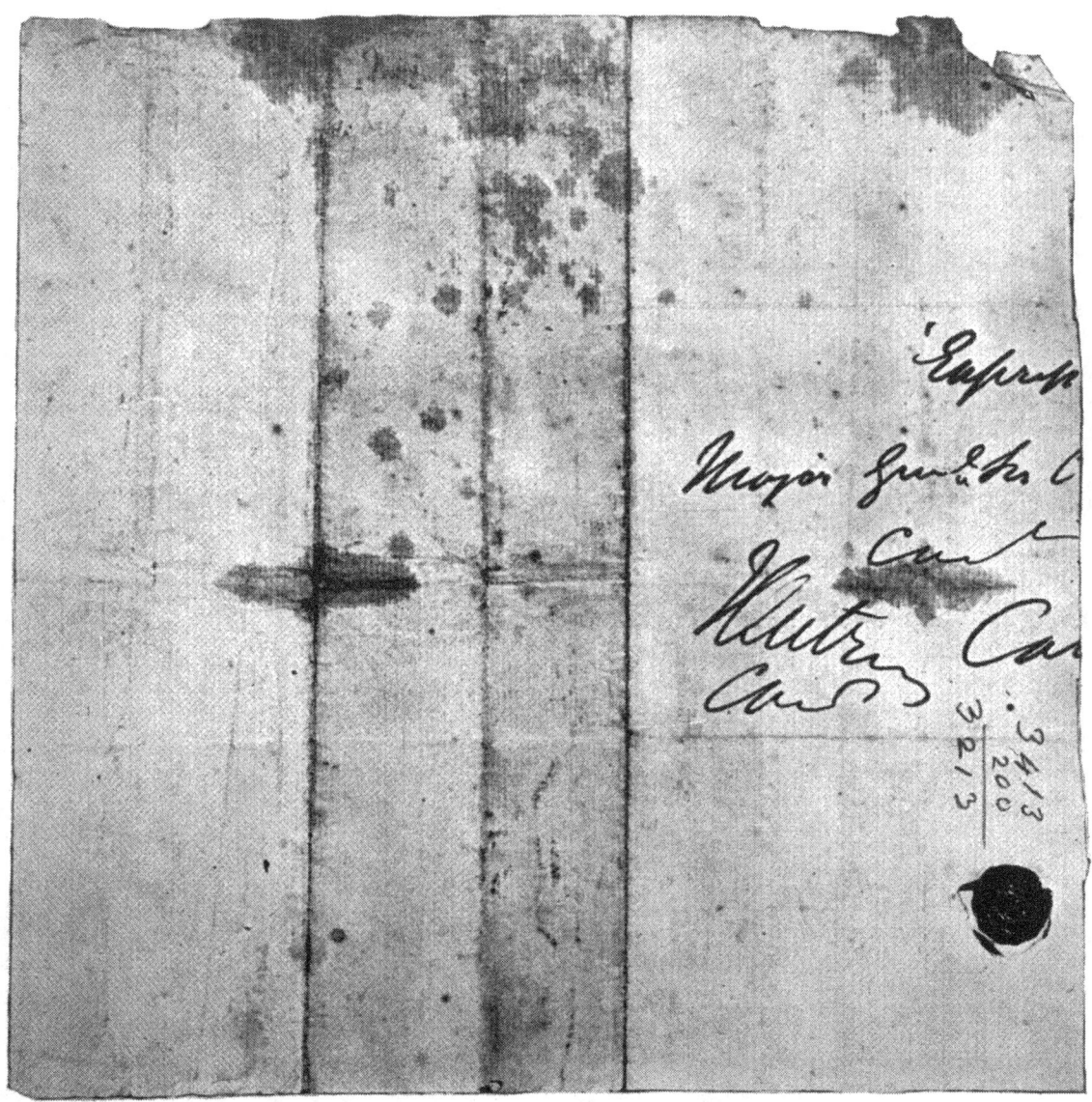

A RELIC OF SIR CHARLES NAPIER—I.

Envelope of a letter from Outram, on the back of which Napier had written
some notes for the conduct of the Battle of Meeanee.

A RELIC OF SIR CHARLES NAPIER—II.

APPENDIX VIII

A RELIC OF SIR CHARLES NAPIER

THE two illustrations are those of a Napier relic, and show an addressed envelope of a letter from Outram, on the back of which Sir Charles had written some notes for the conduct of the Battle of Meeanee.

The figures would seemingly have some reference to the numbers available for the battle.

Memo. 16 Feb^{ry} 1843.

At 4 I leave the camp.

At 9 attack the wood.

At 9 Outram drops down to the wood.

Send Outram 150 Sepoys under an European officer.

Send Prisoners on board the steamer.

Send the sick on board the flat immediately.

Dispatch to Col. Roberts for reinforcements.

Baggage guard.

Treasure on board steamer.

March at 4 a.m.—in order of Battle, left in front—22nd Regt. hold on to the River.

Pound the enemy's right with guns—charge it with all my Cavalry—if our men prevail we shall shove the enemy in masses into the River.

APPENDIX IX

CORRESPONDENCE

Masnières—The Canadian Cavalry Brigade

20th November, 1917

Copy of letter from General Greenly, *re* the holding up of the Canadian Cavalry Brigade advance at Masnières.

My memory is extremely defective, and I can only tell you what my impressions are. I would be sorry to swear to their accuracy and I would not pit them against anything like authentic notes made at the time. Of such, unfortunately, I have none.

As far as I can recollect I was not responsible for deciding when General Seely's Brigade was to cross, or I imagine I would have been much closer up and in close personal touch with Seely throughout the day. This seems curious to me now, but I do remember the whole question of command was a little involved but think I did NOT go forward to see Seely except the once, probably as you say about 3.0 or 3.30 p.m.

It was mid-November, and the days were short and by that time I was thinking that if we were to get across at all by daylight we should have to be on the move very soon. When I did go forward, I found Seely at his H.Q. It was a small house in the low-lying bushy country not far from the canal, and from where the general line of the canal could be seen by the trees, etc., but nothing else, and a thoroughly bad place to see anything from.

I am pretty sure Seely had come back from the actual canal or very near it just before I got there, as I remember his telling me there was nothing to be gained by my going farther on and I should see nothing more. It was essentially a low-lying bushy bit of ground, I think, and no look-out points in it.

I certainly formed any opinions I did form on Seely's information, and personally saw nothing more than I had seen before.

My impression is that his information was to the effect that they had found a small (I think) footbridge and had to some extent repaired it; that he had sent some men across on foot, that the bridge was under machine-gun fire and that one or two horses had passed over (I believe by moving through the water while men crossed by the bridge), and that they were still dribbling over in small numbers like that.

I am quite sure that Seely was unaware that anything like a squadron was across or thought it in the least probable that anything of that sort could be got across in the near future, or that any mounted action was in prospect on the far side. My impression is that his men were on foot, fighting alongside the infantry in so far as they were fighting at all, and that possibly a few horses were over and waiting under the canal banks.

I know I left Seely without the slightest idea that anything which could possibly be described as a forward movement was going on, and it certainly never entered my head to stop any such movement. I am as sure as I can be of anything that I never gave any sort of order that could possibly be construed into " cancelling a forward movement," as I did not believe any such thing was going on.

On the contrary, I have a hazy idea that I told him that he must hang on to anything he could gain on the far side of the canal, and take every opportunity of pushing forward if he possibly could do so. That, anyway, would have been a platitude, as Seely was not a man who wanted gingering up into going forward.

It is possible, though I do not recollect it, that I may have advised against dribbling horses over as I understand he was doing, until there was a reasonable chance of getting a number over together and being able to act on the far side.

My impression was that there was still an infantry battle, for the crossing, and that some of his men were engaged in it on foot.

I believe I came back thinking it was a practical certainty that the 2nd Cavalry Division would not be able to cross by daylight, as I did not in the least expect Seely's Brigade to be going to be able to do so.

I think I had a Staff Officer with me. Who? and does he remember what occurred? perhaps de Burgh?

I am also sure there was a Brigade-Major and the Staff Captain of an Infantry Brigade with Seely, perhaps of the 85th Brigade. Has that Brigade War Diary anything on the subject?

APPENDIX X

THE SILLADAR SYSTEM IN INDIAN CAVALRY

The Silladar System, on which all regiments in India, with the exception of the three old Madras Cavalry regiments, were based prior to The Great War, in a measure resembled that of the Yeomanry in the old days.

It was the method adopted in India, from time immemorial, for raising and maintaining bodies of irregular horse.

The employer paid the trooper, or silladar as he was called, a certain wage, in return for which the man provided, not merely his arms, rations, uniform, and equipment, but his horse, with its food, and the necessary transport.

The true silladar can now be seen in the levies that accompany Political Officers on the Frontier, and the original silladar cavalry were merely a collection of these levies, usually under their own chiefs.

In the early days no serious fighting was expected from corps raised on these lines, and their duties were confined to convoy protection, police work and similar jobs. Meeanee would appear to be the first general engagement in which irregular horse took a really decisive part.

In the great cavalry fights, like Assaye and Laswari, and in the operations generally of Sir Arthur Wellesley and Lord Lake, it was the British Light Dragoon, with regular native cavalry, who did all the heavy work. The same thing is noticeable in the Mahratta War of 1817. At Sitabuldi, the only serious cavalry fight, it was a " regular " Bengal Light Cavalry regiment which saved the situation.

The longer the units of irregular horse remained embodied, the more the necessity for a certain degree of " regularisation " became obvious, and it became the custom for the silladar to purchase his horse, etc., from the regiment. On leaving the service, the man received back all the money he had paid in, and he handed back his horse. In order, however, to obtain a new horse when his own became non-effective, he had to pay in to the regiment a certain subscription as an insurance. This he did not get back. The " horses," originally, were only ponies of the type the well-to-do zemindar now rides, hardy and wild. The stamp improved as time went on, but the mounting of even the best regiments was never as good as that of the three " regular " Madras Cavalry regiments, whose horses were Government property.

The arms and equipment, moreover, differed in every regiment, and, in most cases, could not compare with Government stuff. Finance was at the bottom of this, and a commanding officer always had this bogey before him.

Furthermore, the scope allowed commandants in selecting patterns of equipment did not always tend to efficiency, owing to the idiosyncrasies of individuals, and what one colonel might select his successor might reject, with a consequent lack of uniformity throughout the unit.

The financial aspect, again, led to the retention of both indifferent equipment and useless animals. In almost every regiment there were horses which hardly did an honest day's work in their lives but which were retained for the mere purpose of drawing pay.

The interest the trooper had in his horse and mule might, on the surface, appear to have been to the advantage of the State. In practice, however, it militated against efficiency, for the man, with some reason, disliked his animals and gear being used by others, and in very many cases his chief idea was to make money over the feed.

The interests of the State being high war efficiency, demanded both well-found and well-trained troops, and this could not be obtained without hard work both for horses and men, and wear and tear of kit.

The financial interests of a silladar unit thus clashed with the requirements of the Service, for more money could be made, both for the regiment and for the silladar, if only very little work was done.

The unsatisfactory state of the mounting, clothing and equipping of silladar units was amply revealed at the outbreak of The Great War, and it is difficult to see how this can ever be completely surmounted, even if units are compelled to make all their purchases from Government, as has been suggested.

From the pre-War Indian Government point of view the system had the ineffable advantage of cheapness, and this was the dominating factor. It was possible to maintain thirty-six moderately mounted and equipped regiments with transport, for the same money as is required for the twenty good units now in existence, but without transport. These thirty-six units were capable of coping with Internal Security, and with petty war not of a lengthy duration, or one which did not make serious demands on horse-flesh and equipment. They were, most emphatically, incapable of a prolonged campaign in a hard country, or of *la grande guerre*.

The question now arises, What is the Indian Army for? Is it for the Empire at large, or is it merely a kind of glorified police?

INDEX

Abbeville, at, 67–69, 84, 88
Abu Naj, action of, 227–230
Abyssinia, 19
Aden Troop, The, formed, 16
Afghanistan (1878–80), 19–35
Aleppo, 237–240
Amalgamation, the, 304, 311
Amiens, near, billets, 69
Arab Rebellion, The, 264–310
Armistice (Turkey), 240
Army reorganization, 41, 311–312
Artillery, shortages, 59–61, 66, 103, 105, 130, 133, 145, 170
Authuille, in the line at, 66

Baghdad, at, 307
 N.E., operations, 283–288
Basra, return from, 309
Battle-Honours, v., 34, 182, 242, 310
Beaumont Hamel, 85
Beisan, at, 220–226, 237
Beled Sinjar, 304–305
Brigades, composition of :—
 Lucknow Cavalry (France), 49
 7th Cavalry (Mesopotamia), 257, 258
 11th Cavalry (Palestine), 185
Bullecourt, 113–114

Cambrai (1917), Battle of, 134–139
Casualties, 110, 236, 333–335
Commandants of The Regiment, 322–323
Communiqués, value of, 132
Craters, shell, 89–91
Crecy, area, 69, 84–85
Croissilles, operations, 95–109
Cutchee, 3–5

Damascus, 233, 237–240
Depots, requirements, 207–208, 247
Divisions, composition of :—
 4th Cavalry (France), 49, 78
 4th Cavalry (Palestine), 185–186
 5th Cavalry (Palestine), 186–187
Diwaniyah, 251–257
Doullens, billets, 117
Drafts, 48, 178, 243

Education, system of, 258
Efficiency of Indian Cavalry (1914), 42–47, 58, 72, 80
Egypt :—
 Concentration, 183–187
 Move to, 174–182

El Afule, 213, 219–221, 227
Epéhy :—
 Battle of, 139–171
 Line, the, near, 130–133
Esdraelon, Vale of, 213

Festubert, trenches, 54
Footwork, importance of, 45, 69, 71, 88, 248
Formation, 1
France and Flanders (1914–1918), 48–177

Girishk, at, 21–25
Goojerat, 13–14
Great War, The, 48–242

Helmets, steel, issued, 74
Hillah, 264–288
Hinaidi, 257–262
Hindenburg Line, advance begins, 86
Honours and Awards, 336–339
Horse mastership, 44, 69, 222
Hyderabad, 9–11

India, departure from, 17, 49, 248–249
 return to, 17, 240, 309
 East, Company, Hon., arms, 17
Indian Frontier, conditions on, 258–259
Infantry, strength, 172
Iraq, 308, 310

Jacob, Brig.-Gen. J., 3–19, 40, 315–321
Jerusalem, 192, 205, 206
Jezreel, Vale of, 220
Jordan Valley, 191–212
 Camouflage, in, 211

Kandahar, 19–35
Kantara, Depot, 187, 205–208
Khushk-i-Nakhud, 21–33
Kifl, 267–277
Kotah, Siege of, 18
Kufah, Relief of, 289–295

Lance v. Sword, 208–209
Loeuilly, at, 174
Loos, 67, 83, 188

Maiwand, action at, 24–34
Manchester Column Disaster, 267–277
Marches, 36, 221
Marseilles, at, 174–178, 187
Masnières, tanks at, 137
Meeanee, 7–9, 343
Megiddo, Battle of, 219
Mekran, 36–41
Mendali, bivouac, 297

Mesopotamia (1920–1921), 247–310
Mooltan, 13
Mosul, 298–304

Neuve Chapelle, 55
Neuville St. Vaast, 74–77, 89

Officers :—
 Nominal Roll, 324–329
 The Great War, 330–332
Omignon, The, 118–123, 139, 172–173
Outline of Services, 1–23, 35–41

Palestine (1918), 188–242
Patrols, 124, 131, 200
Persia, 17
Philistean Plain, 192, 205, 237
Précis, historical, 340–342

Rations, 52, 107, 129, 204
Regiments :—
 Scinde Horse, The, 1–41
 3rd Scinde Horse, 323, 329
 14th (P.W.O.) Scinde Horse, 311–313, 323
 35th Scinde Horse, 243–310, 322, 324–326, 335–336
 36th Jacob's Horse, 48–242, 323, 327–334, 337–339
 42nd Cavalry, The, 244
Rumeitha relieved, 265

St. Quentin, N.E. of, 118–129
St. Riquier, training at, 58, 71–73
Salvage, 112
Seistan, 41
Services, outline of, 1–23, 35–41
Sharon, Battle of, 212–219
Silladar system, the, 16, 46, 312–313, 346–347
Somme (1916), Battle of, opening, 78
Standards, captured, 9, 14
Sword exercise, taught, 19.

Tel-el-Kebir, 183
Titles of Regiment, xx
Transport, Indian Army, 7, 12, 13, 52, 56
Trench-feet, 54

Valour, deeds of, 115, 169
Vauchelles, billets, 117
Villers Guislain, 140–171

Wales, H.R.H. Prince of, 81, 311, 323

Ypres Salient, 57–62.

www.ingramcontent.com/pod-product-compliance
Lightning Source LLC
Chambersburg PA
CBHW080540230426
43663CB00015B/2649